The New York Times

Guide to Listening Pleasure

The New York Times

Guide to Listening Pleasure

Edited and with an Introduction by

HOWARD TAUBMAN

A NEW YORK TIMES BOOK

THE MACMILLAN COMPANY, NEW YORK

COLLIER-MACMILLAN LTD., LONDON

Library of Congress Catalog Card Number: 68-27038

FIRST PRINTING

The Macmillan Company, New York
Collier-Macmillan Canada Ltd., Toronto, Ontario
Printed in the United States of America

UNTIL HIS RETIREMENT IN MARCH, 1968,

Norman S. McGee,

EXECUTIVE VICE PRESIDENT,

WAS FOR THIRTY-ONE YEARS A MAJOR CONTRIBUTOR TO

THE GROWTH AND DEVELOPMENT OF WQXR.

THIS BOOK FILLS A NEED THAT HE

WAS FIRST TO RECOGNIZE AND TO HIM IT IS

AFFECTIONATELY DEDICATED.

Contents

PREFACE, *Ivan Veit*   ix

EDITOR'S INTRODUCTION   xiii

CHAPTER

1   *Opera*, ROBERT LAWRENCE   1

2   *Orchestral Music*, MARTIN BOOKSPAN   39

3   *Music of the Baroque*, IGOR KIPNIS   69

4   *Sonatas and Chamber Music*, MARTIN BOOKSPAN   84

5   *Piano Music*, JASCHA ZAYDE   102

6   *Choral Music*, DAVID RANDOLPH   117

7   *The Art Song*, DAVID RANDOLPH   134

8   *The Musical Theater*, ALFRED SIMON   146

9   *Light Music*, ROBERT SHERMAN   169

10   *Jazz*, JOHN S. WILSON   184

11   *Folk Music*, ROBERT SHERMAN   200

12   *Music from Latin America*, PRU DEVON   210

DISCOGRAPHY—LISTINGS OF SELECTED RECORDINGS   225

INDEX   321

Preface

WQXR has been called "radio with a soul" and many other complimentary things. Those of us who are associated with this good-music station believe that these pleasant epithets are all well deserved. We must admit, however, that it all started by accident. The idea for WQXR was the unexpected by-product of experiments whose real purpose was the technical development of TV.

It happened back in the early 1930's. John V. L. Hogan, a radio engineer with scores of patents to his credit, had techniques in mind for simultaneous image and sound broadcast, and he obtained an FCC permit for an experimental station, W2XR, to carry his sound signals. The radio frequency granted was well above the normal end of the broadcasting range, so listeners weren't expected to be bothered by whatever Mr. Hogan put on the air to go along with his test pictures.

As a fortunate coincidence, in addition to being an engineer, Hogan was a lover of good music. It was perfectly natural for him to draw on his own record collection to provide the sound for his experiments. When he broadcast pictures of a waterfall, he put on Handel's *Water Music,* for example. This was just a private indulgence, he thought, because no one would hear the music on his unfrequented frequency. Anyway, he was in operation only an hour or so in the evening.

To his astonishment Hogan began to hear from the unknown

listening public "out there." First a trickle, than a torrent of cards
and letters: "This is great"; "Keep it up"; "At last." A few dial
fiddlers had found the spot and spread the word to their friends.
W2XR had an audience, an audience in which each member felt
he had his own personal, secret radio station.

Although they had scientific value, the television efforts came
to naught, chiefly because there was no one to receive them. But
Hogan thought he had made another discovery of importance.
There must be a place in the radio spectrum for a station that offered good music and other selected programming for an intelligent, cultured audience. Friendly radio professionals tried to set
him straight. They urged him not to be misled by the odd-ball
fans who had communicated their thanks. "Who wants to listen
to records on the air?" they asked. Anyone who wanted to hear
recordings would play his own. He didn't need a radio set for
that. Radio was for *Amos and Andy, The Goldbergs* and the
A & P Gypsies.

But Hogan persisted. Good-music programming did have a
future, he felt, even though there already were about twenty-five
radio stations in New York. He received enthusiastic support
from his friend Elliott M. Sanger, and in 1936 the two men
formed the Interstate Broadcasting Company.

The start was inauspicious. Headquarters consisted of a desk
for Sanger in Hogan's engineering offices at 41 Park Row. The
transmitter was located on the second floor of a garage in Long
Island City, near Queensborough Bridge. There, if you looked
carefully, you would have seen a wooden pole on the roof which
was W2XR's homemade antenna. You would have said that the
whole venture looked pretty precarious, and it was, except for
one thing: Hogan and Sanger were absolutely right; there *was*
a great, unsatisfied thirst for good music on the air. Although
W2XR (later in 1936 it became WQXR) had power of only 250
watts, just about enough to reach midtown Manhattan and
parts of Queens, the response to its programming brought suc-
cessive power increases to 1,000, 5,000, 10,000 and 50,000 watts,
enabling WQXR to reach an audience of millions throughout the
East.

Interstate was a pioneer on the FM scene, and its experimental
station, W2XQR, the first FM affiliate of a commercial broad-

caster in New York, went on the air in 1939. Today it has one of the largest FM audiences in the city.

The New York Times purchased WQXR in 1944 and has steadfastly maintained the station's basic good-music policies. Elliott Sanger joined *The Times* as executive vice president of WQXR and supervised its operations until retirement in 1967.

In the course of this compressed history, the phrase *good music* has popped up several times. It might be well to define that term, as WQXR sees it. It is not a synonym for high-brow or even classical. To us, any music that has lasting value is good music: symphonies, concertos, chamber works, opera, of course; but also the best of the lighter forms, including operettas, Broadway show tunes, folk music, and the world of jazz. WQXR listeners have wide and varied tastes. They like all kinds of music: they only demand the best of each kind. Serving them through the years has been an education for all of us on the station. Our special audience, difficult and impatient whenever standards sag, has helped us learn a lot about music and recordings. We're glad to pass on some of what they have taught us in this book.

Ivan Veit
President
WQXR

Editor's Introduction

HOWARD TAUBMAN

Dʀɪᴠɪɴɢ alone to New York from my place in the country one morning, I switched on the car radio—naturally, to WQXR. Not that I am in the habit of casually listening to music, certainly not to great music. I could not, even if I wanted to do so. Music has a way of seizing and holding my attention. Once in a while I am unlucky enough to visit a home where fine music is used as a backdrop to conversation, and I find myself in an uncomfortable quandary. I want to be polite and share in the talk, but the music, like the ancient mariner, fastens me in its grip, and I end by seeming distant and abstracted, like an absent-minded professor. However, I can understand how people turn to music while they are occupied with routine tasks. My route to New York is so familiar that the music from WQXR beguiles my journey.

On the particular morning of which I speak, I snapped on the radio to hear what I could hear. I had not looked at the program listings in advance, and I did not know what to expect. It happened to be the hour for *Piano Personalities,* and the music that filled my car was unfamiliar. It was sunny and lilting and capricious in its turns of phrase and mood. What could it be? Obviously there were more than ten fingers at work. Two pianists? Yes. Two pianos? Not likely, probably something for four hands on one piano. Mozart and Schubert, I knew, had written lovely things for this intimate form of music-making, designed for the delectation of their friends in their homes. Hardly anyone plays these pieces in public these days, and one can spend a long lifetime of devoted concert-going without encountering even the best pieces in this form. This piece, I was sure, could not have been on many programs. But how appealing it was! And how it shortened the miles! When it was over, I listened carefully for the announcement of title and author. *Divertissement à la Hongroise* by Franz Schubert, for four hands. The composer was not too great a surprise, but the music? I confess I had never heard it before. WQXR had done me and anyone interested in a different musical experience a good turn.

There is another dividend I get from tuning in WQXR. Actually it is a game I play to challenge myself. I do not look at the programs in advance, and I am pleased when I turn on the radio after a piece has begun. The first requirement of the game is to identify the composer. The next is to name the composition. The third is to say who is playing, and that is often the tough part of the game. It is not too difficult when one hears an orchestra playing with a wonderful momentum, with a tone that never fails to sing, with a Mediterranean clarity, in which attacks and releases have a dazzling crispness, and the inner voices are so cannily articulated that they are both clearly defined and deftly blended into the tonal pattern as a whole. It must be Toscanini at the helm, and I am rarely mistaken. Or the piano has a tone that caresses or bursts with power, without ever sacrificing its songfulness, while every resource—sensitivity to form, regality of rhythm, and freedom of phrase—is directed to a total experience of the music, whether it be an étude or a sonata. Several distinguished pianists have the skill and penetration for such an achievement, but the little touches, as well as the grasp of the grand design, are the hallmark of only one man: Horowitz. Or the violin strides forth with a poise, an elegance, an aristocratic style which are in the command of one man: Heifetz. Or the cello manages as many as four gradations of tone in what can only be one bow, while the music is proclaimed with sovereign power or unimaginable serenity. Who but Casals? But these are the relatively easy ones to recognize. In a lifetime of professional concert-going, I have sat at the feet of these men, have listened again and again to their recordings, and I feel that I am as acquainted with their musical personalities as I am with the traits of my family and best friends. There are others with whom I have had as long a musical intimacy, and I have little difficulty identifying them: Bruno Walter, Artur Rubinstein, Rudolf Serkin, Nathan Milstein, Lotte Lehmann, Enrico Caruso. After all, I was virtually weaned on Caruso records. I heard that magnificent voice on the primitive records of my youth and did not realize how truly magnificent it was until electronic advances made it possible for the engineers to let us hear something approximating what the tenor had sounded like on a stage. But new performers of quality keep coming along, and recordings have grown into a flood. There are musicians I could not possibly identify; I had never heard their names until the WQXR announcer spoke them. There are pieces, not only new, but old—think of the torrents of baroque music that have been poured onto discs—I could not possibly recognize, for the simple reason that I did not know they existed, and I am not unfamiliar with the baroque literature.

Failures and frustrations do not discourage me from testing myself in my WQXR game. Better ears than mine have been fooled by recordings. There is the authenticated story about Toscanini and an unheralded conductor whose work he first heard on a disc. This chap had made several recordings with a pick-up group of exceptionally skilled orchestral players, and the result was truly impressive. Toscanini could not be blamed for getting excited over the quality of the ensemble tone and the perceptive style of the interpretation. There was the record to prove that it had not been accomplished with knobs or mixers. And it hadn't, though we know that musician-engineers can do wonders for performers, from converting pipsqueak voices into thunderers to substituting the right note for a false one. What was exhilarating on these discs was the interpretations, and these had to be the conductor's. But were they? Well, Toscanini invited the conductor to do some guest appearances with the NBC Symphony during the summer series, and it turned out that the man was what Maestro called an *assasino*. It was the crack musicians under the man's temporary command who had contributed the quality to the discs.

If the record was misleading about the conductor's gifts, it was nothing of the sort about the music. And that is what counts. Music is our theme. Indeed, it is a vast congeries of worlds. One may find it in everything from trifling charm to exalting sublimity. One may dwell always on the heights amid apocalyptic masterpieces, or one may romp happily along the gentle valleys with the humble works that have no ambitions other than to amuse and entertain. Or one can be tolerant and wise and choose to relish the exalted and the modest at different times, depending on one's mood and taste.

For myself I am not doctrinaire about any school, form, or epoch. All I seek is excellence, which, of course, is a great deal to ask, and I am happy to find it in any style or genre. For me, music has been and is an endless source of enjoyment. I get a kick out of a tenor singing a thrice familiar aria, provided it is a tenor like Caruso doing an aria like "Vesti la Giubba" from *Pagliacci,* and I can get a lift out of a Sousa march, a Strauss waltz, or an honest and evocative treatment of an old jazz fixture like "The Saints Go Marching In." More often my preference is for a late Beethoven quartet, with its relentless searching for the elusive, mysterious truth of our common mortality and our uncommon reach for immortality, or a Chopin ballade, with its unexpected refractions of the sweetness and heartbreak of the human predicament. But I exclude no area. I welcome new experiences in the concert hall and opera house, on the radio and through the phonograph and tape recorder in my home.

It is the aim of this book, as it is of WQXR itself, to encourage you to be as ardent an explorer as you wish or dare to be. The writers of the individual chapters have been guides to the public on the air, and they now have given their enthusiasms a more permanent form. If you follow them into any section of the musical cosmos, you will find their personal distillations of years of experience. If you take advantage of their discographies, you can become as knowledgeable—well, almost as knowledgeable—as they are. I don't mind confessing that I intend to take some of the hints of my colleagues in fields where I have less experience than they.

I don't pretend that I agree with every judgment in these chapters. I have great respect for Robert Lawrence's command of opera, and I join in most of his views. But I do not agree with his estimate of either *Carmen* or *Otello*. I grant that he makes his points cogently, and I feel that when Bizet stops to let Micaela, that innocuous milksop of an ingenue, sing a long, showstopping aria, he is less than true to the passion and intensity of his subject, and that Verdi retrogresses to his earlier style when he pauses to have Iago sing the surefire *Brindisi*, or drinking song. But even as I agree with the need for rigorous artistic standards, I find myself recalling the pleasure I have derived from a Bori singing Micaela or a Leonard Warren belting out the *Brindisi*. But what about my demands for excellence? Well, the singing is excellent, and I welcome any manifestation of grace.

I am especially pleased with the independence of judgment to be found in these chapters. Does Mr. Lawrence dare to declare his preference for Kappel over Flagstad? Bravo for him! I, too, felt that Flagstad often sounded like some inhumanly glorious machine when she poured out those shining cascades of rich, dark tone, but there were moments when her power to transcend apparently human limits of sound were unbelievably thrilling—and right. In the *Liebestod*, when her voice, with its unearthly coolness, pierced and surmounted the surging orchestra, she seemed to me to achieve the transfiguration—the passage beyond human desire and the merging with a kind of brooding, exulting world spirit—that Wagner intended.

Each of us has his own treasured memories. Like Mr. Lawrence, I have a higher opinion than most connoisseurs of *Fidelio*, and like him, I recall with admiration Flagstad's Lenora and René Maison's Florestan. I have grateful recollections of a more recent *Fidelio* with Nilsson in the title role and John Vickers as Florestan. But the *Fidelio* I remember best is the one I heard in Salzburg in 1935, during one of those brief, magical years when Toscanini, who had turned his back on a Bayreuth dominated by Hitler, joined Bruno Walter and others to make the Austrian festival the most unforgettable of my musical experiences. Lotte Lehmann was the Maestro's Fidelio, and though her voice never had the sheen and amplitude of either Flagstad's or Nilsson's, it had a humanity, a vulnerability that enhanced the character's courage, that was immensely touching. With Toscanini holding everything together with a tight, yet incandescent force, Lehmann sang with a tenderness and intensity remarkable even for her. At that year's Salzburg Festival, if I may permit myself to wallow in rich memories, Toscanini also conducted a *Falstaff* of incomparable lightness and radiance, and Walter presided over a luminous and enchanting *Don Giovanni*. I have always regretted that those performances were not captured on discs. I know that Toscanini did another *Falstaff* years later with the NBC Symphony Orchestra, not long before his retirement, and I feel that in this performance he caught more of the sunset glow and undercurrent of melancholy that are so clearly part of Verdi's operatic swansong than in the Salzburg performance. But it would be wonderful to have records of both performances, as well as, say, a much earlier Toscanini *Falstaff* from his first Scala years at the turn of the century. I am sure that one would discover unexpected subtleties of interpretation in each version, and one would learn something about the growth and change in attitudes of a great performer as well as discover different views of a lovely and abiding masterpiece.

My colleagues have confined themselves for the most part to recommendations of one performance of certain works, though there may be dozens of different recordings. The purpose is to simplify difficult decisions for you. But no one will be offended if you go your own way and select a different recording. I would recommend that occasionally you might try different versions just for the fun of checking how much difference you can discern. Jascha Zayde, in his chapter on the piano, its literature and interpreters, has brought an expert musician's discrimination to an analysis of the individual excellences as well as the differences between the Horowitz and Rubinstein performances of the *Waldstein Sonata*. I would also suggest that you investigate the differences in a great pianist's various interpretations of the same piece. I have spent some time comparing Horowitz's old Victor recording of Chopin's *B flat Minor Sonata* with his more recent Columbia recording. I thought I had a distinct notion of the pianist's way with this sonata; I was astonished to find how much alteration and penetration had developed in the years between the two versions. The Funeral March movement in the later one has arrived at a dignity and nobility that leaves one humble and grateful. If there is any music that has become shopworn from reuse, this is it. One does not need to hark back to meetings of a provincial Kiwanis Club of decades ago where grown men stood up and bleated the words, "Where will all be a hundred years from now? Pushing up the daisies, pushing up the daisies," in an embarrasing caricature of Chopin's music. Heaven alone knows how many times in my thirty years of music criticism I sat through overly sentimental or deliberately unsentimentalized and arid treatments of this movement. I developed, I fear, a kind of instant nausea at the thought of having to endure another traversal, even by a fine pianist. But listening to the later Horowitz version, I was led to rediscover the shattering simplicity and purity of Chopin's emotion.

I hope that you will give yourself a chance to broaden the range of your musical interests by accepting the counsel of my colleagues to try a variety of styles and performances in whatever fields your interest lies. I happen not to be an admirer of the operettas of Romberg and Friml, but I am gratified that Alfred Simon is willing to defend their good qualities at a time when it is unfashionable to do so. I might just go back and listen to his recommendations and find that he speaks with the voice of wisdom.

I would also hope that if your first preferences are for music that is readily accessible, whether a Gilbert and Sullivan song or a Tchaikovsky symphony, you will take chances and try other and more challenging things. You might find yourself on an unexpectedly adventurous course. I recall a friend of years gone by, a man whose principal preoccupation was sports, whom I sent one night to see and hear his first opera. I don't think he was at all interested, but here was a pair of tickets down front on the aisle for *Lucia di Lammermoor* at the Met. The next day my friend was shiny-eyed. Why hadn't anyone told him about her? I wondered for an instant whether he was talking about Lucia. Not at all; he was ecstatic about Lily Pons, and if he remembered that a chap named Donizetti had had something to do with the occasion, he did not mention him. Well, my friend, a meticulous man, not only caught every Pons performance at the Met that season, but also kept a log with the dates and the roles. For several seasons he was a dedicated Pons follower; if he could not get away for the entire performance, he managed to hear at least an act, for he could not bear to have his log remind him that he had missed a Pons evening. Was this the fidelity of a man in love from a distance? Who knows? I do know that my friend was exposing himself to all the operas in which Miss Pons sang. And then, one year, Miss Pons was away from the Met for quite a long time, and my bereaved friend decided that he might as well as try another singer. This time he hit on Verdi's *Traviata,* and another enchanted world opened up for him. Thereafter he became the slave of Verdi, and presently he broadened his experience—and the scope of his log—to embrace nearly all the Italian and French operas. I assumed that his zeal would stop there, but it was not many years before he thought he ought to venture on Wagner. Strauss followed, and then almost anything new or different that the Met did. In time the Met became inadequate to his curiosity, and he began to attend other performances when they were available, in and out of New York. Finally, the thing happened that I would have regarded as most unlikely: He decided to explore something besides opera. Toward the end of his enormously enriched life he went to all sorts of concerts—recitalists as well as ensembles—and he had lovingly accumulated a record collection of amazing diversity and catholicity.

I daresay that many of us have had comparable, if not similar, adventures with music. I remember that as a high-school lad in New York in the twenties, I sat in the cheapest seats at Lewisohn Stadium. They cost twenty-five cents in those days, and there was the nickel fare each way in the subway. But like so many New Yorkers, I had my first experience of the staples of the symphonic repertoire at the Stadium. The inevitable echo was an annoyance, and the performances were often routine, if not downright slipshod. But how could you quibble when you found yourself listening to marvels of eloquence for a total outlay of thirty-five cents? Radio in those days, you must remember, was a primitive affair; you were lucky to get a shadow of a voice or an instrument if you held your earphones snugly to your ears. I remember that my dream of felicity was to have a season pass so that I might attend every Stadium concert every summer. Alas, for the disillusionment of maturity. I reached the point where I did have a season pass, and I used it only when I had to go to the Stadium in the line of reviewing duty. By then I knew that there were better ways to hear symphonic music. By then I was also eager for much greater variety.

I have learned that there are no limits to the ways in which people discover and respond to music, and I am constantly reminded of the rewards for those who come unexpectedly upon something moving or stirring. I remember spending summer vacations in the late thirties in the White Mountain area of northern New Hampshire. My wife and I rented a little wooden shack on a knoll surrounded by sloping fields, with the Presidential range in the distance. We brought with us one summer a portable phonograph, not bad in quality of sound for its time, but thoroughly rudimentary by present-day standards, and a limited number of albums. I need hardly remind the old-timers among my readers how brutally heavy a load of the old shellac 78-rpm discs could be. I have forgotten exactly what was in the collection, though I know it was diversified, including several big pieces, some works for soloists, a Beethoven quartet, a Mozart quintet, some songs. Among the items on my list was an acetate disc of Toscanini's performance of Sibelius's *Second Symphony.* I admit readily that this was a pirated recording, and if my friends among the Toscaninis think they have a cause for action, so be it. It was a full-voiced, dramatic performance of a symphony that may sound corny to impatient and sophisticated ears, and somehow it was perfect for our porch on the knoll, with all of northern New Hampshire to absorb the sound of the phonograph played at top volume and to give back a reflection of Sibelius's affinity for the forests and hills. It happened that our house was on a road over which a group of young actors—members of the newly installed company at the Chase Barn Playhouse—passed each afternoon, on foot I might say, on their way to dinner before the evening's rehearsal or show. It became habitual for them to pause on our knoll and stretch out on the grass while we regaled them with a spot of music from the portable. We went through our tiny repertory several times, but the piece they nearly always demanded was the Sibelius *Second.* Its drama and its orotundity thrilled them and picked them up better than a cocktail could have done. I have run into some of these actors and actresses in later years, and they have told me that no music reached them so readily and that Sibelius's *Second* became, no matter how they fared in their careers, a kind of symbol of how it felt to aspire to a grand utterance.

Music was for me not only a career but a way of life for so many years that I was desolated at the thought of being without it. When *The New York Times* requested in 1960 that I shift from the post of music critic to that of drama critic, I knew I would miss enkindling experiences in the opera house and concert hall, and I did. But I did not miss music, because I sought after it. If my evenings were occupied with theatre openings, I could turn to my record collection and to the radio, especially WQXR, for things I wanted to hear when the mood struck me.

I found that I rarely listened to the familiar repertory. While my blood could still be stirred by a grand performance of Beethoven's *Eroica,* I rarely turned to it of my own accord. If it was Beethoven I wanted to hear again, I went to the less frequently performed pieces. I listened to the piano sonatas, especially the late ones, that are not on every recitalist's program. I lived on intimate terms—and still do—with the late quartets; repetition does not diminish their spiritual strength. I can go back to Mozart's *G Minor Quintet* without fear of being disappointed. In its passion and anguish it tells me as much as any work of art, whether Shakespeare's *King Lear* or a Rembrandt self-portrait of the later years, about the truth of human suffering and courage. And on the same level of greatness is Schubert's *C Major Quintet.* I find inexpressible beauty in all sorts of places—in the slow movement of a Bach concerto, like the one for two violins, in a Corelli concerto grosso, in a long, declamatory, and piercingly emotional passage by Monteverdi, in a spacious, sunny air by Handel, in a moment of shy tenderness of a Schumann piano piece, in the exuberant playfulness of a Mendelssohn scherzo, in the heartbreak of a Schubert song, in the fragmented, eerie pointillism of Webern, in the rarefied atmosphere of the late, still adventurous, Stravinsky, as exemplified in a piece like *Threni.*

The rewards of music are unending, and the directions one can take in seeking them are unlimited. Familiar pieces can yield new discoveries, and unfamiliar ones can provide unexpected delight and illumination. The other day I decided to try Prokofiev's *Quartet No. 1*, Opus 50, which was written in 1930 on commission from the Library of Congress and Elizabeth Sprague Coolidge, that great and good benefactor of music of our century. I must have heard this quartet at one time or another during the years I haunted the concert halls, but it struck me with the force of an utter and agreeable stranger. I was particularly taken by the lovely slow movement.

Another evening I selected Horowitz's record of twelve Scarlatti sonatas. You will notice, when you read Igor Kipnis's chapter and discography, that he recommends Landowska and Kirkpatrick, both harpsichordists, for the Scarlatti sonatas. There is no doubt that this was the instrument for which Scarlatti wrote, and that each interpreter has something worthwhile to reveal of the composer and his music; but I would also suggest listening to a pianist like Horowitz bringing his own resources and those of the modern piano to bear on Scarlatti. The result is entrancing. Listen to Horowitz play the *F Minor Sonata*, Longo 118, and note the poignancy and sweetness of Scarlatti's enamoring inspiration. This music is like the prefiguring of a melting aria by Bellini. Then listen to Joan Sutherland reviving the glories of bel canto in Bellini, and perhaps even as you relish the commanding control of the singer, note how this music bears a slight, incipient kinship to Chopin, who was touched and influenced by its composer.

As you read through the ensuing chapters and consult the accompanying discographies, you will observe that there are some duplications. Thus David Randolph and Igor Kipnis list Handel's *Messiah,* but in different interpretations. I welcome such differences of opinion, and I hope that you will have the opportunity to take advantage of them by testing various performances for yourself. I suppose that you will dissent from some of the choices our experts have made. I know that I do. I could argue with Martin Bookspan, for example, about interpreters of Beethoven's symphonies. I could certainly want people to have some idea of the way Toscanini conducted these works. But there is no doubt in my mind that the recommended discs in all categories are deserving. Our object in limiting ourselves to a minimum of suggestions was to provide immediate guidance to the reader who is not yet sure of his own predilections. In time he will make his own way, ignoring the hints of his advisers. That is as it should be.

Let me make another confession. I am a little unhappy that we have not done more with contemporary music. I happen to think that one of America's distinguished composers is Elliott Carter and that his string quartets, though novel in structure and difficult to apprehend on first acquaintance, are works of stature, which will repay repeated hearings. But in our desire to range over the vast literature in all the forms, we found we had to make choices, lest the discographies themselves form a book as thick as the Schwann catalogue. We were mindful of our purpose—to provide a guide for family listening pleasure. We assumed and hoped we would be reaching into families for whom the vast, overflowing worlds of music remained largely to be explored. We are confident that those individuals and families well on their way in musical exploration will also find these pages useful, and that they will be encouraged to leave us for bypaths we have not mapped. We hope that you will get fresh ideas from these chapters, and that you will keep telling WQXR how it can continue to enhance your family's listening pleasure. In your home, in the opera house and concert hall, in the schools and churches, and on the airwaves, especially WQXR's, AM and FM, happy listening!

1

Opera

ROBERT LAWRENCE

Opera is less an art than a state of being. The allegiance it exacts is total, engulfing, lifelong. Emotion reigns as in a cult; logic is secondary; even the most objective critic, in framing his verdict, will start from only one of several possible viewpoints. The charm of opera—and its strength—lies in the power to disunite, stir aesthetic conflict among all who prize it. Learned men have stated, from time to time, that opera is dying; but no moribund organism could possibly generate such passions.

The word *opera*, really an omnibus term, has been used rather loosely across the years—especially in this country, where "Grand Opera" is still taken to mean any sung and staged work calling for expensive soloists, large orchestra, chorus, and production by a multiple staff. This is an illusion. Style, not size, is the determining factor in opera's identity; yet size alone seems to have written its calling card in the United States. Any art taken up by the rich and highly placed (as opera has been in the past) is assumed to be "grand"; and the inflating process, inspired by the word *opera* and its association with crystal chandeliers, imposing halls, elegant audiences, went down the line during the last century until most small towns in America called their largest theater—housing vaudeville and occasionally a spoken drama—the *Opera House*, not because opera was being given there, but because the place was grander and more sumptuous than any other in town.

The majority of works produced in a season of "Grand Opera" are, technically speaking, not *grand* at all. Most of them may be classified as *lyric drama*, with a libretto (generally the equivalent of a modern play) set to music which not only sounds well in itself but continually heightens the action. There are few, if any, formal arias. Historical pageantry does not exist; ballet, infrequently. The scale of production, despite a few big scenes, is generally intimate. All the scores of Puccini, with the exception of *Turandot*, are *lyric drama;* and so is the preponderance of those by Massenet.

An even more intimate style, closely connected with the French theater, is *opéra-comique*, which features set numbers (as in modern Broadway musicals) linked by spoken dialogue. *Carmen* and *Mignon* are perhaps the best known examples. Their German cousins—*The Magic Flute, Fidelio, Der Freischütz*—are put together in exactly the same way, though designated across the border as *singspiel*. It should be noted that despite the French term *comique*, this type of opera is not so lighthearted (plenty of the plots are tragic) as it is intimate, evoking life at close quarters, and reminiscent of the *genre* paintings of Greuze as opposed to the monumental canvases of a Rubens.

Opera buffa, a style beloved of the Italian theater (this time read *buffa* for real comedy), also uses set numbers; but instead of being linked by spoken dialogue, they are bound together by a freely moving song-speech called *recitativo*. The numbers themselves concentrate on antic, often zany farce. *Folk opera*—a mood rather than a style, often comic, sometimes rich in pathos—draws on national coloring, ranges widely in repertoire from *The Bartered Bride* to *Porgy and Bess*.

There are many avenues of approach to this flexible and diversified art. Richard Wagner spurned old-fashioned opera (*arias* alternating with *recitativo*) in favor of *music drama*, with its uninterrupted chain of melody and symphonic dominance of the orchestra. Musorgski, using much but not all of the same philosophy (voice and orchestra are equally prominent in his scores), created the *chronicle* type of music drama: short historical scenes varying sharply in characterization, wild humor contrasting with bleakest tragedy.

Most of the great Verdi scores (and a majority of those by Rossini, Bellini, and Donizetti) are labeled simply *opera*, no less, no more—a design of formal numbers known as *arias* alternating with *recitativo* in convincingly dramatic sequence. *Lucia di Lammermoor, Luisa Miller, Rigoletto, Il Trovatore,* and *La Traviata* are among the masterpieces that come to mind. As for the redoubtable style labeled *grand opera*, only the giant machines of Spontini, Meyerbeer, late Rossini (*Mosè, William Tell*), early Verdi (*Nabucco, I Lombardi, Macbeth*), quite late Verdi (*Simon Boccanegra, Don Carlo, Aida, Otello*), Ponchielli's *La Gioconda* and a few twentieth-century loners, such as Puccini's *Turandot*, conform technically to the concept of historical background, vast concerted numbers, frequent use of ballet, and elaborate pageantry which make it very special.

This variety of approach strengthens, in the long run, the fascination of opera. The diverse types of work, such as *grand opera, opera buffa, opéra-comique*, complement rather than vie with one another. There is plenty of room in the musical theater for every sort of style. No basis for conflict here. The real battle line, over which many wars in opera have been waged, has to do with the relative importance of words and music. Which comes first? Which rates a priority? For centuries we have had tugs of war between admirers of the vocal melodists—Handel, Scarlatti, Bellini, Donizetti—and champions of the dramatic reformers—Gluck, Wagner, Musorgski, Berg—with fans of some of the greatest composers (Mozart, Verdi, Strauss) standing dead center.

Allied with this conflict—on a performing rather than a compositional level—is the question of how singers should behave when the music comes first. How far can they go in milking a climax and yet stand within the bounds of good taste? These are issues that can still bring opera buffs to blows, or at least to the breaking of long-time friendships.

Since all of opera is a personal experience, and every writer—subconsciously or otherwise—advances his own point of view, I trust the reader will permit me to present my own, imbedded in reminiscences of New York performance. Light—admittedly subjective—may thereby be shed on certain styles and artists.

Personal Memories

My first preparations for listening to opera took place in movie palaces. It is almost impossible today to imagine the quantity of good music performed in New York, thirty-five or forty years ago, in the vast, cathedral-like motion picture theaters. Every one of them had its permanent orchestra of from sixty to seventy-five players, expert musicians all. The Capitol Theater's ensemble provided a base of development for Eugene Ormandy, first as assistant concertmaster, later as associate conductor.

These orchestras at the Strand, Capitol, Roxy, Rivoli and Rialto, under the direction of competent leaders and with musical programs arranged by men of taste and imagination, played a widely ranging repertoire of overtures, tone poems, and excerpted symphonic movements. During a brief stint as usher at the Rialto I came to know Bruckner's *Fourth Symphony* as incidental music for a silent film featuring Emil Jannings, "The Way of All Flesh." This score was performed by the orchestra at two of the five shows daily (the organ took over at the other performances). I was so drawn, night after night, by the symphony's opening horn call that I stood listening in the aisle, forgetting the flow of patrons waiting for seats.

Vocally, too, the movie houses had interesting things to offer. They maintained, in addition to resident orchestra and ballet, a permanent chorus and often very good soloists. We had Verdi—the triumphal scene from *Aida*—on the stage of the Capitol and the beauties of Russian opera, in excerpted form, at the Rivoli.

New York in those days was starting on its career as a cultural beehive. My musical background was formed at popular roots not only in the movie houses but the ball parks (a first encounter with *Aida* took place one night long ago at the Polo Grounds), open-air concerts in Central Park by the Goldman Band, and at the Lewisohn Stadium by the New York Philharmonic. A first memory of the Stadium—and an operatic one—goes back to the night following the death of President Harding, when the Philharmonic played "Siegfried's Funeral March" in memoriam. So heroic a send-off may not have been warranted; but to the youngster drinking in this music as a new experience, the evening lent Warren G. Harding a special aura. I wonder if he ever heard of Wagner.

The most vivid preparation for life as an opera buff came with a musical play imported from Berlin: *Johannes Kreisler*. It was based on short stories by E. T. A. Hoffmann, some of whose tales had already inspired the famous piece by Offenbach. Years have gone by since this production in the early twenties, sumptuously mounted, with Jacob Ben-Ami as the protagonist. I have tried checking with any number of contemporaries, brought up in New York, as to their impressions. No one today recalls *Johannes Kreisler*.

There were over sixty scenes, made possible through a revolving stage and the ingenious use of cutouts. At one point, as the platform swung around, the interior of a rococo opera house came into sight, while on the stage within a stage, Mozart's *Don Giovanni* was being performed. Indeed the central theme of the play was the art of Mozart, and its crowning point the moment when Johannes Kreisler—in love with the soprano who sings the rôle of Donna Anna—returns late at night to the empty opera house. He sits brooding in his box, suddenly perceives the ghost of the soprano on the stage below, hears her sing a spectral "Non mi dir." In a surge of feeling which defies gravity itself, he soars (on wires) from the box, descends to the stage, and holds out his arms to the phantom, who disappears. Exaggerated, ridiculous? Not at all. A way of life eternally operatic, illusory, expressive.

Then at last came an encounter with opera at the Metropolitan. Newspaper pictures of Maria Jeritza as Turandot, wearing a cloth-of-gold train that spread from the top of a majestic staircase to footlights apparently hundreds of feet away, led me to the spectacle by Puccini. I bought a ticket in that part of the old house perpendicular to the stage, from which one could see very little of what was happening on stage. Moreover I was poorly prepared, having read only a brief synopsis, instead of the libretto word for word. Yet certain elements in the performances made their mark: the clatter of the xylophone in the opening bars; the entrance of Turandot, silent and implacable, extending a hand tipped with clawlike nails to signal death for the Prince of Persia. These were among the externals that impressed. The work itself, as I learned later, suffers from variations in quality.

Even before attending *Turandot*, I had succumbed to that love for the music of Wagner, which, once it sets in, holds one captive for years. There were weekly visits to the shelves of the New York Public Library, borrowing piano-vocal scores of the *Ring*, playing them through. I resolved to hear every work of Wagner then being offered by the Metropolitan. To raise funds for standing room, I tutored in Latin; but my mind was not much on the work. What held me fast were *Tristan und Isolde*, *Götterdämmerung*, *Parsifal*, and a dramatic soprano, new to the Metropolitan, who sang in all of them: Gertrude Kappel.

The night of January 16, 1928, was a significant one for me. Life, at the age of fifteen, seemed to hold no limits. The thrill of a first *Tristan*—toward which I had built through months of studying the score, playing it, dreaming it—was about to be realized. I stood in back of the house, impatient for the opening notes of the prelude. When the music began, my critical sense told me this was not a good orchestra (Metropolitan instrumental standards have risen immeasurably since then); but once the soprano from Munich, who was making her debut that evening, had embarked on Isolde's first-act narrative, the performance cast its spell. There were other aspects that have stayed with me: the intensity of Artur Bodanzky's conducting, despite the poor ensemble he had to work with; the sumptuous singing of Karin Branzell as Brangaene; the vigor and authority of Friedrich Schorr as Kurvenal; the cast-iron sound of Rudolf Laubenthal as Tristan; but my chief impression was of the Isolde, a performer I was rarely to miss from that night until her departure from the Metropolitan eight years later. Gertrude Kappel, from the other side of the footlights, taught me more about drama through vocal coloring than any artist in recall.

Was this just a puppy love, the indiscriminate worship of a youngster taking his first steps in opera? I do not think so; for on the basis of much that was told me later, there were other articulate, sensitive opera-goers growing up at that time who felt the same way. Some three decades after that memorable first *Tristan*, I was seated at a performance of *La Traviata* with a group that included the conductor Erich Leinsdorf and his wife, Anne, who as a child had been taken to almost all of the Bodanzky performances. That night we were hearing Renata Tebaldi's first New York Violetta—a mellifluous study in surface gloss. Suddenly Mrs. Leinsdorf shot me a glance and muttered, "*We* heard Kappel!" An odd remark, evoking the name of a soprano who had never in her life sung Violetta; but I understood at once what was meant: the chasm between that beloved voice, which had come from the soul, and the well-negotiated singing of the moment.

I often disagree about opera with George Marek, author of *Puccini* and *Richard Strauss,* but never about Kappel. He and his wife were standees in that era; they too were held by the vocal colors Kappel used for revealing psychological states, and they still talk about it. The late Robert Bagar, a perceptive music critic, told me that on a Sunday afternoon in April, 1934, when Kappel sang Brünnhilde's Immolation at Carnegie Hall with the New York Philharmonic under Toscanini's direction, he was so unstrung following the concert that he walked miles before recovering himself. In short, I did not stand alone as an enthusiast.

Why was it, then, that this remarkable artist, for all her gifts, never reaped the public acclaim of a Flagstad? I should say in answer—and this is a question over which I have pondered long—that one had to tune in, provide one's own reception on her very special wave length. Before hearing her sing, one had to know the *word.* It was the extension, the transformation of this word into music that melted one. The voice itself had superb natural beauty, especially in the deeper tones, with a dark opulence I have heard from no other soprano. Then just before the emergence of the extreme top it had a fullness, richness, eloquence, which haunt one in retrospect. If my words, at this point, read like those of a physician recounting a case history, it is because this voice etched itself on my mind and heart, because I knew—just as the lover knows every impulse of the woman he has been courting—the most minute responses of this instrument in performance. There were passing technical lapses; the top tones, basically thrilling, were sometimes strained, for this great interpreter varied perceptively from one evening to the next. Her voice did not possess the Niagara-like plenitude that marked the Flagstad tone, the metallic gleam of Frida Leider or Germaine Lubin, other leading Wagner singers of Kappel's generation.

Yet it had something more to say than any of the voices I have mentioned; it brought—when in best condition—a matchless sense of illumination to the role.

Outwardly Kappel was jovial—blonde, attractive, modest. I have heard it said by those who sang with her that she was among the most considerate of colleagues. The wonderful carriage of her head, the regal bearing of the shoulders were attributes onstage and offstage. One of her most winning qualities as a person was her simplicity, her bubbling and spontaneous warmth.

Yet was she really simple? I cannot believe so; for over the years, my ears attuned to many voices, I have never heard another so mysterious, so elusive. This is perhaps the reason it was never a successful recording voice. The few discs (pallid pre-electrical) that are available can give no idea of its color, its unique overtones. When, in Isolde's first-act narrative, she reflected on the wounded Tristan and sang the words *Er sah mir in die Augen* ("He looked into my eyes"), the voice glided softly, almost opaquely, up those half-steps to the final note, then opened like some fabled flower. Yet this was only one facet of Kappel's art. Loftiness and nobility, as in the *Götterdämmerung* Brünnhilde, were another; and a third lay in the subtle, almost insidious projection of evil. Her Ortrud and Kundry were complex, malevolent creations both, a journey into the extrasensory.

To have summoned this sound out of the depths of her consciousness, projected her inner world to those willing to get in touch, must have demanded a complexity that still has me baffled when I recall the modest, smiling woman offstage. The enigma remains.

If I have dwelled on Gertrude Kappel at length, it is because her singing determined for me the standard by which I still judge opera in performance: expressivity. There are many ways, all entirely personal, of appraising this art. Some listeners prefer vocal brilliance; others, intellectual discipline; a third group, purity of phrasing; and so on down the line. It is possible, of course, for the same buff to prize all these qualities in varying degree; but usually one who lives for opera has his own hard-core approach, his own well-defined aesthetic. And so, with a bow to the intellectual, to the purely musical, to the vocally pyrotechnical, I shall explore operatic values in the remainder of this piece with an ear for the expressive.

Singing Style

Before long the seductive air of the opera house, the desire to be there at all times, no matter what the work to be sung, cut through my limiting Wagnerian preference. I learned that every part of the repertoire can have its special appeal. There came as fresh discoveries the grandeur of *Norma,* pathos of *Manon,* high spirits of *The Bartered Bride.* Three distinguished sopranos were appearing in these works: Rosa Ponselle, Lucrezia Bori, Elisabeth Rethberg—all of them strikingly different in sound, yet almost equally fine. Ponselle, though American by birth, exemplified the tradition of the Italian dramatic soprano: vocal majesty, command of ornamentation. Bori was the singing actress, relying less on opulence of tone than unfailing charm and insight. Rethberg had perhaps the most appealing voice of all—a lyrical instrument, capable of dramatic flight—plus enormous taste and musicality.

When one is new to opera and to the halls where it is given, almost every detail on both sides of the footlights lingers through the years. In those early days as a standee at the old Met, I had my counterpoint notebook before me, propped against the rail. There were exercises to be done for next morning's class, and intermissions were the time in which to get started. As I worked, those idols of my youth, the New York music critics, would saunter up the aisle in the midst of the crowd. These were the mysterious ones, unrecognized by most of the audience, but known to my fellow standees. They ranged through their empire incognito, much as Haroun al Raschid must have gone in disguise among his people. Olin Downes, Lawrence Gilman, Oscar Thompson, journalists all, looked to us, behind the rail, like sages from some Caliphate in space. These were first impressions, refracted and romanticized.

Other great singers held sway in those days—the last of the Gatti regime—in addition to the artists already mentioned. Lawrence Tibbett, at his vibrant best; John Charles Thomas, a model of vocal elegance; Giuseppe De Luca, all suavity and lyricism; Ezio Pinza, one of the noblest bassos in the world. And with the demise of the old Chicago Civic Opera, some of its leading singers came to perform—outstandingly—at the Metropolitan. Frida Leider, Maria Olszewska, Lotte Lehmann, Tito Schipa, and Richard Bonelli established themselves among the elect. There were brief but memorable returns by Claudia Muzio and Edith Mason, both of whom had sung in New York prior to their days in Chicago. This was the firmament of the time, made even brighter by the debut of Kirsten Flagstad in 1935.

It was before the huge success of Flagstad that I had begun to wonder about the aesthetics of opera in performance. Could it be that some of the world's most celebrated artists, the recognized "greats," were not to the taste of all who heard them? Might one concede that stylistic preference, previous education, helped shape one's judgment just as definitely as the sound of the singer's voice?

The lack of an absolute standard for judging operatic artists first made itself known to me during certain performances that featured Beniamino Gigli. Here was a tenor with an indisputably beautiful voice, lionized by the public; yet I found much of his work uncongenial. The compressing of all emotion into the passing sigh, the vulgar sob, put me off then and still does whenever I hear his records—excepting a first-rate *Andrea Chénier,* which, sung straight, shows how great an artist he might have been. In the case of his contemporary, Giacomo Lauri-Volpi, the brilliantly trumpeted top tones, arrogantly held ad infinitum, again could bring offense. There was little real expressivity in either of these men, for all their conventionalized show of it. Their art, though based on quality singing, was contrived; "sold" to a public out front via routine theatrical effects.

One has only to hear a recording by Enrico Caruso with its manly, straightforward account of the music to realize that Italian tenors need not exaggerate in order to make their point. Aureliano Pertile, Giovanni Martinelli, and in our time Carlo Bergonzi have upheld the dignity and emotional directness of the Latin performer, with such distinguished foreigners as the late

Jussi Bjoerling, Jan Peerce, Nicolai Gedda, and Richard Tucker seconding their approach. Franco Corelli, who continues to grow artistically from one season to the next, still has enough of the Lauri-Volpi vocal strut to alienate me in part. The point of view is admittedly subjective. Which school of singing, in short, does one prefer? Best make a choice and judge accordingly.

Now back to Kirsten Flagstad, with that same subjectivity as guide. There can be no doubt that hers was one of the phenomenal voices of the century. The grandeur of sound, ease of emission, and feeling of limitless reserve made her art—from the technical standpoint—unique and unsurpassable. On occasion the size and splendor of the voice created an aura that matched the excitement of the music—as in Brünnhilde's oath on the spear, Leonora's rapture at the freeing of Florestan. In general, however, her acting and much of her singing lacked (for me and for others) that inner expressivity one had cherished so greatly in Kappel and found in the art of a Frida Leider, a Lotte Lehmann.

Recently I have studied several Flagstad recordings with a view to playing them on the air; and in almost every case, though admiring the tone and musicianship, I have been put off by their austerity, the separation of notes within the phrase, so that the climactic ones come out detached and sometimes dry. A more basic source of alienation lies in the small amount of nuance, the limited gradations of color. Yet I am aware, more now than ever before, that it is not so much the individual singer who determines the listener's reaction as the school he or she represents. Substitute, in this year of publication, Christa Ludwig and Régine Crespin for Kappel and Leider; replace Flagstad with Birgit Nilsson, and the lines are clearly drawn. Here are two opposing schools of thought, their patterns running from one generation to the next: the expressive and the overwhelming. Take your pick, and mark X on the ballot.

There comes a time in the life of most opera fans when the focus of energy and admiration shifts from their contemplation of the singer to the work itself. This, in short, is maturity; and, regrettably, some of the more impassioned bobby-soxers never make it. They end as they started—with a permanent crush on performers, endless talk about singers, their fees and foibles. To them, opera is a parlor game, a checkerboard of personalities; or a sport, with high C's bearing the same importance as a home run or a matador thrust.

Turning away from all this, one can concentrate on *opera*—the sum rather than its parts—the most complex and fascinating of theatrical arts. Having reached expressivity as my critical norm, with the understanding that certain great singers fall within this category and others do not, I began to approach the art of the performers with less personal involvement, learned to take their achievements more in stride. It was the music itself that held me more than before.

This is not to imply a lack of major artists during the regime of Edward Johnson, who followed Gatti-Casazza as general manager. The brief but fiery presence of Maria Caniglia, an outstanding dramatic soprano, and of Mafalda Favero, a cherishable lyric, just before World War II, helped maintain international standards. The success of such American singers as Helen Traubel and Eleanor Steber did much for the development of native talents. Zinka Milanov, vocally authoritative in the big Verdi roles, brought a special glow to the 1940's, as did those two admirable lyric sopranos, Licia Albanese and Bidu Sayao.

There followed, after the war, a gifted group of Italian singers who bloomed dramatically and faded too quickly: Giuseppe Di Stefano, Mario Del Monaco, Cloe Elmo, Fedora Barbieri (now enjoying a resurgence as "character" mezzo)—all prime voices lacking in the moderation that preserves. Then, well into the administration of Rudolf Bing, came Maria Callas (expressive school) and Renata Tebaldi (overwhelming) with their famous rivalry.

At the risk of being charged with inconsistency, I must admit to playing few recordings by Callas on the air, for the fine intelligence, the creativity of her singing do not always neutralize what for me is an unpleasant sound. I respect her artistry, but choose not to live with it. Yet Callas holds, and deserves, a stature that will never be lessened by adverse reaction from any critic. She has given significantly of herself in dramatic projection and musical splendor. Her case illustrates again—more strikingly than most—the hotly subjective nature of one's feelings about opera. The recordings of her rival, Madame Tebaldi, though smoother and more luscious, disaffect me from another standpoint. They have little to offer interpretatively. Tebaldi is the surer vocalist, Callas the greater artist.

Still one further credit, a large one, must be chalked on the Callas scoreboard: her versatility in portraying many roles, and more important, her enterprise in reviving single-handedly a whole branch of the repertoire fallen into disuse: the *bel canto* operas, which concentrate on vocal agility as well as expressive song. *Anna Bolena, Il Pirata, I Puritani, La Sonnambula* are among the works that have returned to life through this singer's initiative. Whether or not one relishes their music is another question, part of the eternal subjectivity of opera, but her contribution is undeniable.

It remained for Joan Sutherland to follow the road opened by Miss Callas and to add certain dazzling accomplishments of her own. Starting purely as a vocalist (the overwhelming school), Miss Sutherland has developed the expressive side of her art until she now stands among the best-rounded of today's performers.

These conflicting elements of expressivity and vocal glamor may sometimes overlap in the same artist—as with Miss Sutherland and the excellent basso, Nicolai Ghiaurov—but more often they occur singly. Then it is up to us and our tastes, how much the performer pleases. Along such basic lines, Evelyn Lear—with a good voice and superb theatrical instincts—would be ranked among the leaders of today's expressive school. Leontyne Price, with wonderful vocal equipment and routine acting ability, would be hailed for her eminence in song. Each, according to the reader's lights, will have filled a valid place.

Worship of the prima donna, for many years in eclipse, is being revived for commercial reasons. A group of operatic susceptibles (turbulent fans) has been indoctrinated into nostalgia for a bygone era when princes, archdukes and railroad magnates drank champagne out of a diva's slipper and students unhitched the horses from their favorite soprano's carriage and bore her in triumph on their shoulders. This neogaslight cult—set in motion by a skillfully handled advertising campaign for recording artists—has been under way since the early 1950's. No more unhitched carriages, of course; and we are too hygienic to drink out of slippers. But florid titles, suggestive of old-time Havana cigars, have been invented for modern singers: *La Divina, La Stupenda, La Diva Imperial.* Recording companies, out to surround their artists with the type of fervent mystique that greeted Jenny Lind on a tour of America in the 1850's (whipped up by her New York representative, P. T. Barnum), would seem to have convinced some of our buffs that it is history relived to turn the opera house into a bedlam of shouts and cheers *during* the act. They rip the music as it sounds, smash the mood before its spell has ended, and take over the show in a belief that exhibitionist madness can restore the fabled past. This group has been spoiling opera at its source, driving many devotees to give up live performance for the privacy of stereo in the home, which no bellowing extrovert can mar. (The sale of discs has ironically been increased by all this, but not on the basis of divas.) Certainly the LP recordings of today offer an ideal, uninterrupted listening experience, which most opera houses (with the exception of Bayreuth, where special festival conditions prevail) would find it hard to match.

Another good reason for listening to records at home is one's own choice of repertoire. In this country, where the major opera houses are not—as in Europe—state-supported, an impresario must be guided by the public's taste in the production of new works or the revival of rare old ones. He depends, financially, upon its preference.

New York's operatic audience is in the main conservative. *Bohème* and *Traviata,* both admirable yet frayed, still reign at the ticket window. Rather than face a new musical experience, many patrons prefer rotating stars in the same old works. It *is* true, and fortunately, that unfamiliar scores sometimes do take hold. Strauss's *Die Frau ohne Schatten,* given its first New York stage production during the Metropolitan season of 1966-1967, succeeded with the public; and a superb revival of *Peter Grimes* in the same winter also found favor. But when the Hamburg Opera arrived in June, 1967, on an official visit to Lincoln Center, bringing with it a group of works never before presented here, response at the box-office was initially slow and ultimately disappointing. This, in effect, would constitute a mandate to any local impresario for the exercise of caution. Music-lovers with a taste for modern masterpieces will have to go it alone until the public, through its support, permits these works to enter the repertoire. Meanwhile *Lulu, Mathis der Maler,* and *Les Dialogues des Carmélites* make for good listening at home, complete on stereo, or in excerpted form, via radio.

Opera Companies

With the single exception of repertoire—in which they can afford to be more adventurous—the state-subsidized houses of Europe are run on a similar scale and with the same performing ideals as the great opera theaters of the United States. First-class orchestras and choruses are the rule; there is generally elaborate staging; famous singers divide their time among the various companies. Most celebrated today—and this is a rating that can always change—are La Scala, Italy's leading theater at Milan; the Vienna State Opera; the Hamburg, Munich, and Berlin operas; the Paris Opéra (more, perhaps, as a memory than a current achievement); the Bolshoi in Moscow; the Stockholm Opera; London's Covent Garden; in South America, the Teatro Colón of Buenos Aires; and here at home the Metropolitan.

So much for the crystal chandelier division. There remains another type of house, popularly priced, that fills a definite need. Vienna has its Volksoper, London its Sadler's Wells, New York its City Opera—theaters with good, often inventive repertoire and rising young artists to perform it. These companies are stable; their working conditions range from modest to excellent.

Those of us with memories of New York before the advent of the City Opera can recall more sketchy ensembles, which nevertheless gave pleasure. I remember, for example, a traveling troupe known as the *Art of Musical Russia.* This threadbare company brought to many young opera-goers a first, and startlingly wonderful, taste of *Khovantschina* and *The Golden Cockerel.* It mattered little that the orchestra was small, the singers only so-so, the scenery kept standing by the grace of God. The group, in its warmhearted abandon, radiated true musical theater.

Not all production need be luxurious. Low budget in itself is no crime against opera, and only mediocrity of spirit can do real damage. Memories go back to a shoestring venture which shaped the tastes of many buffs in my time. Following its great days as a home for extravaganza, the old New York Hippodrome had been converted into a vaudeville house, the big stage shorn to half its former size, the orchestra pit foreshortened. The auditorium, still overpowering in a moldy sort of way, was taken over during the early 1930's by a showman with a flair: Alfredo Salmaggi. He wore luxuriant black hair almost shoulder length, topped it with a broad-brimmed Borsalino, carried a gold-headed cane, and called himself Maestro. This flashy exuberance marked one side of the man. He also brought to the Hippodrome a vein of idealism for which few have given him credit. Many operagoers heard their first *Otello, Mefistofele, Ballo in Maschera, Andrea Chénier,* during the long years when these works were out of the Metropolitan repertoire, and some very superior performances of *Norma,* all at a widely publicized "ninety-nine-cent top."

Those who recall the workings of this theater from the inside tell me that its operation was filled with intrigue of a low order; but I, from out front, remember with gratitude a large selection of Italian operas done quite acceptably at prices that made it possible for one to attend night after night. When success came to Salmaggi, he did not stint, but extended himself by attempting—like Don Quixote combating the windmills—such formidable works as *Tannhäuser, Die Walküre,* and *Tristan und Isolde.* His productions of Wagner were weird; nor could they have been otherwise. A good *Ring* orchestra is hard to come by even with adequate rehearsals and a balanced budget. More importantly, Wagner cannot be improvised, while within certain definable limits, Verdi and Puccini can. I have heard, when the flame burned bright, a *Trovatore* or a *Tosca* come off at the Hippodrome with tremendous excitement. It was the unpredictability of those performances that made one eager to be there. Many evenings went unbelievably well, and in retrospect one thanks the Maestro.

Some of the rough-and-ready qualities of the old Hippodrome survive today in a company known as the Brooklyn Opera, under the direction of a second-generation Salmaggi: Felix, one of Alfredo's four sons. I go there, drawn by the lure of Brooklyn's

Academy of Music, its cozily fading splendor, perfect sight lines, and fine acoustics. The audience, too, attracts me. Only at the Academy can one still find the unjaded. The star system, its piddling rival camps and sniveling fan clubs, are unknown to these young people who shout with joy as Tosca—*any* Tosca—stabs the villainous Scarpia, for they are totally involved with the drama. The Brooklyn scenery is often wild. The orchestra can sound as if it were reading the music for the first time. And yet the singers are convincing, the performance weaves its spell, conjures up that sense of the homemade, the authentically popular, which remains an endearing part of the Italian operatic world below top performance level.

The control of that top level has shifted with the years. We read a good deal about the Golden Age of Song, during which star singers were virtually in command. Then, fired by enthusiasm, we rush out to buy whatever discs remain of these great personalities, and are often disappointed.

Their voices come off solidly; their technique sounds more flexible, in many instances, than the singing of today; the dramatic intensity is high. Yet the performances, to put it plainly, can be sloppy, wanting in accuracy. Even so famous an artist as Mattia Battistini took signal liberties with the composer's rhythms, and his less talented contemporaries went further. The carelessness to which I refer is not to be confused with the freedom and improvisation so appropriate in the old *bel canto* operas. I have in mind music composed during the artists' own careers. In addition to being lax, their performances bear a trace of arrogance.

Opera Conductors

Centralized control was needed to check such abuses. It came in the person of Arturo Toscanini, who battled for authority over the performance as a whole and won. The singers gradually fell into line, embraced the concept of responsibility. In the recordings of a Caruso may be heard, to an ideal degree, the wedding of the old brilliance and the new integrity.

Then, in the wake of Toscanini's reform, came the golden

period of opera conducting. Singers and musical directors worked jointly for the glory of the performance, the last word emanating from the maestro. Bruno Walter, Fritz Reiner, Otto Klemperer, Erich Kleiber, Fritz Busch and Sir Thomas Beecham were the distinguished men who presided—no mere accompanists, but masters of the orchestra.

This development was in a sense ordained. Had Toscanini not come forward, some other great conductor with fire and initiative would have created the new order, for it was implicit in the needs of the music. Composers, rather than performers, are the ultimate force for change. When the suave *bel canto* operas of Donizetti and Bellini gave way to the fierce, earthy scores of young Verdi, an adjustment in vocal style had to be made. The newer operas called for savage accents, ringing tones, a violence quite alien to what had gone before. The size of the orchestra, too, was enlarged. Singers had to cope with increased instrumental volume, and so the stentorian style still prevalent in Italian opera was evolved. No one performer dictated this transition. It lay in the nature of the music.

It was the composer too, with his new symphonic needs, who shaped the rise of the all-powerful conductor. No mere time-beater or accompanist could do justice to the orchestral intricacies of mature Wagner, middle and late Verdi, Debussy, and Strauss. *Parsifal, Falstaff, Pelléas et Mélisande, Elektra* all demand consummate skill on the part of the musical director, full control of the complicated forces. For every recording today of an operatic masterpiece, there is a famous conductor at the helm.

Ironically, much of the arrogance marking the attitude of the old-time star has more recently crept into the approach of the conductor. We may substitute for liberties taken by the storybook prima donna a rigidity of tempo imposed by the maestro. Even the great Toscanini (as evidenced in his recordings with the NBC Symphony of *Aida* and *La Traviata*) was known in later years to force his singers, instead of breathing with them. This was the whim of a Titan, who instead of relaxing toward the end, recharged his strength excessively and drove not only his colleagues but himself.

In truth there can be no imposed, *absolute* tempo in opera. The speed, the travel of the music, are determined by the physical condition of the singer. One soprano will have shorter breath than another; one tenor, instead of sustaining a top note, will be compelled to cut it relatively short. This is part of the give-and-take in operatic performance, calling ultimately for a meeting of minds in rehearsal rather than a ruthless dictatorship at performance. Many younger conductors, lacking the special gifts of a Toscanini, have captured his outward manner instead of his inner genius, interfered with singers of talent and good will, interrupted or congealed their flow of song.

Yet the wheel still turns in this evolving art, and the power of the maestro today is being largely eroded by a comparative newcomer to the scene: the *régisseur*. It all started with Richard Wagner, who declared his works to be a complete union of music, drama and décor. He acted as his own stage director, bringing what he considered theatrical truth to the scene. For more than sixty years after Wagner's death in 1883, the quest that he had started, for convincing movement and psychological insight, grew mainly in Central Europe, with offshoots in Italy, Russia, and less notably, France and the United States. I am referring not to the great individual acting performances of a Feodor Chaliapin, Mary Garden, Geraldine Farrar, Germaine Lubin, but to the drawing together by one person—the stage director—of *all* the theatrical elements in opera. The popularity of motion pictures, from the beginning of this century, put an additional demand upon the *régisseur*. Scenic credibility and dramatic motivation were called for by audiences in the great opera houses, as well as beauty of song, splendor of orchestral playing.

Then suddenly, as the end of World War II, there began in Germany and spread around the world what might be called the implosion of operatic stage direction. Sparked by the success of Wieland Wagner at Bayreuth—the grandson of Richard Wagner, modernizing the visual texture of the *Ring* in the very theater built for its first performance, fusing singers, conductors and designers into one performing unit on which to work his concept—the *régisseur* soon became king in many places. It was he who would now have the last word in policy decisions and dominate the music as well as the scene. Using this philosophy, Herbert von Karajan, always a controlling force as conductor, extended his sway to lighting, grouping and décor, thus keeping a grip on the entire production. In the cases of other less versatile (or influential) maestri it has been a losing struggle to exercise the old authority from the orchestra pit in the face of steadily growing power from the stage. Tyrone Guthrie, Walter Felsenstein, and Giorgio Strehler are among the masters of this comparatively new element in opera. Their function, in the highest sense, is not so much to illustrate as illumine the music.

Occasionally, as with conductors who have tended to throw their weight around, certain *régisseurs* can go too far. I recall, for example, a production of Poulenc's *Les Dialogues des Carmélites* not long ago in Rio de Janeiro by a visiting Frenchman who deliberately changed the structure of the work. He declared, in a program note, that Poulenc's division into three acts was dramatically weak. Therefore he, the *régisseur*, had arranged matters differently. There would be only two acts, with the intermission coming at a moment of his choice. The intent was presumptuous; the resulting performance, lopsided.

The editing of a work centuries old, launched under conditions that never approximated our own, is, within discretion, justifiable. Tampering with an opera whose composer, a man of the theater, has been dead less than five years would appear to be a crime. At best the modern stage director is a vitalizing force. On a lower level, he could endanger the artistic climate.

Recorded Opera

Thus far we have been considering what happens inside an opera house. When production is transferred to a medium outside the theater—recording—changes in the power structure inevitably take place.

The earliest recordings, primitive by modern standards of presence and fidelity, were based on the star system, on the desire of the public at the turn of the century to hear its favorite artists in familiar excerpts. The voice was everything. Standards of orchestral performance were generally neglected, personnel kept to a minimum. Not until the early 1920's did the practice of recording complete operas under first-class conditions take hold, as in the pioneering series by La Scala of Milan. So gradually have refinements been added since then as to make us forget that the long-playing record, with what would seem its immemorial advantages, is at this time of writing (1968) less than twenty years old. The complete opera albums of 78's were weighty affairs, containing thirteen or fourteen double-faced discs, and often running into two volumes.

LP changed all that. It also brought, on associated technical fronts, a dramatic improvement in orchestral sound. New clarity of texture, of over-all dimension, has added to one's pleasure in listening. And the emergence of another person in command—the producer, as distinguished from the musical director—has altered the sonic face of opera. The conductor no longer controls the blend of voice and orchestra, the ideal balance as he has imagined it. This is determined by specialists. And in their search for recorded perfection, shortcuts may be brought into play. Small voices have been beefed up, ringing top tones substituted for tired ones, by mechanical means. Expediency may here be pleaded. But what is one to say when inner strands of the orchestra, designed as background, suddenly take over and dominate?

This free-swinging approach, the deliberate reshaping of operatic sound in the image of the producer, has rung the bell of controversy. For those who believe—as do I—that the goal of recording is to document, make accessible, translate artistically, not arbitrarily, from one medium to another, the trend is distasteful.

History of Opera

When I first attended opera at the Metropolitan, the company was divided into three wings: Italian, German, and French. The first two units were a matter of nationality, the third (since there were few singers actually from France), of language.

All that has changed. Today we classify operatic production largely in terms of style and period. With a new awareness of history, we are more conscious of the Baroque (an era which, in theater music, would range roughly from 1600 to 1760). Many works of that age have been unjustly neglected. Few have survived in common knowledge, except on library shelves. And all were performed differently from opera in our time. Gone is the pristine *castrato* (male soprano or alto) whose prowess—a combination of agility, sweetness of tone, and muscular brilliance—once inspired so much theatrical song. His music has been arranged, perforce, for other voices. And many of the instruments that played in the early opera orchestras are obsolete. We have had to make do with near-authentic substitutes. For these retouchings, modern scholarship has been called into service.

Again, even in the distant Baroque, we meet the old struggle between the expressive and the decorative in music. Opera began with dramatic truth, and Claudio Monteverdi was its earliest master. The nobility and psychological strength of his stage works would assure their effectiveness in any age. His *Orfeo* moved the princely court of Mantua. And the superb love duet (first of its kind, they say, in the history of opera) that brings *L'Incoronazione di Poppea* to so glowing a close captivates the heart and mind today.

This is the art of the early Baroque. In its later mazes we come upon a more formalized idiom—the operas of Handel. Unlike the starkly sculptured works of a Monteverdi, these are full of floridity, shaped by vocal rather than dramatic line. Elaborate scenic pageantry marks their revival. And in well-handled productions, care is taken that the musical repeats should be embellished, to charm the ear and avoid monotony, as in the time of Handel himself. What emerges in performance (one recalls the beautiful *Giulio Cesare* by the New York City Opera) is a stately and beguiling masque, a melodious ramble on an antique poetic theme. When one has learned to pry oneself loose from motile theater and surrender to the spell of Handel's music, enjoyment can be strong.

This whole tradition of the *opera seria*—the stiff but impressive medium in which Handel excelled—was to continue into the 1700's past the midcentury mark. Even so progressive a composer as Mozart wrote vestigial works in this style (for special occasions)—notably, *Idomeneo* and *La Clemenza di Tito*, last traces of a disappearing age. But in general Mozart cut to the heart of the drama and created characters rather than types. And in this he was preceded, in a lovable mixture of clumsiness and grandeur, by Christoph Willibald Gluck, the oldest composer still represented, season after season, in our standard repertoire.

It was *Orfeo ed Euridice* that established Gluck as a leading composer of opera and has maintained him ever since. Created for male alto at its Vienna premiere in 1762, the work was revised for tenor by Gluck himself when given twelve years later at the Paris Opéra. The form in which we generally hear it today was devised by Hector Berlioz in 1859 for a revival of which he was in charge. Berlioz, known for his devotion to the music of Gluck, combined the finest pages of both the original and the French versions, avoiding the problem of a *castrato* (extinct even then) by assigning the rôle of Orfeo, *en travesti,* to the great mezzo-soprano, Pauline Viardot-García. Eventually the new design was shifted, for international performance, into Italian. In our own time Margaret Matzenauer, Kerstin Thorborg, Kathleen Ferrier, Risë Stevens, Giulietta Simionato, and Kerstin Meyer have followed the Berlioz tradition.

This was the last change for modern performance in Gluck. Once the master, in full career, had settled in Paris and was writing expressly for the Opéra, he composed scores that are given today as they were in his time. Gossec, it is true, reworked Act III of *Alceste;* Richard Wagner edited *Iphigénie en Aulide;* and Richard Strauss, *Iphigénie en Tauride*, but these revisions have gone out of fashion. The works are now performed as Gluck composed them. And especially in *Armide*, the pearl among his operas, brilliantly in touch with the modern theater, no single note might be changed or revised without weakening the drama. *Armide* was last heard in New York (1912) with Olive Fremstad and Enrico Caruso in the leading roles, Toscanini conducting.

As a reformer, a champion of the expressive, Gluck took excess floridity out of opera and tightened the lines of music and plot. His characters, while godlike rather than human, were able to communicate with the public in terms of direct emotional experience. When Alceste, loyal wife of Admète, vows—in the aria, "Divinités du Styx"—to save her husband from the rulers of Hades and yield herself in his place, the nobility and passion of her song can conquer even now.

The closing scene of *Armide*, a work little known to modern audiences and never recorded, is still more interesting in its play of emotion, its range of theatrical effect. The temptress who has laid bare her heart, renounced hatred, and given herself to the Christian knight whom the Saracens have set her to corrupt, finally loses him. Invoking the demons of air to destroy her pleasure dome—an act suggesting the modern death-wish—she vanishes in a chariot of fire, and the music that Gluck has provided matches every changing facet of the text.

For all the nobility that animates his operas, certain pages come off as melodically stilted, striving for dramatic ease rather than achieving it. Yet in the full flight of *Armide*, the grandeur of *Alceste*, and those parts of *Orfeo* that are tinged with a rare sensibility, Gluck must be accounted the first of our modern masters.

Modern—but he was still not idiomatic. His melodies suggest, at times, the old walls of a city, the outer fortifications that once protected the town and are still a part of the urban plan. Now they stand at the periphery—they contain, rather than animate— whereas the operas of Mozart, chronologically on the heels of Gluck, are well inside the walls.

Mozart was not a reformer or a theorist. He worked with existing styles, improved rather than changed them. What made for the radical difference between his operas and all that had gone before (always excepting Monteverdi) was his theatrical grasp of modern man, his ability to fix upon people like ourselves and set them to music. Since Mozart was a genius, the beauty of his scores is to be taken for granted. What astounds freshly, every time one restudies *Don Giovanni, The Marriage of Figaro, Così fan tutte,* and *The Magic Flute,* is the humanity of these operas, their almost Shakespearean understanding of men and women, their commentary—alternately witty and tragic—on our daily lives.

Part of this achievment, it is true, came about through the skill of Lorenzo da Ponte, Mozart's librettist for *Giovanni, Figaro* and *Così.* Here was a man completely of the theater, a dramatic poet to be ranked with—or perhaps above—Arrigo Boito and Hugo von Hofmannsthal for his literary contributions to opera. But da Ponte only set the stage. Mozart took over psychologically where his collaborator stopped. The sophistication of a *Così fan tutte* could never have been achieved by text alone without the knowing poise and sparkle of the music. That Mozart was equal to any demands of the theater, in whatever style, is shown by his triumphant treatment of the libretto given him by Emmanuel Schickaneder for *The Magic Flute*. Fantasy, pathos, farce, Masonic ritual, all side by side; and the composer evoking every mood with mastery.

Mozart did not wear his heart on his sleeve. For all the expressivity to be found in his scores, there exists a patrician manner that cannot be denied. His music is not to be barked, its subtleties made obvious. Neither is it served by performers too precious in voice and bearing. The hallmark of the great Mozart operas is their humanity. Affectation has no place in them. Neither has the vocal poverty that masquerades as refinement. If a performer cannot sing out, if he takes refuge from technical requirements in an elegant crooning, then—just as surely as the singer who belts—he is unsuited to this repertoire.

Still another demanding element enters the picture with Mozart: the need for an *ensemble* in which all the leading artists —while maintaining their individual skills—must unite in a singing and acting style that brings gloss to the performance as a whole. Too often the word *ensemble* has been taken to mean an amalgamation of vocal mediocrities. The true galaxy in these operas must be made up of stars who, instead of colliding on their courses, unite for greater brilliance. The finest festival performances at Glyndebourne and Salzburg have operated on this principle. And star conductors are always in charge of such events—from Bruno Walter and Fritz Busch of earlier times to Carlo Maria Giulini today.

With the passing of the Mozart era, European opera entered the nineteenth century by splitting into two main streams— German Romantic and Italian *bel canto*—with further tributaries —French and Slavic—opening up in the years that followed.

There were a few works, stirring and important, that fitted into none of these categories: the *Médée*, for example, of Luigi

Cherubini. This powerful opera, first given at Paris in 1797, started as an *opéra-comique*, spoken dialogue alternating with the musical numbers. Then, on the German stage, it underwent plastic surgery, being provided in 1855, at Frankfurt am Main, with musical recitatives composed by Franz Lachmann (these are still in use), to replace all spoken dialogue. By virtue of this new material, the work came to be considered a full-dress opera. Its most famous revival has taken place in our own era (Florence, 1953)—in Italian translation as *Medea*—with Maria Callas a brilliant interpreter of the title rôle.

Another anomaly, from the standpoint of the revisions it has undergone since the Vienna premiere of 1805, is Beethoven's *Fidelio*. Twice revised by the composer, provided by him with no fewer than four different overtures (three of them named *Leonore*, after the heroine, and the fourth, *Fidelio*), the score remains technically a *singspiel*, with spoken dialogue linking the set numbers. After Beethoven's death, still others tried to reshape the work.

More than one prominent musician (Michael Balfe in London, Artur Bodanzky in New York) composed his own recitatives to replace the spoken dialogue—with no lasting result. The original lines are still spoken. And Gustav Mahler, in a celebrated Viennese revival, changed the face of the opera by establishing a custom followed even now: beginning the evening with the *Fidelio* overture, then using the *Leonore No. 3* as a bridge, a kind of Wagnerian interlude, between the two scenes of the second act (prison cell and castle gate). Since the opera is symphonic by nature, the interpolation of *Leonore No. 3* does no violence to the styles; but dramatically it is a point-killer. The offstage trumpet announcing the Minister of Justice has already sounded. Its reintroduction a few minutes later, in the midst of an interlude, weakens the theatrical impact, no matter how overpowering the music.

As for the score itself, how many detractors it has had across the years! Because Beethoven composed nine symphonies and only one opera, historians have taxed him with a lack of dramatic flair, basing their judgment for the most part on the ratio of nine to one rather than any considered examination of the music. This opera, in reality, is shot through with the strongest, most cogent kind of theater, and one special moment ranks among the exalted in any medium: the passage (Scene 1) for divided violins and cellos that precedes the canon quartet, "Mir ist so wunderbar." Outwardly poised and serene, these measures transmit a throbbing inner life.

Fidelio has also been called unvocal. This, I submit, depends upon who is singing it. When the test has been joined, the result can be glorious. Among the renowned Leonores of our time have been Lotte Lehmann, Kirsten Flagstad (her most convincing role), Birgit Nilsson, Leonie Rysanek, and Christa Ludwig. Jon Vickers and René Maison stand as the most ardent Florestans, and Alexander Kipnis as the ideal Rocco, the benevolent jailer. I have never heard a Pizarro quite equal to the demands Beethoven put upon this villainous character, but Michael Bohnen, in the recording of a single aria, "Ha! welch' ein Augenblick!," made in the 1920's, suggests how fearsome his full-length version of the part must have been. Ironically, Bohnen sang Rocco, not Pizarro, during his years at the Metropolitan.

In the short space of time between Beethoven's *Fidelio* and Karl Maria von Weber's *Der Freischütz*, the structure of German opera did not change—it was still based on the *singspiel*—but the style was remarkably transformed. The new Romanticism that was sweeping Europe found in Weber a musical apostle. His stage works, filled with stirring scenes of the superhuman (as, in the Wolf's Glen episode of *Der Freischütz*, the casting of the magic bullet while infernal hounds bay in the darkness and firewheels roll by), the knightly feeling of the Middle Ages, and the evocation of old peasant festivals, were to lead directly—through their fantastic musical coloring—into the youthful operas of Richard Wagner.

Der Freischütz, however, is by no means to be taken as just a historical link. It remains, on its own account, a work of genius, full of marvelous melodies, a superb hunting chorus, and thrilling orchestral effects. With his next, *Euryanthe*, Weber moved into the field of full-dress opera, abandoning the spoken dialogue so characteristic of the *singspiel*. He replaced it not with *recitativo* but with a fluid connecting tissue that anticipates the finest type of music drama. Indeed *Euryanthe* is a splendid work, worthy of modern revival. I heard it in 1937 at Salzburg, under the direction of Bruno Walter; and the beauty of the score rings in the memory. Weber's *Oberon,* set to an English text for Covent Garden and conducted by the master in the last year of his life, was never completed to his satisfaction. It survives as a problem piece, subject to editing of one sort or another (usually a condensation of the numerous scenes and characters), but the great moments, such as the heroine's "Ocean, thou mighty monster," are equal in grandeur to anything in opera.

While Weber and Romanticism were holding the stage in Germany, the type of opera known as *bel canto* began its reign in Italy, spread to the Théâtre-Italien in Paris and from there to Covent Garden. It should be noted at once that the expression *bel canto* has less connection with style or form than with sound. In this kind of opera, entirely vocal in inspiration, the singing—even when dramatic—had to flow purely. Technical hurdles were set up in advance for the singer, so they might be surmounted with bravura. As for structure, it was the traditional full-dress opera: *arias,* concerted numbers (duets, trios, quartets), and choruses, linked by *recitativo.*

The *bel canto* operas developed a formula that became in time a stereotype. At its heart lay the solo number, allocated to most of the leading singers in turn. This consisted of an opening *recitativo* (to display the artist's feeling for dramatic accent), a *cavatina* (proof of his ability to spin out a slowly moving melodic line), and a concluding *cabaletta* filled with fast, dazzling runs and scales. The three-part entity was known, in sum, as a *scene and aria.* It had been used more passionately, and with greater orchestral complexity, by Mozart, Beethoven, and Weber. In *bel canto* the emphasis was frankly on voice.

Masterpieces could spring from this restricted soil. Rossini's *Otello,* Bellini's *Norma,* and Donizetti's *Lucrezia Borgia* are commanding works by virtue of the melodic sweep and dramatic intensity that transcend their conventional design. All are vehicles for singing stars, and *Norma* in particular has maintained a tradition of stellar performance. Within a span of memories dating from the late 1920's, no other diva has approached Rosa Ponselle in the vocal grandeur needed for Bellini's heroine.

Norma, however, was only an isolated opera in the twenties.

The modern *bel canto* revival had yet to come. Set in motion thirty years later by Maria Callas, it became a platform for other singers of outstanding ability: Joan Sutherland, Montserrat Caballé, Leyla Gençer. Audiences roared their approval of works and of artists, both in concert and opera. To meet a demand for fresh vehicles, forgotten operas by Bellini, Rossini, and Donizetti were taken off the shelf, and almost every salient musical idea was stalked by a smothering formula.

These noted composers at their best—Rossini (in his Italian period) with *Otello, The Barber of Seville,* and *Cenerentola,* Bellini with *Norma,* Donizetti with *Lucia, Don Pasquale,* and *L'Elisir d'Amore*—offer treasures of beautiful sound, and occasionally, dramatic glory. But they wrote in bulk. Their lesser, grade B, products, dusted off hastily for recent revival, fizzed not only in our era, but even in their own. Most of the *bel canto* repertoire disappeared quite naturally, its sighing elegance replaced by the new vigor of Giuseppe Verdi.

During the ascendancy of *bel canto* in Italy, the beginnings of *grand opera*—in its technical sense as a style—were stirring in France. I must point out, of course, that theater music in Paris and Versailles had enjoyed an illustrious history for well over a century before the Revolution. Lully and later Rameau had set a dignified, dramatic, and often imaginative tone. Then Gluck had come from Austria, under the patronage of Marie Antoinette.

After the Terror had passed, and years later, Napoleon had gone into exile, Paris became the first city of Europe. A newly enriched bourgeoisie supported the arts. Writers, painters, musicians, and dancers formed an ambiance unique in modern times. Chopin, Liszt, Berlioz, George Sand, Balzac, Delacroix, de Musset, Flaubert, Gautier, Taglioni, Grisi, Heine, Meyerbeer, Auber, and Rossini (in his French period) brought a cosmopolitan outlook, a large-scale interest in the theater that made *grand opera* inevitable. This was the concept of the "big machine": a story with historical background, calling for mammoth pageantry, brilliant ballet, and grandiose vocal and orchestral power.

Gasparo Spontini, the Italian composer who settled in Paris and later moved on to Berlin, was a pioneer in the field with *La Vestale* and *Fernand Cortez;* but the first *grand opera* to make an absolute and overpowering contact with its audience is said to have been Auber's *La Muette de Portici* in 1828. One year later, Rossini—then living in Paris—had *William Tell* produced in the French capital. Like the work of Auber, it became a beacon in the development of epic style. I say "style" rather than form because *grand opera* differed not at all structurally from the traditional Italian opera. There were the same arias, concerted numbers, choruses, but less vocal display, with the melodies more tightly drawn and a heightened sense of dramatic awareness.

These qualities came to stay in French *grand opera*. No matter how elaborate the framework, the music is spare, often severe. And this type of writing found its apogee in the works of Giacomo Meyerbeer, born in Berlin, educated in Venice, triumphant in Paris. The wild fantasy of his *Robert le Diable*, with its ballet of unfrocked nuns, burst upon the public in 1831; *Les Huguenots*, based on the massacre of St. Bartholomew's Day, came five years later; then *Le Prophète*, taking for its story the infamous career of John of Leyden; and finally *L'Africaine*, with Vasco da Gama and a fictional Indian queen as its central figures. This last work was given a posthumous premiere in 1865, a year after the composer's death.

Most of the estimates of Meyerbeer's music still in print today were launched over sixty or seventy years ago. They came from critics indoctrinated by Wagner's well-known (and highly personal) dislike of this composer. There is only one way in which to form a valid estimate of Meyerbeer, and that lies in studying his scores first hand. Unfortunately, none of his operas has been recorded complete, and few of the great scenes, except in German on sonically faded discs. There are indications that some of the big works will presently be revived, at least in concert form.

It is easy, of course, to go along with condemnations of the sensational element in Meyerbeer. His plots, to attract the public, had their bizarre and erotic moments (but is this not also a tendency of well-respected opera in our time—the orgy in Schönberg's *Moses and Aaron* and the voluptuous events in Ginastera's *Bomarzo*?). Some of the music is plodding on occasion. Yet when it soars, as in the grand duo of *Les Huguenots*, the final act of *L'Africaine*, the closing scene of *Le Prophète*, and a miraculous trio (unaccompanied) in the third act of *Robert le Diable*, this is writing of supreme imagination. The framework is definitely grand; and with Meyerbeer the structure of the "big machine" is established in five acts, one of which contains a large-scale ballet.

It will be noted that Spontini, Rossini, and Meyerbeer, all practitioners of Parisian *grand opera*, were foreigners. A great native Frenchman Hector Berlioz tried his hand at the style— in *Les Troyens*—and turned out a work of full-blown genius. The entrance of the Grecian horse into Troy, hailed by an enormous chorus, with three stage bands converging stereophonically upon the scene, and the tragic Cassandra crying out her prophecies in vain, affords the noblest example of how *grand* opera can become, with no literary element distended, no part of the music banal or overblown. In those portions of the work taking place in Carthage, there is a softer, more lyrical quality, culminating in a nocturnal septet by the sea that has remained one of the glories of the French repertoire. The work is too long—not for its content, which is almost continuously beautiful, but for the staying power of the audience. Cuts are usually made; when discreet, they prove successful. *Les Troyens* has yet to be heard in stage form at the Metropolitan Opera House.

Secondary composers of French *grand opera* include Halévy (*La Juive*), Saint-Saëns (*Samson et Dalila*), Reyer (*Salammbo*). Massenet, whose glowing skill lay in lyric opera, attempted the grand in *Hérodiade*, but his most winning achievements stem from the intimacy, poetry, and theatrical flair of *Manon, Werther*, and *Le Jongleur de Notre Dame*. I vibrate personally to this composer, to the economy of his orchestral scoring, his supple writing for voice and refinement of dramatic style. Charles Gounod in *grand opera* (*Faust*) I salute with more respect than affection, Delibes, in *Lakmé*, with neither. It was in the lyrical sphere that Gounod was to win out with a captivating version of *Romeo and Juliet*.

Masterpieces of French lyric opera have been those in which music and the stage are as one—song, action, and orchestra fused with absolute equality: the finer works of Massenet, Charpentier's *Louise*, Debussy's *Pelléas et Mélisande*, Poulenc's *Les Dialogues des Carmélites*. In *opéra-comique* one must mention

Carmen, if only for the sake of the record. I have never enjoyed it, except for that dramatic last act, finding in its music too many diabetic turns of phrase. The lyric operas bring no over-all stress on voice, no stentorian underlining by the orchestra. The fusion of elements is complete, the balance perfect.

Yet Gallic elegance, though gaining in favor today, is still a specialized taste. If one were to point out the heartland of opera, one's finger would inevitably move toward the works of Giuseppe Verdi. This great composer, who with Mozart and Wagner remains among the pillars of musical theater, outstrips his rivals in one important respect: his scores, like the Bible, speak with equal persuasion to men of all intellects. The simple and sophisticated are inspired by them. There is, in this music, a miraculous force that dignifies the crude, refines but never softens.

After the suave and long-lined *bel canto* operas, Verdi's output came upon the scene with violence. His early works had a vein of rugged exaggeration, a gusto that bordered on the uncouth. Yet cheek by jowl with exuberance, as in his first big success, *Nabucco*, lay enormous nobility. We still hear the threadbare advice to bypass early Verdi and start admiring him with *Don Carlo;* one cannot protest too strongly the assumption that this genius, in his younger years, was writing only trash. Grave inequalities do exist in *Rigoletto;* yet consider the strength of *Il Trovatore* (I have reference not to an addled libretto but the unfailing excitement of the music); the warmth of *La Traviata*, marking a new threshold of sensitivity in this master's approach; the splendor and *terribilità* of a *Macbeth*, flawed though it be in certain pages.

Personally I take keenest enjoyment in Verdi's experimental works that followed the "popular" period of *Trovatore* and *Traviata*. Here was a famous man reaching for new devices, sometimes failing, more often succeeding in an attempt to broaden his horizons. It is the flux of this period, the trial and achievement, that makes it so vivid and brings such power to a work like *Don Carlo*, which incorporates not only music and drama but psychology on a scale not attempted in the Italian theater since Monteverdi. *Don Carlo*, to be accurate, has a few substandard pages. These are, however, exceptional and minimal. The ability of Verdi to read the human soul and communicate his findings has never been more explicit (or polished) than in this masterpiece, written for the Paris Opéra and then translated, revised, and improved for its place in the Italian repertoire.

La Forza del Destino, of this same period, represents the master at white heat. No matter the extravagances of the plot! Into no other score did he pour such molten melody. Skill of characterization, too, runs high. All of the principals are strongly painted; the secondary figures—such as the gypsy girl, Preziosilla; the muleteer, Trabucco; the whining friar, Melitone—have a sharpness of definition never before encountered in Verdi's supporting roles. There is humor—incisive and mature—in addition to tragedy. And the orchestra mirrors superbly the darkling Spanish background of the first two acts and the brio of the military scenes in Italy.

Simon Boccanegra, also of this era, has top pages—the Prologue, Council Chamber scene, final duo (unforgettably sung, in our time, by Lawrence Tibbett and Ezio Pinza)—along with others which might better have been suppressed when Verdi revised the work. I feel less drawn (a minority of one) to *Un Ballo in Maschera*, where great places—the scene in the fields, Renato's "Eri tu!," the quintet that follows—yield to crashing disappointments, notably the masked ball itself.

As for Verdi's final period, this was largely glory. *Aida* is perfection from almost every standpoint. It has become the archetype of Italian *grand opera* (in four acts, rather than the five of the Parisian stage), with a carefully worked historical background, grandiose solo and concerted numbers, rousing choruses, spectacular pageantry, and a glittering ballet. The humanity of *Don Carlo* is still there, limited only by a somewhat stiff libretto. Aida herself and Radames stir us musically rather than through drama; but Amonasro, the father of Aida, comes fiercely to life; and Amneris, torn by pride and jealousy, yields to few other operatic characters in total rapport with the listener.

It has for so long been the fashion to consider *Otello* as the greatest of Verdi's works that I must with apologies name it an overrated opera. The score contains dramatic music of high quality: the whole of the first act, much of the last. Yet aside from the famous Kiss motive, the melodic ideas fall below the best of *La Forza, Don Carlo, Aida,* even *Trovatore* in appeal and spontaneity. They are superbly worked, but tired. Characterization is skillful—in the case of the Moor, eloquent; but Iago sounds more orotund than evil (exception: the delicately spun, insidious page known as "Era la notte"). And I should question the finale of Act III, a big old-fashioned number that is out of joint in style and pacing with the rest of the opera.

It is a different story with *Falstaff*. Youth regained, and at the same time made wise, hovers over the music—joyous, spare, modern. Verdi is here in tune with the contemporary world. And in the stunning fugue that ends the opera ("Tutto nel mondo è burla") he has put, as in a time capsule, the best of his musical heritage together with a prospect of things to come.

Wagner is not so much a branch of the repertoire as a way of life, and there remains little to be written that can throw new light on this most engulfing of composers. In youth, one submits almost totally to the power of *Der Ring des Nibelungen, Tristan und Isolde, Die Meistersinger von Nürnberg,* and *Parsifal.* Inevitably the confirmed Wagnerite will revolt against the system; but just as surely he will return, armed with reservations, yet basically loyal. My own residue of disquiet about Wagner has to do with the *Ring*, which I feel—despite page after page of magnificent music—is orchestrally inflated, its counterpoint forced. No such hesitancy stays me in the other great works.

The Wagnerian music dramas stand or fall through their performers. We are told, for example, that Gurnemanz, aging knight of the Grail in *Parsifal*, is a bore, and he usually is, when sung by the average basso. But those who have heard a Kipnis in this role will recall not a measure that might be spared. And as to the long scene of Tristan's death, so often undersung and overacted: for the listener who doubts its power, I recommend an old recording, made in Buenos Aires over a quarter-century ago, by Lauritz Melchior. The splendor of his voice is not matched by the sonics of the disc, but what tremendous intensity comes through!

Above all, we have been losing in most performances of Wagner the lyricism and the introspection that mark his music at its finest. We are settling for volume in place of depth. I am averse, by nature and training, to the chilly, monumental sound. These works can be sung intimately, warmly. Kappel and Leider succeeded in the past. Perhaps Christa Ludwig and Régine Crespin will do it again.

The operas of Richard Strauss—an extension orchestrally, vocally, and dramatically of Wagnerian principles—can still, in our time, stir men to battle. One army of buffs declares that Strauss's inspiration stopped short after *Salome, Elektra, Der Rosenkavalier,* and *Ariadne auf Naxos.* The opposing side claims that his inspiration only began at that point. Their argument is inconclusive, since so much of value may be found in Strauss on either side of the Great Divide. *Die Frau ohne Schatten* and, among his later works, *Arabella* and *Capriccio,* have reservoirs of enormous worth.

My own feeling is that Strauss's operas at their shortest are also at their best. *Salome* and *Elektra,* each in a single act, each a study in dramatic conciseness, go on to magnificent climaxes. Some of the details in *Salome*—especially the music of Jochanaan, with its revivalist overtones—are coarse. But in *Elektra* the Furies are at work, driving music and drama forward, flaying the participants, beating the audience into ultimate, pleasurable insensibility. *Elektra,* when paced by a great conductor (Fritz Reiner!) and sung by an inspired singing-actress, can furnish one of the stirring theatrical experiences of this century.

Brevity also enhances *Ariadne auf Naxos.* Strauss's idea of scoring this opera for an orchestra of only thirty-seven, resulting in a chamber atmosphere throughout, makes for a work that can charm on a number of levels. And its prologue, with the portrait of a young composer tricked into sacrificing art for expediency, brings us Strauss at his most moving. As for *Der Rosenkavalier,* having once loved the work, I must confess to finding it too long, repetitive, and (for a comedy) ponderous. While the superb moments remain—the Marschallin's monologue, the presentation of the silver rose, the final trio—the acres of "situation" music grow less interesting to a listener not bound up with Ringstrasse tradition.

Again too long, though irresistible in its finest pages, is *Die Frau ohne Schatten.* The score has enormous power; most of the action sweeps one forward—but Strauss's great librettist, Hugo von Hofmannsthal, is often grandiosely obscure, bringing to mind those famous words by an Emperor of Japan:

> All prosy dull society sinners
> Who chatter and bleat and bore,
> Are sent to hear sermons by mystical Germans
> Who preach from ten till four.

The least familiar part of the repertoire is the Slavic division. Of these operas unsurpassed for emotional surge, only *Boris Godunov* has become standard. Because the composer, Musorgski, was notoriously lacking in skill as an orchestrator, we have heard it at the Metropolitan—within a span of twenty years—in three different editions: by Rimski-Korsakov, by Karol Rathaus, and by Shostakovich. Rimski, in addition to reorchestrating the opera, softened certain of its harmonies, and deleted an amount of basic material. In spite of these indignities, his version surpasses the other two. It sounds; it conveys the gorgeous, barbaric essence of medieval Russia. As for the work itself, any performance with a prime singing-actor must impress the listener, and when played for ensemble (*every* part is important), the result can be extraordinary.

Musorgski's other great opera, *Khovanshchina*, is also a chronicle play, dealing with that dark part of Russian history in which three factions—the old nobility, a fanatical clergy, a liberally minded prince—wrestled with and destroyed one another, all disappearing in the upheaval that gave rise to the Romanov dynasty. Despite loose ends, caused by its sprawling structure, *Khovanshchina* is magnificent music drama: superb choruses, imaginative solo scenes, and a finale—the mass suicide of the Old Believers—the recollection of which may never be shaken off, once it has been seen in the theater.

There are other fine works in the Russian repertoire, but they reach us only intermittently. Borodin's *Prince Igor*, Rimski-Korsakov's *Sadko* and *The Snow Maiden*, once popular in New York, have vanished from the scene. *The Golden Cockerel* comes and goes. We have had, to be sure, revivals of those Tchaikovsky masterpieces, *Eugene Onegin* and *Pique Dame*, but neither in a performance that touched the springs of their greatness.

As to Czech opera, we live in twilight. Smetana's *The Bartered Bride* has not been given these many years on a professional level. The same composer's epic *Dalibor* does not exist for us, nor does Dvořák's *Rusalka*. The works of Leoš Janáček (save for a very occasional *Jenufa*) stand apart. Ambitious music schools sometimes attempt them, but thoroughly skilled productions of *Katya Kabanova, The Sly Little Vixen,* and *The Makropoulos Affair* are still awaited in New York. From reports in other places, they are said to match one's expectations.

Save for the big pieces of Verdi, there have been few *grand operas* out of Italy in almost a century. Among the few, one would note Ponchielli's *La Gioconda,* Boito's *Mefistofele* and *Nerone,* and Puccini's *Turandot.* These are, generally, relics. The trend has run to works of an intimate nature, some realistic, others sentimental.

Mascagni in *Cavalleria Rusticana* and Leoncavallo in *Pagliacci* produced operas that broke with the romantic past and emphasized the everyday aspects—some of them grim—of small town life in Italy. Their heroes were the poor and illiterate. Refinement was not their aim, but violent impact. And their best works, despite moments of outhouse vulgarity, cannot be dismissed on grounds of taste, for they also have dramatic truth and compassion. When these operas are given straight, free of hamming, with the Sicilian or Calabrian countryside bearing in relentlessly on the actors, they come off with power—and with empathy for an audience of today. There is not much difference, really, between this dispossessed *verismo* world of the nineties and the convulsed, unromantic Italy cast up by World War II (well known to us through the early films of De Sica). Life in both was hard, fundamentally tragic.

Umberto Giordano was a glossier composer than the others, cross-pollinating realism with the last vestiges of *grand opera.* The combination worked. One tends in our time, without justification, to underrate *Andrea Chénier,* that gusty score inspired by the French Revolution, the scintillating *Madame Sans-Gêne,* a comedy set in the same period and in the Napoleonic era that followed, and *Fedora,* based on a lushly old-fashioned stage play of Sardou and worth reviving for a white-gloved, tiara-topped diva.

Since these judgments are personal, I trust the reader will

indulge me in a one-sided approach to the theater of Puccini. I am not a fan. The excitement is there; so are the hit tunes; so is the sentimentality. We know from his letters that Puccini, a gifted composer, took great pains with his operas. He had an expert sense of theater, a unique flair for melody, but he often wasted these assets on the obvious. There are, of course, stunning exceptions: the superb score for *Il Tabarro;* the climax of Act II (the poker game) in *Girl of the Golden West*, where the power of the music transcends the hokey plot; and most of *La Bohème*, with its very special flavor of young love. What has prejudiced me against certain of the Puccini works—notably large parts of *Tosca* and almost all of *Madama Butterfly*—is their literalism, their show biz exploitation of the surefire. Counter in spirit runs the motto inscribed on the proscenium of the Royal Opera House in Copenhagen: MORE THAN ENTERTAINMENT.

I am for contemporary opera. Out of experimentation must come the great new works of which we have need, if music theater is to stay alive. Today's undisputed masterpieces are Berg's *Wozzeck*, Prokofiev's *The Flaming Angel*, Britten's *Peter Grimes*, all represented—not equally well—in New York during the past decade, and, fortunately, all superbly recorded. I cannot admire the elegant conceits of *The Rake's Progress*, despite the prestige of its composer, Igor Stravinsky. I find infinitely more rewarding the modest but penetrating little music drama by Luigi Dallapiccola, *Il Prigioniero*.

American opera? Coming up, hopefully.

2

Orchestral Music

MARTIN BOOKSPAN

IT is only during the past four hundred years that music for a combination of instruments has become prominent in Western civilization. During the first fifteen hundred years of the Christian Era, the literature of music was largely for the human voice—and mostly for the church, at that. Two sixteenth-century Italian composers named Gabrieli—Andrea and his nephew Giovanni—are generally credited with expanding the horizons of music to include instruments within the framework of choral writing; it was not long before the Gabrielis were composing music for instruments alone, and the whole course of music history was changed.

The earliest of Andrea Gabrieli's works for combinations of instruments bore the designation Sonatas, literally, *sounded pieces* (as contrasted with Canzonas, *sung pieces*). Pivotal works produced by the Gabrielis are Andrea's *Sonatas for Five Instruments* and Giovanni's *Sonata pian' e forte* in which contrast between loud and soft is explored for the first time in instrumental music.

Giovanni Gabrieli died in 1612, and for the most part the composers who followed him during the seventeenth century experimented with the concepts and forms first formulated and codified by him and his uncle. Orlando Gibbons and William Byrd, both of whom outlived Giovanni Gabrieli by about a dozen years, were important composers in England who seized upon the newfound emancipation of instrumental music and wrote a considerable body of works for combinations of stringed instruments. One of the most fascinating musical figures of the period was the Frenchman Jean-Baptiste Lully, who was born Giovanni Battista Lulli in Florence, Italy, in 1632, but who was brought to France at the tender age of about twelve to teach Italian to the niece of a French nobleman. Lully spent the rest of his life in France and became her most famous and influential musician, an intimate of Louis XIV, for whose court he composed innumerable ballets, and a friend of Molière, with whom he collaborated in the composition of many ballets. Lully was also an expert dancer and a comic actor of considerable ability.

During the last fifteen years of his life, Lully was the director of the Paris Opéra, and he ruled the musical life of France with an iron hand that was reinforced by royal edict. The King proclaimed that no opera could be performed anywhere within the kingdom without Lully's permission. Along with his administrative and other musical activities at the Opéra, Lully also took it upon himself to conduct many of the performances. This he accomplished by standing in front of his instrumentalists and rapping a long wooden pole on the floor in order to establish the tempo and keep the musicians playing together. Legend has it that he clubbed himself right out of this world: In mid-performance, one day, he missed the floor and came down hard with the pole on one of his feet; the resulting wound abscessed, and Lully died from the infection.

During the century between the death of Andrea Gabrieli in 1586 and the death of Lully in 1687, instrumental music developed rapidly. Certain principles of form were already well established, and the basic foundation of orchestral music as an expressive medium had been well laid. It remained for three composers, all of them born just a few years before Lully died, to bring this particular phase of musical history, the Baroque period, to its finest flowering. In his chapter on Baroque, Igor Kipnis details the facts and the figures of this fascinating epoch, but I must touch briefly on the music of Johann Sebastian Bach, George Frederick Handel, and Antonio Vivaldi. The veteran among them was Vivaldi—his birth date is given variously as

1669, 1675, and 1678; Bach and Handel were both born in 1685.

Not until the post-World War II period was the musical community fully aware of Vivaldi's importance as a composer. Recent scholarship, along with vigorous championing of Vivaldi's music by the recording companies, has revealed the true dimensions of Vivaldi's art. He was a seminal influence in the development of two musical forms—the concerto grosso and the solo concerto—and he even pointed the way for the later development of the symphony itself by Haydn and Mozart.

Vivaldi left behind him an astonishing profusion of compositions—operas, choral works, sonatas—but my concern is with his instrumental music, particularly the concerti grossi and the solo concerti. The concerto grosso form was pioneered by Italian composers toward the end of the seventeenth century, notably Arcangelo Corelli and Giuseppe Torelli. It was Torelli who created the standard form of Baroque concerto grosso with three movements, fast-slow-fast. In textural design, the concerto grosso pits a small group of soloists (called the *concertino*) against a larger group of players, usually strings only (called the *tutti* or *ripieno*). With these as the basic ground rules, Vivaldi produced dozens of masterful orchestral concerti grossi, distinguished by rhythmic vitality and drive and requiring brilliant precision work from the performers. Similarly, Vivaldi's dozens of solo concerti are remarkable examples of a music bursting with energy and vitality. His best-known orchestral score is *The Four Seasons*, a cycle of four violin concerti deliberately calculated to conjure up visions and emotions associated with the four seasons of the year. "Program music"—both descriptive and narrative—existed before Vivaldi composed *The Four Seasons*, but this is the oldest example of the genre still in the active repertoire.

If Vivaldi's greatest accomplishments as we know them today were in the field of instrumental music, then surely the major contributions of Bach and Handel were their large-scale choral works, as discussed by David Randolph in this volume. Yet the contributions of both composers to instrumental and orchestral music are among the glories of the literature. The principal works of Bach's output for orchestra are the six *Brandenburg Concerti*, the four *Suites for Orchestra*, and the various concerti for solo and multiple instruments. Handel's orchestral works include two famous sets of concerti grossi, along with the *Water Music* and the *Royal Fireworks Music*.

Bach composed his set of six orchestral concerti on commission from Christian Ludwig, the Margrave of Brandenburg, who was a deeply committed musical amateur. The composer seized upon the opportunity offered him, and the six scores that he produced represent the ultimate in Baroque concerto grosso expression. Each is scored for a different group of solo instruments—the *Third* and *Sixth* for strings only, the other four for various instrumental combinations. They are endlessly fascinating, and repeated hearings only increase the listener's respect for the fertile inventiveness of Bach's creative genius.

The four *Suites for Orchestra* seem to have been composed by Bach at about the same time he produced the *Brandenburgs*. During the six-year period between 1717 and 1723 Bach was in the service of Prince Leopold of Anhalt-Cöthen, where an orchestra of eighteen musicians was placed at his disposal. It is not hard to imagine with what joy Bach threw himself into the task of providing music for the ensemble; and the players, in turn, must have been first-class virtuosi, for the works are by no means easy to play. The *Second Suite* has a prominent part for solo flute and the *Third* contains the long-breathed song for strings that became famous as the "Air for the G String" by virtue of August Wilhelmj's arrangement for violin solo. Structurally, each of the *Suites* is built along the same lines: an elaborate French Overture (in the slow-fast-slow Lully tradition), followed by a series of dances popular in Bach's time—bourrées, gigues, gavottes, and the like.

No less inventive and stimulating than the *Brandenburgs* and the *Suites* are Bach's numerous concerti for solo and multiple instruments. Chief among these are the *Violin Concerti in A minor* and *E Major* and the *D Minor Concerto for Two Violins*, the *Concerto in C minor for Violin and Oboe*, several of the concerti for solo keyboard instrument, the two for two solo keyboards, and those for three and four solo keyboards. The principal keyboard instrument of Bach's time was the harpsichord, and it was for the harpsichord that the Bach keyboard concerti were composed. Until the Baroque revival of recent years, these scores were more often than not given in performances utilizing the modern piano. Today, however, performances on the harpsichord are the rule rather than the exception.

The most important of the concerti grossi that Handel composed are the eighteen contained in two sets: Opus 3, made up of six works for woodwinds and strings, and Opus 6, twelve concerti for strings alone. Much of the music in both sets was freely adapted and rewritten by Handel from earlier works. It remains astonishing, nevertheless, that the twelve superb Baroque concerti of Opus 6 could all have been completed in a single month during 1739.

The *Water Music* and the *Music for the Royal Fireworks* were both composed for the entertainment of the King and his court. During the early years of the eighteenth century, the Thames River served not only as London's main commercial artery, but also as the city's chief pleasure arcade. King George I frequently organized barge parties on the river and for one, probably in July, 1717, Handel composed a series of brief pieces, later collected under the generic title *Water Music*. According to an account in the London *Daily Courant* at the time of the King's party, his entourage was accompanied by another barge "wherein were fifty instruments of all sorts," which performed "the finest symphonies, compos'd express for this occasion by Mr. Hendel, which His Majesty liked so well that he caused it to be played over three times in going and returning."

More than thirty years later Handel composed his other great piece of "outdoor" music, the *Royal Fireworks* score written for the celebration of the Treaty of Aix-la-Chapelle, which ended the War of the Austrian Succession. Because of the festive nature of the occasion, Handel seized the opportunity to score the work for an enormous body of winds which included twenty-four oboes, twelve bassoons, nine trumpets, and nine horns. A special pavilion was built in London's Green Park to house the "machine" that would set off the imposing fireworks display at the climax of the celebration. Suddenly there was a totally different kind of climax: the hundred-foot high wooden pavilion caught fire, panic ensued, and in the turmoil the architect of the building engaged the director of the fireworks in a duel. No one apparently considered substituting the *Water Music* for the *Fireworks* score to help quench the flames.

During this period composers throughout central Europe were busy creating instrumental works of increasingly elaborate proportions and formal structure. The most important activity along these lines took place in the court of Mannheim, whose elector, Karl Theodor, was a devoted music lover. A first-class orchestra came into being there during the middle of the eighteenth century, and the place was alive with orchestral composition and performance. The most important composers active in the Mannheim group were Richter (1709–1789), Holzbauer (1711–1783), Johann Stamitz (1717–1757), and his son Carl (1746–1801), Filtz (1725–1760), and Cannabich (1731–1798). Their influence extended far beyond Mannheim, and their attitudes and stylistic designs are to be found in the orchestral scores of their contemporaries all over Europe: William Boyce and Johann Christian Bach in England, Giuseppe Sammartini in Italy, Carl Philipp Emanuel Bach and F. A. Rössler (who composed under the name of Rosetti) in Germany, Carl Ditters von Dittersdorf in Austria. Each of them produced instrumental music in abundance, with special emphasis on the newly emerging form, the symphony.

Haydn and Mozart

In defining the symphony, *Grove's Dictionary of Music and Musicians* and the *Harvard Dictionary of Music* agree that it is the most exalted form of instrumental music. The word is derived from the Greek and means merely "a musical ensemble." By the time of the Mannheim composers and their contemporaries, the symphony had come to represent its creator's noblest and most advanced musical thoughts. The first truly great symphonic composer was Franz Josef Haydn, whose *Symphony No. 1* appeared in 1759, nine years after Johann Sebastian Bach died.

Over the next thirty-five years Haydn produced more than one hundred more symphonies, many of which are staples of the concert repertoire today. His last twelve, composed in sets of six each for two different visits to London during the 1790's under the auspices of the impresario Salomon, have always figured in the mainstream of symphonic life. The Haydn revival of the past couple of decades has served to focus attention on many of the composer's earlier symphonies and to enrich our experience and knowledge of his incredible output. My own favorites among the lesser-known symphonies are the trilogy of works titled *Morning, Noon,* and *Night* (the *Symphonies Nos. 6, 7,* and *8*); the *Symphony No. 13* (whose last movement's principal theme is a remarkable anticipation of the main theme in the last movement of Mozart's *Jupiter Symphony*); the *Symphony No. 22*, called the *Philosopher,* because of the weighty and serious aspect of its first movement; the dramatic and impassioned *Symphony No. 39 in G minor;* the intense *Symphony No. 44 in E minor,* which is known as the *Mourning Symphony;* the turbulent and storm-tossed *Symphony No. 49 in F minor;* the *Symphony No. 80 in D minor,* which begins as a serious contemplative work and ends as a lighthearted romp; and the *Symphony No. 86 in D,* alive with spontaneous sparkle and joy, especially in its captivating last movement.

Haydn also left us a large body of instrumental concerti, including several for solo violin, cello, horn, organ, harpsichord, and flute. But perhaps his most widely played concerto today is the irrepressible *Trumpet Concerto in E flat,* a virtuoso player's paradise. Another gem for solo instruments is the *Sinfonia Concertante in B flat,* scored for orchestra with principal solo parts for oboe, bassoon, violin, and cello. As with Vivaldi, our present broader knowledge of the total creativity of Haydn is due in no small measure to the sense of creative repertory adventure shown by the recording industry in recent years. Many of the works by Haydn listed in the discography at the end of the book were not available in recordings until fairly recently.

During the year when Haydn produced his *First Symphony,* there was a three-year old boy named Wolfgang Amadeus Mozart in Salzburg, Austria, who was astonishing his musician-father with an incredibly precocious display of musical gifts. He would sit for hours at the family harpsichord and play by ear the pieces he heard his older sister, Marianne, practicing. The father began to give his son music lessons as a game, but the game quickly became serious business as the full measure of the child's capacities made themselves known. Soon the father began to take young Wolfgang on concert tours all over the continent, exhibiting him as a prodigy pianist and violinist. The nomadic concert life was the only existence young Wolfgang knew for many years, and other circumstances of his personal life were anything but sanguine. And yet in a life-span that barely covered thirty-five years, Mozart composed more than six hundred works in nearly every conceivable musical form. The percentage of masterpieces is astonishingly high; and even the slightest among Mozart's creations radiates a quality of elevated invention and superior craftsmanship. In recent years New York's Lincoln Center for the Performing Arts has undertaken month-long festivals of Mozart's music which have surveyed its wealth and dynamism; I can think of no other composer whose works could sustain such concentrated scrutiny without falling victim to the law of diminishing returns.

I could single out two dozen or more of Mozart's works which are special favorites of mine for discussion in these pages; the problem is that at least an equal number of favorites would go neglected. I propose, therefore, merely to mention some that come to mind immediately. Since I am a frustrated violinist from way back, perhaps a good place to begin would be with the violin concerti. Mozart often produced works in clusters, either because he was commissioned to produce series of scores in the same genre, or because an inner need compelled him. Between April and December of 1775, in his twentieth year, Mozart composed no fewer than five violin concerti; the *Third, Fourth* and *Fifth* have been standard concert fare almost from the moment of their creation. Each has its individual character—the *Third* has as its centerpiece a deeply felt, melancholy Adagio which is one of the most moving of all Mozart's works; the *Fourth* is a sunny outpouring of joy; and the *Fifth* is a frolicsome romp which in the last movement introduces a raucous orchestral episode borrowed by Mozart from music he had earlier composed for a ballet appended to his early opera, *Lucio Silla.* These three violin concerti stand at the apex of Mozart's music for solo instrument and orchestra.

Another absolutely unforgettable Mozart masterpiece is scored for two solo string instruments and orchestra; this is the *Sinfonia Concertante in E flat for Violin, Viola, and Orchestra.* Alfred Einstein, in his authoritative study of Mozart's music, calls the *Sinfonia Concertante* Mozart's "crowning achievement in the field of the violin concerto." Like the *Third Violin Concerto*, the *Sinfonia Concertante* has a profound and elegiac slow movement, which scales the heights of nobility and passion.

There is another *Sinfonia Concertante in E flat* by Mozart, this one scored for four solo woodwind instruments and orchestra: oboe, clarinet, bassoon, and French horn. Some doubt exists concerning the authenticity of this score, but I am prepared to include it unquestioningly in the Mozart canon. If this score is not authentic Mozart, whoever *did* write it deserves a place in music history alongside Mozart. This is music that overflows with a wealth of rich and inspired melody, and its blending of the four solo instruments is the work of a master.

When we come to Mozart's piano concerti, we are faced with works incredibly rich in quantity and quality. It could almost be said, indeed, that Mozart created the piano concerto as a form. When he came upon the scene, it was little more than a sonata for keyboard instrument with a modest string accompaniment. He left it a full orchestral vehicle, more complex even than a symphony, for the two elements of solo instrument and orchestra had to blend or alternate in perfect integration. Any one of Mozart's later piano concerti is fully symphonic in character—often richer in color and variety than a symphony. He "composed" his first four piano concerti when he was ten years old; the quotes are around the word *composed* because these four works are actually nothing more than concertolike arrangements of keyboard sonata movements by several now-forgotten composers popular during Mozart's early youth. But from his first original concerto onward (the *Concerto No. 5 in D*), he produced a body of music that is perhaps unrivaled in the orchestral repertoire by any other group of works by any composer. *Numbers 9, 12,* and *14* are my own favorites among the earlier ones, and from *No. 15* through the last, *No. 27,* there is an unbroken string of masterpieces. If I were pinned against a wall and forced to name my unqualified favorite, my choice would be the *Concerto No. 20 in D minor.* The epic-heroic nature of this particular concerto made it for years not only *a* Mozart piano concerto but *the* Mozart piano concerto. My own reasons for my special love for this work are quite personal, however. I have already alluded to my violin playing days. When I was about twelve, I was a member of the second violin section in the symphony orchestra of the Boston Music School. The climax of each year's activities was the annual recital on the stage of Jordan Hall in Boston—and one of the pieces on the program my first year in the orchestra was this concerto, with my friend Bernie Siff as soloist. Not only did that performance open up for me the whole magical world of the Mozart piano concerto literature, but I am convinced I have never heard a better performance of it than the one Bernie and I played!

Before continuing with the Mozart orchestral music, let me at this point introduce the mysterious letter *K*. It has taken considerable restraint for me thus far to refrain from using *K* numbers in connection with the several Mozart scores we have already discussed. Concert programs, record catalogues, and all other reference material always append a capital letter *K*, followed by some combination of numbers in their listings of Mozart's works. What is this strange mumbo-jumbo? Nothing more than the indication of the catalogue number assigned to every known Mozart composition by the nineteenth-century musicologist and scholar, Ludwig Köchel, who devoted years of research to cataloging, codifying, and chronologically listing Mozart's entire output. Thus Mozart's first original piano concerto, the *No. 5 in D*, carries the number 175 in Köchel's catalogue, and the *Concerto No. 20 in D minor* is numbered 466 by Köchel's reckoning.

Prominent in Mozart's orchestral output is a series of works titled variously Cassation, Divertimento, or Serenade. The titles, really interchangeable, refer to a body of entertainment music. But even here Mozart was incapable of turning out music automatically, and some of his most inspired musical creativity is to be found in these works. My favorites? Four in the key of D Major among the Divertimenti—K 131, K 136, K 251 and K 334—along with the *Divertimento No. 15 in B flat*, K 287, an endlessly melodic and inventive work, scored for strings and two horns. Among the Serenades I particularly treasure the little

Serenata Notturna, K 239, with its antiphonal effects and drum flourishes; the mighty *Serenade in B flat for Thirteen Wind Instruments*, K 361; the two that follow it, also scored for woodwind instruments (K 375 and K 388); and the *Serenade in G Major* for strings only, K 525, titled *Eine kleine Nachtmusik—A Little Night Music.*

And so we come to the Mozart symphonies; again the fertility of the total output is astonishing. The first two symphonies, K 16 and 19 (K 17 and 18 are copies of works by other composers), were written while the eight-year-old lad was recuperating in London from a serious childhood disease, and the last three—the great *Symphonies Nos. 39 in E flat, 40 in G minor,* and *41 in C,* the *Jupiter*—were created in one enormous gush during a six-week period in the summer of 1788. From the *Symphony No. 32* onward, each one exerts some special claim to my affections. Among the earlier ones my favorites are the *Symphony No. 20 in D;* the *No. 25 in G minor,* an absolute miracle of concentrated drama and passion; *No. 28 in C;* and *No. 29 in A.*

Beethoven and the Romantics

When Mozart was creating his last three symphonies during the summer of 1788, a youth of seventeen was playing viola in the opera orchestra in Bonn, the place of his birth. A year earlier he had spent several weeks in Vienna, and may even have taken a few lessons in composition from Mozart—the record is unclear—but he had hurriedly returned to Bonn because of the serious illness of his mother. His name, of course, was Ludwig van Beethoven, and by the turn of the nineteenth century he was to become well established in Vienna as her most famous musical figure. No only did Beethoven usher in the nineteenth century literally, he was also the figure who dominated and pointed the way toward the whole musical philosophy of the century. In all the arts, the nineteenth century was the era of Romanticism. In music this meant that composers gave free expression to their own emotional urgings; it also meant the slow dissolution of many of the principles of form and structure established by composers during the two previous centuries.

By and large Beethoven worked on a broad musical canvas. His ideas could not be contained within the framework of eighteenth-century thought, hence there is a visionary quality about much of his music. He wrote in all forms and left his personal stamp on every one. In this chapter, of course, we are concerned with his orchestral music—which is to say that we shall be dealing with the very backbone of the orchestral repertoire.

Beethoven's nine symphonies may be said to be the cornerstones of Western symphonic culture. It has been traditional to divide the composer's creative life into three definite periods—early, middle, and late. Where the symphonies are concerned, this almost works, but not quite. The symphonies numbered 3 through 8—composed during the decade between 1803 and 1812—can legitimately be called "middle period," and the monumental *Ninth,* a product of the six years between 1817 and 1823, certainly is representative of the impulses of Beethoven's "late period." What of the first two? It has been convenient in the past to pigeonhole them as youthful muscle-flexing: the emerging composer taking a fling at the form so gloriously developed by Haydn and Mozart. The trouble with this theory is that it ignores the impact and daring of Beethoven's first two symphonies; each represents a significant break with the traditions of the past, and both herald the arrival of a great and original creator.

It has been observed that in his even-numbered symphonies Beethoven sought after gentler beauties, reserving his defiances, his true depths of passion, for the odd-numbered ones. Let us take a brief look at the nine Beethoven symphonies with this thought in mind. The *First* immediately breaks with the past by ambiguously hovering in two rather alien keys before it settles down to its fundamental tonality, C Major. It is a virile, extroverted work that has a particularly playful last movement. The *Third Symphony* is the mighty *Eroica,* dedicated at first to Napoleon Bonaparte, but then dedicated simply "to the memory of a great man" after the Little Corporal had proclaimed himself Emperor. The *Eroica* has been called by Paul Henry Lang in his admirable *Music in Western Civilization* "one of the incomprehensible deeds in arts and letters, the greatest single step made by an individual composer in the history of the symphony and in the history of music in general." The colossal score stretched all the symphonic ground rules. Its length, for example, is about twice that of the average Haydn or Mozart symphony; the first movement alone is as long as many complete four-movement symphonies written during the eighteenth century. And in its harmony, rhythm, and formal structure, the *Eroica* looks ahead to a new era of music. The *Fifth Symphony* is that bold, fist-shaking score that opens with the four-note motif that has been characterized as Fate knocking at the door. During World War II the opening motif of the *Fifth Symphony* was adopted by the Allies as the musical signature of the coming victory, and at the Victory Concert played by the Israel Philharmonic Orchestra in Jerusalem in June, 1967, to celebrate the cessation of the six-day war against the Arab countries, it was again Beethoven's *Fifth Symphony* that marked the occasion. The *Seventh* is a rhythmic romp from first to last. Characterized by Richard Wagner as "the apotheosis of the dance," the *Seventh* is one of the most spontaneous and vigorous works in the entire literature. The *Ninth* is the symphony in which instruments no longer sufficed; Beethoven had to turn to the human voice for the expression of his muse. The last movement is a setting for orchestra, chorus, and four vocal soloists of the *Ode to Joy* by the German playwright and poet, Friedrich von Schiller.

Performances of the *Ninth Symphony* have taken on special meaning because of the unique message and significance of the music. It is not uncommon for conductors to open or close their annual subscription series of concerts with the *Ninth Symphony*, or for the score to figure on Pension Fund or other such special programs. I have heard the *Ninth* under many different circumstances and in many extraordinary situations, but the performance that remains indelibly engraved on my memory is the one given in Symphony Hall, Boston, on the last Saturday in April, 1945, with chorus, soloists, and the Boston Symphony Orchestra conducted by Serge Koussevitzky. At that time the last remnants of the German war machine were being overwhelmed by the United States and its Allies, and the war in Europe was rapidly rushing to its triumphal conclusion. Koussevitzky had scheduled the *Ninth* for the final concerts of his season as an act of rededication to the higher principles of humanity. Promptly at the scheduled starting time, he strode out to the podium, acknowledged the welcoming applause of the audience, and then with a motion of his arms silenced us and indicated that he had something to tell us. "Germany has surrendered!" he proclaimed, "and I now dedicate this performance of Beethoven's *Ninth Symphony* to the victorious Allies and to the cause of universal peace!" Pandemonium broke loose in Symphony Hall as strangers hugged and kissed each other; the members of the orchestra cheered and shouted, and tears streamed down Koussevitzky's face. And then he wheeled around on the podium and led his combined forces in a performance of the *Ninth Symphony* that I can only describe as apocalyptic. It was of little consequence that we learned after the concert that the radio reports on which Koussevitzky had based his announcement were a bit premature; it was not until a week later that the unconditional German surrender was finally effected. But the high emotion of that Saturday evening in Symphony Hall will live with me forever—as will that performance of Beethoven's *Ninth Symphony*.

Beethoven's *Second Symphony* may be termed a transitional work from the *First* to the great *Eroica*. It treats its material in a more relaxed manner; perhaps its most distinctive section is the long and lyrical slow movement. The *Fourth Symphony* was called by Robert Schumann "a slender Greek maiden between two Norse giants"—a reference to its position in the Beethoven chronology between the *Eroica* and the *Fifth*. It, too, is a free-flowing, lyrical outpouring whose mood is always sunny. The *Sixth* is the *Pastoral Symphony*, modeled in its formal and pictorial outlines after a similar symphony by one of Beethoven's contemporaries. But how marvelously Beethoven characterizes the pastoral scenes portrayed in the music! The *Eighth* is altogether a more robust and rambunctious score than any of the other even-numbered ones, but it, too, deals with superficial pleasures rather than profound ones. As the reader may by now have gathered, I consider all nine of the Beethoven symphonies completely indispensable in any representative home library of the great musical masterpieces of our civilization.

Similarly indispensable are Beethoven's concerti for solo instrument and orchestra—five for piano and one for violin. One can almost apply to the piano concerti the same generalization applicable to the symphonies—the odd-numbered ones are the heaven-stormers, the even-numbered ones, the more placid and lyrical expressions. The last is the so-called *Emperor Concerto*, a nickname attached to it by a soldier, who at one of its first performances is reputed to have shouted, at its conclusion, "This is the Emperor among concerti!" The *Violin Concerto* is a more rhapsodic, elegiac work. In Beethoven's output it came into being between the *Fourth* and *Fifth Symphonies;* in spirit and content it relates more closely to the *Fourth.*

Beethoven also composed a sizable body of instrumental music for performance with dramatic works in the theater. For Goethe's drama, *Egmont,* there is incidental music, including an overture that is one of Beethoven's most powerful and concise scores. Similarly, his overture to Collin's drama, *Coriolan,* is a miniature tone poem of the conflicting elements in the makeup and personality of the central figure of the play. And there are no fewer than four different overtures to Beethoven's only opera, *Fidelio*—the *Leonore Overtures Nos. 1, 2,* and *3* and the *Fidelio Overture* itself. They are all staples of the active symphonic repertoire, and each has its individual character.

In the five years between 1812 and 1817, when Beethoven composed no symphonies, a young Viennese musician named Franz Schubert produced his first six symphonies. Schubert was seventeen years younger than Beethoven, and he admired the older composer with a fervor that bordered on adulation. There is much to admire in these first six Schubert symphonies—especially in the rollicking *Second,* the darker-hued *Fourth* and the easy and genial *Fifth.* In 1821 Schubert drafted a *Seventh Symphony* in quite some detail, but dropped it and never returned to it. The following year he turned again to the composition of a symphony, completed two movements, sketched out a third, and orchestrated a few measures, then dropped that symphony too. Did he intend to return to it? Did he indeed return to it and complete two more movements, which were subsequently lost? Neither question has yet been satisfactorily answered; the fact remains, however, that the two-movement torso of a symphony, which was discovered some years after

Schubert died, and which has been known ever since as his *Unfinished Symphony*, is an unquestioned masterpiece. It is utterly different from any symphony that had been composed before it; the music is extremely dramatic and passionate, yet at all times under complete control. It is an "unfinished" symphony only in the sense that it consists of two movements rather than the four that were customary in Schubert's time. In every other respect, however, the work is a fully developed, completely fulfilled gem. Schubert's last symphony, composed during the last year of his tragically brief thirty-one-year life span, is the *Great C Major Symphony*, so called because of its magnitude and content, and to distinguish it from his earlier *C Major Symphony*, his *Sixth*. The *Great C Major* Schubert *Symphony* is one I particularly love; it is a symphony that soars constantly, ever striving to burst its bonds and go careening off into space. Because of its magnitude it has sometimes been called "The Symphony of Heavenly Length." As far as I am concerned, the score could just as easily sustain a one-word mark of identification as the "Heavenly" symphony.

Two years after Schubert completed his *Great C Major Symphony* there appeared another epoch-making symphony of heroic dimensions. This was the *Fantastic Symphony* by the twenty-six-year-old Frenchman, Hector Berlioz. If Beethoven, in the *Pastoral Symphony*, had created pictorial effects, then Berlioz' *Fantastic Symphony* is the first hallucinogenic score in music history. Berlioz is very explicit on this point; outlining the program for the *Fantastic Symphony*, he wrote: "A young musician of morbid sensibility and ardent imagination is in love and has poisoned himself with opium in a fit of desperation. Not having taken a lethal dose, he falls into a long sleep during which he has the strangest dreams, in which his feelings, sentiments and memories are translated by his sick brain into musical ideas and figures." The *Fantastic*, with its vividly descriptive tone painting, was as influential a work in its way as Beethoven's *Eroica*.

One of the most hilarious experiences I have ever had in the concert hall occurred in a performance of the *Fantastic*. Charles Munch is single-handedly responsible for the great revival of this score during our time; his white-hot, impetuous reading of the symphony has influenced a generation of conductors and audiences and has set the standard for current performances. During the summer of 1956 Munch toured Europe and the Soviet Union with the Boston Symphony Orchestra, and one of the most frequently scheduled works was the *Fantastic*. A highlight for Munch was the concert scheduled in his home town, Strasbourg; understandably, he was especially anxious to "wow" his fellow Strasbourgians, and the *Fantastic* was scheduled as the central focus of the program. As luck would have it, one crisis after another conspired to bring orchestra, instruments, and conductor into Strasbourg almost literally at the last minute. The stage crew hurriedly arranged the chairs, stands, and instruments on the stage and finally the concert began—with the *Fantastic*. One of the most chilling episodes in the music occurs in the last movement— "Dream of a Witches' Sabbath"—when two large bells, tuned to C and G, are struck successively just before and during the playing of the theme of the *Dies Irae*, the Roman Catholic liturgy for the dead. In their haste to assemble the stage, unfortunately, the stage crew had reversed the positions of the two bells, so that the C bell was where the G bell was normally positioned—and vice versa. Came the time for the two bells to be struck, and the percussion player made a mighty hammer blow in the direction of the C bell—except that the note that came out was not C but G! By the time the poor player realized that the position of the bells on stage was reversed, a sequence of G-G-C (instead of C-C-G) had been intoned. You can imagine the range of emotions that gripped everyone on stage! First there was incredulity, then rage, then uncontrollable shock, and finally contorting, aching inner laughter. Mr. Munch's face changed colors several times, from ashen white to tumultuous red to apoplectic purple. During his thirteen seasons with the Boston Symphony, Munch led many extraordinary performances of the *Fantastic*, but surely this one in Strasbourg was the most unforgettable!

In many respects Berlioz was the archetypal Romantic composer. He was the possessor of a perfervid imagination, he was brilliantly gifted as a writer and critic, and he was in touch with all the movements in the artistic ferment of his time. His

Harold in Italy Symphony, scored for solo viola and orchestra, is a depiction in sound of the adventures of Lord Byron's hero, Childe Harold. And Berlioz composed many operas on literary subjects—among them the *Faust* legend, *Romeo and Juliet, Beatrice and Benedict,* and *The Corsair.*

Another musician whose temperament and talents closely resembled those of Berlioz was Robert Schumann, who was born seven years after Berlioz and died thirteen years earlier. Schumann, too, was a man of extraordinary literary accomplishments as writer, editor, and critic. And he, too, was drawn to literary subjects for some of his compositions: Goethe's *Faust* and Byron's *Manfred* were among them. Schumann's most important orchestral scores, however, were his four symphonies and his individual concerti for piano, cello, and violin. Schumann was also a remarkable pianist, and until recent years it was fashionable in certain circles to denigrate his orchestral music as amateurish in scoring. That attitude has undergone considerable change of late, and some conductors—notably Leonard Bernstein—find it possible to conduct the Schumann symphonies without tinkering with the scoring at all. Schumann's *Piano Concerto* is one of the best known and best loved of all works for piano and orchestra. It began its life as a single-movement *Fantasy for Piano and Orchestra,* written for the composer's wife, Clara; Schumann later added two movements and created the *Concerto.* The *Cello Concerto* likewise is a staple of the literature; and the *Violin Concerto,* after nearly a century of neglect, is beginning to find its champions.

An almost exact contemporary of Schumann was Felix Mendelssohn, who was born in 1809 and died in 1847. Into his short life Mendelssohn crammed a wealth of musical activity, including important conducting accomplishments, reviving some of the great works of Bach. As a composer Mendelssohn produced no fewer than seventeen symphonies. The first dozen are juvenilia, however, and are not generally counted in his over-all output. Of the five that are, two are masterpieces: the *A Minor Symphony* titled *Scotch* and the *A Major Symphony* titled *Italian.* Both reveal a fertile imagination and a sure hand for orchestral color. Mendelssohn also composed two concerti each for violin and piano. The early *D Minor Violin Concerto* is something of a curiosity, but his later *Violin Concerto in E minor* has been called "the most perfect" concerto for the violin ever written. It sings all the way and has a quality of innocent purity that sweeps all before it. The *First Piano Concerto* has a similar quality of simplicity, but it has not been able to maintain as consistent a hold on the affections of performers and public as has the *Violin Concerto.* By far the best known of Mendelssohn's works is the *Wedding March* he composed as part of a set of instrumental pieces for Shakespeare's play *A Midsummer Night's Dream.* Interestingly, the music for the play came into being in two installments: the Overture was composed as an independent work when Mendelssohn was all of seventeen; the other pieces were composed seventeen years later, on commission from the King of Prussia, for a scheduled performance of the Shakespeare play.

One of the most fascinating musical figures of the nineteenth century was Franz Liszt. No less important than Liszt's piano music is his output for orchestra. As an innovator, he created the symphonic poem. Taking Berlioz' *Fantastic Symphony* as his model, Liszt achieved a new kind of musical and poetic unity in his thirteen symphonic poems. The best known are *Les Preludes* and *Mazepa,* the former being a musical reflection of Lamartine's philosophy that life is but a series of preludes to death, the latter depicting a wild ride across the Ukrainian steppes by a Cossack hero. Liszt's two piano concerti are brilliant display vehicles for a virtuoso pianist, as is his *Hungarian Fantasy for Piano and Orchestra.* By far his most ambitious score for orchestra is his *Faust Symphony,* a three-panel musical canvas on which are delineated the characters and personalities of the story's principal figures: Faust, Gretchen, and Mephistopheles.

During the second half of the nineteenth century there were five great composers of symphonies: Brahms, Bruckner, Dvořák, Mahler, and Tchaikovsky. At the same time there were many composers all over Europe writing music for orchestra that can generally be categorized within the broad framework of the political climate that was sweeping the continent: nationalism.

Brahms's four great symphonies are in the direct Beethoven

tradition. They are visionary, heroic, noble—and quite outside the mainstream of the music of his time. We tend to take it as a sign of admiration that someone at the time called Brahms's *First Symphony* "Beethoven's Tenth." And yet was it admiration, or was it a comment of condescension, a criticism of Brahms for looking to the giants of the past and away from the musical currents of his own time? A bitter rivalry existed between the supporters of Wagner and the admirers of Brahms; the Wagner champions considered Brahms old hat and reactionary. Yet there is little question that the music of Brahms has stood the test of time.

Along with the four symphonies, Brahms's orchestral output consists principally of two companion concert overtures, the *Academic Festival Overture* and the *Tragic Overture*, and four concerti—two for piano, one for violin, and one for violin and cello. Brahms himself, speaking of the two overtures, said the first laughs while the second weeps. Although this characterization may be simplistic, it conveys the essential nature of the two pieces. Each of the concerti is a score of large and sweeping dimensions, and each engages in an intense musical confrontation, emerging at the end on a note of high triumph and affirmation.

One of my own most exciting adventures as a broadcaster occurred during a performance by Rudolf Serkin of Brahms's *Second Piano Concerto*. Serkin, as is well known, is not a reticent performer. He almost literally throws himself into his playing, and the piano absorbs a good deal of physical punishment. On the day in question I arrived at the hall several hours prior to the start of the concert, and there was Serkin on stage, practicing some of the trickier passages and flailing away at the piano for all he was worth. After a dinner break I returned to the hall and prepared for the broadcast. The first part of the concert consisted of music by Aaron Copland conducted by the composer, with Serkin and the Brahms concerto conducted by Charles Munch following after intermission. I had some matters to discuss with Copland, and after I introduced the concerto, I left my broadcast booth and proceeded to the conductor's room to chat with Copland. Shortly after the third movement of the concerto began, the stage door leading to the conductor's room opened and one of the double bass players of the orchestra ambled slowly offstage, to be followed in an instant by one of the assistant managers of the orchestra, who came bounding backstage through another door. I didn't know what had happened, but quite obviously something had gone wrong. I immediately bounced up from my conversation with Copland, ran to the other side of the stage and then up the two flights of stairs that led to the broadcast booth, picking up en route the information that the lyre mechanism at the bottom of the piano had literally torn away from the main body of the instrument! When I arrived at my microphone, I was as thoroughly out of breath as though I had run the mile in three minutes. Between gasps for air I signaled for the engineer to let me tell the radio audience what had happened, and then after some seconds of "dead air" while I caught my breath, I described to the audience the various stages of piano repair work that were taking place on stage. After a delay of about fifteen minutes a makeshift arrangement was completed that allowed the performance to proceed to its conclusion. To this day I cannot hear Brahms's *Second Piano Concerto* without uttering a silent prayer that the piano and the soloist will hold out until the very end of the music!

Finally, I must mention Brahms's two *Serenades* for small orchestra and his *Variations on a Theme by Haydn*. The *Serenades* are easy-going, genial works that reveal a far more relaxed side of their composer's nature. I defy anyone to listen to the last movement of the *Second Serenade in A Major* and not break into a smile of pure joy. The *Variations on a Theme by Haydn*, Brahms's last purely orchestral work before he produced his *First Symphony*, is actually a misnomer; the so-called Haydn theme on which the music is based is actually an old Austrian peasants' hymn, the *St. Anthony Chorale*. A more accurate title would be *Variations on the St. Anthony Chorale*—and the score is so listed in the WQXR library.

The case of Anton Bruckner is another instance of modern-day revival. During his own time Bruckner was admired by some, reviled by most, and did not experience the joy of public acceptance of his music until fairly late in life. When he died in 1896, much of the interest in his music died with him. During his lifetime Bruckner was so grateful for whatever performances his music received, he allowed conductors and editors to retouch and reorchestrate his symphonies. The modern-day interest in Bruckner began with a Munich performance in the early 1930's of the original version of the *Ninth Symphony*. It was seen that the variously edited and reorchestrated editions had wiped away much of the power and originality of Bruckner's music. From that time on, the swing was back to Bruckner's original scoring. Bruckner today enjoys unprecedented popularity. His nine symphonies are massive splashes of orchestral weight and sound; they are repetitious and long; and there are patches of dull note-spinning in nearly every one. Yet the best contain pages of exalted musical inspiration that cannot fail to impress any fair-minded listener. My own choices among the Bruckner symphonies are the *Fourth, Seventh, Eighth,* and *Ninth*—each a monolith, but each exerting a strong and cumulative impact.

Dvořák, for my money, is the most underrated symphonist of the nineteenth century. For years his last symphony, the one called *From the New World*, quite obliterated his other works in this form. Indeed, for years he was credited with only five symphonies, because his first four works in the form remained unpublished. Now the nine symphonies of Dvořák—isn't it amazing how many composers produced nine symphonies?—are seen as a total symphonic output of heroic proportions. The recent publication of the four early Dvořák symphonies has brought about a renumbering of the other five; the *Symphony From the New World*, for example, formerly bore the number 5—now it is correctly identified as the *Ninth;* the old *No. 4* is now the *No. 8*, and so forth. Dvořák's *Symphonies Nos. 6, 7, 8,* and *9* (the old *Nos. 1, 2, 4,* and *5*) form a quartet of exuberant and exhilarating works on the very highest level, and among the four newly mined Dvořák symphonies, my favorites are the *Third* (in E flat, Opus 10) and *Fourth* (in D minor, Opus 13).

Dvořák also composed symphonic poems, concerti, concert overtures, and a series of *Slavonic Dances*. His *Cello Concerto in B minor,* supposedly suggested to him after he had attended a performance in New York of Victor Herbert's *Second Cello Concerto,* is the *locus classicus* of the literature for cello and orchestra. The *Violin Concerto* is a less successful work but it nonetheless is a full-blooded expression of Dvořák's rich melodic invention and is beginning to find increasing favor with performers and audiences. The *G Minor Piano Concerto* went virtually ignored for years, partly because of the thickness of its orchestral scoring, but now this work, too—thanks largely to the championing of Rudolf Firkusny and Sviatoslav Richter—is beginning to make its way in the repertoire. An interesting trilogy is formed by the three overtures, *In Nature's Realm, Carnival,* and *Othello.* Dvořák created them as a group, and they share some thematic material, but they can be, and often are, played separately. The Dvořák symphonic poems are perhaps his least frequently played orchestral compositions. They carry fanciful titles—*The Golden Spinning Wheel, The Watersprite, The Wood Dove,* and so forth—and are full of inventive orchestral imagery. There are two quite extraordinary *Serenades:* the *First, in E Major,* is scored for strings and is a lyrical outpouring of irresistible charm; the *Second, in D minor,* is scored for woodwinds, cello, and double bass, and is a darker-hued but equally affecting score. The *Slavonic Dances* run the gamut of expression from the boisterous extroversion of the first, in C Major, to the atmospheric calm of the last, in A flat.

Tchaikovsky (1840–1893) produced what is probably the most popular body of orchestral music in the whole of the literature. Symphonies, symphonic poems, concerti, overtures, concert pieces, ballets—Tchaikovsky wrote them all, and he left his mark on every form. There is a quality of melancholia about much of Tchaikovsky's music, and this has tempted some interpreters to go overboard in "emotionalizing" their performances of Tchaikovsky. For me, the most successful performances are those that take full advantage of the sentiment without swooning. The last three Tchaikovsky symphonies, *Nos. 4, 5,* and *6,* are his most popular. The *Fourth* builds to a cumulative excitement which can be quite overwhelming, the *Fifth* is in the victory-through-struggle tradition of Beethoven's *Fifth,* and the *Sixth* is the gloomy, despairing *Pathétique.* Before he composed the *Pathétique,* Tchaikovsky sketched out another symphony and then abandoned it. In 1956 the Soviet musician Semyon Bogatyryev reconstructed this abandoned symphony from

Tchaikovsky's sketches, and it now has some currency as Tchaikovsky's "*Seventh*" *Symphony*.

Tchaikovsky composed one *Violin Concerto*, one score for cello and orchestra titled *Variations on a Rococo Theme*, and three concerti for piano and orchestra. The first is probably the best-known of all works for piano and orchestra. During the 1940's, when composers of Tin Pan Alley appropriated a good many of Tchaikovsky's works for their own purposes, the majestic opening of Tchaikovsky's *First Piano Concerto* turned up on the Hit Parade as "Tonight We Love." Tchaikovsky's *Second Piano Concerto* is a far more serene score, but it is full of typical Tchaikovsky melodies, and it is beginning to be heard in our concert halls more frequently. The *Violin Concerto* is one of the half-dozen most popular works of its kind and the *Rococo Variations* is a charming and subtle score.

Many other Tchaikovsky compositions are part of the bread-and-butter orchestral repertory: the *Romeo and Juliet* and *Francesca da Rimini* fantasies, both extremely dramatic and melodious; the *Serenade in C Major for Strings*, with its liquid waltz movement; the *Capriccio Italien*, a dazzling display of colorful orchestration; the *March Slav* and *1812 Overture*, two intensely nationalistic scores. But there are those who maintain, and with considerable justification, that the essence of Tchaikovsky is to be found in his three great ballet scores: *Swan Lake*, *The Nutcracker*, and *The Sleeping Beauty*.

Unlike Tchaikovsky, who composed in many different musical forms, Gustav Mahler was primarily a symphonist. A superb conductor of the operatic and symphonic literature, Mahler was forced for the most part to be an avocational composer during his summer vacations. Despite this restriction, however, he managed to produce nine symphonies—there is that magical number "nine" again—which are truly colossal in mystical and philosophical terms. "A symphony is like the world," Mahler once stated. "It must embrace everything." And the nine Mahler symphonies go into the recesses of wild and secret territory, probing and challenging established truths about the nature of the universe. In an extraordinary letter to Mahler in 1904 Arnold Schönberg wrote: "I must not speak as a musician to a musician if I am to give any idea of the incredible impression your symphony made on me: I can speak only as one human being to another. . . . I felt it as an event of nature, which after scouring us with its terrors puts a rainbow in the sky. . . . I believed in your symphony. I shared in the battling for illusion; I suffered the pangs of disillusionment; I saw the forces of evil and good wrestling with each other; I saw a man in torment struggling toward inward harmony; I divined a personality, a drama, and truthfulness, the most uncompromising truthfulness." What characterizes the specific also serves the general. Mahler's symphonies, all of them, are immense frescoes of life, which we are only now beginning to understand.

Because of his mystical and superstitious nature, Mahler hesitated to put a number *nine* on a symphony—out of fear that it would be his last. He dodged the issue for a while by putting a title with words onto what actually *was* his *Ninth Symphony*—this is the sublime song-symphony *Das Lied von der Erde* (*The Song of the Earth*). But then he did put the number nine onto his next full-blown orchestral score, and he even sketched out a *Tenth*, which was painstakingly reconstructed recently by the British Mahler connoisseur, Deryck Cooke, and performed and recorded. The year 1960 marked the centennial of the birth of Mahler; it also marked the real beginning of a wide public appreciation of Mahler's importance in music history.

The Nationalists among the composers of the latter half of the nineteenth century were responding to the prevailing political climate throughout Europe. The Bohemian Bedřich Smetana rebelled against the repressive measures of the Austrian Empire in his native land and fled for a time to Sweden, where he could more freely function as a creative artist. When he returned to his homeland, he created a series of Czech national scores, including the cycle of six symphonic poems titled collectively *My Country*. The second and fourth—*The Moldau* and *From Bohemia's Meadows and Forests*—are the best known.

In Russia, Mikhail Glinka was the founder of the Russian school of nationalist music, which ultimately brought into being the group of composers who banded together as "The Five": Balakirev, Cui, Rimski-Korsakov, Borodin, and Musorgski. Each of them composed orchestral music chiefly distinguished by exotic and colorful orchestration. The most prolific was Rimski-

Korsakov, whose *Scheherazade, Capriccio Espagnole,* and *Russian Easter Overture* are perennial favorites.

In Norway, Edvard Grieg became the national musical spokesman, and his incidental music for Ibsen's fantasy *Peer Gynt* is one of his nation's richest natural resources. Also reflective of Grieg's national character is his *Piano Concerto in A minor*—solid, tough and richly romantic.

A Spanish national music was beginning to emerge under the impetus provided by the success of the music of Albéniz and Granados, and toward the very end of the century Sibelius appeared in Finland as that country's representative of a national musical expression.

In France, too, there was a musical ferment, though it would be overstating the case to say that the composers active in France were creating a distinctive French musical nationalism. Rather, each was expressing his own musical point of view, and in the aggregate what they came up with are some of the qualities we today characterize as being typically French: wit, urbanity, polish, and meticulous craftsmanship. To this group of composers belong such figures as Franck (though Belgian-born), Chausson, d'Indy, Lalo, Fauré, Bizet, and Saint-Saëns.

In the Austrian Empire the musical nationalism that reigned supreme was the waltz, and its chief apostle, of course, was the man who quickly came to be dubbed The Waltz King, Johann Strauss the Younger.

Although his life span covered the first half of the twentieth century, Richard Strauss (no relation to the waltzing Strausses from Vienna) must be evaluated in the context of his orchestral output as a composer of the nineteenth century. Though he composed a delectable *Oboe Concerto* and a few other instrumental scores late in life, his principal orchestral scores date mostly from the last decade and a half of the previous century. That he was a Romantic to the core is proven by his addiction to literary subjects for many of his works—*Don Juan, Macbeth, Don Quixote, Thus Spake Zarathustra,* and even *Death and Transfiguration* all have literary programs. So does *Till Eulenspiegel's Merry Pranks.* The symphonic poem *Ein Heldenleben* (*A Hero's Life*), which may be said to sum up the first period of Strauss's creativity, is similarly tied to an explicit program, albeit one of Strauss's own devising. All these scores have a plush and luxuriant sound and a truly sensual impact.

The Twentieth Century

In our own century orchestral music has flourished. There have been many different trends along the way, to be sure, and the situation seems constantly to be changing. I label as nonsense the dire predictions of those who forecast the disappearance of the symphony orchestra through atrophy. Before we examine some of the most recent contributions to the orchestral literature, let us briefly look at some of the great composers of the recent past.

During the early years of this century Debussy, Schönberg, and Stravinsky were busily enriching orchestral literature. Debussy's *La Mer, Nocturnes,* orchestral *Images,* and *Jeux* are highly evocative scores, which seem to challenge all the senses at once. Schönberg's first orchestral works are in the style of lush Romanticism—*Pelleas and Melisande,* the *Gurre-Lieder,* and *Transfigured Night.* And the three great ballet scores Stravinsky composed between 1910 and 1913—*The Firebird, Petrouchka,* and *The Rite of Spring*—are all brilliantly scored orchestral tours de force very much in the Rimski-Korsakov tradition—yes, even the savage and barbaric *Rite of Spring.* Similarly, the orchestral works of Ravel are natural outgrowths from the evolving French style of the 1880's and 1890's and the early 1900's.

What makes the music of the twentieth century such a fascinating and complex literature is its many-sidedness. Composers like Nielsen, Bartók, Prokofiev, and Britten have worked within traditional frameworks and formal concepts, and each has enriched the art with the power of his own musical thought. Free spirits like Ives and Varèse have cast aside the motivational principles that have guided other composers, and have struck out in their own new directions. Composers like Copland and Shostakovich have consciously striven to communicate directly to their audiences while others, of whom John Cage is perhaps the principal example, seem to devote their energies toward finding new ways to confound the public. In short, there is something for every taste.

To conclude this chapter, I would merely like to touch upon some of the music of the present and the recent past that I find particularly satisfying.

The emergence of the Danish composer Carl Nielsen as a powerful figure in twentieth-century music is especially gratifying to me. Nielsen was a unique figure, and his six symphonies are among the most engaging in the entire realm of music. My own favorites are the graceful and pastoral *Third* and the sardonic, menacing *Fifth*.

Bartók, who died so tragically unappreciated in New York as recently as 1945, left us a heritage of many superb orchestral creations. Chief among them are the *Concerto for Orchestra;* the *Music for Strings, Percussion and Celesta;* the *Second Violin Concerto;* the *Divertimento for String Orchestra;* the *Dance Suite;* and the *Second* and *Third Piano Concerti.*

Bartók's *Concerto for Orchestra* was composed on commission from Serge Koussevitzky for the Koussevitzky Music Foundation. Its first performances were given in Boston under Koussevitzky's direction by the Boston Symphony Orchestra early in December, 1944, and a few weeks later Koussevitzky took the unprecedented step of repeating the score in the same subscription series. Precarious health had prevented Bartók from attending the first performances, but when the repeats came along a few weeks later, he journeyed to Boston to be present at the rehearsals and performances. Koussevitzky saw to it that Bartók was comfortably seated in Symphony Hall's first balcony, overlooking the stage, for the rehearsals. No sooner did the conductor begin to rehearse the concerto than the composer, seated directly overhead, interrupted with the suggestion that the tempo was a bit too slow for what he had in mind. Koussevitzky began again, this time with a slightly faster tempo. Before long, however, Bartók again interrupted with another comment, and then another and another. After a while Koussevitzky patiently suggested to Bartók that perhaps he could write his comments down on a sheet of paper, and then the two of them could discuss matters during the rehearsal's intermission, rather than using up valuable rehearsal time for their deliberations. To this Bartók readily agreed, and a pad of paper and pencil were brought to him. The rehearsal proceeded without further interruption from Bartók, but he was observed to be writing furiously, filling page after page with notes. When the intermission break arrived, composer and conductor closeted themselves behind the locked door of the conductor's room to go over Bartók's notes and suggestions. Only Koussevitzky and Bartók know the details of the discussion that followed, and neither, unfortunately, is around today to offer testimony. Not a sound was heard by the bystanders who were stationed outside the door, but in a very few minutes the door was unlocked from the inside, and Bartók and Koussevitzky emerged wreathed in smiles. When the rehearsal session was reconvened on the stage, the conductor announced beatifically: "Gentlemen, during the intermission of our rehearsal I was able to go over the score of this masterpiece with its inspired composer, and I am happy to report to you that he agrees in every detail with *my* interpretation. Let us go now to the fourth movement!"

Prokofiev was an extremely important creative figure of this century, and his symphonies, concerti, and incidental scores form one of the richest lodes of the music of our time. His *Classical, Fifth,* and *Sixth Symphonies* are true classics, his two violin concerti and five for piano are endlessly fascinating, and several of his miscellaneous orchestral scores, including the *Scythian Suite,* the *Lieutenant Kije Suite,* and *Peter and the Wolf,* are among the best-known works of our time. Prokofiev was also a superb composer of music for the ballet, and his *Cinderella* and *Romeo and Juliet* are full-scale masterpieces.

Of the output of that other great Soviet composer of the twentieth century, Shostakovich, I particularly recommend five of the symphonies: the *First, Fifth, Sixth, Eighth,* and *Tenth.* Each packs a powerful and long-lasting message.

In addition to the three great ballets, there is much other Stravinsky music worth cultivating: the *Symphony in C* and the *Symphony in Three Movements,* the *Capriccio for Piano and Orchestra,* the *Violin Concerto, The Soldier's Tale,* the *Symphony of Psalms, Card Game,* and *Oedipus Rex.*

Of Aaron Copland's music I particularly like *Appalachian*

Spring, Billy the Kid, El Salon Mexico, the *Dance Symphony,* the *Piano Concerto, Rodeo,* and *Music for the Theater.*

Though Benjamin Britten's major reputation rests on his operas and other theater works, I would additionally commend to your attention his *Sinfonia da Requiem,* his *Variations on a Theme by Frank Bridge,* the *Young Person's Guide to the Orchestra,* and the *Symphony for Cello and Orchestra.*

The symphonies by Sibelius and Ralph Vaughan Williams are distinguished twentieth-century additions to the form that so dominated orchestral music during the nineteenth century. In addition, both Sibelius and Vaughan Williams composed much other orchestral music of outstanding and lasting importance. Chief among Sibelius' output in this area are the symphonic poems *Pohjola's Daughter, Tapiola, En Saga, The Swan of Tuonela,* and *Finlandia;* Vaughan Williams' principal orchestral scores in addition to his symphonies are the *Fantasia on a Theme by Tallis,* the *Fantasia on "Greensleeves,"* the *Romance for Violin and Orchestra* titled *The Lark Ascending,* and the *English Folk Song Suite.*

Finally, I would call to your attention some of the music of the Czechoslovakian-born composer, Bohuslav Martinu, who spent the years of the Second World War in this country. Unfortunately, not much of Martinu's music is performed or recorded. His was a distinctive voice, however, and he had a rich sense of orchestral color and symphonic design. Of the available recordings of his works, perhaps the most representative are his *Fourth Symphony,* the *Third* and *Fourth Piano Concerti,* and the *Violin Concerto.*

This brief panoramic survey of four centuries of orchestral music is of necessity highly condensed. Many important composers have not even been mentioned. I hope, however, that the reader will be encouraged to do some exploring of his own, for only through personal discovery can one fully participate in what Leonard Bernstein has so rightly termed *The Joy of Music.*

3

Music of the Baroque

IGOR KIPNIS

To some listeners Baroque music represents a somewhat vague historical period, somewhere around the time of Bach or earlier. To them this is music of a faintly antiseptic nature, anti-emotional in content, usually involving reduced performing forces, who are utilizing antiquarian instruments. The bulk of compositions stemming from this time is looked on as an early and undeveloped form of expression. It is regarded as music still in a fairly primitive state, music that has not yet attained the full flowering it would achieve with the rise of the symphony in the age of Mozart or Beethoven.

Another company of music lovers has a somewhat less restricted view of that era. But they look upon Baroque music as a passionless antidote for the Romantic excesses of the late nineteenth and early twentieth centuries. They appreciate their Vivaldi or Teleman because they think that these composers have the characteristics of classicism, purity and formalism. Even Mozart has been viewed by this school of listeners as an essentially classical composer, whose emotional penetration is seldom profound.

This attitude, like the first, is a limited one. It applies neither to the early Baroque (the beginnings of the seventeenth century—the time of Giovanni Gabrieli and Monteverdi) or to the late (the Baroque in music is usually said to end with the death of Johann Sebastian Bach in 1750). The one distinguishing characteristic that emerges from any study of this period, whether it deals with music or the visual arts, is an unusually strong element of passion. This quality, of which a great many music lovers are unaware, runs throughout the entire 150-year span of what we call *Baroque music*. What I would like to stress here most of all is that in this period of music history, with its tremendous concentration on the emotions, there was an immense amount of vitality. There was, to be sure, an occasional undercurrent of classicism, but by and large it was an era of overt expression. This passionate communication was not couched, however, in the Romantic style, a rhapsodic revelation of a later century, but rather in the controlled expression of an exceptionally rhetorical and brilliantly varied age, an age whose intensity and desire to explore very much matches our own.

What we think of today as a historical period of music was originally a descriptive term, and not a very complimentary one at that. First used over three centuries ago in reference to irregularly shaped pearls, *Baroque,* by the middle of the eighteenth century, had attained a derogatory meaning that was applied to art, implying something contorted, eccentric, bizarre, and even tasteless. The word did not lose its pejorative connotation until close to the beginning of this century, when *Baroque* began to be used to describe a stylistic period in the visual arts. The attachment to music did not come until around 1918, but several decades had to pass before its general acceptance as a stylistic label for the music of the seventeenth and first half of the eighteenth centuries.

This style of composition was an outgrowth of the Renaissance, the aesthetic ideal of which was the discovery and control of the world and mankind. The Renaissance concept was one of serene formalism and reality; the Baroque involved an exaggeration, a striving beyond formal structure. The Renaissance held its own equilibrium, the Baroque pushed out of it, but without entirely foregoing the formalistic elements.

Music between 1600 and 1750 may be pictured as involving two opposing forces, a formal structure (fugue, aria, concerto) and an equally powerful desire to escape the structure (the free cadenza at the conclusion of the aria, the spontaneously embellished repeats of a formal dance movement in an equally formal setting of the suite, the virtuosic flights of fancy of a toccata). The interaction between these two forces results in tension; tension is also achieved by a new harmonic language, in which the emphasis is rather more strongly on the discord than the concord (the reason why trills begin on the upper note rather than the main note). There is, of course, relaxation as well, but tension, the driving impulse of the Baroque, is always present to some degree. One may hear it in a 1610 *Magnificat* by Monteverdi, a keyboard lament for the death of a lutenist by the mid-seventeenth-century Austrian, Froberger, or a French-styled suite by Bach. In the Monteverdi work, which derives from a musical setting of the Vespers for the Feasts of the Blessed Virgin, the symmetrical spirit of the Renaissance has been magnified, even distorted, with the most grandiose results.

Innovations

Monteverdi, who parallels the beginnings of the Baroque, was also intensely interested in a new development of musical composition—monody; here the concept of melody and accompaniment displaced an earlier polyphonic style, where all voices (or parts) of a composition has equal importance. The manner in which Monteverdi approached this idea, with its supreme emphasis on the importance of the text, sometimes resulted in an affective expression that becomes manneristic, which of course is Baroque exaggeration carried to its furthest extreme (for instance the highly chromatic passage of some of his madrigals, or one hundred years later, the strange harmonic progressions of a Bach chorale prelude).

Monody was to have far-reaching influence, for out of it came the opera aria. Opera developed at the beginnings of the Baroque, as did another important principle from Italy (this country was the musical leader throughout not only the Renaissance but also the Baroque): the idea of contrast (*concertato*). Early examples of such contrast in Baroque music are particularly stimulating for stereo-minded listeners, for such composers as Giovanni Gabrieli wrote both instrumental and choral pieces involving spectacular antiphonal effects. *Concertato* eventually developed into the concerto, in which either a single instrument or a group was pitted against a larger, accompanying body. So far as Baroque composers were concerned, the solo forces involved in a concerto could not only be variable (ranging from a single violin, oboe, or even, as in the renowned Bolognese school, the trumpet, all the way to a small ensemble, as in a concerto grosso), but the principle of contrast could be achieved as well by dynamics and differing tonal characteristics. Perfectly in keeping with the concerto principle are works of that name by Bach (the *Italian Concerto* for a solo harpsichord with two keyboards), by the early eighteenth-century French bourgeois favorite Joseph Bodin de Boismortier, who wrote a delightful *Concerto in E minor*, Opus 37, just for flute, oboe, violin, bassoon, and continuo, and by Vivaldi, who composed numerous concertos for orchestra without any solo instruments at all.

The Baroque age is sometimes called the period of the continuo, or to use its full name, the basso continuo. This was the system of the figured bass or thorough bass, and it refers to the harmonic underpinning for any piece of music. Composers developed a musical shorthand for indicating with each bass note what harmony was to be required at any given moment, a method that has its counterpart today in the system of guitar chords for popular music. "Continuo" really refers to the bass line of a composition, a part that has considerable aural importance. That line would normally be played by the low stringed instruments, together with one or more keyboard instruments, such as harpsichord and organ and even lute or harp. The instruments that were capable of playing more than just the bottom line would also fill out the indicated harmonies from the figures. So far as the execution of the harmonies was concerned, this was an entirely improvisational system.

Among other innovations developed during the Baroque age was the instrumental sonata (solo plus continuo, or more instruments, as in the trio sonata, where two soloists are heard above the continuo—in other words, involving three separate parts, although as many as four or five players may be participating). Then there was the suite, which derived from pairings of dance movements. The Renaissance Pavan and Galliard metamorphosed, roughly speaking, into the Baroque Allemande and Courante. To these were added a slow and stately Sarabande and a bouncy Gigue (as in a Froberger suite); eventually additional movements were provided, some free, some not dance movements at all, but descriptive pieces (as in the harpsichord suites of Couperin and Rameau), and some movements that could serve as introductions (Prelude, Fantasia, Toccata, or French Overture).

The French Overture, itself a highly stylized form, consisting of a slow section with dotted rhythms, followed by a fast fugal section with, usually, a return to the slow pompous opening material, was developed by Lully in the latter half of the seventeenth century. It was used both orchestrally and instrumentally by composers both French and non-French, and it is one of the most common musical forms to be found during this era (*viz.*, Handel, *Royal Fireworks Music;* Telemann, *Don Quichotte Suite;* Bach, *Goldberg Variations, No. 16*). The Sinfonia, a more Italianate development, was made up of three movements in a fast-slow-fast sequence, and it eventually became transformed in the later eighteenth century into the classical symphony.

Among the innovations, it might be wise to mention the development of certain instruments, notably the violin. Music for it began to be written at the very outset of the Baroque, although not until the end of the seventeenth century could it be considered a serious rather than a popular instrument whose function had to be restricted mainly to dance music. By the close of the Baroque, Corelli had ennobled the violin through his sonatas, Vivaldi had helped to develop the violin concerto and broadened its technical capabilities, Tartini extended them even further, and Locatelli (whose *L'arte del violino*, Opus 3, appeared in 1733) provided opportunities for violin virtuosity that were not to be equaled until the time of Paganini.

The lute and the viols, however, proceeded rather in the opposite direction. Their heyday was at the close of the Renaissance, when they were beloved by amateurs. By the close of the seventeenth century both had diminished considerably in appeal. The lute had evolved from an instrument any gentleman could play to an incredibly complex device, which might be effective only in the hands of the most skilled virtuoso (for example, Bach's intricate lute pieces).

Among the keyboard instruments, three held sway: the harpsichord, which could be played solo, in ensemble or with orchestra (in its continuo as well as in a concerted function); the organ, whose main use was connected with the church; and the clavichord, an intimate-voiced home instrument.

As a harpsichordist I cannot refrain from adding a few remarks about my own instrument. Contrary to the popular belief, the harpsichord is not an ancestor of the modern piano; it is, however, a kind of great granduncle, for the simple reason that it bears the same approximate shape as the later instrument and because it uses a keyboard. Mechanically, however, the harpsichord has its strings plucked, as against the struck strings of the piano. In that respect, the clavichord, for all its tiny dynamic span, is the true ancestor of the piano, since its strings are struck, by metal tangents, to produce a tone. That instrument, incidentally, is the only keyboard instrument able to produce a vibrato, which the player can accomplish by gently wiggling any key up and down. Both the harpsichord and clavichord possess an enormous repertoire, most of it, of course, Baroque, though modern composers have become attracted to them as well. The new enthusiasm for the harpsichord has been only one of the factors in the Baroque revival that indicate to what extent musical tastes have shifted.

The Baroque Revival

The enormous interest in, and appreciation of, Baroque music, which has reached peak proportions in the last few years, could hardly have been envisaged a mere two decades ago. At that time the standard repertoire for concerts or records lay almost exclusively within nineteenth-century boundaries, with only occasional forays into earlier or later fields. There were eloquent spokesmen for these fringe areas, but so far as an enlightened public response might be concerned, a phonograph representation or concert performance of Schönberg's *Pierrot*

Lunaire had about as much general appeal as Handel's *Semele* or Monteverdi's 1607 opera *Orfeo,* which is to say hardly any at all, certainly not enough curiosity to make such a performance commercially worthwhile.

In the late 1940's the situation changed dramatically. A wealth of unusual repertoire, embracing music of many different periods, became available, and a public that for so long had been content with oft-performed Beethoven, Brahms, and Tchaikovsky suddenly became aware of names and works that, though largely unfamiliar, were no less attractive. This repertoire explosion can be ascribed partly to changing tastes, but it got its principal impetus from a commercial development—the long-playing record.

For many listeners the chance to venture beyond standard fare came as a relief after a surfeit of Beethoven *Fifths* and Tchaikovsky *Pathétiques;* there was a reaction against the excesses of Romanticism—overlush harmonies and an overdose of sentimentality. Perhaps because we live in a scientific age, the clarity of Baroque writing, as exemplified in a Vivaldi concerto, had much to do with its appeal. As much may be said about interest engendered in the pointillistic effects of a twentieth-century Webern composition. The music was different, and this in itself was a source of attraction. However, curiosity in this drastically different repertoire remained largely unexpressed, until record producers in the late forties discovered that a Vivaldi concerto was far less expensive to make than a nineteenth-century piece. Baroque music (as well as a good deal of contemporary material) was akin to chamber music in its demands of manpower. A Bach *Brandenburg Concerto* not only did not need the resources of a full-scale symphony orchestra, it sounded better with the small ensemble for which the composer intended it.

A large number of the Baroque works that were finding their way into the hands of record buyers originated in Europe, where recording costs, primarily musician's fees, were lower. The result was that a number of young, small firms began making excellent reputations and achieving respectable, if not overwhelming, sales based on releases of this repertoire. As more records were sold, the repertoire widened and was duplicated by other companies. The larger companies began to realize that there was money to be made in this area, though the biggest began to make their inroads into the Baroque only a few years ago. Once the momentum began to be felt, the effects on the record market were startling, to say the least. At latest count, according to the Schwann LP-record catalogue, there were twenty-three recordings of the Tchaikovsky *Nutcracker Suite,* as against twenty-one of Vivaldi's *Four Seasons.* Schwann lists thirty-three Beethoven *Fifths* compared with twenty-four sets of the complete Bach *Brandenburg Concerti.*

The Four Seasons and the *Brandenburg Concerti* are the evergreens of their fields. With the more esoteric pieces, the numbers are far less, though in a few curious instances (for example, there have been four recordings of an early Baroque oratorio, Carissimi's *Jepthe*) there exist more duplications than one might reasonably expect.

Because recordings have so dramatically broadened the standard repertoire, there has also been a striking change in live concert programming. To be sure, the Beethoven symphonies have not been displaced, but symphony orchestras do occasionally delve into orchestral repertoire of the early eighteenth century. Instrumentalists no longer are content to begin their recitals with the usual Handel sonata; they even go so far as to program a piece by the seventeenth-century Biber. I might mention here in passing that instruments once considered museum curiosities—the viola da gamba, lute, recorder, viola d'amore, and of course, the harpsichord and clavichord—have successfully been revived and are now appreciated on their own merits and no longer thought of as inferior ancestors of our "improved" modern instruments. A manifestation of the remarkable Baroque advance occurred at the 1967 Berkshire Festival at Tanglewood when an all-Vivaldi orchestral program attracted an audience of over six thousand.

Vivaldi may be considered the key composer responsible for the Baroque revival. It was around 1950 that the first recording of *The Four Seasons* was issued on long-playing discs. People who had never heard a note of Vivaldi suddenly were charmed by that Italian composer's marvelous rhythmic verve. They began investigating other Vivaldi works available in the record stores. They asked for more, and they discovered, especially after the record companies realized that there was a huge potential Vivaldi market, that this early eighteenth-century Venetian wrote hundreds of orchestral pieces, most of them concertos for almost every instrument available at that time (bassoon, cello, flute, lute, horn, mandolin, oboe, piccolo, recorder, trumpet, viola d'amore, violin, as well as combinations of these and other instruments).

A wag once observed that Vivaldi didn't write four hundred concerti, but merely wrote one concerto four hundred times. Though exaggerated, the comment has a slight touch of truth. When one is forced to listen to a great deal of Vivaldi at one time, the harmonic patterns and sewing-machine sequences (those energetic rhythms so typical of nearly all late Baroque Italian music) do begin to pall, but cannot one say the same of nearly all other composers?

If Vivaldi began as one of the principal heroes of the Baroque revival during the fifties, today he seems to have been supplanted at least partially by Telemann, who was even more prolific. Georg Philipp Telemann (1681–1767) not only outlived Johann Sebastian Bach by seventeen years, but was in his time considered a far greater composer; it was he who was offered first choice at the position Bach eventually attained, cantor of the Thomaskirche in Leipzig. When the Bach revival began, toward the middle of the nineteenth century, Telemann also came in for investigation (Bach had transcribed some of Telemann's concertos for keyboard), and in comparison with the astounding Bach, he was found wanting. He was considered facile (how could one not consider the creator of some eight hundred orchestral suites facile?) and unprofound, a poor runner-up to the great composers of the epoch—Bach, Handel, Corelli, Vivaldi, Couperin, and Rameau, to mention only some of the late Baroque names. Even at the start of the LP era, Telemann was vastly underrepresented on records. Today the situation is quite changed; within the last few years there have appeared three separate recordings of Telemann's three *Tafelmusik* productions (music for banquets, consisting of both orchestral pieces and chamber works, each set of which lasts about an hour and a half), not to mention a plethora of discs involving almost every aspect of the composer's widespread activity, from Passions and that favorite chamber music form of the eighteenth century, the trio sonata, to orchestral suites and concertos. If Telemann still cannot be considered an equal to Bach (and who can?), there is often far more to his writing than can be glossed over by the superficial description "eighteenth-century Muzak." Certainly equal in intrinsic musical merit to some of the best Vivaldi (*The Four Seasons,* the *D Minor Concerto Grosso,* Opus 3, No. 11, or the *Concerto in C Major for Ottavino* [usually played on the piccolo], *Strings, and Continuo*) are Telemann's *A Minor Suite for Recorder, Strings, and Continuo,* the *Don Quichotte Suite,* or his *Concerto in B flat Major for Three Oboes, Three Violins, and Continuo.*

Johann Sebastian Bach has not been neglected since the early nineteenth century, though the variety and scope of his compositions did not achieve representation in performance and recordings for many years. The Baroque revival has helped immeasurably. There is now not only a multitude of recordings of such standard works as the *St. Matthew* and *St. John Passions,* the *B Minor Mass,* the *Magnificat,* the cantatas, such as *No. 140* (*Wachet auf!*) or *No. 4* (*Christ lag in Todesbanden*), the suites, concertos, keyboard and instrumental pieces (the *Italian Concerto,* the *D Minor Organ Toccata and Fugue,* the unaccompanied violin *Chaconne*), but there has been added to the recorded and concert repertoire a considerable number of curiosities, from a thirty-three-bar exercise for organ pedals to such spurious attributions as the *St. Luke Passion.* There was a time when, to propagate the greatness of Bach, composers, arrangers, and conductors resorted to transcriptions, and indeed, a great many music lovers came to know such works as the *D Minor Organ Toccata* from Leopold Stokowski's orchestration, or some of the chorale preludes from the piano transcriptions of Busoni. Today, with a change in tastes and aesthetic attitudes, the arrangements are often looked upon as passé; one can hear the originals with a better appreciation of the music and the instrument for which it was written.

If the Baroque revival has succeeded in broadening the Bach repertoire to an amazing extent (I sometimes think that our era's mania for completeness is a kind of library neurosis), it is a little surprising to find that not all the two hundred-plus cantatas have yet been committed to discs. With George Frederick Handel, the other giant of the late Baroque, the public's appreciation has been rather more narrowly centered on fewer works. These pieces—*Messiah, Israel in Egypt,* the *Water Music, Royal Fireworks Music,* and some instrumental favorites—have long been held in affection. While Bach in his own day was esteemed by only a small body of connoisseurs (mainly for his organ playing) and was known but regionally, Handel was widely admired on an international level; he was an impresario of opera and oratorio performances, he hobnobbed with royalty, made money and lost it, and not least, was one of the most cosmopolitan of composers. The popularity of his music—primarily certain oratorios—has never diminished, not so much because of the style of his writing but, curiously, because of social and religious reasons. The works the public refused to relinquish were invariably connected with the idea of music being good for the uplift of the soul.

Handel had considerable difficulties with his operatic productions. Audience tastes were changing in the first half of the eighteenth century, and the lavishly staged but incredibly stylized opera of the day was rapidly losing appeal. The Puritans considered the form sinful, while oratorio, which was musically almost identical with opera but basically unstaged, was considered morally acceptable. It must be remembered that from the standpoint of entertainment opera and oratorio stood about equal in Handel's eyes. In the years after his death in 1759, however, the dramatic character of the composer's oratorios became sadly diluted in favor of the concept of the oratorio as a religious experience. This metamorphosis, evidence of which may be heard in most seasonal presentations of *Messiah,* is the principal reason Handel's name did not fade out by the nineteenth century, as did Bach's. On the other hand, what remained, in its pompous and inflated way, was principally, due to the participation of vast performing organizations, choirs and orchestras, a far cry from the dramatic entertainment Handel had originally intended.

Fortunately, the vestiges of the Victorian approach to Handel are dissolving today, and his sacred and secular music is again being performed and admired on its own terms. Even the operas, so different in their relatively static quality from the conventional opera we know, are being revived with success.

So far I have singled out for specific mention four composers—Vivaldi, Telemann, Bach, and Handel—who in the eyes of the casual onlooker might epitomize Baroque music. There are of course many other distinguished names, even though they might not have attained the same level of popularity: Domenico Scarlatti, the composer of over 550 harpsichord sonatas; Jean Philippe Rameau, whose opera-ballet productions are slowly being revived, and whose clavecin (harpsichord) music, along with that of his earlier contemporary, François Couperin, is a mainstay of Baroque keyboard literature; and Giovanni Battista Pergolesi, whose fame after his early death at the age of twenty-six eclipsed that of the majority of his contemporaries. There is also a host of less important Italians, whose liberal outpourings of concerti and orchestral pieces have brought them into the Baroque popularity boom: the Marcello brothers (Alessandro and Benedetto—Alessandro is now believed to have written the popular *Oboe Concerto*), Geminiani, Tartini, Sammartini, Locatelli, and Albinoni.

Not all these composers are equally outstanding, but all have become virtually household names in the fields of Baroque music. It is essential to realize, however, that everyone of them, from Vivaldi through Albinoni, belong to the *late* Baroque. For the neophyte listener approaching the Baroque from other later musical interests, these are the personalities he will find most congenial. From the popular Bach, Handel, and Vivaldi to the more esoteric Geminiani or Rameau is not too big a step, though there are fairly profound stylistic differences among them, especially between the fairly clear-cut Italians and the more sophisticated, rhythmically complex French. It is logical to assume that if one becomes familiar with the late Baroque, the music of the previous one hundred years or so can also be assimilated without too much feeling of strangeness.

The music of the Baroque, viewed as a whole, had incredible variety. Much of it was composed for specific occasions. In this category we may include not only all the sacred literature and many large-scale operatic undertakings designed for royal patronage, but also a large variety of spectacular display pieces composed for wedding, victory, and peace celebrations (my own favorite is Handel's *Royal Fireworks Music*).

Different Styles

It was an age for strong trends in musical fashions and tastes. There were two principal styles of writing, and both had nationalism as their basis. The Italian manner was fairly clear cut rhythmically, songful in slow sections and highly energized in fast ones. Melodiousness was much admired. The typical Italian "sound" may be easily traced through 150 years in such works as a Gabrieli canzona, a Frescobaldi ballo, a Corelli concerto grosso, or a Tartini sinfonia. The opposing style was French, and it was characterized by complex rhythms, an intricate manner of writing which was far more subtle in expression, often convoluted, and quite stylized, with a great profusion of ornaments. Whereas the Italians glorified in the voice, the French preferred the ballet. A representative cross section of the French Baroque "sound" might include a Lully ballet suite, lute pieces by Denis Gaultier, a Charpentier *Te Deum,* one of Couperin's *Leçons de Ténèbres,* and a Rameau suite for harpsichord.

These two principal national schools (there was also the German polyphonic style) had enormous influence over virtually all composers of the period, no matter what their country of origin. There was, in addition, a considerable interchange of influences, so Couperin and Rameau wrote French music with some distinctly Italian elements, while Vivaldi and Geminiani delved into French dotted rhythmic patterns from time to time. As for non-French and non-Italian composers, they took liberally from whatever they liked. In England Henry Purcell wrote vocal and instrumental pieces based on Italian models but with strong French characteristics (including much use of the French overture).

Incidentally, Purcell may, along with Monteverdi, be the next Baroque hero. His writing is quite extraordinary in its appeal and expression. I would strongly recommend that anyone not

familiar with this composer sample his *Dido and Aeneas,* some
of the incidental music to his plays, and several of the fantasias
for string consort.

Toward the close of the Baroque, one can see the nationalist
influences in French and Italian movements coexisting side by
side in, for instance, the concerti grossi of Handel and the cantatas of Bach.

Near the end of the first quarter of the eighteenth century
a new style became manifest, and this shift in taste signaled the
end of the Baroque. This was the *galant,* a supersensitive, elegant, sighing, polite manner of composing, in which sensibility
rather than deep emotions was stressed. It developed through
the latent classical qualities of the Baroque, and as a style it
may be heard in many works of Telemann (who, in contrast
to Bach, was rather an avant-gardist; the two men were close
contemporaries, but Bach was distinctly conservative), in the
post-Baroque works of the Bach sons, and in the music of Haydn
and Mozart. Another offshoot of the Baroque was the Rococo,
in which the intricate ornaments of music and the visual arts
became more convoluted and overembroidered; it was a typically French development, a heightening not of the essential
structure but of the purely decorative. Although François Couperin may be considered an example of a late Baroque composer (he died in 1733), his music features very obvious Rococo
elements.

Of the different styles of writing during the Baroque era,
the Italian is the one easiest for present-day audiences to assim-
ilate; perhaps this is why Vivaldi has made such a conquest
in our own time. On the other hand, the considerable quantity
of Vivaldi-like pieces of the late Baroque—those by Marcello,
Albinoni, Torelli, Corelli, Geminiani, Manfredini, Locatelli, and
the like—can begin to pall after a while. At their best they can
be most enjoyable, but one cannot deny a certain repetitiveness
when they are taken in large quantities.

When these works pall, it is time to explore earlier periods
and men—Monteverdi, Purcell, the great German sacred composer Heinrich Schütz (his *Christmas Story* is one of the gems
of the entire period), and the French school. The French,
whether in their stylized ballets, somewhat overpompous sa-

cred music (I am thinking particularly of Charpentier), often effete but refined harpsichord pieces, or deliberate and quite delightful cultivation of rural or pastoral atmosphere (hence the many musettes and tambourins in basically aristocratic music, such as Boismortier's *Daphnis et Chloë*), are perhaps more difficult to appreciate, but the extra effort may be worthwhile in terms of eventual enjoyment and understanding.

4

Sonatas and Chamber Music

MARTIN BOOKSPAN

In this chapter we shall be dealing with the vast body of music scored for solo or ensemble players. Ensemble music for small forces, whether for two or ten players, requires the most perceptive and delicately balanced teamwork in performance, hence the medium has frequently served composers as the vessel into which they have poured some of their most deeply felt and intimate musical thoughts.

There was a time, in the not too distant past, when the chamber music literature was regarded by large segments of the music-loving public as a kind of rarified, untouchable commodity, which yielded its innermost secrets only to the most sophisticated of listeners. Nothing could be farther from the truth. Much of the chamber music literature came into being because composers of the past and present created music that could be played by small groups of their own friends and colleagues, often with their own personal participation in the performances. Haydn, Mozart, Schubert, Schumann, and Mendelssohn all composed the great bulk of their chamber music for immediate performance by ensembles comprised of their dearest friends. And though the chamber music literature does contain some of the most profound and sublime music ever written, one must never lose sight of the fact that in chamber music, perhaps more than in any other serious compositional medium, the aim of the composer is to communicate.

For the performer there is no musical satisfaction quite like the one to be derived from playing chamber music with a small ensemble of one's peers. It is for this reason that Jascha Heifetz and Gregor Piatigorsky have in recent years limited their public music-making almost exclusively to chamber music, or that such distinguished individual artists as Isaac Stern, Leonard Rose, and Eugene Istomin devote part of their professional lives to public performance of the great piano trios.

The annals of musical legend and lore are full of amusing anecdotes relating to the performance of chamber music. Before we get to the historical elements, a few of these anecdotes might not be out of place.

Brahms, who was an inveterate chamber music participant as a pianist, was playing one of the Beethoven cello sonatas with a friend when he rather enthusiastically came down hard on the pedal. "Softer," pleaded the other musician, "I can't hear my cello." To this Brahms is supposed to have replied, "You're lucky. I can."

The pianist Moriz Rosenthal used to take along on his tours a dumb piano that produced no sound, but which contained a full eighty-eight-note keyboard, so he could practice fingerings. A maid in a Southern hotel room, seeing him so occupied, asked what he was doing. He replied that he was playing on a magic piano that could be heard only by people who had not sinned within the past twenty-four hours. She hesitated for a moment, and then bolted out of the room!

Fritz Kreisler and Sergei Rachmaninoff often played violin and piano sonatas for their own amusement; occasionally they consented to appear in public together. On one such memorable evening in New York's Carnegie Hall, Kreisler had a memory lapse in the middle of a piece and could not extricate himself from his difficulty. Inching over to his partner at the keyboard he managed to whisper, "Where are we?" To this came Rachmaninoff's instantaneous and dead-pan response: "In Carnegie Hall."

And so to the literature of chamber music and sonatas. It is always hazardous to generalize, but the composers who loom largest in the creation of symphonies, tone poems, and concerti

are also those who have enriched the repertoire of smaller concerted ensemble music.

Bach, Haydn, Boccherini, and Mozart

We have seen how the symphony as a form evolved from
the rather modest beginnings of the sixteenth and seventeenth
centuries. Because of the development of expert violin makers
in the little Italian town of Cremona during that time, the
evolution of the solo sonata was principally of Italian origin
and largely violin-derived. Some of the leading composers of
violin sonatas three and four hundred years ago were Corelli,
Tartini, Geminiani, Vivaldi, Locatelli, and Veracini. That the
art was not wholly an Italian monopoly, however, is proved by
the appearance in other countries of composers who toiled in
the same vineyards as their Italian colleagues—Heinrich von
Biber in Bohemia, or Henry Purcell in England. By the time
of Bach and Handel, the violin sonata had become pretty well
established as one of the most popular musical forms of the
day, and Domenico Scarlatti, also born in 1685 (the year of
birth for both Bach and Handel), was composing harpsichord
sonatas by the dozens.

Bach's principal works for solo violin are the six *Sonatas and
Partitas for Unaccompanied Violin* and the six *Sonatas for Violin
and Harpsichord*. Handel, for his part, composed many sonatas
for violin and harpsichord, and both composers also contributed
a vast body of music for other solo instruments with harpsichord accompaniment and for harpsichord alone. Not until the
second half of the eighteenth century did the ultimate form of
so-called chamber music come into being with the development by Franz Josef Haydn of the string quartet.

Composers before Haydn employed the combination of two
violins, viola, and cello for concerted and intimate musical conversation. Haydn's great leap forward was the assigning of
equal weight to all four instruments and in freeing the small
ensemble from the control of an extra continuo instrument
which filled in the composer's figured bass line. Further, Haydn
set the formal pattern for the structure of the string quartet, a

structure that proved to be fundamental to the advancement of the medium. Before he was finished, Haydn composed more than eighty string quartets, not to mention other works for different combinations of four instruments. He also produced piano sonatas by the yard. What is incredible is the astonishingly high level of inspiration he was able to maintain throughout his overflowing output. Because of some special characteristic, many of the Haydn string quartets have identifying nicknames: the *D Major Quartet* of Opus 64 is called the *Lark* because of the first violin's singing, soaring solo melody in the first movement; the *C Major Quartet* of Opus 76 is called the *Emperor* because its slow movement is a set of variations on an original Haydn melody, which later became the Austrian national anthem. Haydn also composed more than two dozen trios for piano, violin, and cello—fifteen after 1790, the year of his first visit to England. The best-known is the *G Major* with a Gypsy Rondo as its final movement.

Before we move on to Mozart, there is one other significant composer of chamber music who must be mentioned: Luigi Boccherini, who was born in 1743 and died in 1805. Boccherini, too, was extraordinarily prolific; he composed twenty-one symphonies, eight sinfonias concertante, and assorted concerti for solo instruments. But he was primarily a composer of chamber music! In addition to a large body of duos, trios, quartets, and quintets for combinations that included wind instruments, Boccherini composed ninety-one string quartets and 113 string quintets. The famous "Boccherini Minuet" is the third movement from his *String Quintet in E Major,* Opus 13, No. 5.

Though the list of Mozart's sonata and chamber music output is not so voluminous as that of Haydn or Boccherini—about sixty completed works of chamber music, along with the piano sonatas, the sonatas for violin and piano, and for other instrumental combinations—it contains one masterpiece after another in many different combinations: string trios, piano quartets, string quartets, string quintets, and so forth. The fertility of Mozart's musical imagination was truly beyond belief!

Of the string quartets there are perhaps a dozen that I particularly cherish; among them are the six that Mozart dedicated to Haydn (*Nos. 14* through *19*) and the final four (*Nos. 20* through 23). The *G Major Quartet, No. 14,* has a particularly frolicsome final movement full of fugal passages; the *D Minor Quartet, No. 15,* is an impassioned work with a concluding movement—a set of variations—which has about it an unsettling feeling of urgency; the next quartet in the series, *No. 16 in E flat,* opens arrestingly with absolutely no harmony at all—the theme is stated at the beginning in octave unison—and then a few bars later the opening is restated, this time fully harmonized and with some dissonances that are like needle pricks; the fourth quartet of the "Haydn" series is the *No. 17 in B flat,* called the *Hunt Quartet* because the opening somewhat resembles a hunting call; *No. 18 in A* has a particularly free theme and variations as a slow movement, which culminates in a coda of sheer magic; the last quartet of the series, *No. 19 in C,* is called the *Dissonant Quartet* because of the harmonies in the slow introduction.

Mozart's two *Quartets for Piano and Strings,* in *G minor* and *E flat,* also deserve special mention. The *G Minor* is the more dramatic and hence the better known. Both, however, reveal Mozart's unending source of inspired melody and his constant ability to thrill us with unexpected surprises—for example, the episode in five-beat meter in the first movement of the *G Minor Quartet.*

Speaking of unexpected surprises in Mozart's chamber music brings me to the *Divertimento in E flat for String Trio* (violin, viola, and cello), K 563. The texture these three instruments afford the composer is not very broad, and the fourth of the six movements of this work is again a theme and variations. Mozart deliberately further restricts the texture of the opening of the movement by casting it principally for violin and viola in octave unison, with a rather pedestrian bass line in the cello. Just when the ear begins to question the wisdom of this restricted tonal framework, the music bursts into three-part writing that now seems all the richer. Further adding to the suddenly expanded sound is the frequent scoring of double stops for the viola, so that in many places the trio sounds like a quartet.

Of Mozart's six string quintets, those in *C Major,* K 515, and *G minor,* K 516, are especially rewarding. The addition of a second viola to the string quartet gives the whole sound a richer, more vibrant quality. The *G Minor Quintet*, indeed, is one of the most tragically beautiful things in all music. Two other quintets I must mention are the *E flat for Piano and Woodwinds* and the *A Major for Clarinet and String Quartet*. Mozart himself, in a letter to his father, wrote that he considered the *E flat Piano Quintet* his finest work to date; it is certainly one of the most perfectly organized and unified works in the literature—a joy for both performers and listeners. The *Clarinet Quintet* is perhaps the perfect introduction to chamber music; its mood is all sunshine and warmth, and its quality of spontaneity and freshness, always self-renewing.

There are so many marvelous sonatas by Mozart for various instruments, we can only scratch the surface. The piano sonatas I leave to Jascha Zayde. Where the violin sonatas are concerned, the one in *A Major*, K 305, used to be my big show-stopper in my violin-playing days; hence, I retain a special affection for it, even though it is admittedly one of the slighter sonatas. The biggest are the two in *B flat*, K 378 and K 454, in which the two instruments operate at equal levels of musical interest.

Beethoven

And so to Beethoven, whose collective chamber music output is among the most varied in the entire literature. At the center, of course, are his sixteen string quartets and the *Great Fugue* for string quartet. Beethoven's string quartets fit very handily into the early, middle, and late categorization. The first six were composed during the years 1798–1800, before Beethoven was thirty; they were published in 1801. The next three, the so-called *Rasumovsky Quartets* of Opus 59, were composed about 1806 on commission from the Russian ambassador to Vienna, Count Rasumovsky. Two more quartets followed in 1809 and 1810. And then in the last years of his life, between 1824 and 1826, Beethoven returned once again to the string quartet to produce his final five visionary quartets and the *Great Fugue*. These were the last works Beethoven wrote, and he composed no other music at this time.

All seventeen works are indispensable to any chamber music lover; I merely wish to point out a few highlights. The first quartet in the Opus 18 group is the biggest and the boldest of the six; the second, in *G Major,* is the gentlest and perhaps the most charming of the group; the fourth, in *C minor,* is the most passionate and the one that makes the most immediate impression. The first of the *Rasumovsky Quartets* is bigger in conception than its two companions, and it is, arguably, the finest of the three. The second, in *E minor,* has a kind of Slavic melancholy—and in the trio section of the third movement Beethoven incorporated the well-known "Slava" ("Glory") theme that later was to form the central musical material in the Coronation Scene in Musorgski's *Boris Godunov.* The last of the *Rasumovsky Quartets* is perhaps the most accessible of the three, especially its muscle-flexing and athletic last movement. The next two quartets, Opus 74 and Opus 95, have won for themselves identifying nicknames because of particular characteristics: the many pizzicato accompaniments in the opening movement of the Opus 74 *Quartet in E flat* have led to its being dubbed the *Harp Quartet,* and the serious nature of the Opus 95 *Quartet in F minor* has brought about its *Serioso* identity.

The last five quartets are the work of a master far removed from temporal affairs. It once was fashionable to regard these five works with a respectful but distant awe—as though their inner being and meaning could not be comprehended by mortal man. I take violent exception to this point of view. True, all require concentrated listening and study, but there are no abstruse secrets in these works; they are merely the ultimate expression of Beethoven's remarkable imagination. Interestingly, three of the five are multimovement affairs: the *B flat Quartet, No. 13,* has six movements; the *C sharp Minor, No. 14,* has seven; and the *A Minor, No. 15,* has five. The *Quartet No. 12 in E flat* is a genial, contented work, with an especially moving slow movement; the *Quartet No. 13* is a headlong plunge into the unknown, whose fifth movement is a tragic Cavatina about which Beethoven is supposed to have remarked, "Never have I written a melody that affected me so much"; the *Quartet No. 14 in C sharp minor* is perhaps the most consistently "other-worldly" and sublime—its seven movements are played without pause, and more than one symphony conductor (Mitropoulos and Bernstein among them) has included the *C sharp Minor Quartet* on symphony concerts by assigning the four voices of the music to the massed orchestral strings; the *Quartet No. 15 in A minor,* among many special features, has two that are outstanding—the slow movement carries with it the heading "Song of thanksgiving to the Deity on recovering from an illness, written in the Lydian mode," and the quartet concludes with a rather gentle movement whose main theme Beethoven at one time had intended for the last movement of the *Ninth Symphony;* the last quartet, in *F Major,* is a relaxation from the tremendous emotional and intellectual challenges of its companions—it is about half their length and poses none of the refined problems presented by the others.

A word about the *Great Fugue.* This was originally the last movement of *Quartet No. 13.* Beethoven's publisher, however, insisted that it made an already long work quite undigestible. Beethoven, in an unexpectedly conciliatory gesture, set about composing a new last movement for the quartet (which became the last music he completed) and the *Great Fugue* assumed an independent life of its own. It is a craggy, granitelike score, which taxes the playing capacities of four instrumentalists almost to the breaking-point. Like the *C sharp Minor Quartet,* it, too, is sometimes played at symphony concerts by the combined strings of an orchestra.

In addition to the string quartets there is a considerable body of chamber music by Beethoven, including piano trios and quartets, five string trios, a septet for strings and winds, a string quintet, a quartet for piano and strings, a quintet for piano and winds, and a sextet for winds. Chief among the piano trios are the two of Opus 70, in *D flat* and *E flat,* and the *B flat Trio,* Opus 97, titled the *Archduke.* The first of the Opus 70 trios also has an identifying name: because of the low rumblings in the piano part it has come to be known as the *Ghost Trio.* The *Archduke Trio* is so called because Beethoven dedicated it to the younger brother of the Austrian Emperor, Archduke Rudolf, who was a devoted amateur musician. It was the Archduke who in 1809 set up an annual annuity to be paid to Beethoven by the government, the only condition of which was that Beethoven could not accept employment outside Vienna. The

Archduke Trio is a constantly inventive and fascinating score and marks the high point of Beethoven's music for piano and strings. Another masterpiece for the combination of violin, cello, and piano is the *G Major Trio,* called the *Kakadu Variations* because the basis for the music is a silly little tune titled "I Am the Tailor Kakadu" from an opera by a Viennese contemporary of Beethoven's, one W. Müller. The variations that Beethoven contrives for the tune are remarkable, and they include one for piano alone, one that shows off the violin, one that spotlights the cello, and one for violin and cello together with no piano at all.

What about the *Septet,* scored for clarinet, bassoon, horn, violin, viola, cello, and bass? From its very creation the work has been extremely popular, which caused Beethoven himself to downgrade it. He did it a disservice, however; it is one of his finest ensemble pieces, blending together in masterful fashion the seven different sonorities. Its Minuet is one of the most familiar of all Beethoven's creations.

In the fashion of his day, Beethoven allowed his violin and piano sonatas to be published as works for piano "with violin," or for piano "with violin accompaniment." The implied secondary role for the violin is not at all justified, however; the two instruments are equal partners even in the early sonatas, and in the later ones it is the piano that gets the shorter end of the stick. The first really arresting sonata among the ten is the *Fourth, in A minor,* Opus 23; rather than flowing along in the accepted classical mould, this piece is full of stops, starts, and surprises. The *Fifth, in F Major,* appeared in the same year as the *Fourth,* 1801. Its easy-flowing lyricism long ago earned for it the nickname *Spring,* and it seems particularly appropriate. The last two are the brilliant *Kreutzer Sonata,* Opus 47, and the much more relaxed *G Major Sonata,* Opus 96. The *Kreutzer* comes by its subtitle from the name of the French violinist, Rudolphe Kreutzer, to whom Beethoven dedicated the work.

The *Third, Fourth,* and *Fifth* of Beethoven's five cello and piano sonatas come from the composer's middle and late periods. The *Third, in A Major,* Opus 69, is a broad, singing work; the *Fourth* and *Fifth,* which together form the composer's Opus 102, are more in the form of free fantasias, rhapsodic and improvisational in nature. As the Beethoven sonatas for violin and piano form the backbone of the violin recitalist's repertory, so the cello and piano sonatas serve the solo cellist.

Schubert, Mendelssohn, and Schumann

Franz Schubert left us about thirty works of ensemble chamber music, some among the most beloved in the entire literature. His last three string quartets—in *A minor, D minor,* and *G Major*—are profoundly melancholy works but with a particular and pervading beauty; that the three were composed by a lad still in his twenties is one of those miracles of the creative process. Each plumbs emotional depths, and each is an ennobling listening experience. The *D Minor Quartet, No. 14,* is known as *Death and the Maiden,* because its second movement borrows the melody of the second half of the song Schubert had written seven years earlier.

On a similarly exalted level of spiritual communication is the great *Quintet in C Major* for strings by Schubert. In range of emotion, quality of material, and perfection of form there is little question that the *Quintet* is Schubert's chamber music masterpiece. Where Mozart employed an extra viola in his string quintets, Schubert went back to the model of Boccherini and employed an extra cello. The added velvety texture contributes in no small measure to the over-all impact of the music. The heart of the *Quintet* is the long and almost unbearably poignant slow movement marked "Adagio," one of the most serenely beautiful creations in all music.

Another Schubert quintet that offers a different kind of pleasure is the *A Major* for piano, violin, viola, cello, and double bass—the *Trout Quintet,* so called because the fourth movement is a set of variations on Schubert's song, "The Trout." If the *C Major Quintet* is an impassioned, stormy work, the *Trout* is all headlong rapture. Because of the odd scoring, the *Trout* is not heard in the concert hall nearly frequently enough; several supremely good recordings of it exist, however.

Another blissfully happy Schubert chamber work is the *Trio in B flat* for violin, cello, and piano, Opus 99. The first movement has a blustering extroversion which sweeps all before it; the second is a freely developed extension of the simple cello melody announced at the beginning; the Scherzo is a brusque, dancelike affair, which becomes an out-and-out waltz in the middle section; the concluding Rondo is full of bustle and excitement.

Nor should we forget Schubert's *Octet* for clarinet, horn, bassoon, string quartet, and double bass. The score was commissioned by Count Ferdinand Troyer, an amateur clarinetist in the court of Archduke Rudolf. Troyer wanted from Schubert a score like Beethoven's *Septet,* and he got it. The *Octet* has six movements and is delightful entertainment.

Schubert also composed a variety of music for violin and piano. The three sonatas of Opus 137 are particularly outstanding. They were composed when Schubert was nineteen and are really sonatas in miniature. The first is amiable and gentle, the second is dramatic and fiery, and the third has elements of both.

Felix Mendelssohn contributed several outstanding works to the chamber music repertoire, among them the *Octet for Strings,* the *D Minor Piano Trio,* and several string quartets. The *Octet* is scored for double string quartet, with each part a vital element in the fabric. The music has a marvelous swing and lift. The third movement is one of Mendelssohn's winged Scherzos, all gossamer and shimmer. The English pianist, composer, and musical scholar Sir Donald Francis Tovey wrote of this movement: "Eight string players might easily practice it for a lifetime without coming to an end of their delight in producing its marvels of tone color." The *D Minor Piano Trio* has had its ups and downs in public affection; right now it seems to be in an "up" period. Much of the effect of this music can be vitiated by performers insensitive to the fragile beauties it contains. But I have heard Isaac Stern, Leonard Rose, and Eugene Istomin play this score to perfection. Fortunately, we now have a recording of the music from them.

Among Robert Schumann's five chamber music works are three string quartets, the magnificent *Piano Quintet in E flat,* the *Piano Quartet* in the same key, and three piano trios. Astonishingly, Schumann's *Quintet* was the first work ever composed for that combination of instruments. The work is one of Schumann's perfect inspirations. After an impetuous first movement comes a slow movement rather like a funeral march; impetuosity returns in a Scherzo which makes much of ascending and descending scales, and the last movement is a tour de force of contrapuntal dexterity: in the coda the main theme of the first movement returns as the subject of a fugal section, with the first theme of the Finale as the countersubject. In spontaneity, daring, and manipulation of musical materials, the *Piano Quintet* is probably Schumann's most successful large-scale work.

Brahms, Smetana, and Dvořák

We move on to Brahms. This most self-critical of composers once stated that he had written twenty string quartets before he produced one that he considered good enough to publish. At least four sonatas for violin and piano were composed and then destroyed before he allowed the appearance of the one we label his *First, in G Major,* Opus 78. His most important works in the field are three string quartets; two string quintets; two string sextets; three piano trios; three piano quartets; a piano quintet; a trio for clarinet, cello, and piano; a trio for horn, violin, and piano; and a quintet for clarinet and strings. In addition there are three sonatas for violin and piano, two for cello and piano, and two for clarinet (or viola, interchangeably) and piano. Considering the lengths to which Brahms went to destroy many of his own compositions, the list of chamber music and sonata scores that survives is quite formidable!

The kinship of Brahms with the musical impulses that motivated Beethoven and Bach is to be found everywhere in his music, but nowhere more pointedly than in the chamber music. The string quartets, though characteristic of Brahms, follow directly in the path trodden by Beethoven. In the string sextets one finds Brahms constantly shifting the texture to lighten it, in the manner of Bach. With but a single exception, the *Horn Trio*, the first movement of every chamber music work by Brahms is in classical sonata form. The *Horn Trio*, a magically rhapsodic and elegiac work, occupies a special place not only in the Brahms catalogue but in all chamber music literature. The quartets for piano and strings are gems for that combination of instruments, with a special nod in the direction of the *First, in G minor*, with its Gypsy Rondo final movement. Despite my abiding love for this score as Brahms cast it for piano and three strings, I consider Arnold Schönberg's orchestral version an overwhelmingly successful realization of the music's character, and I wish more symphony conductors would program it. Finally, I want to direct special attention toward Brahms's *Clarinet Quintet,* a work of his later years that has the sweet autumnal quality of Brahms's final works.

Brahms's two Bohemian contemporaries, Smetana and Dvořák, also composed works of importance in the chamber music medium. Smetana's mature years saw him produce only three chamber music compositions, the *G Minor Piano Trio* and two string quartets, of which the *First, in E minor,* was titled by Smetana himself *From My Life.* Smetana appended a fairly detailed program to the quartet: the first movement is about the composer's youth, his yearnings and aspirations and his love of art; the second movement, a rustic polka, finds Smetana reminiscing about the days of his youth when he composed much dance music (he himself was an expert dancer); the slow movement recalls the esctasy of his love for the girl who became his first wife; and the final movement deals with his ability to be a national spokesman through his music—toward the end of the movement a high, sustained note is introduced, signalizing the whistling in Smetana's ears that preceded his deafness, and the autobiographical quartet ends in a mood of painful regret. This quartet, like the Brahms *G Minor Piano Quartet,* has been transcribed for orchestra most successfully; the arranger in this case is George Szell, and it is time that we had a new recording of the music from Szell and the Cleveland Orchestra. Though infrequently performed, Smetana's *Second Quartet, in D minor,* is also quasiautobiographical. Smetana stated that the quartet was his attempt to put on paper "the whirlwind of music in the head of one who has lost his hearing."

Dvořák's chamber music list is long and largely neglected.

He composed at least fourteen string quartets, several piano quartets, string quintets, a quintet for piano and strings, and several trios for violin, cello, and piano. The popularity of three works—the *Piano Quintet*, the *American Quartet*, and the *Dumky Trio*—tended until recently to overshadow Dvořák's other chamber music works, much as the *Symphony From the New World* all but obliterated Dvořák's eight other symphonies. There are now encouraging signs that some of Dvořák's other chamber music creations are beginning to emerge from the shadows. The *Quartet No. 3 in E flat*, Opus 51, and the *Seventh, in A flat*, Opus 105, to name just two, are fully mature, deeply expressive works which deserve to be far better known. This is not to deny that the *American Quartet* (*No. 6 in F Major*) is a gorgeous, colorful and exciting score, or that the *Piano Quintet* is a vibrant, melodious, rhythmically vital composition. What I am suggesting is that a healthy curiosity about some of the lesser-known Dvořák chamber music compositions will pay the listener handsome dividends.

Though the second half of the nineteenth century was the period of the bestirring of Russian composers in the field of orchestral music, there was comparatively little activity by these men in the chamber music area. There are only two nineteenth-century Russian string quartets in the international repertoire—Tchaikovsky's *First* and Borodin's *Second*, both in the key of *D Major*. Both have individual movements that have been taken out of context and arranged for every possible (and some impossible!) combination of instruments and voices. In the case of Tchaikovsky's quartet it is the slow movement, marked "Andante Cantabile," which has been butchered. (Does anybody remember a lunatic song on the Hit Parade a quarter of a century ago whose verse ran something like ". . . and it was June, June on the Isle of May"?) In Borodin's quartet it is the third movement, the Nocturne, that has been variously appropriated; in the musical show *Kismet* it turned up as "And This Is My Beloved."

The Late Nineteenth and the Twentieth Centuries

Before we get to some of the important composers of chamber music in the twentieth century—Bloch, Bartók, Schönberg, and Berg—we must briefly touch upon some other nineteenth-century figures. Edvard Grieg in Norway produced a very fine *String Quartet* and four sonatas—three for violin and piano and one for cello and piano. The *Third Violin Sonata* is especially fine; though it seems to hold little interest for the present generation of fiddlers, it was a great favorite of Fritz Kreisler and one of the happiest of all recorded performances is the version played by Kreisler and Rachmaninoff.

César Franck was an important figure in the development of sonata and chamber music composition in France. His *Sonata in A Major for Violin and Piano* is one of the richest products of his entire creative life; it is music of elegance, poetry, and drama, with the two instruments complementing each other to perfection. Franck's two other vitally important works to chamber music literature were the passionate and sensual *F Minor Piano Quintet* and the *String Quartet in D*. The latter, his most ambitious work, was completed just a few months before he died. At the beginning of the last movement Franck borrows Beethoven's technique from the last movement of the *Choral Symphony:* He recalls the themes from the earlier movements before the music settles down contrapuntally on the basic motif of the first movement.

Another important French figure was Gabriel Fauré, whose music includes two violin and piano sonatas, two piano quintets, two piano quartets, a piano trio, a string quartet, and two cello and piano sonatas. The sonatas for violin and piano were composed forty-one years apart; the earlier one, in *A Major*, is one of Fauré's best-known works, sparkling and spontaneous in character. The *First Piano Quartet* has the same qualities of grace and poise; the *Second* is more intense and powerful. In the last year of his life, 1924, the seventy-nine-year-old composer produced his vibrant and impulsive *Piano Trio* and his only *String Quartet*, an enigmatic, fragmentary work that has a beatific, farewell glow.

Claude Debussy composed four principal works of chamber music: his early *String Quartet* and the three late sonatas for different combinations of instruments. The *Quartet* is a marvelously atmospheric piece, full of shifting moods and mosaiclike patterns. The three sonatas, composed impulsively while Debussy was dying of cancer, reveal that he had lost none of his powers of evocation.

The *String Quartet* of Maurice Ravel, composed in 1902—nine years after Debussy's—has many traits in common with the Debussy, yet it is unquestionably the work of a strong and independent new voice. The other concerted piece by Ravel that belongs in the present discussion is the *Introduction and Allegro for Harp, String Quartet, Flute, and Clarinet*—a brilliant display vehicle for a virtuoso harp performer which nevertheless manages to sustain musical interest from first to last. Ravel's *Piano Trio* has a Spanish character, his *Sonata for Violin and Cello* has a sparse severity and the *Sonata for Violin and Piano* finds Ravel composing a "Blues" movement.

Ernest Bloch, with five string quartets, and Béla Bartók, with six, are thus far the twentieth century's principal practitioners in the string quartet medium. True, Dimitri Shostakovich has produced a dozen or so string quartets by the most recent reckoning, but his quartets are wildly uneven, while the four by Bloch that I know and the six by Bartók are all masterpieces. Bloch's *No. 1*, dating from 1916, is a sprawling colossus; an indication of its character is to be found in some of the markings in the score: *frenetico, furioso, feroce,* and *strepitoso.* Some thirty years passed before Bloch turned again to the string quartet. He produced four more quartets between 1945 and 1956. The *Second Quartet* is more controlled, less explosive than the *First;* it makes a devastating impression. The *Third* is closely knit but mellow and profoundly moving; the *Fourth* is lyrical and poetic.

Bloch also left us a superb *Piano Quintet*, several pieces of a descriptive nature for piano trio and string quartet, two violin sonatas, and a suite for viola and piano (which also exists in an alternative version by Bloch himself for viola and orchestra). The *Piano Quintet* was a problematic work when it appeared in the 1920's; its use of harsh dissonance and quarter-tones repelled some listeners. Today it is seen as an uncommonly symbolic work, with an optimistic faith that even the most hopeless and despairing struggle is capable of resolution. At the end of the *Quintet* order and calm have been retrieved out of chaos and trouble, and the work ends on an innocent C Major chord.

The six Bartók string quartets have been likened to the last five of Beethoven in their prophetic vision and their challenge to listeners. They cover very nearly Bartók's entire creative life-span: the *First String Quartet* appeared in 1908, when Bartók was twenty-seven; the *Sixth* is a product of 1939, when Bartók was fifty-eight. In December, 1944, nine months before he died, he sketched out a few ideas for a seventh quartet but was never able to pursue them. The *First Quartet* is an eclectic work—the principal influence would appear to be Beethoven's *C sharp Minor Quartet*—but the wild rhythms of the last move-ment are indicative of the Bartók to come. The *Second Quartet* is essentially romantic and lyrical. The *Third* is the shortest, the most concentrated, and generally considered the most dif-ficult to listen to of the six. The *Fourth* followed the *Third* by only a year, and it has much the same toughness, though not quite the same austerity. The *Fifth* shows a further relaxation, with an ironic parody in the last movement of second-rate Hungarian cafe music. In the *Sixth Quartet* Bartók finally ar-rives at the classical sequence of four contrasting movements. The form is relatively simpler, and the themes have a more sustained, broader nature. It is a short step from the Bartók of the *Sixth Quartet* to the Bartók who composed such popular works as the *Sonata for Two Pianos and Percussion*, the *Concerto for Orchestra* and the *Third Piano Concerto*.

Much of the experimentation of Arnold Schönberg, which ultimately led to the strict twelve-tone method, was accom-plished in various chamber music pieces. In his *First String Quartet* of 1904–1905 the four movements are played without a pause, and the developments are no longer identifiable sec-tions but are fused into the over-all structure. In his *Second String Quartet* (1907–1908) there is no development at all in the first two movements; instead, the third movement becomes the arena in which material from the first two movements is developed. In the last movement Schönberg dissolves all con-tact with a recognizable tonal center. Here was the turning point, and this principle was to motivate all of Schönberg's thinking, as well as that of his disciples, for many years. Among those disciples, Alban Berg and Anton von Webern composed a considerable body of music for chamber ensembles.

Now, in the late 1960's, more and more composers are concentrating their attentions and resources upon music for small ensemble and solo performance. There is still plenty of life in the chamber music medium.

5

Piano Music

I WOULD have an easier time counting the stars at night than trying to cover the gamut of keyboard music. It is my sincere hope, however, that I may be able to give the reader a somewhat clearer insight into some of the great literature written for the one true solo instrument that is able to fulfill totally all musical requirements of the immortal composers. Do not misunderstand me. I am fully aware of the significant contributions made by clavier writers prior to the invention of the piano (by Bartolomeo Christofori about 1707), but with the exception of Johann Sebastian Bach and Domenico Scarlatti, whose keyboard compositions are part of every pianist's repertoire, the works of the other composers are still played mainly on the instruments for which they were originally intended: the clavichord, harpsichord, and organ.

I am always irritated when I hear people say that Bach's music is cold and without feeling. Nothing could be further from the truth. From the relatively simple two-part inventions, the not so simple partitas, the forty-eight preludes and fugues, the French and English suites (nobody really knows why they are called French or English—the music certainly shows no nationalistic tendencies) to the profound and complex *Goldberg Variations*, Bach's clavier music is full of lyric passion, emotion, and monumental architectural construction. There is never a dull moment in any of his works. The melodies or counter-melodies (Richard Wagner was a great admirer of Bach's melodic writing) are always on the move, always soaring and searching for something new to say and a new way to say it. The wonderful and at times daring harmonies hold a special degree of importance in all of the master's works. They never sound jaded or old-fashioned; on the contrary, they are fresh, and vital. Bach wrote magnificent fantasias and toccatas and fugues for the organ, and we can never sufficiently thank Ferruccio Busoni, Eugene d'Albert, Franz Liszt, Alexander Siloti, and others for transcribing them for the piano. I'm sure that they did this so that pianists might also share in the joy of playing these extraordinary works with their organist cousins. Bach's fantasias are exactly what the title indicates. They are written in a free style, unhampered by rigid rules and regulations (Bach broke all conventional rules regarding form and harmony, whenever his inventive mind required it) and display an enormous variety of moods and styles. Some passages are brilliant and fast, and the performer must accomplish incredibly spectacular feats of digital proficiency. Other passages are quite somber and create a chorale atmosphere. But at all times there is a feeling of spontaneity. Therein lies part of the genius of Bach. The *Fantasia and Fugue in G minor*, as arranged for the piano by Liszt, is a choice example of that.

Bach was meticulous in many ways, but when it came to leaving musical instructions on paper for the artist to follow, he was negligent. Take the *Goldberg Variations*. There are almost no indications of tempo or dynamics. When a pianist plays this almost superhuman work, he may do as he pleases with the notes. He may play them loudly or softly, quickly or slowly, smoothly or detached, and he will not transgress the composer's requirements. Bach apparently had a very free attitude toward his music (or tremendous faith in the players of his day) as well as to the compositions of others, which he would change and arrange (sometimes signing his own name to the product without so much as a second thought). He left no detailed instructions as to how he wanted his ornamentations (little signs above certain notes that tell you to embroider them in a special way) executed. One of Bach's sons, Johann Christoph, published a manual for the correct playing of these signs, but there are those who say that young Johann had a minor falling out with his father and spitefully indicated the wrong way to finger the ornaments. Two of the most admired Bach specialists, Rosalyn Tureck (she is "untouchable" in the forty-eight *Preludes and Fugues*) and the slightly eccentric but formidable musician and pianist, Glenn Gould, approach the *Goldberg Variations* with a different outlook. Miss Tureck adds very little to what is on paper. She loves each note and pays fond attention to each, like a mother afraid to show favoritism to any of her young. She takes no liberties with tempo. Once she chooses one, it never varies. But within this strict framework she manages subtle nuances of tone color and phrasing to interpret the mood of each of the thirty variations that make up this colossal masterpiece. It is an unforgettable performance. Gould's version on the other hand (the one I prefer) is more thrilling. He rips into the piece with an enormous amount of vitality and energy. He breathes fire and brimstone. He takes many liberties with tempo and voicing and sometimes adds ornaments of his own. On occasion he even transposes entire passages up or down an octave. Everything, however, is under perfect control. All I can say is *bravo* to both. Each sounds perfectly correct, artistic, and beautiful.

There rises on occasion a rather provocative question: Should keyboard works of Bach be played on the modern piano? After all, Bach conceived his works for the harpsichord or clavichord, and there are those who feel they owe it to history to perform the music on the instrument for which it was composed. I am not among them. I am sure Bach would have agreed with me, had a piano been available to him, that it is much more satisfactory for the expression of a complete musical concept than is the harpsichord. Although the harpsichord can produce various degrees of dynamics by means of coupling or uncoupling octaves with the pedals, it cannot be made to bring out enough different shades of loud and soft. The mechanics of the instrument do not allow notes to be sustained for any length of time or to be played smoothly. The naturally detached sound cannot be altered, nor is there a personal approach to tone quality. One might compare the relationship of the harpsichord and the piano to that of a black-and-white sketch and a color portrait.

I do not mean to belittle the art of a great harpsichordist like the late Wanda Landowska. She was a beacon for twentieth-century Bach interpretation; her understanding and performance of the repertoire for her instrument were sheer magic. Igor Kipnis, Ralph Kirkpatrick, and Rafael Puyana, among our present-day performers, are artists of the highest level and project everything the harpsichord has to offer. Nor do I deny the charm of the harpsichord as an ensemble supplement, but I prefer the piano, which permits the performer to produce dynamic expression and phrasing. Harpsichord or piano, Tureck or Kipnis, Gould or Landowska, does it really matter? I have my preference, you may disagree, but a mutual bond unites us in our veneration of Bach. Although Handel was a keyboard virtuoso, his contribution towards its literature is, unfortunately, quite limited. (The organ, for some strange reason, is not considered part of the keyboard family.)

Alongside these two giants, Domenico Scarlatti, also born in 1685, was a tiny giant who wrote about six hundred works for the harpsichord, which are now played on the piano. Even though they are called sonatas, they in no way resemble the sonata of later development. They are, however, miniature masterpieces. Only a few pages in length, and taking but a few minutes to play, they require extreme dexterity of fingers and arms. In many you have to crisscross your hands in rapid tempo. These sonatas brim over with limpid melodies, excitement, rhythmic pulsation, and many sudden changes of mood and color. If you want to spend an exhilarating hour, I suggest you listen to the twelve Scarlatti sonatas recorded by Vladimir Horowitz. Pay special attention to the extraordinary sequence of sounds in the *D Major*, L 164, the lyric beauty of the *F Minor*, L 187, and the unbelievably rapid hammering of the A *Major*, L 391.

Mozart and Haydn

To the average listener the obvious thing about the music of Mozart is that it seems to be endlessly bright, gay or serene, cheerful, witty and full of spirit. One thinks of Mozart in white wig, lace cuffs, and silk pants. Consider the *Sonata in A Major* (K 331), the one with the "Marcia alla Turca" as its final movement. I remember an unforgettable performance many years ago by Ossip Gabrilowitsch.

Although I was quite young, I was impressed by his playing of the opening theme, soft and songlike, as if he were humming a lullaby. There were occasional slight swells and dips in dynamics, minute waits before stressing certain notes, but an over-all feeling of quiet and contentment. The six variations that followed were handled with a delicacy of fine china, yet each had its own character. The "Marcia alla Turca" (every child plays it as a separate piece of music and bangs like mad, trying to imitate the snare and bass drum) was played in miniature style, but big in scope, so that the whole sonata hung together.

The other side of Mozart is the tragic one, the Mozart of financial difficulties, illness, and frustration, a musician whose music is somber, melancholy, and intense. The superlative and profound *Fantasia in C minor* (K 475) belongs to this category. It offers sudden and extreme dynamic changes, gentle phrases that explode into violent ones, and slow passages followed by rapid ones. It is a true fantasy and a great one. Daniel Barenboim gives it an exceptional treatment in his recording.

Except for the concertos, Mozart's greatest contribution to the piano literature is his *Sonata in F* (K 497) for four hands, one piano. In a letter to his father Mozart wrote that he would prefer to have this piece played on two pianos. He undoubtedly realized the stupendous grandeur of this composition. In view of the limited sound and volume the piano was capable of producing in his time, Mozart probably wished for some striking way to enhance this sonata. For me it is truly a symphony for the keyboard. A gentle slow opening leads into a fast movement, with a heavenly, lyrical second movement, and a boisterous and gay rondo, to complete a masterpiece. The work is so rich in concept, melody, harmony, and rhythmic novelties that after playing it for more than twenty years, I feel I need another twenty before I can be sure I am doing more than scratching its surface.

Included in Haydn's vast output are more than fifty piano sonatas, themes and variations (the one in *F minor* is best known), and shorter pieces. Haydn was highly resourceful and imaginative in the development of his thematic material, if I may say so, and actually more daring than Mozart in exploring and experimenting with new ideas. It's a pity his piano music is heard so rarely on the concert stage. There certainly is a place for it. My colleagues have recorded quite a few of his pieces, and of these I highly recommend Nadia Reisenberg's delightful and ingratiating version of the *Sonata No. 50 in C Major* and the *Sonata No. 52 in E flat Major*, Opus 78. Artur Balsam plays the *Sonatas Nos. 21* and *48*, both in *C Major*, *No. 31 in E Major*, and *No. 32 in B minor*, with impeccable musical taste and technique. The *Andante and Variations in F minor* is performed by Artur Rubinstein. Need I say more.

Beethoven

And now we come to Beethoven. His piano sonatas were twice the length of any previous composer's. He would use two themes where only one had been the practice. He changed piano technique to suit his needs. Into almost all his piano works he introduced new kinds of rhythms, harmonic progressions, and an infinite variety of moods, ranging from deepest sadness to the most radiant happiness.

For me one of his finest piano pieces is the *Sonata in C*, known as the *Waldstein* because Beethoven dedicated it to one of his patrons, Count von Waldstein. This sonata requires the ultimate artistry to do it justice. Certainly Artur Rubinstein and Vladimir Horowitz qualify for the job. Each is a great interpreter, and each seeks to be faithful to Beethoven's wishes. Unlike Bach, Beethoven left many notations, but such are the mystery and wonder that, though Rubinstein and Horowitz play loud and soft where Beethoven indicated, though each plays legato and staccato according to the score, though each follows all the other markings, the two end up with renditions that sound completely different and completely persuasive. How does this happen?

The Horowitz version goes with a great deal of drive and power. Every atom of his being is focused on the task at hand.

The result is an intensity in the pianissimos, as well as the fortissimos, which electrifies the listener.

Rubinstein's interpretation, on the other hand, is broad and relaxed, shimmering with a velvety sonority which beguiles the listener. Horowitz's tempos are barely a hair's breadth faster than Rubinstein's, but because of the differences in tone and concept (his nervous drive compared with Rubinstein's relaxed authority), he seems quite a bit faster. In short, a great artist is always convincing.

Beethoven's sonatas are illustrative of the course of Beethoven's development. The first thirteen, with the possible exception of the *No. 8 in C minor,* the *Pathétique,* belong to the first stage, where the influence of Haydn and Mozart is clearly evident. With the *Sonata No. 14 in C sharp minor,* Opus 27, No. 2, or *Moonlight* as it is popularly known, we see Beethoven making a clean break with tradition and settling into his own style. I remember the magnificent conception of Josef Hofmann, who made this sonata a personal message from the pianist to the composer, especially the first movement, which took on an improvisational flavor, as if it were being thought of for the first time. This middle Beethoven period reached its peak with the *Waldstein* and the *Sonata No. 23 in F minor,* Opus 57, the *Appassionata.* These titanic works require vast imagination plus gorgeous tone quality and lots of nervous energy. They sound best when a Horowitz brings his power and infinite varieties of dynamics to them.

The "unpianistic and unplayable" *Hammerklavier,* the *Sonata No. 29 in B flat Major,* Opus 106, marks the third and last Beethoven period, intense and introspective. The *Hammerklavier* abounds in technical nightmares for the performer. It is a sonata that should be played only by the elite. Then it becomes Beethoven's greatest contribution to the piano literature. I am most satisfied by the Rudolph Serkin and Daniel Barenboim performances, but hasten to add that the lesser-known Hans Richter-Hasser's reading is also to be greatly admired. For these artists the *Hammerklavier* is certainly not unpianistic or unplayable.

I have been asked whether I thought Beethoven could adequately handle it. I most certainly think so, for he was renowned as a virtuoso pianist. Like all great creators writing music for their own instruments, he invariably wrote for his own capabilities.

Another aspect of Beethoven's genius as composer and pianist was his remarkable ability to improvise. He would on occasion give public demonstrations of this wonderful gift. I can very well imagine how these extemperaneous works sounded. There must have been glory in his melody and harmony, as well as power, vitality, force, and even the brute strength of a demonic artist seeking to enlarge the instrument's capacities and extract every last ounce of delicacy and sonority from it.

Weber through Brahms

During Beethoven's lifetime, there occurred six wondrous musical events. A seventh came six years after his death. What were they? The birth of seven of the most illustrious pianists and composers of all time.

First came Carl Maria vón Weber (1786), then Franz Schubert (1797), Felix Mendelssohn (1809), Frederic Chopin and Robert Schumann, (1810), Franz Liszt (1811), and last, Johannes Brahms (1833). Although all the composers were ardent admirers of Beethoven, they felt the need to create new forms and a new language of musical expression. They exploited new harmonic structures, and this resulted in an extraordinarily varied palette, expressive devices and dynamic exaggerations. The piano itself was improved. Keys were added at both ends of the range, and the action was accelerated, making possible increased sonority. Pedals for the sustaining, blending, and muting of sounds were invented, and made an indispensable contribution to the evolution of new, creative ideas.

Weber, with large hands and slim fingers, must have been a virtuoso pianist. His compositions offer many opportunities for the pianist to display pyrotechnics. Huge, rapid leaps, intricate finger passages, and immense chords are characteristic of his piano works. He wrote brilliant polonaises, excellent themes and variations, attractive sonatas, and other fine music for the instrument. His melodies, full of charm and grace, are unmistakably original. His fame today rests on his operas and overtures; unfortunately, his solo piano music has been discarded as concert fare and relegated to the practice room.

Schubert left imperishable compositions for almost every form and combination, but none surpassed in quality his works for the piano. Whether one listens to his delightful short pieces, the impromptus, *Moments Musicaux,* waltzes, the great *Fantasy in C minor* known as the *Wanderer* (the Artur Rubinstein version is the most beautiful I've ever heard), the sonatas, or the compositions for one piano, four-hands, certain basic traits are always in evidence. The melodies have unutterable loveliness in their mixture of sensitivity, strength, dignity, emotion, and dramatic intensity. He succeeded in imparting to all his music a feeling of youthful romance, poetic tenderness, variety, and charm.

Some people complain that Schubert's sonatas are too long. I disagree. I enjoy the soulful melodies and distinctive modulations. They are sublime. Long-windedness in some composers may be a sin, but with Schubert it is a blessing.

The wolf that seemed to howl at Schubert's door did not exist for Mendelssohn. His music reflects his taste and culture. It makes me think of a young gentleman, immaculately dressed, exuding personal charm, refinement, and suavity, completely capable of handling any situation. Mendelssohn has never been given enough credit for his talent; he was a first-rate and individualistic composer. His scherzi, capriccios, and rondos are in a class by themselves. They are gay and lighthearted in spirit, elfin in character, and very humorous. His beautiful, lyrical *Songs Without Words* are a permanent part of the pianistic repertory. Of his more serious works for solo piano or piano four-hands, the *Andante and Rondo Capriccioso,* the *Variations Sérieuses,* and the *Allegro Brillante* are among his finest. Two recordings of the *Andante and Rondo Capriccioso* are absolute standouts: one by the immortal Hofmann and the other by Serkin. The interpretations are vastly different, but both are superb. The *Variations* are given a glorious treatment by Horowitz.

If I had to say whom I regarded as the greatest writer of music for the piano, I would nominate Chopin. He wrote almost exclusively for the instrument, and in the handful of compositions where the piano is not the prime factor, it is effective. He is the perfect poet and lyricist of the keyboard. He experimented with new and subtle harmonies. He investigated and brought into focus the full sonority of the piano. Novel and original forms and a new piano technique were his creations. All of his works have boldness, richness, exuberance, and charm. They remain unalterably attractive, brilliant, and daring; the critics of his day called them barbaric, wild, and dissonant.

To Chopin must go the credit for bringing to the fore a new style of performance called *rubato* playing. According to Chopin, *rubato* means that the right hand plays freely while the left plays in strict time. What happens in practice is that a little is taken away from the time value of one note and added to another, thus giving the latter note unexpected importance. The musical effect is to permit greater freedom of expression and a more rhapsodic style. Without *rubato* the compositions of the Romantic school, from Schubert through Brahms, would be dull and mechanical, and would be false to the mood and contour of the melodic line. It would be wonderful if we had discs or tapes of Chopin playing, for we would then know exactly how he conceived his *rubatos* rather than having to rely on the conflicting and not always dependable authorities.

There is an abundance of recordings of Chopin's piano music. If I were starting a collection, I would certainly include some of the following compositions played by artists who most closely approach what, I imagine, were Chopin's own interpretations: the stately and vigorous polonaises, the ones in *A Major*, Opus 4, No. 1, and *A flat Major*, Opus 53, No. 6, played by Rubinstein; the coquettish *Waltz No. 1 in E flat Major*, better known as the *Grande Valse Brilliante*, and the one in *C sharp minor*, again Rubinstein; the *Etudes in G flat Major*, Opus 10, No. 5 (*Black Key*), *C minor*, Opus 10, No. 12 (*Revolutionary*), the *G flat Major*, Opus 25, No. 9 (*Butterfly*), and the *A Minor*, Opus 25, No. 11 (*Winter Wind*), excitingly performed by Vladimir Ashkenazy; the *Fantaisie in F minor*, Opus 59, Van Cliburn; the *Sonata No. 3 in B minor*, played by the late Dinu Lipatti with ravishing subtlety of nuances. Although the name Moura Lympany may not be too well known to the average music lover, she is nonetheless a first-rate artist, and her performances of the delicious and beautiful *Nocturnes in E flat Major, A flat Major, F sharp Major,* and *C sharp minor* are exquisite. However, if I had to start with just one recording, my choice would be the *Scherzos Nos. 1, 2,* and *3,* dazzlingly played by Josef Hofmann.

Schumann did not write for the virtuoso school of piano playing. His conceptions demand a variety of tone and contrasts of color and pedal effects. His music is brimful of poetic inspirations. His imagination is fanciful rather than profound; he delighted in writing about subjects of fantastic grace. He developed what we call program music, music that expresses a definite, firm, and external idea. In almost all his best-known piano compositions, such as the *Kinderscenen, Papillons, Carnaval, Davidsbündlertänze,* and *Fantasiestücke,* Schumann paints charming vignettes. Each vignette is a complete composition; yet a series may be held together by a single, binding thought. (By the way, don't miss Rubinstein's playing of *Carnaval.* Sheer heaven!)

While Schumann was writing program music, and Chopin was developing and enlarging the sonorities and capabilities of the piano, Liszt, a pianistic cyclone, was sweeping the world. As an interpreter his blazing drive, unbelievable virtuosity, and diabolic strength overwhelmed all who heard him play. As a creator his exotic harmonies and original forms opened new doors not only for composers of his generation but also for those of later periods.

Liszt played for Beethoven and Schubert and was still giving concerts when Bartók and Stravinsky were starting to take piano lessons. He is yet another example of an outstanding creator whose worth has never been fully recognized by the public and who has, save in rare instances, been neglected by concert pianists. The monumental *B Minor Sonata* (a terrific performance by Emil Gilels), a few etudes, a nocturne or two, one of the *Mephisto Waltzes* (the William Kapell recording is superb), a half-dozen rhapsodies, and some of the pieces in *Années de Pèlerinage* are about all we are likely to get during an entire season of piano recitals. Yet the number of original works Liszt wrote for the piano is immense and diversified. Not all of his pieces are bombastic, as you might think from a glancing acquaintance with his music. Many contain some of the most exquisite melodies and delicate improvisations anyone ever conceived for the piano. There are those of his compositions that prefigure the dawn of the twentieth century and its use of dissonant harmonies, and some are the foundation for styles used by Debussy and Ravel. Liszt's transcriptions of operatic themes and arias for solo piano set a trend for the future in their virtuoso demands. These transcriptions call for great surety in leaps, crossing of the hands, brilliant and elaborate runs in single and double notes, and chords in each hand played at breakneck speed. He transcribed the great organ fugues of Bach, the songs of Schubert, and many symphonic works, including all the Beethoven symphonies, four-hands, one piano. His influence was widespread. He started societies to publish the music of Bach, Handel, and Mozart. He gave free piano lessons to gifted students (I was fortunate to call two of his students my friends, Moritz Rosenthal and Alexander Siloti). He was the patron of Schumann, Chopin, Wagner, Tchaikovsky, Dvořák, Grieg, Borodin, and a host of others. He originated the piano recital, doing away with the custom of performing publicly only with orchestral accompaniment. I am sorry he did not record for the old cylinder discs; after all, the phonograph was invented when he was sixty-six and still, I am sure, a giant as a pianist. I would dearly love to hear him, even on a scratchy, primitive recording.

Liszt always enjoyed the music of Brahms, especially the short compositions. It is strange but nonetheless true that Brahms wrote his longer works for solo piano before he was forty, and for the rest of his life was content to compose, at least for the piano, poetic gems like ballades, rhapsodies, intermezzi, and capriccios; and for piano duet, a simple and charming cycle of waltzes and Hungarian dances. I feel particularly close to Brahms, since I studied for many years with the great and benevolent Carl Friedberg, who was a pupil of Brahms and Clara Schumann.

Brahms's place in music has caused a great deal of controversy, perhaps because he did not seek new forms or harmonies. He was no revolutionary; he worked along traditional lines, using the sonata form and that of the variations for big piano compositions. Tchaikovsky pronounced him "ungifted, pretentious, and lacking in creative power." Is it possible that Tchaikovsky was jealous of Brahms? Although Brahms may have been conservative, his works overflow with romantic inspiration, technical interest (he was a virtuoso pianist), and vitality. I find it difficult to sit through an entire program devoted to the works of one composer. Yet I listened gladly to a series of four programs, presented within a few days, encompassing all Brahms's piano music. The recitals were not only enjoyable but exhilarating. The dignity, force, and nobility of the large works, contrasted with the lighthearted merriment and childlike gaiety of the smaller pieces, gave each concert an endless variety of moods. Julius Katchen, who played the series, was superb.

The Late Nineteenth and the Twentieth Centuries

While Brahms in his mature years was writing some of his loveliest romantic-lyrical compositions, a young generation was striving to find new ways of translating their impressions and emotions into music. Claude Debussy, who was to become perhaps the greatest harmonic innovator of the late nineteenth and early twentieth centuries, succeeded by avoiding clear-cut pictures and by resorting to misty sonorities and a revolutionary approach to the pedals, giving them unprecedented importance and using them in heretofore unimagined combinations. (I was told by a pupil of Debussy that the composer spent at least an hour a day improving and advancing pedal technique.) Logically, the most effective way to create a misty, veiled impression is to superimpose sonority upon sonority; thus each detracts from the clarity of the other and leaves details to the imagination of the listener. It is the moon under many thin layers of clouds, or a forest as seen through a frosted pane of glass. Debussy loved to paint pianistic tonal pictures of colorful subjects. *Footprints in the Sand, Gardens in the Rain, Fireworks, Sails, Goldfish, Reflections in the Water:* These are among the pieces in his marvelous set of twenty-four piano preludes. His many piano works under the fingers of masters like Robert Casadesus or Walter Gieseking are priceless.

With modified variations in harmony and form, the piano music of Maurice Ravel is in many ways quite similar to that of Debussy. I find in Ravel a great deal more absolute music (compositions without any extramusical association, written purely for the beauty of their sound) than in Debussy. However, in *Gaspard de la Nuit* there is the same building of veiled sonorities, important and intricate pedal manipulations, and sparkling colors (let me recommend a dazzling performance on a disc by Vladimir Ashkenazy). Ravel sometimes reverts to strict and old musical forms like those of Bach's partitas and suites. A striking example is *Le Tombeau de Couperin*.

The polar opposite of Debussy's innovations was created by Arnold Schönberg. He devised a new system of musical structure, which produced harmonies and tonal colors previously unheard. But where Debussy's are blurred and veiled, Schönberg's intensify sonorous images, defining them to a point of jagged distortion and harsh dissonance. Most of Schönberg's music is without title and specific program. It can best be described as an expression of anger or frustration, sometimes illuminated in a wild outburst, sometimes in subdued brooding and melancholia. It is his musical way of showing his dissatisfaction with the world. The *Piano Pieces*, Opus 33, as recorded by Glenn Gould, reveal the special creativity of Schönberg.

His disciples Alban Berg and Anton Webern branched out in opposite directions. Berg took the Schönberg doctrines and shaped them toward the conservative side, while Webern, with a far more liberal viewpoint, crystallized and intensified them to a point that went beyond Schönberg, as disclosed in his *Piano Variations*, Opus 27.

It is difficult to describe the music of Stravinsky, Bartók, or Prokofiev without going into great detail. Dissonance is flaunted as never before, often with two or more alienated harmonies used at the same time. There are compelling rhythms, deriving from a kind of barbaric and brutal primitivism, with an inexhaustible supply of energy and extraordinary coloristic effects. The melodic line is as romantic and lyrical as any ever written, but because of the harshness and caustic fence built around the melody, the beauty and elegance of the phrase are often difficult to discern. Try Stravinsky's

Concerto for Two Solo Pianos (Gold and Fizdale), the *Out of Doors Suite* by Béla Bartók (Leonid Hambro), and the Prokofiev *Sonata No. 7* (Vladimir Horowitz).

Of the piano works being written today, little can yet be said authoritatively. They must be given a chance to stand the test of time. You and I may or may not like what we hear, and audiences may hiss, boo, and deride some of the new works. But I believe that much thought and originality are being shown by some of today's young composers. I discern imagination and organization in the works of Boulez, Stockhausen, Babbit, and Carter. History will be the judge. I hope that this generation's creators will compare favorably with those of the past.

What impresses me as I go back in history over the long and noble line of creators is how many have been superlative keyboard artists. All these men I have mentioned in this chapter were wonderfully at home at the keyboard. So were such composers as Granados, Albéniz, Nin, Turina, and scores of others. Among contemporaries, Copland, Gould, Shostakovich, Kabalevsky, Britten, Barber, and Bernstein belong to the line of composer-pianists. How many of the great symphonists and opera composers were not pianists? Very few indeed. Wagner, though known primarily for his operas, was an accomplished pianist. Saint-Saëns, De Falla, Fauré, Richard Strauss, who are known for their symphonic, chamber, and choral music and not especially for piano works, were fine pianists, and the list goes on and on. Where, I might ask, would music be without the piano?

6

Choral Music

DAVID RANDOLPH

Strange as it may seem, my enthusiasm for choral music started rather late. I had, I suppose, the average music lover's lack of interest in choral music and much preferred symphonies, concertos, chamber music, and opera. Curiosity impelled me to visit a rehearsal of a glee club. However, that single rehearsal discouraged me, partly because of the low quality of the music, and partly because of the undifferentiated shouting that passed for singing.

A radio broadcast of Beethoven's *Ninth Symphony* served to bolster my slight interest in choral music and, in turn, made me more receptive to a fellow student's suggestion that I join a chorus that was being formed at the New School in New York City. I wasn't much of a singer and was not even particularly interested in singing, so I approached the experience rather warily. The fact that I became as enthusiastic as I later did is a tribute to the taste and musicianship of the conductor, Arthur Lief. The repertoire he chose served to open a whole new world of beauty to me. It included Bach's *Cantata No. 106, God's Time Is Best*, madrigals by the early English composers Dowland, Wilbye, and Morley, Handel's *Acis and Galatea*, Purcell's *The Fairy Queen*, Mozart's *Requiem*, Brahms's *Schicksalslied*, Bartók's *Slovak Folk Songs*, and Howard Hanson's *Lament for Beowulf*.

I can still recall my sense of wonderment as each new work

revealed a new facet of the composer's musical personality. Bach, in his cantata *God's Time Is Best,* emerged with a more "human" quality than I had known in his instrumental music, and the rich romanticism of the symphonic Brahms took on another dimension when applied to voices in his *Schicksalslied.* I found in the sound of concerted voices an additional sensuous satisfaction that was not present in purely instrumental music.

One other factor contributed to my enjoyment of the medium —one that I often refer to in my rehearsals with my own choruses. I have often pointed out to, let's say the baritones, that the cellos are capable of making equally beautiful sounds. But the singer has an advantage over an instrument. He can evoke feelings by the use of words and their attendant emotional connotations. For example, if the text contains the word *bitterly,* the cellos might accent the beginning of the passage. But that would not evoke the same emotional response as the singers could by intensifying the first syllable of the word. In addition, the listener actually has more in common with vocal music than with instrumental music, since it is with the voice that he most readily expresses his own feelings.

Vocal music developed earlier than did instrumental music, for the simple reason that man was able to manipulate his own voice more easily than he could the crude instruments at his disposal in early times. In fact, in the "Golden Age" of vocal music, the Elizabethan period, when the madrigal reigned supreme, instrumental music was largely an imitation of vocal music. True orchestral music developed long after choral music had attained a great degree of polish and sophistication.

Let me return to my first enthusiasms in the choral field. The work that reached me with the greatest impact was Mozart's *Requiem.* The drama and excitement of that music were the equivalent of any I had known in his orchestral output. Moreover, there was the exhilaration of making the music myself! I can very clearly recall that I was able to close the score for about sixty consecutive pages and sing from memory. Participating in that performance was probably my greatest musical experience up to that time, even though the accompaniment was played on an electronic organ. Later there was the thrill of singing Howard Hanson's stirring *Lament for Beowulf* under the composer's direction, and with full orchestra. Not long after, I wrote a work that had the distinction of being the second student's composition ever performed by the Teachers' College Choir of Columbia University. (The first was by William Schuman.) Years later, at a meeting with Howard Hanson, I told him how greatly my composition had been influenced by his work.

Curiously, my first encounter with the best known of all choral works was the result of an unusual circumstance.

The story begins in New York City's Washington Square Park on a beautiful spring night. A gentle rain was falling—the kind of soft, caressing rain in which young people in love enjoy walking. I was a young person in love—aged seventeen, and I was walking with the first girl whom I ever loved. Quietly, yet with an intensity I could not hide, I confessed to her that I had been in love with her for a year and a half, only to be told that while she liked me, her feelings toward me were merely those of a close friend.

We completed the walk around the park in silence, and then, perhaps in order to ease our embarrassment, we stopped in at one of the churches on lower Fifth Avenue, where an oratorio was being presented. I was in no state to notice the name of the work being performed, but the first sound to greet our ears was a tenor voice, singing a slow, expressive melody to the words "Thy rebuke hath broken His heart"! This was my first exposure to Handel's *Messiah.*

I have since conducted that work any number of times in Carnegie and Philharmonic Halls. It is not difficult to imagine the thoughts that go through my mind each time we reach that section.

Handel and Bach

Messiah is the most popular single large choral work ever written. It may be said to hold the position in choral literature that Beethoven's *Fifth Symphony* occupies in the symphonic repertoire. This, in spite of the fact that it has been the victim of more mishandling, by major and minor performers alike, than any other choral work.

It is the British who are largely responsible for the prevalent misconceptions regarding the manner in which *Messiah* should be performed, though they love choral music and have adopted the German-born Handel as their own. It is they who fostered the custom of performing his *Messiah* with ever-increasing forces. This megalomania began with the first Handel Festival in England, which took place in 1784, twenty-five years after the composer's death. Since then the tradition of the ponderous performance has grown, reaching a climax in a performance given in 1859, by a chorus of 2,765 singers (almost the capacity of Carnegie Hall) and an orchestra of nearly four hundred!

The English scholar Sir Richard Terry wrote in 1927 about the British Handelian as follows:

> He has evolved a heavy, lumbering carthorse-like method of singing Handel. He calls this big bow-wow "the Handel tradition". . . . You may tell him 'til you are black in the face that Handel was (musically) an Italian by training, that he has all the Italian grace and elegance of style that will not stand rough handling. All to no purpose; he will return to his "Messiah" and bellow out "And He shall purify" for all the world like a corpulent Dutch galliot wallowing in the trough of a heavy sea.

Fortunately, within the last decade, we have realized that Handel was a composer of the Baroque era, and that his style was closer to Vivaldi's than Verdi's. Thus Thomas Beecham's recording of the work, rescored for a full nineteenth-century symphony orchestra (such as Handel never knew), and the equally stodgy versions by Malcolm Sargent and Adrian Boult have been supplanted recently by no fewer than three recordings, all of which restore the authentic texture of the work. All are listed in the discography.

Messiah is by no means the only oratorio Handel wrote. In fact there is even more dramatic music in such works as *Israel in Egypt*, which contains many exciting double choruses.

An unaccountably neglected work is *Solomon*, which contains some of Handel's most beautiful writing, both for soloists and chorus. Here I must agree with Beecham, who in his recorded version has omitted certain portions of the work and rearranged the order of the remaining numbers. Having investigated the score in preparation for my own performances, and having found it too long and of uneven quality, I discovered that Sir Thomas's omissions largely reflected my own tastes. I do regret, though, the fact that Beecham did not allow Handel's original scoring to speak for itself, but as in the case of *Messiah*, he reorchestrated the work for a symphonic aggregate of romantic proportions.

I would especially commend to your attention the so-called "Masque" in *Solomon*. Under the guise of presenting an entertainment for the Queen of Sheba, Solomon proposes a series of highly contrasting choruses, one more beautiful than the next. Another high spot is the so-called "Nightingale Chorus," which in its delicacy of treatment is nothing short of entrancing.

There are riches to be found in other Handel oratorios. *Judas Maccabaeus* contains a most moving opening chorus, as well as the famous bravura aria for tenor, "Sound an Alarm." And did you, as I did when a pupil in grammar school, sing "See the-huh conq'ring he-he-he-he-hero comes"? Well, that comes from this oratorio, and it turns out to be quite appealing when properly sung.

Another oratorio, *Saul*, contains many felicities that are worthy of investigation. And if you'd like to hear a shorter work, which is an absolute gem, locate a performance or a recording of Handel's so-called *Chandos Anthem No. VI*. This is a setting of the Forty-second Psalm, and it represents Handel in a tender vein, with some meltingly beautiful music.

One cannot mention Handel without thinking of the other giant of the Baroque period: Bach. Needless to say, his four "big" works—the *Mass in B minor*, the *Passion According to St. Matthew*, the *Passion According to St. John*, and the *Christmas Oratorio*—are musts for any lover of choral music. That does not mean I don't find occasional dull spots in some of these works. My devotion to the truth compels me to report that in the *St. John Passion*, I find the tenor aria "Erwäge" too long— and I could point out a few more such examples. My reason for making this declaration is solely to make all the more convincing my expressions of enthusiasm for the remainder of the music. Perhaps one way to convey my admiration is to confess that each time I conduct one of those four works, I feel as if I were approaching it for the first time. They are such endless sources of wonder that each rehearsal and each performance reveals something new.

Of the four, the *Mass in B minor* is to me the greatest source of musical riches. The *St. Matthew Passion* is the warmest and most human, while the *St. John Passion* is more compact and possibly the most dramatic. Let me stress, though, that these opinions are subject to change—and above all, they are not meant to influence your own reactions.

With this brief bow in the direction of the four "big" Bach choral works, let me call your attention to the beauty in the cantatas—that body of about 250 works that Bach was *required* to write for the church holidays, and of which 199 are still in existence. Note that I used the word *required*. The composer of Bach's era was not just "expressing his inmost feelings" when he wrote music. He was responding to a specific need for music— music for a specific time and place. Under those circumstances it is all the more amazing that Bach was able to maintain such a high level. To be sure, he often borrowed from himself; several portions of the *Mass in B minor* were simply taken from previously written cantatas, with the original German words replaced by the Latin text.

Let us investigate some of the cantatas. There is one cantata for which I have a soft spot. It is *No. 106, Gottes Zeit ist die allerbeste Zeit (God's Time Is Best)*, also known as the *Actus Tragicus*. For a long time I felt this was "my" cantata. It was the first cantata I had ever sung and the first Bach work I had ever conducted. When a recording of it was issued, and it was my duty to write a criticism of the performance, I approached it almost defensively—as if to say: "Who dares perform *my* cantata?" But I was completely captivated by the performance, which I found to be a revelation. It was conducted by Hermann Scherchen. I would strongly recommend this disc for its insight into the stylistic requirements of a Bach performance.

Some years after this record appeared, I was introduced to Scherchen at a gathering after one of his New York concerts. I told him about my proprietary feeling toward Bach's *Cantata No. 106*, and that I was, nevertheless, completely won over by his recording. A smile gradually appeared on his face. His only answer was to sing the melody of one of the choruses: "Es ist der alte Bund: Mensch, du musst sterben" ("It is the old decree: Man, thou must perish"), making the appropriate conductorial gestures, as if he were directing an imaginary ensemble. I nodded in recognition, and our conversation was interrupted there. About a year later, Scherchen died. How curious that he should have chosen that particular phrase to sing that evening!

Here are a few more of the Bach cantatas I have found particularly appealing. *Number 104, Du Hirte Israël, höre* (*Thou Guide of Israel, Hear Us*), has a lilting opening chorus. *Number 140, Wachet auf!* (*Sleepers, Wake*), explores a single chorale melody in its opening movement, and again in a later movement, where it is combined with a beautiful melody in the violins. I'm quite certain that you will recognize the latter treatment of it. There is also an expressive duet for the bass and soprano soloists in this cantata.

Cantata No. 76, Die Himmel erzählen die Ehre Gottes (*The Heavens Declare the Glory of God*), is one of the longer cantatas. As the title implies, some of it is rather exuberant in feeling. There is a most delicious opening chorus in the little-known *Cantata No. 8, Liebster Gott, wann werd' ich sterben*. Unfortunately, the only recording of it at this writing uses boy sopranos and altos, who, for me, leave something to be desired. However, the sound of the solo flute weaving its florid melody above the plucked strings of the orchestra is not easily forgotten.

The opening chorus of *No. 12, Weinen, Klagen*, is the original from which the "Crucifixus" of the *B Minor Mass* was taken. *Number 50, Nun ist das Heil*, is a brief, single-movement work that makes up in power what it lacks in length. But there is no end to the possible recommendations of Bach cantatas. Dip in. They are an endless source of pleasure.

Let us go back in time to an era preceding that of Bach and

Handel: the Italian Renaissance, a source of much beautiful music. One of the supreme masters of this period is Claudio Monteverdi, who lived from 1567 to 1643. One of my favorites for many years has been his "Lagrime d'amante al sepolcro dell' amata" ("Tears of a Lover at the Tomb of the Beloved"). In fact, I was so haunted by it that I could not rest until I had published my own edition of the printed score and had recorded it. As the title indicates, the work is a somber one. It was composed upon the death of an actual person, a beautiful and talented young student of Monteverdi, Caterina Martinelli, who died in 1608 at the age of eighteen.

In my rehearsals of the work with The Masterwork Chorus, in preparation for making the recording, I warned the singers that in the beginning, they might not be aware of the beauties of the work. It is scored for five-part unaccompanied chorus, and it seems for a time as if nothing happens. Only gradually do the subtleties and the expressive qualities of the music emerge. Just as I had predicted, though, the members of the chorus came to me to tell me that they were being haunted by the music, even between rehearsals.

I cannot leave the pre-Bach era without mentioning a few other composers who have produced some beautiful music. The French had an individual style, sometimes· ceremonial and at other times greatly expressive. For example, the moving "De Profundis" by Lalande, the "Dies Irae" and "Miserere Mei Deus" of Lully and the "Te Deum" and "Grand Magnificat" of Marc-Antoine Charpentier, not to be confused with the nineteenth-century's Gustave Charpentier, composer of *Louise*.

Haydn, Mozart, and Beethoven

It would be pleasant to linger over the early composers, but we must move on to the two great representatives of the classic period, Haydn and Mozart.

Haydn's two best-known choral works are *The Seasons* and *The Creation*, but we are just beginning to be aware of the beautiful music in his various masses. The *Mass in Time of War* is a fine work, as is the *Lord Nelson Mass in D minor*, which sometimes goes under the name *Imperial Mass*. The *St. Cecilia Mass* is a large-scale work, which begins most beautifully, and most originally, with a hushed opening. Any of these works is well worth exploring.

Mozart's best-known single choral work probably is *Ave Verum Corpus*, simple and appealing enough to be done by many amateur choruses. The *Requiem*, I suspect, would come next in popularity. Certain it is one of the greatest works in the choral literature, though Mozart left it unfinished at his death. Parts of it were completed by his student Felix Süssmayer, who did a most excellent job. Süssmayer left a clear indication of those portions that had been completely written by Mozart, those in which he carried out Mozart's intentions, and those he composed completely by himself. One of the sections I find extremely appealing, the "Benedictus," is entirely the work of Süssmayer.

If you'd like a chilling experience, play the recording of the "Lacrymosa" of the *Requiem*, up to the climax at the words "homo reus," and then stop the music suddenly. Those were the last notes ever composed by Mozart! The remainder of the movement was completed by Süssmayer.

Then there is the *Mass in C minor*, again a work left incomplete by Mozart. But what a powerful opening chorus it contains, and what a wealth of other beauties! For Mozart in a truly relaxed mood, there are his canons. Some of the texts are so free, however, that the literal translations are seldom supplied in present-day performances and recordings!

After Haydn and Mozart, the next great figure is Beethoven. It has become the custom to denigrate almost all Beethoven's choral music, with the exception of the *Ninth Symphony* and the *Missa Solemnis*. While I acknowledge the existence of weak spots in the output of the greatest composers, I should like to guard against the too-easy dismissal of certain works *in toto*, merely because writers and commentators repeat the generalizations of their predecessors, without taking the trouble to investigate the music. The mere fact that Beethoven sometimes wrote without consideration for the comfort of the singers is not sufficient reason, in my opinion, for consigning his choral music to the scrap heap. (An analogy comes to my mind: Once, when a violinist complained to Beethoven about how difficult some of his music was for the violin, Beethoven replied, "Do you think that I'm thinking about your puny little fiddle when I write?" In all likelihood, he took the same attitude toward the singers, when he composed some of those fiendishly high passages.)

Those who are familiar with Beethoven's *Ninth Symphony* and its famous choral finale may be interested in his lesser-known *Fantasia in C minor for Piano, Chorus, and Orchestra,* Opus 80. In effect, this was a "study" for the choral finale of the *Ninth Symphony*. Its closing section for chorus and six vocal soloists sounds very much like the later symphony, since it, like the rest of the *Fantasia,* is the exploration of a theme which is very similar to the famous "Ode to Joy" melody of the *Ninth.* In addition to the pleasure obtainable from the music itself, this work is of great historic interest, since it gives us an insight into Beethoven's own development. The entire piece, which lasts about nineteen minutes, is in essence a series of variations on the melody. Moreover, while this is a rather strange combination, the first three-quarters of the work actually amounts to a concerto for piano and orchestra.

I have a fond personal recollection in connection with this work. I had trained The Masterwork Chorus for a performance of it with The Philadelphia Orchestra under Eugene Ormandy. At the single rehearsal of the chorus and orchestra together, late in the afternoon on the day of the performance, Mr. Ormandy read through the work once. He then turned the baton over to his assistant and walked to the rear of the auditorium to listen. I recall that both of us were standing in the center aisle, and after a few minutes of listening, he turned to me slowly and quietly uttered one word: "Beautiful!" That constituted the entire rehearsal.

I omit discussion of Beethoven's *Ninth Symphony,* because it is so familiar. I prefer to call your attention to a lesser-known work, his *Mass in C Major,* Opus 86, which is not to be confused with the better-known *Missa Solemnis.* The later work has overshadowed the *Mass in C Major* to the point where many music lovers are not even aware of its existence. This is a pity, since it is a beautiful, melodious work in Beethoven's middle-period style, and while it does not reach the heights of the *Missa Solemnis,* it does generate its own excitement. Of course, the *Missa Solemnis* is not to be overlooked. I grant that it is not as immediately accessible as some of Beethoven's other music. Yet it more than repays the time spent getting to know it. And did you know that Beethoven composed an oratorio? This is his *Christus am Oelberg* (*Christ on the Mount of Olives*), Opus 85. Fate seems to be unkind to certain works by even the greatest of composers. This work merits a hearing.

Nineteenth Century

The romanticism of the nineteenth century made itself felt in choral music. Berlioz, one of the prime influences in this movement, is a composer who affords me increasing pleasure. His *Requiem* was described by an early critic as "beautiful and strange, wild, convulsed and dolorous." True, there is a spot where the flutes are bunched up high in their register and are accompanied by eight trombones in the lower part of their register. And what a weird effect they create! But that same imagination served him well in the creation of many arresting passages in the *Requiem* and the exquisite *Romeo and Juliet.*

Of special appeal is *L'Enfance du Christ.* For a man who was capable of some of the greatest excesses, his restraint in this work is nothing short of remarkable. Indeed, Berlioz originally pretended that some of the music of *L'Enfance du Christ* was the work of an unknown, earlier composer!

Should your mood call for drama, I would suggest the *Requiem* by Verdi. Do not expect any of the restraint so often associated with religious music. It is my feeling that Verdi has here written another opera, without scenery and without action. It is one of the most overpowering works in the entire choral repertoire. In judging any recording of it, by the way, I suggest you turn immediately to the second movement, the "Dies Irae," or "Day of Wrath," section. If your room doesn't shake with the power of the music, then reject the recording. There is a part for a bass drum that will be a good test of your equipment.

The *Requiem* of Brahms—to me, surely one of the most beautiful nineteenth-century compositions—has overshadowed another work of his which I regard as equally fine. It is the *Shicksalslied* (*Song of Destiny*), Opus 54. Brahms himself was said to have been especially fond of this work. It begins with a slow, lyrical opening followed by a very turbulent section. Curiously, though, this second portion leaves the chorus "up in the air," so to speak. The music has a feeling of uncertainty, which is resolved only by the orchestra, as it returns to the consoling opening portion.

If there is any composer whose music can be said to lack "heroic" quality, he is Gabriel Fauré. His aesthetic creed apparently had no place for the "monumental." Instead he substituted a refined lyricism. But within his self-prescribed limits, he is a minor master. Listen to his *Requiem*. There are no huge crescendos, no overpowering climaxes. Even the violinists sit there for most of the performance, doing nothing. Fauré prefers the muted sounds of the lower strings and the darker woodwinds. But what a hypnotically beautiful work it is, with its graceful melodies and exquisite harmonies! In 1887, the year in which he composed his *Requiem*, Fauré also wrote his *Pavanne*, Opus 50, for chorus and orchestra. This is a work lasting about five minutes, but its beauty will haunt you. It exists in two versions—with and without chorus. Either version is beautiful, but the chorus adds the distinctive quality that only the human voices can impart.

Twentieth Century

The twentieth century has seen the creation of a number of exciting choral works. In fact, the 1920's and 1930's alone have accounted for at least a half-dozen compositions that are all-time favorites for me as both conductor and listener.

A work I found intriguing from the moment I first heard it is the *Slavonic Mass*, or as it is also known, the *Glagolitic Mass*, by Leoš Janáček. Written in 1926, when its composer was seventy-three years old, it was performed for the first time two years later, shortly after Janáček's death. Two years later, on the occasion of its first New York performance, the conductor,

Artur Bodanzky, remarked: "I can realize that anyone who comes to hear this Mass of Janáček's with the Masses of Mozart or Palestrina or the Passions of Bach in mind will be shocked by the barbaric peasantlike strength of this new music."

I would suggest that in approaching this work you banish from your mind all preconceptions of how religious music should sound. To me the work suggests Stravinsky's *Sacre du Printemps*, as it might sound if it had been filtered through Moravian folk music. As one commentator aptly said: "An old man had here flung before the world a work filled with tempestuous vitality."

Speaking of rough-hewn music inevitably brings to my mind one of the most exciting choral works of the twentieth century: William Walton's *Belshazzar's Feast*. It should be borne in mind that when this work was given its *premiere* in 1931, its composer was only twenty-nine years old. It is an interesting commentary on the taste of the times that Walton's composition was accepted for performance at the Leeds Festival only after considerable controversy, because its idiom was considered so extreme; this, despite its use of a Biblical text. Since then it has caught on in England, though performances in the United States are unfortunately still a rarity. Perhaps the British love of choral music has helped the work to gain a foothold there. The scarcity of performances in the United States may be attributable to the unusually large orchestra required. Besides a full symphonic complement, including an organ and a piano, with extra wind instruments, the score calls for an amplified percussion battery: bass and snare drums, cymbals, triangle, tambourine, gong, glockenspiel, a slapstick, a Chinese block, and an anvil! In addition, Walton calls for no fewer than two extra brass bands, facing each other from opposite sides of the chorus! Sheer economics make it difficult, if not prohibitive, for the average American choral society to engage the requisite number of players. But when the text comes to the words "Make a joyful noise," the effect of these enormous forces is overwhelmingly exciting.

Another outstanding section is the one in which, after a tremendous climax and a moment of silence, the baritone soloist (the only solo voice) intones, entirely without accompaniment:

"And in that same hour, as they feasted, came forth the fingers of a man's hand, and the King saw the part of the hand that wrote." Then, against a quiet but foreboding accompaniment, he continues: "And this was the writing that was written: 'Mene, mene, tekel upharsin.'" A four-part male chorus, singing fortissimo and reinforced by four French horns, translates: "Thou art weighed in the balance and found wanting." The soloist returns with another unaccompanied recitative: "In that night was Belshazzar the King slain," with a momentary pause before the final word—a pause that sends shivers up one's spine. Immediately upon the completion of that phrase, the full chorus of men and women, supplemented by the brass and percussion instruments, shouts the single word "Slain!" For sheer dramatic impact, this is a most thrilling moment.

Also English, but at the opposite end of the emotional scale, is the lovely *Mass in G minor* by Ralph Vaughan Williams. It is well known that Vaughan Williams had great admiration for the music of his compatriots of the sixteenth century, an admiration reflected in his beautiful *Fantasia on a Theme by Thomas Tallis,* which is based on a hymn composed by Tallis in 1567. The *Mass in G minor* might be said to be the vocal counterpart of the *Tallis Fantasia,* which is composed for two string orchestras and a string quartet, while the *Mass* is written for two unaccompanied choruses and a vocal quartet. The similarity in textures is readily apparent. In both works the two choirs (whether of strings or voices) are treated antiphonally—that is, they answer one another from different locations. At times they are used as one massive choir. In addition, the presence of the string quartet and the vocal quartet in the respective works supplies a contrast in weight of sound. It should be obvious that in the cases of both of these works the composer's intentions are best realized in a stereophonic recording, which reproduces the spatial relationships of the two choirs.

While the *Mass* evokes the feeling of early English music, it should not be thought that Vaughan Williams attempts merely to imitate the old composers. The work bears the unmistakable stamp of a twentieth-century musical personality. (And just in passing, lest any choral conductor be led to the conclusion that the work, with its many serene sections, is an easy one to perform, let him be forewarned. Behind the *apparent* simplicity of the music lie many pitfalls for the chorus. It takes quite some time for a chorus to accustom itself, not only to the notes, but also to the stylistic requirements of the music.) There is frequent fluctuation between major and minor harmonies, which together with the "false relations" (the presence of, say, an E flat in one part, followed immediately by an E natural in another part), lends the work a modern feeling, at the same time evoking the old modal style. The chorus is sometimes divided into as many as ten or twelve parts, with a consequent richness of sound. This, contrasted with the sections given over to only the four solo voices, makes for some exquisite contrasts. Listen to Vaughan Williams's setting, in the "Crucifixus," of the words "passus, et sepultus est," in which both choruses combine, in some extremely soft and simple chords. It is an absolutely magical moment.

While we are in the period of the 1920's and 1930's, I must mention Ernest Bloch's *Sacred Service,* composed in 1933. Aside from the inherent beauties of the music, the work occupies a unique place historically. The various Catholic and Protestant services have been set numerous times by great composers, but the *Sacred Service* is the first large-scale choral-orchestral composition written for Jewish worship by a composer of stature.

The work has a power and drive which will come as no surprise to anyone familiar with Bloch's earlier composition, *Schelomo,* a rhapsody for cello and orchestra. The scoring has a richness which matches that of the earlier work, combined at times with a fine lyrical quality. A wonderful excitement pervades both chorus and orchestra at the words "Yimloch Adonoy leolom," with its irresistible rhythmic drive. The only portion of the work that is given over to the unaccompanied chorus (the hushed setting of the words "Yihyu L'rotzon" ["May the words of my mouth"]), coming immediately after, supplies a beautiful contrast in mood.

Stravinsky has contributed an exciting work in his *Symphony of Psalms,* which I regard as one of the major choral compositions of this century. It contains a rhythmic propulsiveness and a fine lyrical quality. I regard myself as fortunate in having been present to hear the composer himself conduct the work during Lincoln Center's Stravinsky Festival in the summer of 1966.

Another Stravinsky composition that can afford considerable pleasure is *Les Noces*. The accompaniment of four pianos and percussion gives some idea of the texture of this music, which is characterized, above all, by rhythmic vitality.

Three works by the twentieth-century French composer Francis Poulenc have been most gratifying to me. They are the *Mass in G* of 1937, the *Stabat Mater* of 1951, and the *Gloria*, which dates from 1961, only two years before the composer's death. Poulenc seems to have two different musical personalities. He often appears to aim for nothing more than witty effects, peppering his music with what sound like Paris music-hall tunes. One example that comes to my mind occurs in the closing movement of his *Concerto for Two Pianos and Orchestra*. But these three choral works reveal another side of him. Always the superb craftsman, here he shows a more serious face as well. His is a distinctive voice—no mean accomplishment in an era that boasts so many composers. My own feeling is that he has been somewhat underrated because of the urbanity and playfulness of so many of his compositions. Dip into any of the three works I have listed—the first is for *a cappella* chorus, the other two are with orchestra, each with a soprano soloist. I think you will be gratified by the results.

Speaking of unaccompanied choruses, I must mention a few groups that have given me great pleasure, not only for the charm and appeal of their musical fare, but also for the high caliber of the performances. One is the Agrupación Coral de Pamplona de España, under Luis Morondo. I suspect there is very little music of any school to which this virtuosic group of nine women and seven men could not do complete justice. There seems to be no end to the variety of tone quality they can produce. Listen to their performance of *Five Songs* by Manuel de Falla—music you will probably recognize—and as you do so, you will gradually become aware of the fact that the guitar accompaniment you are hearing is produced by the voices! Their technical polish is truly outstanding. Moreover, the solos are sung by various members of the chorus.

Another remarkably fine group is the National Chorus of

Russian Song, a ninety-five-voice mixed chorus which was founded during World War II. How artistically these performers sing even so popular a war horse as "The Volga Boatmen," and what tonal richness they bring to the soft opening and close! However, their most outstanding contributions are two songs called "On the Mounts of Manchuria" and "The Little Birch Brooms." The first is one of those typical sentimental, lilting Russian folk melodies sung by the tenors to a simulated guitar (or is it balalaika?) accompaniment—with the basses singing the "oomp" and the women supplying the "plink, plink." Words can hardly convey the beauty of the music or the artistry with which it is sung. I have almost worn out my copy of the recording of this number as a result of repeated playings for both myself and my friends. The other number is a humorous song about the tied-up bunches of birch twigs used for sweeping and scrubbing in every peasant household. Listen to the wonderful ensemble achieved by the chorus and its conductor, A. V. Sveshnikov, as the music speeds up and slows down. Here is real musical excitement!

I cannot leave the field of folk music without mentioning another group—the Mazowsze Choral Ensemble and Orchestra, conducted by Tadeusz Sygietynski. There is a naïve but refreshing charm to their arrangements and performances. The tone of the chorus, and especially of the soloists, is hardly what we would consider polished, "professional" quality. Yet it has the ring of authenticity, and it fits the music perfectly.

Here is a quick mention of other choral works I would recommend without hesitation. Zoltán Kodály's *Missa Brevis* and *Te Deum* are first rate, alternating power with appealing melody. Bernstein's *Chichester Psalms* is a surprisingly accessible work, considering the amount of avant-garde music that its creator has espoused. Dvořák's *Requiem* and his *Stabat Mater* are rewarding works, with many felicities. He is another composer who is not sufficiently appreciated. Then there are *Trois Chansons de Charles d'Orléans* for unaccompanied chorus by Debussy, Ravel's *Trois Chansons*, Erik Satie's *Mass for the Poor*, the appealing work called *Psalms* for chorus and two pianos by Lukas Foss, and *The Christmas Story* by Hugo Distler, and . . . and . . .

7

The Art Song

DAVID RANDOLPH

ONE cannot think of the art song without immediately thinking of German Lieder. In fact, I suspect the German word for *songs* has almost replaced the English word in the minds of most devotees of this art. If this is so, the reason is not hard to find. The art song has been brought to its greatest heights by four composers: Franz Schubert, Robert Schumann, Johannes Brahms, and Hugo Wolf, all of whom set German poems to music. Other composers and other nations have made significant contributions, but nothing can approach the extent to which these four composers devoted themselves to the creation of songs. Schubert alone wrote over six hundred!

Why is it that we so readily expose ourselves to sadness and tragedy in art when we go out of our way to avoid them in real life? Be that as it may (and to answer that question would lead us into an involved discussion of the nature of the artistic experience), I shall start with one of the last and most somber of Schubert's song cycles. It is his group of twenty-four songs known collectively as *Die Winterreise* (*The Winter Journey*). The text has to do with a man who is sick at heart because he has been betrayed in love. He travels through the snow-covered countryside, assailed at every turn by desolation. The streams are frozen, nature is lifeless. At night he hears the prolonged barking of dogs, the creaking of the weather vane. He pushes on without hope, finally encountering an organ-grinder, whose one tune becomes his own song.

Out of this pessimistic cycle of poems, Schubert has fashioned some of the most touching music ever written for solo voice and piano. Each of the twenty-four songs has some musical felicity to recommend it. For me the crowning touch is the final song, "Der Leiermann" ("The Organ Grinder"). In its very simplicity, it is the most moving of all. The entire song is accompanied only by a drone bass, intended to suggest the hand organ. The mere snatches of melody allotted to the voice help to intensify the sense of loneliness. As a musico-dramatic entity, this is a masterpiece of writing.

Another of my favorites, and one of the best known, is "Der Doppelgänger" ("The Double"). What subtle musical wonders Schubert creates in this work! The introduction consists of four somber chords, which are repeated almost identically for fully two-thirds of the song. But notice the magical effect produced near the end of the song, when Schubert changes just the fourth chord! This song is one of fourteen which comprise the cycle known as the *Schwanengesang* (*Swan Song*)—a title given to the set not by Schubert but by his publisher. The cycle also contains the now famous "Serenade."

Let us leave the rather somber feelings expressed in these Schubert song cycles for the emotional relief afforded by a slightly less pessimistic cycle composed by Schumann, the *Dichterliebe* (*Poet's Love*), to poems by Heine. While it does seem characteristic of the German romanticists always to be lamenting a lost love, there are some lighter works in this collection of sixteen songs. Listen to the third song in this collection, "Die Rose, die Lilie, die Taube, die Sonne," a brief but ecstatic outpouring of love. And there is certainly an infectious excitement in "Das ist ein Flöten und Geigen" and "Aus alten Märchen winkt es," with their powerful piano accompaniments. And what a felicitous touch Schumann imparts to the entire cycle by ending it with a thoughtful postlude in the piano, after the poet has gradually become disillusioned by his faithless sweetheart.

Another beautiful cycle by Schumann is *Frauenliebe und Leben* (*Woman's Love and Life*). As the title suggests, this group of eight songs runs the gamut from the ecstasy of a woman in love, to her sadness upon the death of her beloved. It is one of the pinnacles of the romantic song literature.

There were, of course, songs before those by the four I have mentioned. Let me touch briefly on two of their predecessors. Although he is acknowledged as one of the most universal of composers, because he wrote so superbly in nearly all the forms, Mozart is not regarded as preeminent in the field of the song; nor is Beethoven. The art song did not become an important aspect of music until the later, romantic period. Nevertheless, both giants wrote songs that, while they may not possess the intimate, personal quality of the songs by the later composers, are worthy of attention on their own terms. One of Mozart's songs, "Die Alte," represents a woman who is lamenting the fact that "everything was better in the old days." Mozart directs that the song is to be sung "a little bit through the nose"!

Beethoven composed a group of six songs titled *An die ferne Geliebte* (*To the Distant Beloved*). Because the subject matter of the texts is related, and because Beethoven linked several of the songs by reusing some of the musical material, these are considered to be the first "song cycle" and are of importance in the development of the art song.

Mozart's songs reveal the approach of the classic period—an almost folklike simplicity in which the piano accompaniment supplies mostly harmonic background.

Later in the nineteenth century it fell to the lot of Brahms to carry on the Lieder tradition. For years I have been in love with his *Vier Ernste Gesänge* (*Four Serious Songs*). As the title indicates, their subject matter is rather somber. But there is a richness about the music that makes these songs irresistible to me, regardless of the texts. I invite you to listen especially to the culmination of the fourth song. For beauty of melody I know of few things that match it.

Of perhaps even more immediate appeal is his "Immer leiser wird mein Schlummer." The melody of this song will be familiar to those who know the composer's *Piano Concerto No. 2*, since it appears in the second movement as a cello solo. His "Ständchen" is a light-hearted serenade, while the dramatic "Auf dem Kirchhofe" finds Brahms in a somber mood. Perhaps his best-known work in this genre is the familiar "Wiegenlied," the cradle song. Although it is not readily apparent to us, the piano accompaniment of this work incorporates a traditional Viennese love song. While Brahms was the conductor of the Hamburg Ladies' Choir, one of its members brought the song to his attention. Some time later, on the birth of her second son, Brahms dedicated this cradle song to her and her husband. Accompanying the music was a note saying that "since the song is suitable for boys or girls, you need not order a new one each time."

The fourth of the great pinnacles in the field of German Lieder is Hugo Wolf. Curiously, despite the fact that both Brahms and Wolf occupy comparable positions as song composers, Wolf was nothing short of vitriolic in his opinions of the music of Brahms. These opinions were expressed in print, since Wolf was a music critic for one of the Viennese newspapers. His hatred of Brahms's music extended into a detestation of Brahms the man, with the result that his reviews reached the heights (or should we say the depths?) of critical invective. Incidentally, the last few years of his relatively brief life were spent in an insane asylum.

Be that as it may, Wolf did compose many magnificent songs. In one period of a little more than two years, he wrote more than one hundred and sixty songs. I would call your attention to just two. They are the very lyrical "Benedeit die sel'ge Mutter," and the vigorous and outgoing "Fussreise."

Another composer who has contributed some of the most beautiful songs to the literature is Gustav Mahler. Many of his songs, however, are written with orchestral accompaniment. Where to begin? Let us start chronologically, with the *Lieder eines fahrenden Gesellen* (*Songs of a Wayfarer*), composed when Mahler was in his twenty-third year. These four songs are tremendously appealing. In addition, a melody in the second song served as the principal theme of the opening movement of his *First Symphony,* and a refrain in the fourth song appears in the slow movement.

There is a later cycle for contralto, baritone, and orchestra, called *Des Knaben Wunderhorn* (*The Youth's Magic Horn*). Here, too, we find beautiful music as well as the source material for another symphony. You'll find the origin of the scherzo of the *Second Symphony* in the song "St. Anthony and the Fishes," and the song "Urlicht" ("Primeval Light") serves as the basis of part of the fourth movement.

Early in the twentieth century Mahler composed his *Kindertotenlieder* (*Songs on the Death of Children*), and again we find some of the most magnificently expressive songs ever conceived. Here indeed, in Mahler, is a fitting successor to Schubert and Brahms as a creator of the romantic song.

If you would like to follow the German song into more recent manifestations, I would recommend the three *Geistliche Motetten*, composed in 1941 and 1944 by Paul Hindemith. There is a simplicity to these three works that makes them immediately accessible, and at times they are downright haunting.

Italian, Spanish, and French

So much for songs in the Germanic tradition. There are many beauties to be found in the songs of Spanish, Italian, and French composers. Some of the very earliest examples, even those going back as far as the fourteenth century, contain music that should not be overlooked.

It sometimes happens that one particular song will appeal to us above all others of its kind. This has been my experience in the case of a two-and-a-half-minute song by the early eighteenth-century Italian composer Alessandro Scarlatti, called "Cara e dolce." I have played it on radio broadcasts numberless times and have always had requests that it be repeated, thanks to its haunting quality. For those who are interested in the vocal music of sixteenth-century Spain, I would recommend two composers: Luis Milan and Alonzo de Mudarra. The latter's "Triste estaba" is a dignified yet moving setting of David's Lament for Absalom.

French composers seem to have been attracted to the song almost as much as the Germans. There is a cycle of six by Berlioz called *Les Nuits d'Été* for soprano and orchestra, which is one of my all-time favorites. Here is Berlioz at his best. Not only is the vocal line at all times expressive, but the orchestra is used so imaginatively that the ear is constantly being ravished. There is none of the bombastic Berlioz here—no attempt to bowl you over with tremendous orchestral forces. This is intimate music—music that envelops you with a bittersweet sadness, as it conveys the essence of Theophile Gautier's romantic poems.

One cannot discuss the songs of French composers without mentioning Gabriel Fauré and Claude Debussy. Fauré, who was treated with mere respect during his lifetime, mainly because of his position as a pedagogue, has still not fully come into his own. Yet for those listeners who are sensitive to his subtleties, his music can afford considerable pleasure. I would particularly recommend his cycle of nine love songs called *La Bonne Chanson*.

Debussy, too, brought all his individual genius to his songs. His "Beau Soir," "Green," and "Mandoline" have justly become favorites among devotees of this type of music. There is one song in particular whose text I have found especially moving, since it deals not with some imagined poetic situation but with real life. It is "Noel des Enfants Qui n'Ont Plus de Maisons"—"Christmas of the Children Who Have No Home." The song was composed during the First World War as Debussy's protest against the inhumanities of war. It was the last song he ever wrote, and one of the few for which he wrote his own text. By showing the effects of war upon homeless children, he brings the horror down to a personal and intimate level. The text reads, in part: "We have no house any more, the enemies have taken all, taken all, down to our little bed!" The words "taken all"—in French, "tout pris"—are repeated at each appearance, to a brief descending musical figure that becomes quite heartbreaking in its effect.

The words continue: "To be sure, papa is at war and poor mama is dead. Before she could see all this. What are we going to do?" What a far cry this is from the typical romantic descriptions of the beauties of nature which form the texts of so many songs! The music has a restless quality that matches the plaintiveness of the children's outcry, and the piano accompaniment, with its constant motion, adds to the emotional impact.

The songs by another French composer, Francis Poulenc, reveal both his originality and lyricism in full measure. His settings of four brief poems by Guillaume Apollinaire are delightful. I recommend especially "Avant le Cinéma." The heights of soaring lyricism are attained in his "Tu Vois le Feu du Soir," with its fiendishly difficult range. "Main Dominée par le Coeur" has a wonderful sense of urgency, and each of his seven brief *Calligrammes by Guillaume Apollinaire* is more expressive than the last.

I cherish the memory of my only contact with Poulenc, which took the form of a brief telephone conversation with him in the 1950's, during one of his visits to New York. My purpose was to ask him whether at one place in the opening movement of his *Concerto for Two Pianos and Orchestra* he did not consciously attempt to imitate the Balinese gamelan, despite the fact that the jacket notes on the recording made no mention of it. His answer was an impetuous "But, of course!"

Should you wish to venture even farther into the byways of French song, I would call to your attention the songs of Emanuel Chabrier, and Erik Satie's *Trois Melodies.*

Middle European and Slavic

The songs I have discussed so far make relatively little use of folk melodies. Generally speaking, it was the middle European and Slavic composers who seemed to draw to a greater degree upon their folk heritage in their art songs.

A truly unconventional song cycle is Leoš Janáček's *Diary of One Who Vanished,* composed in 1916. The text deals with the mysterious disappearance of a young Moravian peasant. A group of short poems were found in his room. They were at first thought to be folk songs, but a legal investigation revealed that they were an account of his love affair and his subsequent suicide. These poems form the basis of the text of this song cycle. The greater part of the twenty-two songs are sung by a tenor, but the girl is represented by a mezzo-soprano voice. A few magical moments are supplied by two brief appearances of three women's voices.

A precursor of Janáček is Modest Musorgski, whose *Songs and Dances of Death* are a must for any lover of the art song.

I can still recall the chills I experienced upon first hearing an old 78-rpm recording by the baritone Igor Gorin of "The Field Marshall," the final song in this cycle of four. Both Musorgski and Janáček made use of the folk music of their respective countries without attempting to prettify it. They preserved the simpler aspects of their native music, which other composers might have rejected as too crude. This authenticity of feeling, coupled with the observance of the inherent rhythms of their respective languages, imparts a tremendous sense of conviction to the works of both men. When Musorgski deals with death in four different guises in his song cycle, the effect is dramatic in the extreme. The first, "Trepak," is about a toil-worn peasant. The second, "Lullaby," is concerned with a mother nursing a sick child. "Serenade" finds death in the form of a lover courting a maiden, and in the final song, death appears on a battlefield as a field marshall, crying out: "Struggle no more, the fight is over. I am the conqueror of all . . . In life you were bitter enemies, but in death you are joined together . . . I will rule over you, all powerful." The emotional tension is in marked contrast to the relatively restrained feelings found in the typical German Lied or the French Song.

Another aspect of Musorgski's art is represented by his *The Nursery*, a cycle of seven songs of great charm and originality. It would be difficult to imagine a greater contrast in emotional tone than that supplied by this cycle. There are also two other delightful songs by the same composer—"The He-Goat" and "Hopak."

Are you willing to seek out the unfamiliar in song literature? You will find a delightful surprise in a cycle of eleven songs called *From Jewish Folk Poetry*, the Opus 79 of Shostakovich. The Soviet composer has set eight old Jewish folk texts and has added three more from recent times. The result is most appealing. Shostakovich employs a soprano, a mezzo-soprano, and a tenor, using them in solo capacity and in various combinations.

Another prominent Soviet composer, Dmitri Kabalevsky, has made a setting for bass voice and piano of three of Shakespeare's sonnets. How strange to have Shakespeare emerge as Russian music! In its own terms, however, the music is gratifying to hear.

English and American

Let us not overlook the considerable contribution of English and American composers to the song literature. The undisputed master of the art of setting the English language to music is the seventeenth-century English composer Henry Purcell. Four of his works display several facets of his genius. Dramatic declamation is the basis of "Not All My Torment," while in contrast "If Music Be the Food of Love" contains some appealing lyricism. (The words of the latter song, by the way, come not from Shakespeare, but from a poem by a Colonel Heveningham.) A variety of moods is to be found in "From Rosy Bowers." It was composed for D'Urfey's *Don Quixote* and is a fairly lengthy *scena* in which Altisidora attempts to seduce the knight from his allegiance to Dulcinea. In its five parts, it is alternately dramatic and lyrical, and it ends with a section intended to illustrate the lady's frenzy when she discovers that her attempts are in vain. "Man Is for the Woman Made" is a jocose work whose original text is so free that some modern record versions are discreetly bowdlerized.

In our time some of the most gratifying music for the human voice has been composed by Benjamin Britten. Indeed, Britten has been spoken of as the first English composer to match Purcell in his ability to set the English language to music.

One of his most rewarding works is *Les Illuminations*, for high voice and string orchestra, written in 1939 when the composer was only twenty-six. What color Britten draws from the strings, right from the start of the opening movement, called "Fanfare"! And what excitement is created as the voice intones over the strings, as if in defiance, the opening line of Arthur Rimbaud's poem "I alone hold the key to this savage parade"! At the opposite end of the scale is the exquisite setting of the poem "Being Beauteous," in which the voice floats above a quietly sustained accompaniment in the strings. This is one of the truly outstanding examples of twentieth-century lyricism. Immediately following, and in the sharpest contrast possible, is the movement called "Parade," in which both voice and strings seem to pile color upon color, as they match the feelings of the wildly exotic text.

Two other song cycles dating from this period in Britten's life have been sources of pleasure to me, though they both take more time to yield their riches. They are his settings of *Seven Sonnets of Michelangelo*, and *The Holy Sonnets of John Donne*. In the latter set Britten gives us some intensely passionate writing for the voice, in the sonnet beginning "Since she whom I lov'd hath payed her last debt to Nature." And there is a dramatic and powerful setting of the sonnet beginning with the words: "Thou hast made me, and shall thy work decay?"

For some years I have been intrigued by a novel work of the American composer Henry Cowell, who died in December, 1966. It was composed in 1938 for the unusual combination of soprano voice, flute, cello, and piano. But more noteworthy than the instrumentation is the fact that the voice sings a wordless vocalise and is treated simply as one of the instruments in a chamber group. I am in favor of this approach to vocal music, since it frees the composer from the strictures of a text. At the same time it enables him to take advantage of the warmth inherent in the human voice, and thereby to imbue his music with human expressiveness.

Cowell's work is titled *Toccanta*. This is a rather clever combination of the word *toccata*, which since Bach's time has meant a rhapsodic show piece for an instrument, and *cantata*, meaning a work for voices. Its five short movements employ the voice in a variety of manners which are unusual and quite appealing.

Henry Cowell subsequently returned to his idea of writing wordless music for voices. Some years ago he agreed to compose a work for The Randolph Singers, a madrigal group of five voices that I conducted. The result was his "Hymn and Fuguing Tune No. 5," which contained no text and not even any indication of the sounds to which the notes were to be sung. We experimented with various sounds, and finally decided to hum the opening "Hymn" and sing the faster and more complex "Fuguing Tune" to the syllables "la-la-la-." This made possible the clearer articulation of the faster notes. For contrast we also hummed a few of the interludes in the "Fuguing Tune," thus achieving changes of color. The results are preserved in the recording we made of *English Madrigals and American Part Songs,* a disc which has since become a collector's item.

Twentieth-century America also boasts the songs of Samuel Barber. His *Hermit Songs* were first performed in 1953 by the soprano Leontyne Price at the Library of Congress, with the composer accompanying at the piano. The text consists of ten short poems by Irish monks and scholars of the eighth to thirteenth centuries. They are actually observations written on the margins of manuscripts they were copying. I quote here the complete text of one of the songs, called "Promiscuity":

I do not know with whom Edan will sleep
But I do know that fair Edan will not sleep alone.

The songs display Barber's lyrical talents and contain enough dissonance to enable them to be considered "modern."

I have also enjoyed two more modern song cycles. They are *Pomes Penyeach,* to words by James Joyce, and *Thirteen Ways of Looking at a Blackbird,* to words by Wallace Stevens. Both are by the American composer John Gruen, and both reveal a genuine feeling for vocal writing.

In the interest of accuracy, let me amend somewhat the statement I made earlier about the relative lack of folk melodies in the songs by the German composers. There are some, notably in Brahms. If you would like to share the pleasure I have received from Brahms in a folk mood, try his *Zigeunerlieder* (*Gypsy Songs*), Opus 103. He set these songs in two forms—for solo voice and piano and for four-part chorus and piano. I have conducted the works in their choral setting, but I must admit that the solo version is equally satisfying. If you can resist the infectious quality of these songs, perhaps you don't like music after all.

The Art of Singing Lieder

A final word about the art of Lieder singing. It is not to be assumed that every singer—even among famous opera stars—is necessarily a good Lieder singer. This is a specialized art, requiring not only a flexible voice but also great understanding of the emotional implications of the text. In place of the sheer volume so often required for opera, the art song demands a variety of tone colors and great control of the voice, often in *pianissimo* passages. This is a more severe test of musicianship than is the more brilliant kind of singing called for in opera. To me, the outstanding Lieder singers of our era are Dietrich Fischer-Dieskau, Gerard Souzay, Ernst Haefliger, Hermann Prey and Pierre Bernac. Among the women, I find Elisabeth Schwarzkopf, Maria Stader, Evelyn Lear, Régine Crespin and Judith Raskin pre-eminent.

8

The Musical Theater

ALFRED SIMON

Wʜᴇɴ I was eight or nine, a cousin presented me with a phonograph record—the first I could call my own. It was Jerome Kern's "Babes in the Wood" from *Very Good Eddie*, as pounded out relentlessly by the Emerson Military Band. Hardly the most sensitive performance for this tender, caressing melody, but at that point in my life it did not matter. There was a folklike simplicity about "Babes in the Wood" which I loved, and the record would be played over and over until the hissing surface noise made the music almost unrecognizable. The name Jerome Kern, or indeed, any other name in the musical comedy world, had no significance for me. But from that record on, I was hooked for life on show tunes. On succeeding birthdays and Christmases I'd acquire more records of theater music for my small, but growing collection. These were set forth in quite traditional style, as solos and duets, by Miss Lucy Isabelle Marsh, Mr. Lambert Murphy, and other genteel sopranos and tenors with beautiful voices.

Even better were the *Gems from . . .* records, a series of vocal medleys, sung by the Victor Light Opera Company, which in a fat four minutes would race through four or five songs (plus a reprise of the hit number) from each of the better Broadway musicals of that era. What a marvelous way to learn the highlights from the new shows, through the earliest ancestor of today's original-cast albums. Happily, almost every new

Victor list would include a new *Gems* record, for in those days there was no scarcity of fine songs. Not only were there the current musicals, but sometimes new versions of earlier operetta scores. In that way I discovered the lilting melodies of Lehár, Kálmán, Oscar Straus, Herbert, Friml, and Romberg. Though born and musically trained in Europe, the last three of these masters achieved their great and lasting fame in the Broadway theater.

During the last generation or so it has become fashionable to be contemptuous of anything as sentimental as operettas. Indeed, there was a period during my adolescent days when I would not dare admit liking such frankly romantic melodies as "Will You Remember?" from Romberg's *Maytime,* or "Only a Rose" from Friml's *The Vagabond King,* or "When You're Away" from Herbert's *The Only Girl.* Pure hypocrisy, of course, but I had to pretend to go along with the snobbishness of my contemporaries, or risk their ridicule.

There is no doubt that indifference or disdain for operetta music is completely genuine in many instances; with that I do not quarrel. But far too many people find it necessary to apologize for really liking the songs from *The Student Prince, Rose Marie,* or *The Red Mill.*

One basic and unfortunately valid reason for the prevailing disdain of operetta music could well be the inept and uninspired performances by some of our light-music maestros. Because the music is old-fashioned, must it always be orchestrally gimmicked-up with echo chambers and other studio tricks? Such treatment is justified when the songs are dull and cheap, but the operetta boys were gifted composers, and they deserve to be properly preserved. Let us at least have room for *both* approaches.

Victor Herbert himself, to judge by some Victor recordings he made in the early years of the century, was a top-notch conductor and had a joyful, yet sensitive way of conducting his music, as well as that of other composers. What a boon it would be to have some of these vintage performances restored on LP's.

Among today's conductors the only one who seems to have the knack for performing Herbert is Eugene Ormandy. His now-deleted record with the Philadelphia Orchestra of selections from *Naughty Marietta* and *The Fortune Teller* has all the zest and understanding the music should have.

While on the subject of authentic operetta records, it is interesting to listen to music by Rudolf Friml as performed by the composer. There is still one disc available, which consists of individual songs played by a large orchestra, with Friml ostensibly conducting from the keyboard. His piano playing is rather charming in an overflorid style, with many pianistic flourishes and ornamentations. Were it not for the presence of the orchestra, one would have the impression of listening to him play in an old-fashioned parlor, surrounded by overstuffed furniture, autographed photos of operetta stars, heavy draperies, and the inevitable scarf on the piano.

That traditional stage performances of period pieces can be commercially successful was delightfully demonstrated as recently as the mid-1940's, when Herbert's *The Red Mill* was produced at New York's Ziegfeld Theater without any tongue-in-cheek staging, and still managed to run for fifteen months. *The Merry Widow* and *Die Fledermaus* also enjoyed long runs about that time. Unfortunately, though, most revivals of famous operettas, other than Gilbert and Sullivan, have not fared too well in New York.

The summer theater is another matter. Since audiences in a vacation mood go to the theater with less rigid standards, it is much easier to please them with simple sets, a small orchestra, and good voices singing familiar melodies. And so the theaters-in-the-round, the converted barns and larger auditoriums, like those in St. Louis, Kansas City, Fort Worth, San Francisco, and Los Angeles, are filled with audiences returning year after year to wallow in the nostalgic pleasure of the music they know and love. They can almost be forgiven for humming along and tapping their feet against the back of your chair, completely out of rhythm!

The great vogue for operettas during the early years of the century diminished as the pace of life quickened. Nevertheless, there has always been a substantial audience not only for the old standards, but for such newer favorites as Noel Coward's *Bitter Sweet, Up in Central Park* by Sigmund Romberg and the Griegoriented *Song of Norway* and Borodin-oriented *Kismet,* both by Wright and Forrest. Thanks to Jerome Kern, Richard Rodgers, and particularly to Oscar Hammerstein II, the operetta form has grown into a newer, more mature, and infinitely more satisfying theater experience through masterpieces like *Show Boat, Carousel,* and *The King and I.*

Years ago the need for swifter-paced musicals was satisfied to some extent by the brash, breezy works of George M. Cohan, the source of the first truly American show tunes. "Give My Regards to Broadway," "You're a Grand Old Flag," "Mary's a Grand Old Name," and "The Yankee Doodle Boy" are still being sung, but are often thought of as folk songs rather than show tunes. The shows were hardly distinguished in themselves; they were just cheerful showcases for the talents of the song-and-dance man and his engaging parents and sister.

Jerome Kern

Unlike most of his colleagues on Broadway, Kern was brought up in a household where there was much music. His mother, a proficient pianist, was his earliest teacher. Being of Bohemian descent, she taught him gay and charming folk tunes, and these served him well much later. He used one for the march played by the stage band that accompanies Cap'n Andy's first entrance in *Show Boat.* Another is a little polka Kern adapted for "Pick Yourself Up," in the Astaire-Rogers film *Swing Time.* This polka, by the way, served not only Bedřich Smetana in "The Merry Chicken Yard," but also Jaromir Weinberger in "Schwanda."

Kern's earliest professional experience was at the music publishing firm T. B. Harms, which later became his publisher. Once his flair for composing was discovered by the head of the firm, Max Dreyfus, Kern got the job of adding new songs with an American flavor to the scores of foreign musicals. The songs he added were not outstanding, especially compared with what was to come, but they had a distinctive quality. Alan Dale, a leading dramatic critic of the day, wrote about one show: "Its music by Jerome D. Kern towers in such an Eiffel way above the hurdy-gurdy, penny-in-slot primitive accompaniment to the musical show that criticism is disarmed."

A British importation to which Kern added music was called *The Girl from Utah.* For it he wrote his first great hit, "They Didn't Believe Me," the song that opened the door to a flood of offers. Kern responded with a succession of intimate musical comedies, full of endearing ballads, comedy numbers, and danceable tunes. Kern was represented on Broadway in the year 1917 by no fewer than five shows. Two of these, *Have a Heart* and *Love o' Mike,* opened five nights apart, and *Oh, Boy!* came along just five weeks later!

Kern was well aware of the importance of intelligent lyrics to go with his new musical style. Guy Bolton and P. G. Wodehouse—both British—collaborated effectively with him in breaking away from the stilted operetta pattern. Their lyrics were models of charm and wit. As far back as 1917 Kern said, "It is my opinion that the musical numbers should carry the action of the play and should be representative of the personalities of the characters who sing them. Songs must be suited to the action and mood of the play."

Although not as productive in the 1920's, each year Kern brought forth new scores, most of them head and shoulders above anything else being produced at the time. While still retaining his lyrical, flowing style, he was able to keep up with changing styles and fads in rhythms. Songs like "Look for the Silver Lining," "Ka-Lu-A," and "Who?" became great favorites, even perennial standards. To no one's surprise, it was Kern who, with Oscar Hammerstein II, created from an Edna Ferber novel the finest musical play of the 1920's, *Show Boat.* Here at last was the perfect blend of libretto, lyrics, and music. Six of the songs have become a part of our heritage; in addition the incidental music is full of wonderfully tender and joyful themes. On records there are excerpts from the score, but *Show Boat* deserves a complete version.

Great as *Show Boat* was, Kern later wrote two musicals that are in some ways even superior. *The Cat and the Fiddle* does not contain as many well-known songs, nor does *Music in the Air,* but each show is more fully developed musically. No matter how often I play through these two piano scores, I marvel at the beauty and variety of the melodies. *The Cat and the Fiddle* and *Music in the Air* have been even more shabbily treated on records, with not even one set of excerpts available today.

It is often difficult to pick one's own favorite among the songs of any composer. But oddly enough, in all that wealth of Kern music, I do have one favorite—"All the Things You Are," with a lyric by Hammerstein to match the endearing melody. It was gratifying for me to learn from Hammerstein himself that this happened to be both his and Kern's favorite among all they had written.

This composer's place in American music is well demonstrated by the fact that no matter how strongly fanciers of show music may differ about other men, they almost invariably agree in their estimate of and affection for Kern.

Richard Rodgers spoke for all of us when he wrote in *The New York Times* some years ago:

> Kern was typical of what was and still is good in our general maturity in this country in that he had his musical roots in the fertile European and English school of operetta writing, and amalgamated it with everything that was fresh in the American scene, to give us something wonderfully new and clear in music writing in the world. Actually, he was a giant with one foot in Europe and the other in America. Before he died, he picked up the European foot and planted it squarely alongside the American one. . . . If we were to look for one example of each extreme of his geographical range, we might find *Look for the Silver Lining* with its almost beer hall simplicity at one end, and discover *Ol' Man River* with its deep turmoil and strong native inflection at the other. Both are fine music and both are Kern.

Irving Berlin

Because Irving Berlin wrote many hit songs not intended for musical comedies, he is often overlooked in discussions of theater composers. The truth is that his contribution to musical theater is more impressive and spans a longer period than any contemporary. The 1911 edition of the *Ziegfeld Follies* contained the first Berlin show music. Fifty-five years later, well into his seventies, Berlin added the hilarious show-stopper "An Old-Fashioned Wedding" to an already bountiful score for *Annie Get Your Gun,* when the show was revived at Lincoln Center in 1966. Captious critics have complained that Berlin keeps reverting to the same old formula, that he never breaks new ground. Perhaps so, but the breaking of new ground is not necessarily a criterion for evaluating a song writer. Even though Berlin has played it safe, he has managed to keep up with the times, writing topical songs for such satiric shows as *Face the Music, As Thousands Cheer,* and *Call Me Madam.* But it is for his disarmingly simple ballads that Berlin will always be remembered. Composers in the current theater are able to write simply, sometimes, but the results are just not the same as "A Pretty Girl Is Like a Melody," "Say It with Music," "Easter Parade," or "They Say It's Wonderful." There is something basic and wonderfully down-to-earth in Berlin's music and lyrics when he expresses the soldier's plight in "Oh, How I Hate to Get Up in the Morning." Despite the fact that much of his fame springs from Tin Pan Alley and Hollywood, the man who wrote "There's No Business Like Show Business" is very much of the theater.

George Gershwin

The particular magic George Gershwin has always held for me is quite indescribable. It probably began when I discovered something unusual about his song "Somebody Loves Me." If you are familiar with the melody, you will note that after the rising, affirmative melody of the first line, there is a sudden doubting effect in the second line, as a beat comes before "I wonder who," and another beat before "I wonder who he can be." This imaginative blending of music and lyric intrigued me, though it seems to be lost on many pop singers, who insist on beginning the song with the beat. As time went on, I became increasingly bowled over by the combination of humor, wistfulness, vitality, and invention in song after song, from show after show. What a joy it is to discover songs like "Fascinating Rhythm," "The Man I Love," "Do Do Do," "Someone to Watch over Me," "My One and Only"—each with its own innovations.

Yet it is interesting to note that it was Kern whom Gershwin called his greatest influence. Gershwin's biographer, Isaac Goldberg, quotes the composer as follows:

> Kern was the first composer who made me conscious that most popular music was of inferior quality and that musical comedy music was made of better material. I followed Kern's work and studied each song that he composed. I paid him the tribute of frank imitation, and many things I wrote at this period sounded as though Kern had written them himself.

Indeed, Gershwin was imitative of Kern, as I discovered in the obscure "Some Far-Away Someone," from the 1924 musical *Primrose*, a song Kern could well have written.

Playing the piano versions of Gershwin songs, with their often intricate arrangements, made me an avid student of all show music, and improved my facility at the piano as well. In the fall of 1931 I had the incredible audacity to ask Gershwin, whom I had met through my oldest brother, whether I could be of any use to him playing piano for rehearsals of his new show, *Of Thee I Sing*. He told me that rehearsal pianists had already been engaged, but kindly and generously recommended that I drop in at the theater any time to watch rehearsals, that it would be an interesting and instructive experience, if I wanted to get into the musical comedy field, which I did, desperately. As things turned out, I was soon put to work, playing mostly for the chorus numbers, headed by George Murphy, a young dancer who later made good in Hollywood, and still later in Washington.

Listening to Gershwin himself take over the piano was a memorable feature of rehearsals. There was a special kind of electric excitement in everything he played. Fortunately for everyone who listened, he loved playing his own music. George S. Kaufman once remarked, "George's music gets around so much before an opening that the first-night audience thinks it's at a revival."

Gershwin recorded several piano solos of his songs for English Columbia; hopefully these will some day be reissued, for they capture marvelously his own joy in playing. His recorded up-tempo performance of "Someone to Watch over Me" is unusually interesting historically. Ira Gershwin's fascinating book, *Lyrics on Several Occasions*, has this to say about the song:

> As originally conceived by the composer, this tune would probably not be around much today. At the piano in its early existence, it was fast and jazzy, and undoubtedly I would have written it up as another dance-and-ensemble number. One day, for no particular reason and hardly aware of what he was at, George started and continued it in a comparatively slow tempo; and half of it hadn't been sounded when both of us had the same reaction; this was really no rhythm tune, but rather a wistful and warm one—to be held out until the proper stage occasion arose for it.

That "proper stage occasion" turned out to be Gertrude Lawrence's unforgettable performance of "Someone to Watch over Me" in *Oh, Kay!*

In view of Gershwin's ability to compose in such a wide variety of moods for the theater, and his gratifying success in the concert field, it was not surprising that he combined these talents for the creation of an opera. *Porgy and Bess* was rather cautiously received by the critics and public when it first opened on Broadway. Theatergoers seemed wary of the term *opera;* the opera world reacted condescendingly to a modern work which dared to include so many accessible tunes, and was hardly opera in the traditional sense. It is not in my province to argue whether or not the term *opera* applies to *Porgy and Bess*. The fact remains that it is an exceptional theater achievement. It is hard to think of any musical play that so effectively portrays varied emotions as does *Porgy and Bess* in the tragic song "My Man's Gone Now," the carefree "I Got Plenty o' Nuttin'," the soothing "Summertime," the soaring "Bess, You Is My Woman Now," or the menacing "There's a Boat Dat's Leavin' Soon for New York."

Generosity toward his colleagues was a trait of Gershwin's which is rare in the theater. He was especially enthusiastic about the music of Vincent Youmans (exactly one day younger than Gershwin, incidentally), and he was directly responsible for Youmans' receiving his first Broadway assignment, *Two Little Girls in Blue*. That show had lyrics by one Arthur Francis, who later forsook the pseudonym in favor of his actual name, Ira Gershwin.

Vincent Youmans

Of all the major theater composers, Youmans had the shortest career—eleven years, during which he managed to turn out twelve shows. *Wildflower, No, No, Nanette,* and *Hit the Deck* were outstanding hits, which is not a bad percentage, and out of them came such classics as "Tea for Two," "I Want to Be Happy," "Hallelujah!" "Sometimes I'm Happy," and "Bambalina." Even when Youmans had little commercial luck on Broadway, his songs survived. Most of us are familiar with "Time on My Hands," "More Than You Know," "Without a Song," "Great Day," and "Through the Years," but how many of us realize that these songs were introduced in disastrous shows?

Even during his short career, Youmans developed a style peculiarly his own, and oddly enough, it has never been imitated. There is a quiet, inner strength and great inventiveness in his songs. Even when the melody is not particularly original, his insinuating harmonic and rhythmic effects are often quite striking. While the main opening theme of "Tea for Two" is not outstanding in itself, the sly variations are arrestingly ingenious, and they have had much to do with the song's enduring popularity.

Youmans' own favorite was "Through the Years," the title melody from one of his last shows. This ambitious and beautiful score represented a marked advance over what he had done before, and it points up the great loss that was Broadway's and ours when the composer's frail health forced him to retire at the age of thirty-five.

Richard Rodgers

The *Garrick Gaieties* of 1925 and 1926 made theatergoers aware of music by Richard Rodgers and lyrics by Lorenz Hart. However, I am somewhat proud of having discovered their talents for myself as early as 1920 in the Columbia Varsity show *Fly with Me;* their gay, lilting songs danced in my head for months and months. Two of the Rodgers melodies in that college show had lyrics by Oscar Hammerstein II. *Oklahoma!,* their first professional collaboration, was twenty-three years in the future.

Despite the early Kern influence on him, Rodgers, even at seventeen, was definitely developing a style of his own—an easy, graceful melodic line. One of the songs in *Fly with Me,* called "Peek in Pekin," is completely Rodgers, not at all like Kern. (Larry Hart, never averse to puns, later wrote new lyrics for "Peek in Pekin," and the song, now called "Love's Intense in Tents," appeared in the show *Poor Little Ritz Girl.*)

Between the first and second editions of the *Garrick Gaieties* Rodgers and Hart were represented on Broadway by an exceptionally charming period piece called *Dearest Enemy.* Set in New York City during the American Revolution, it was perfectly, if surprisingly, suited to the partners' light, airy style. The only song that may still be familiar to you is "Here in My Arms," but the score is full of characteristically lilting ballads and infectious production tunes, with wonderfully literate and sly lyrics, the likes of which are almost unheard of in a costume piece. Very possibly this was the progenitor of the Rodgers and Hammerstein era; it would be gratifying to have *Dearest Enemy* revived both on the stage and on records.

It is hard to pick one favorite in the Rodgers and Hart show catalog. I particularly like *On Your Toes,* with its devastating satire on ballet; *Babes in Arms,* full of such marvelous songs as "Where or When," "My Funny Valentine," "The Lady Is a Tramp," and "Johnny One Note"; *Pal Joey,* with one of the most adult books any musical ever had; *The Boys from Syracuse,* which contained "Falling in Love with Love," "This Can't Be

Love," "Sing for Your Supper," and the beautiful and less familiar "You Have Cast Your Shadow on the Sea."

The last Rodgers and Hart collaboration, *By Jupiter*, enjoyed the longest run, but was less inspired than those listed previously. The songs seemed to be oversophisticated and labored, with the notable exception of "Wait Till You See Her," which was cut from the show soon after it came to Broadway. How good it was to hear that lovely waltz, now restored, stop the show when *By Jupiter* was revived Off-Broadway in 1967.

When Rodgers began collaborating with Hammerstein on *Oklahoma!*, the sprightly quality of his music remained, but there also appeared a new open-air freshness, an added warmth and maturity. Hammerstein's previous experience with warm, believable characters in *Show Boat* and *Music in the Air* gave Rodgers a new dimension on his musical life. The sunniness of *Oklahoma!*'s opening song, "Oh, What a Beautiful Mornin'," established the show's mood brilliantly; it also set the appropriate tone for the start of the collaboration itself.

Instead of following with another musical in the breezy vein of *Oklahoma!*, Rodgers and Hammerstein turned to the poignant, bittersweet *Carousel*—as wise a move as it was triumphant in accomplishment. The score for *Carousel* represented Rodgers' greatest advance, with its abundance of wonderful melodies and its complementing of the tender glow of Hammerstein's lyrics. The music for *South Pacific* is not in the richly romantic vein of *Carousel*, nor should it be, but it is exactly right for the predominantly exuberant mood of the show.

The most beautifully conceived of all their shows, for me, is *The King and I*. The touching story of *Anna and the King of Siam* seems to have been made to order for their particular talents. Each of them had pertinent things to say about the adaptation. Hammerstein said, "What was required was the Eastern sense of dignity and pageantry—none of this business of girls dressed in Oriental costumes and dancing onto the stage and singing 'ching-a-ling' with their fingers in the air." Rodgers maintained that "a too-accurate reproduction of the sound of 1860 Siam would give less than small pleasure to an Occidental ear, and an evening of it would drive an American audience howling into the streets. The score makes an occasional pass at the five-tone scale, but only in the interest of color. I finally decided to write a score that would be analagous in sound to the look of a series of Siamese paintings by Grant Wood. I myself remained a Broadway character, not somebody disguised in Oriental get-up."

If *The Sound of Music* is not up to the mark set by *Carousel, South Pacific,* or *The King and I,* it does have much of the warmth and simplicity so typical of Rodgers and Hammerstein. One of its songs, the folklike "Edelweiss," has a lyric that reminds me of "I've Told Every Little Star," which Hammerstein wrote with Jerome Kern for *Music in the Air.* There is even a feeling of Kern in Rodgers' gentle melody. This was their last song; a tenderly appropriate one to mark the end of a memorable collaboration.

Admirers of Rodgers sometimes feel they must take sides on the subject of Hart versus Hammerstein. This is nonsensical, for both were wonderful in their completely disparate styles. Hart would scarcely have done right by *Carousel* or *The King and I,* and Hammerstein would hardly have been the ideal lyricist for *Pal Joey* or *On Your Toes.*

Never content to repeat a formula, Rodgers followed *The Sound of Music* with *No Strings,* a breezy affair which reverted in some ways to the sophisticated quality of the Rodgers and Hart shows, but with some inventive effects in staging and orchestration. Another recent score, the one for *Do I Hear a Waltz?,* is once again in a relaxed, melodic vein. Altogether, Rodgers has been a refreshingly adventurous man in the musical theater.

Cole Porter

Cole Porter's first song hit gave no hint of the sophistication for which he was to gain his greatest fame. That first song was "An Old-Fashioned Garden," introduced by Lillian Kemble Cooper in a revue called *Hitchy-Koo, 1919.* This was a frankly sentimental ballad, undoubtedly setting the scene for a lavish production number. Though Cole Porter was the most sophisticated and worldly of all songwriters, there was more simplicity in him than his devotees would have us believe. There was also enormous variety. Most typical are the sparklers, like "You're the Top," "I Get a Kick Out of You," "Let's Do It," "My Heart Belongs to Daddy," and "Just One of Those Things." But when the occasion called for it, he could turn out a clog-waltz like "Me and Marie," a quasihillbilly tune called "The Ozarks Are Calling Me Home," or an outrageously corny duet like "Friendship." As something of a sentimentalist, I melt at such haunting ballads as "So in Love," "Night and Day," and the neglected "Ev'ry Time We Say Goodbye."

As for the shows themselves, there is little, if any, argument about what is Porter's masterpiece. *Kiss Me, Kate* has a succession of marvelous songs of infinite variety and imagination. Until *Kiss Me, Kate* came along, most lovers of show music considered *Anything Goes* his best score. Not I. My vote goes to *Jubilee*, which contains not only one of the greatest show songs by any composer, "Begin the Beguine," but also "Just One of Those Things," "Why Shouldn't I?" and a host of other winning numbers which may be a bit too special outside of the show itself to get much recognition. Notable among these is "When Love Comes Your Way," an affectionate takeoff on a typical Noel Coward waltz ballad. As for *Anything Goes*, it contains four fine standards: "You're the Top," "I Get a Kick Out of You," "All Through the Night," and "Blow, Gabriel, Blow." The other songs for the most part are second-rate Porter. When the show was revived Off-Broadway some seasons ago, the producers wisely substituted several other obscure songs by Porter for the ones in the original score. Ordinarily, I do not approve of indiscriminate substitutions; but in this case it was warranted.

There was another team that contributed a great deal to the gaiety of Broadway during the 1920's and 1930's. This was the trio of Buddy De Sylva, Lew Brown, and Ray Henderson. Like Irving Berlin, they played it safe, but also like Berlin, they wrote many attractive and breezy songs. George White's *Scandals* contained "The Birth of the Blues," "Black Bottom," and "Life Is Just a Bowl of Cherries." Then there were such high-spirited shows as *Good News, Follow Thru* and *Hold Every-*

thing. For these they wrote "The Best Things in Life Are Free," "The Varsity Drag," "Button Up Your Overcoat," and "You're the Cream in My Coffee."

Schwartz and Dietz

If Rodgers and Hart proved in the *Garrick Gaieties* that revue scores need not be just a hodgepodge of sentimental ballads and rhythm numbers to accompany production numbers and dance routines, Arthur Schwartz and Howard Dietz continued and developed the intimate revue tradition. Their first success, the litlting "I Guess I'll Have to Change My Plan," was introduced by Clifton Webb in *The Little Show* in 1929. The next year came the first Schwartz and Dietz song to become a lasting hit: "Something to Remember You By," which Libby Holman sang in *Three's a Crowd.* Like Gershwin's "Someone to Watch over Me," this lovely ballad started life as a fast dance tune under a different title by another lyricist. But Dietz suggested to Schwartz that he slow down the rhythm to accommodate the romantic mood of the new lyric he had in mind.

Their greatest triumph was *The Band Wagon,* which starred Fred and Adele Astaire, and which even today is remembered as something perfect in the way of revues. While the show was running, RCA-Victor issued a 33⅓-rpm record (the term *long-playing* had not yet entered the vocabularly), which featured Leo Reisman's Orchestra and the Astaires performing "I Love Louisa," "New Sun in the Sky," and the unforgettable "Dancing in the Dark." Arthur Schwartz supplied a piano solo for "White Heat." This, then, was the first original-cast LP. *The Band Wagon* was never produced in England, but as recently as 1966 the enterprising English branch of RCA-Victor issued this treasurable disc as a modern LP. A note to record collectors: the English number is RD-7756.

Adept as he was in the revue form, Schwartz was even more effective in writing romantic songs. In 1934 came *Revenge with Music,* a lavish version of *The Three-Cornered Hat.* The Spanish locale afforded him and Dietz the opportunity for richly melodic and colorfully exciting numbers. Two exceptionally fine ballads came from this show; one, "If There Is Someone Lovelier Than You," is Schwartz's own favorite among his songs. The other, "You and the Night and the Music," was initially banned from radio broadcasting because of its suggestive opening lines: "You and the night and the music/Fill me with flaming desire/Setting my being completely on fire." The fire has long since died down, and the song is one of our most respected and respectable standards. Twenty-five years after *Revenge with Music*, Schwartz and Dietz were still in top form, writing bubbling numbers for *The Gay Life*, with slightly but appropriately Viennese touches.

Aside from the score for *The Band Wagon*, the most appealing songs Schwartz has written are those for *A Tree Grows in Brooklyn*. The gay, tender quality of the lyrics by Dorothy Fields were beautifully caught by her collaborator. Each song seems exactly right—lyrically and musically.

Harold Rome

Like Schwartz, Harold Rome made his first impact on the musical theater with bright topical revues. *Pins and Needles,* produced by the International Ladies Garment Workers Union, contained, not unexpectedly, songs of social significance, as one song put it plainly in its title, but the big hit turned out to be a pleasant little item, which had little bearing on social consciousness—"Sunday in the Park." Quite different, and most rousing, was "Franklin D. Roosevelt Jones," a choral number from Rome's next show, *Sing Out the News*. The joys and problems of GI's returning to civilian life after World War II were dealt with penetratingly in *Call Me Mister*. The best-remembered of Rome's songs in that show is the riotously funny "South America, Take It Away."

By the end of the 1940's, when the revue form seemed to have been absorbed by television specials, Rome turned his attention and talents to book musicals. His first try was also one of his most resounding hits—*Wish You Were Here*, a good-natured musical about life in a summer camp for adults. The wistful title number summed up the mood of the show well, in addition to becoming the most popular song in the Rome catalogue. The composer's diversified talents were heard next in *Fanny*, far more ambitious than anything he had tried before. The result was a charmingly colorful and melodious set of songs, which beautifully underscored the many varied emotions and characters created by Marcel Pagnol in the film trilogy on which *Fanny* was based. Ironically, not a note of Rome's score was sung in the film version adapted from the musical; however, its themes served most handsomely in the background score.

Destry Rides Again, another stage adaptation of a famous film, was far more conventional, and had a most disappointing set of songs. The most recent score by Harold Rome, for *The Zulu and the Zayda*, found him in an unusual setting—the tense atmosphere of South Africa. Unlikely as this might seem for a musical play, the songs were properly atmospheric. And not surprisingly, the most effective were those he wrote for Menasha Skulnik, the Zayda.

Harold Arlen

Certain show composers, despite their considerable accomplishments, are not nearly as well known by name as they should be. Vincent Youmans, mentioned earlier, was one in that category. Another is Harold Arlen. Many of Arlen's greatest songs, like "Stormy Weather," "Over the Rainbow," "Blues in the Night," and "That Old Black Magic," did not originate on the Broadway stage. Perhaps that is why he is not immediately thought of with Gershwin, Rodgers, Kern, and Porter, when the illustrious musical names of the theater are mentioned. But Arlen has written memorable songs for Broadway. The most famous, "Come Rain or Come Shine," is from *St. Louis Woman*, which had indifferent success. *House of Flowers* did not fare much better on Broadway, but it had a hauntingly lovely score, including "A Sleepin' Bee" and "I Never Has Seen Snow," as well as the more exotic and exciting "Bamboo Cage."

Little of the wistful, deeply felt blues quality that is usually associated with Arlen's music is to be found in *Bloomer Girl*, a period piece about the Civil War. But the score has charm and grace, and it is a pity the songs are not heard more often these days.

Arlen, fortunately, is a persuasive singer of his own songs, whether something as plaintive as "Stormy Weather" or as jubilant as "Ac-cent-tchuate the Positive." The many records he has made of his own songs should help toward making him as well known as he should be.

Weill, Styne, Sondheim, Loesser

The notable career Kurt Weill achieved in Germany during the pre-Hitler years was matched by the remarkable way in which he was able to adapt to the American theater. The bitter, sardonic feeling of his German music was still evident in *Johnny Johnson,* his first Broadway show, produced in 1936. Indeed, it was appropriate to the antiwar theme of the plot. But by 1938 and *Knickerbocker Holiday,* his composing style, to some, seemed to have softened; to me it seemed to have acquired some degree of beauty and warmth, especially in the memorable "September Song." Two seasons later came a landmark in his career, as well as in the history of musical shows: *Lady in the Dark.* Weill's experience writing music for the theater and his incredibly rapid grasp of Broadway styles had resulted in a rich, broadly varied score (including such masterpieces as "My Ship" and "The Saga of Jenny"), which matched the incomparable lyrics by Ira Gershwin and book by Moss Hart. *One Touch of Venus* was a pleasant score in a rather more conventional style, notable mostly for another all-time favorite, "Speak Low." Weill resumed collaboration with Ira Gershwin in *The Firebrand of Florence.* Colorful as it was, the show itself was hardly a masterpiece, but the seldom-heard score had much interesting material and deserves more recognition.

Weill's two most impressive scores are the highly dramatic *Street Scene* and *Lost in the Stars,* a singularly moving work. It was during the run of the latter that Weill died. What irony that he could not have lived to enjoy the tremendous American success of his greatest European hit, *The Three-Penny Opera,* when it was revived Off-Broadway. Its "Mack the Knife" also proved to be the great hit of Weill's American career. Thus, in a sense, his entire professional life came full cycle.

Among the most prolific contributors to the Broadway scene is Jule Styne, responsible for the scores of such hits as *High Button Shoes, Gentlemen Prefer Blondes,* and *Bells Are Ringing.* There is a professional, craftsmanlike, and occasionally dynamic quality about his songs, but they are seldom distinguished. The exception is *Gypsy,* in which he captured so vividly the brashest, gaudiest, and seamiest aspects of show biz, and provided Ethel Merman with some rousing material. Of tremendous value in making the songs so effective were the sharp, funny, and knowing lyrics of Stephen Sondheim. Although Sondheim is recognized for his lyric writing (*West Side Story* and *Do I Hear a Waltz?* particularly), his musical gifts are not so well known. The songs he wrote for *A Funny Thing Happened on the Way to the Forum* were rightfully subordinate to the comedy, but the music had some quietly sly twists. Some day when he is given the opportunity to write a show in which music plays a prominent part, Sondheim may turn out to be one of the theater's most important composers.

Few composers have had as much interesting and original versatility as Frank Loesser. After beginning with *Where's Charley?* in 1948, he switched from its conventional formula to *Guys and Dolls,* which portrayed superbly the raffish characters and atmosphere of the Damon Runyon stories. Next he turned almost operatic with *The Most Happy Fella.* Perhaps there was too much variety in this ambitious score, as if he could not make up his mind about the prevailing mood. But there is no denying that the score contains an immense amount of colorful musical material.

How to Succeed in Business Without Really Trying is far from a memorable score, apart from the production itself, and it has been judged unfavorably on that basis. I suspect, though, that rather than write a series of lively, attractive songs, Loesser decided to write music that underscored the fast-paced and hilarious action in the show, as if he were doing a film background score. In that sense, he succeeded admirably. Unless one has seen and enjoyed the show itself, though, the record album is disappointing.

Leonard Bernstein

Leonard Bernstein has written only four major scores for the Broadway stage, but all four are such exciting experiences that he ranks as one of the musical theater's most impressive figures. Three are set in New York, but each has its own individuality. *On the Town,* an off-shoot of Bernstein's ballet *Fancy Free,* is full of dance music, with a humorous, quasi-Gershwin flavor, but still a good quota of romantic moods. *Wonderful Town* reveals Bernstein in a more satirical mood, with the foibles of the 1930's as his target. *West Side Story,* without question a great masterpiece of the American theater, is a marvelous mixture of highly dramatic songs, ballads, comedy numbers, and ballet music. *Candide* gets away from New York, but not from satire. Although the adaptation of the Voltaire classic left a lot to be desired, the Bernstein score is full of delights. With other serious composers, it could have come perilously close to conventional operetta, but that's just what Bernstein satirized so impishly. The result: a collection of such European rhythms as the waltz, tango, gavotte, and mazurka, all dressed up in totally irreverent style. He does not overlook opera, either, for the highlight is a devastating lampoon of coloratura singing in "Glitter and Be Gay."

Of the composers who have performed their own music on records, Bernstein is incomparably the most brilliant. His conducting of *On the Town* makes the score sound better than it did originally. And to add to the authenticity, four original cast members—Betty Comden and Adolph Green (who collaborated on the book and lyrics), Nancy Walker, and Cris Alexander—participate on this superb disc. Conductor Bernstein should give us more of composer Bernstein on records.

Lerner and Loewe, Burton Lane

The team of Alan Jay Lerner and Frederick Loewe has given great distinction and beauty to the American musical theater. Their first collaborations were amiable shows with a contemporary setting. However, when they broke away from the present and wrote about the past, their brilliance as writers came into prominence. In *Brigadoon*, Loewe, a Viennese, caught the Scottish flavor magnificently in his ballads, and especially in his themes for the ballet sequences and ensemble numbers. Next was *Paint Your Wagon*. Again, hardly the ideal locale for a composer with a Viennese background, but the score was rousing Americana, with a folklike quality in many songs.

My Fair Lady deserves more space in this chapter, and needs less than any show of which I can think. It comes quite close to being the perfect musical in every respect. There are purists who consider it a desecration of Shaw's *Pygmalion*. To me it is a highly respectful and beautiful extension of a brilliant comedy.

Camelot, which followed, was expected to be an anticlimax, and possibly it was to a certain extent; anything would have been. But *Camelot*, on its own terms, was a lovely show to listen to and to watch. Loewe's score is full of delectable melodies, some lilting and gay, and others in the haunting, almost rueful mood of *Brigadoon*.

Loewe's decision to retire from the musical theater is sad, indeed, even if it is hard to blame him for wanting to forgo the rigors it entails. If we are to look for the silver lining, we can find it in the fact that Alan Jay Lerner found a collaborator in the person of a composer who had been absent from Broadway for much too long—Burton Lane, whose delightful *Finian's Rainbow* enchanted us back in 1946. The songs which Lane wrote with Lerner for *On a Clear Day You Can See Forever* were among the most captivating in many seasons. There is nothing ambitious about the score; it just happens to have what the American musical theater so often lacks today—a series of wonderfully tuneful, bouncy, affectionate, and well-constructed songs. E. Y. Harburg, who wrote the lyrics for *Finian's*

Rainbow, once remarked that of all the modern composers, Lane has come the closest to capturing the effervescence so characteristic of George Gershwin. The music for *On a Clear Day* must, if anything, confirm Harburg's observation. It definitely does so for me.

A great many of the best show tunes of the 1930's, 1940's, and 1950's are not actually show tunes at all. They are the songs written by the theater's top composers and lyricists when they migrated to Hollywood during the heyday of screen musicals. De Sylva, Brown, and Henderson were the first to head westward, and they turned out a typically fresh set of songs for the Janet Gaynor-Charles Farrell film, *Sunny Side Up.* Soon they were followed by the Gershwins, Berlin, Kern, Hammerstein, Dorothy Fields, Rodgers and Hart, Porter, Schwartz, and more recently, Lerner and Loewe. These writers did not lower their standards in Hollywood; they turned out some of their most enchanting songs out there, especially in such films as *Shall We Dance, Swing Time, Top Hat, State Fair,* and *Gigi.*

In time, most of these writers returned to New York, but still contributed to the film song literature by long-distance. As this is being written, a number of Broadway musicals are being prepared for lavish screen production. Many will include additional songs by the original writers. And so these may very justifiably be called show tunes, even if they began life on the screen.

Time was when the principal requirement of a Broadway show was a good set of catchy songs and some unrelated comedy scenes, to punctuate as well as disguise the deficiencies of the wobbly book. The average musical would stand a reasonable chance of success, and could even play to half-empty houses for weeks and months without losing a fortune for the producer and his backers. However, today, with the musical theater facing so much competition from television and musical films, and with sky-rocketing admission costs resulting from economic pressures, audiences have become much more selective. Producers therefore have had to be more selective about the quality of the librettos for the musicals they bring to Broadway. The result has been far greater cohesion in book, lyrics, and music. The exception is the musical tailored for a big box-office name. There is a comparatively small group of writers gifted and knowledgeable enough to cope with the exacting requirements of tying together the components of a musical show. Most active are Jerry Herman (*Milk and Honey, Hello, Dolly!, Mame*), Jerry Bock and Sheldon Harnick (*Fiddler on the Roof, Fiorello, She Loves Me*), Harvey Schmidt and Tom Jones (*The Fantasticks, 110 in the Shade, I Do! I Do!*), Charles Strouse and Lee Adams (*Bye, Bye, Birdie, Golden Boy*), and John Kander and Fred Ebb (*Cabaret, The Happy Time*). Admirable as their work is, what I miss about it is an individual style. I miss the pleasure of being able to recognize a characteristic tune by this or that composer. The younger writers are too preoccupied with the integration of the ingredients, and not sufficiently concerned with the importance and permanence of a fine melody with distinctive turns of phrases and harmonies. Consequently, there is a certain sameness about the scores.

I believe that the music should serve as more than a convenient crutch for engaging lyrics. It should have a separate life of its own, away from the theater. That may seem impossible, but it can be done—look at *My Fair Lady*.

9

Light Music

ROBERT SHERMAN

I HAVE always been unhappy with the phrase *light music*. It suggests bits of fluff, unworthy of serious discussion or attention. It calls to mind the sort of faceless tonal wallpaper we find with distressing frequency in department stores, supermarkets, and other places of commercial worship. Its connotation is that of music with little substance and less inspiration, not music to listen to, just music to be heard. Besides, it implies that Mozart and company are "heavy," and I am not ready to concede that either.

How then can we define light music? Simple. We cannot. The term is too vague, and the field encompasses far too diverse a range of material to permit any convenient pigeonholing. Generally speaking, though, I think it's fair to say that marches, dances, orchestral novelties, and all the other categories we tend to call "light," have one important attribute in common: They make their musical points directly, with a minimum of artistic subterfuge. By that I mean that a beautiful melody counts more than intricate thematic interplay, infectious rhythm, more than complex counterpoint. In terms of Sonata Form (to borrow a phrase from those "heavy" composers), light music frequently involves exposition without development, and consequently it flourishes in short forms rather than extended ones. Even the more expansive works in the genre (operettas, for example) are usually made up of comparatively concise, uncomplicated segments. A piece of light music, however, is not inherently any less imaginative or creative than a full-scale symphony. Brevity, as Shakespeare remarked in one of his heavier plays, is the soul of wit, and a miniature like "The Beautiful Blue Danube" is, in its own way, as perfect a work of art as the *Eroica*. This is not, of course, to credit Johann Strauss with the profound inspiration of Beethoven, but merely to point out that it would be pretty tricky to waltz to the *Third Symphony*.

The idea of music for casual entertainment is not exactly brand new. Cleopatra had her household musicians, Nero loved to play the lute (he once won first musical prize at the Olympics, possibly because he thoughtfully stationed the judges right next to his soldiers, where they could hear better), and Elizabeth I could not really enjoy her supper unless an ensemble of fifes, trumpets, and kettledrums came by to serenade her.

In bygone eras, like today, many of the most skilled and famous composers were engaged in producing this type of "light" music. We tend to think of Handel in rather staid, reverent terms, but old George Frederick wrote pieces to shoot off fireworks by. Telemann churned out dozens of suites of dinner music, Boyce concocted nearly two dozen birthday songs, and Bach devised a set of harpsichord variations to help out a fellow who could not get to sleep at night.

Long before the Strauss family got the idea, Mozart, Beethoven, and Schubert were keeping the Viennese well supplied with dance music. The stage comedies of Europe, from Shakespeare's day on, came equipped with songs and dances by all the big names: Lully, Purcell, Mendelssohn, Sibelius, *et al.* Saint-Saëns and Satie wrote music for the movies; so, more recently, have Copland, Walton, and Shostakovich.

Light music, then, cannot and should not be equated with inconsequential music. A waltz may be easier to understand than a symphonic poem, it may require less concentration, it may serve a subsidiary purpose aside from pure listening enjoyment; but it is not necessarily a less valid or important part of the musical scene. It is for this reason that we at WQXR program Coates or Offenbach or Gilbert and Sullivan with pride and conviction, and why we feel that a light-music wing is a logical adjunct to any well-rounded library of classical recordings.

Having established the fact that light music is a Good Thing, we are now faced with the far trickier task of coming down to specifics. As previously noted, the term embraces such a diversity of styles and musical types that completeness, or even comprehensiveness, is virtually out of the question. As it happens, four prime divisions of light music (folk, theatrical, Latin American, and jazz) are taken up in separate chapters; what I would like to do, therefore, is merely to go poking about the rest of the field, name-dropping composers, arrangers, and performers who have contributed to it in some special fashion, and talking about a few of the pieces I have found especially appealing.

Pop Concerts

Let us begin with the Pops Concert, a colorful institution, which surprisingly enough was not invented by Arthur Fiedler. In England they had Promenade Concerts as far back as 1838, the name apparently deriving from the informality of the occasion, which allowed the audience to walk about during the program. The musical menu was not terribly exciting—according to one contemporary report, the fare almost invariably consisted of four overtures, four quadrilles, four waltzes, and one solo number—but the concerts themselves were quite successful. About twenty years later the famous Monday Evening Pops were organized "to collect a permanent audience from the lovers of music resident in London and the suburbs." They did precisely that, flourishing for the rest of the nineteenth century, and eventually attracting such topflight guest artists as Clara Schumann, Anton Rubinstein, Grieg, and Paderewski.

One of the conductors of the English proms, Louis Antoine Jullien, came to America in the late 1840's, and it was probably this master showman who introduced the pops concert idea over here. I would give anything to have seen this fellow in action. They say he conducted with a jeweled baton, from a crimson podium edged with gold, and if the piece were by Beethoven, he insisted on wearing white kid gloves, which were ceremoniously presented to him on a silver platter. His music stand was formed by a fantastic giltcarved figure, and an ornately decorated velvet throne stood ready to receive his exhausted, collapsing form at the end of a performance. Despite all the gimmickry, however, Jullien apparently was a fine musician, and since he made a point of including symphonic music on all his programs, he did much to popularize the music of the European masters in America.

The earliest American concerts with a definite tie to our own day were organized in 1885, when the Boston Symphony Orchestra, barely four years old itself, began a series of daily "Music Hall Promenades" (the Boston Music Hall being the orchestra's home at that time). When Symphony Hall was built in 1900, these summer concerts were renamed Symphony Hall Pops, and later they became known more simply as the Boston Pops. And now we *do* come to Arthur Fiedler, who took over as conductor of the Pops in 1930 (after fifteen years playing violin, viola, celesta, organ, and piano for the Boston Symphony), and quietly ushered in a new era in American light music.

From the start Fiedler had an uncanny knack for devising programs that appealed to everybody. He made the Pops Concert an eagerly awaited event, not only in Boston but everywhere in the country that his extensive tours took him. He also evolved the pattern that almost all other orchestral pops would follow. I first heard the Boston Pops about twenty years ago (it was at one of the outdoor concerts on the banks of the Charles River, and Fiedler conducted the *Water Music*, which seemed terribly appropriate), and as I recall, the general makeup of the program was about the same as it is today. The first section contains popular overtures, short symphonic suites, and a few novelty encores; the second part ventures into more ambitious literature, perhaps including one of the familiar concertos; and the last segment blends show and film music, popular standards, and humorous medleys into a razzle-dazzle finale. How can anybody have the theme from *Batman* and the Grieg *Piano Concerto* on the same program? I don't know, but Fiedler does it, and it works, and I guess that is all we really have to know about it.

Although Fiedler's thirty-five-year-plus tenure as King of the Pops is altogether unique, a number of other conductors have successfully followed his lead, combining the more entertaining elements of light music and the classics. Louis Lane has done a fine job with the Cleveland Orchestra Pops; so have Howard Mitchell with the Washington National Pops, Frederick Fennell with the Eastman-Rochester Pops, and Carmen Dragon with the summer festival concerts at the Hollywood Bowl.

André Kostelanetz, despite his lack of a permanent orchestral affiliation, has been even more influential. He plays fugues, foxtrots, and everything in between; he has transcribed opera arias, children's pieces, and ballads by The Beatles, and his concert tours have built up a large and loyal following over the years. I find that Kostelanetz is particularly effective as an arranger of popular, show, and movie music, but his interests and energies have taken him far afield. For more than a dozen years, he has been a regular guest conductor of the New York Philharmonic, and he has commissioned and premiered an impressive list of contemporary scores (including the stirring *Lincoln Portrait* by Aaron Copland).

Over in England things have been bubbling too, thanks to such gifted composer-arranger-conductors as Stanley Black, Frank Chacksfield, and Robert Farnon. Their work is known here primarily through recordings, but it is consistently tasteful and appealing. Another famous English light-music man, and certainly the most imitated, has parlayed lush harmonies and cascading strings into a million-dollar empire. It was in 1951 that Annunzio Paulo Mantovani developed his "new music"— arrangements of popular airs and symphonic favorites, which emphasized overlapping violins and a warm, honeyed orchestral tone. Since then his record sales have been phenomenal (more than sixteen million albums in America alone) and his concert tours are invariably sold out. I must confess I used to look down a highly dubious nose at Mantovani's wall-to-wall background music, but I came to respect it more after attending one of his Philharmonic Hall programs a couple of years ago.

Watching him at work, I realized that he is a sensitive musician as well as a clever showman. And if he does go off the deep end sometimes, with soupy arrangements of *Carmen* and other classical items that should have been left alone, many of his lighter selections do have warmth and an engaging lyric sweep.

Composers

Of all the composers who have made light music their exclusive metier (not counting, for the moment, writers for stage and screen), I find Leroy Anderson the most refreshing. Not only does he have a marvelous flair for melody, but his pieces are laced through with sophisticated wit and all sorts of deftly amusing scoring techniques. "Concert music with a pop quality" is how Anderson himself described his work, and probably that is as close as we are going to get to a proper definition of his indefinable style. All I know is that an Anderson miniature is as immediately recognizable as a Strauss waltz, and most often just as captivating. We have used "Forgotten Dreams," "The Typewriter," "Sleigh Ride," "Serenata," and several others as theme music for various WQXR programs, and it is amazing how well they hold up after repeated hearings. In Anderson's case, at least, familiarity breeds added delight.

An English composer whose music has much the same sort of appeal for me is Eric Coates. He too is a superb orchestral colorist, and he shares Anderson's ability to come up time and again with seemingly inconsequential tunes, which quickly give the listener a severe case of can't-get-it-out-of-my-headitis. Not too much of Coates's music has been available on records in America, and I do not know nearly as much of it as I would like, but such gracious little suites as *London, London Again, The Three Elizabeths*, and *Four Centuries* all have their highly attractive moments, as does his charming concert overture "The Merrymakers."

In America we have the three G's of light music: Ferde Grofé, George Gershwin, and Morton Gould. Gould and Gershwin have several points in common: both were, and Gould still *is*, wonderful pianists; both wrote music for films, shows, and the concert hall; both have distinctly American styles, full of buoyancy and exuberance.

Much of Gershwin's most important work was done for the stage, and accordingly is described in the chapter on Musical Theater. The few concert works that come within our purview, however, are scintillating pieces of Americana: *Rhapsody in Blue, An American in Paris, Variations on "I Got Rhythm."* Gershwin once said all music, in fact all art, should be a product of the period in which it is produced, and he wanted his own scores to reflect the spirit of his age, even as those of the old masters had done in earlier times. He was, of course, totally successful. In the pieces just named, the roaring twenties are alive again, ebullient, impudent, and irresistible.

Morton Gould has split his allegiances even more thoroughly than Gershwin. He is a major symphonic conductor, he has made hundreds of transcriptions from both the classical and popular repertoires, he gives lecture-recitals, composes all manner of pieces for films, TV, ballet, and the concert stage, and he generally keeps himself among the busiest musicians in the country today. Gould's style as a symphonist can be severe and quite dissonant, but his music in the lighter vein bubbles along with a wonderfully jaunty spirit, abetted by bright tunes and highly inventive orchestrations. I have always had a particular fondness for *Interplay*, a zesty piano concerto of sorts which borrows the blues and other pseudofolk rhythms, and the *Latin American Symphonette*, with its heady, south-of-the-border lilt.

A fairly high proportion of light orchestral pieces are descriptive in nature, but one man has set up shop as our chief portraitist in sound. Ferde Grofé has sketched profiles of famous Americans (*Knute Rockne, Henry Ford*), captured the vibrant pulsations of the country at work (*Tabloid Suite, Symphony in Steel*), and painted the natural wonders of the land in rich, soaring strokes of instrumental color (*Mississippi Suite, Hudson River Suite*).

The inspiration for his best, and best-known, work dates back about half a century, when Grofé was a young, itinerant pianist, roaming the desert and mountain country of Arizona, playing in hotel bands, vaudeville houses, nickel-a-turn dance halls, and sundry other gathering places of the Western elite. In due course, he fell under the spell of the Grand Canyon. "It became an obsession," he wrote later; "the richness of the land and the rugged optimism of its people had fired my imagination. I was determined to put it all to music someday." That someday was more than a decade coming, but Grofé accomplished what he set out to do—he portrayed the incredibly vast panorama of the Canyon, with its drifting shadows and ever-changing moods. I love the *Grand Canyon Suite*. I know it is corny, and I know it is derivative, and I know it is played to death, and I love it anyway.

Whenever we think of music that is distinctly and uniquely American, we are bound to come around to the March King. John Philip Sousa was an international monarch, of course. At Queen Victoria's sixty-year jubilee celebrations in London, the Regimental Bands struck up a Sousa march, and in Germany, a Sousa tune was played at the dedication of a Wagner monument (some thirty years earlier, Wagner had conned the Philadelphia Exposition out of $5,000 for a perfectly dreadful "American Centennial March," so the turnabout was only poetic justice). Here in the States, no self-respecting parade for the last seventy years or more would have dreamt of stepping off without at least one Sousa march on tap, and for a while Congress debated making "The Stars and Stripes Forever" our national anthem. Sousa's music even sparked a dance fad which pushed the waltz out of favor in America. It turned out you could do a perfect two-step to "Washington Post," and before long, folks were not dancing anything else.

Ironically, Sousa always wanted to write bigger and better things than marches, and though he produced bigger, they were never better. He wrote ten operas, and all sorts of songs, choral pieces, orchestral suites, even a cantata. All are now forgotten, revived as curios once in a while, perhaps, and then allowed to slip gratefully back into oblivion. The march is what Sousa did magnificently, more magnificently than anybody else before him or since. As someone who spent three years struggling through third clarinet parts in an Army band, I can vouch for the fact that really good marches are in shamefully short supply. There are several fine ones by Edwin Franko Goldman, a couple by

Alford (the "Colonel Bogey" man), and some nifty circus marches too, but by and large, the great ones belong to Sousa.

The Waltz and Operetta Tradition

If Sousa ruled undisputedly as the King of the March, there was a bit of a scuffle before the crown settled on the true Waltz King of Vienna. The waltz, as you may know, came to favor over the collective dead bodies of defenders of the public morality, who found it indecent, immodest, scandalous, and otherwise much too enjoyable for comfort. It was, after all, the first dance where the partners actually embraced each other, and as late as 1896 a reformed dancing master, one T. A. Faulkner, published a graphic exposé of the ballroom, that "hotbed of vice, within whose treacherous embrace so many sweet young things have been whirled to perdition." With recommendations like that it was only a matter of time before the waltz became the rage of Europe, and nowhere did it catch on with greater fervor than in the glittering city of Vienna.

Johann Strauss, the elder, was the first Waltz King, and as properly befitting a royal title, it was passed down from father to son (albeit not without quite a struggle on the part of the father). For a while the men were bitter competitors, but by the time the senior Strauss died, in 1849, there was no longer any doubt that Johann Strauss Jr. was the monarch-in-chief. He soon merged his own orchestra with his father's old ensemble, and within a few years had built up a fantastic organization, numbering some two hundred copyists, singers, musicians, assistant conductors, and even press agents. On a busy night Strauss would have three orchestras playing simultaneously at different ballrooms in Vienna, with the Maestro himself merely stopping in for brief personal appearances at each. Waltz King or no Waltz King, Strauss also wrote hundreds of polkas, galops, quadrilles, and polonaises (not to mention sixteen operettas, about which I shall have more to say presently). And behind the ingratiating melodies lie inspiration and craftsmanship of the very first rank. Strauss may have operated within a comparatively limited sphere, but there he reigned supreme.

Although he was one of its most eloquent practitioners, Strauss himself didn't pioneer the operetta form in Vienna. That task fell to Francesco Ezechiele Ermenegildo Cavaliere Suppé Demelli, who quite understandably condensed his name to Franz von Suppé. In 1860 he produced the first of his successful operettas, and many more followed before Strauss began to corner the market effectively about a dozen years later. Little of Suppé's vocal music is heard these days, but you can hardly escape the overtures (nor would you particularly want to do so). "Poet and Peasant," for instance, is a marvelous curtain-raiser and still fun to hear, despite its ritual murder by first-year piano students, and so is "Light Cavalry," without which half the Westerns in Hollywood could never have been made.

As for Strauss himself, he sometimes was a bit ill at ease with the longer, more involved format of the operetta, but at his best he was, as usual, unbeatable. *Die Fledermaus* is a frothy farce, a fast and funny show with more whistleable tunes than anything you will find on Broadway today. Not far behind (musically speaking at least—I have never seen it produced on stage) is another brilliant Strauss creation, *The Gypsy Baron*.

The waltz and operetta tradition that the Strauss family brought to such elegant heights was continued into the twentieth century by several other composers, all operating at a worthy, if necessarily reduced, level of genius. In Paris there was Emil Waldteufel, whose charming "Skaters Waltz" helped earn him the nickname The French Johann Strauss, while in Denmark, Hans Christian Lumbye enticed dancers to famed Tivoli Gardens with a whole raft of tasty tonal bon-bons. He was duly dubbed The Waltz King of the North.

In Vienna itself, the torch was taken by such men as Franz Lehár, Emmerich Kálmán, Oscar Straus, Edmund Eysler, and Robert Stolz, who at the age of eighty-five or so is still going strong. My own favorite among them is Lehár, whose big hit romped into town three days after Christmas in 1905. *The Merry Widow*, of course, has hardly had a day's rest since, and deservedly so. The operetta is not so much fun to see on stage as *Fledermaus* (book trouble, I think the ailment is called), but musically it is every bit as good, with "Vilia" standing among the loveliest songs of all. Lehár also inherited Strauss's mantle in the waltz department, writing such twinkling pieces as the popular "Gold and Silver."

If nineteenth-century Vienna whirled to the graceful rhythms of the waltz, Paris was cavorting to the frenetic beat of the can-can, an escapade Mark Twain once described as "a mixture of shouts, laughter, furious music, gay dresses, bobbing heads, flying arms, and then a grand final riot, with a terrific hubbub and a wild stampede." And what Strauss did for the waltz, Jacques Offenbach did for the can-can: he brought it stage center, gave it cheery tunes to thrive on, and made it the throbbing heartbeat of a fun-loving city. I suppose the best way to enjoy the full flavor of the Offenbach operettas is to hear them in their original form, but I must admit to a personal preference for their enshrinement as songs without words, either in the various overtures, or as the buoyant melodies for Manuel Rosenthal's ballet *Gâité Parisienne*. Rosenthal picked themes from seven Offenbach stage works, and the impudent, saucy tunes, spiced further by the brilliant new orchestrations, seem to evoke perfectly the giddy spirit of La Belle France just about a century ago.

Meanwhile, over in London town, the reluctant team of William S. Gilbert and Arthur Seymour Sullivan was producing the cream of the operetta crop, the pieces that are to the lyric theater what Beethoven's symphonies are to the concert hall. You could write a book on this subject alone (several people have, in fact) without exhausting the fascinating details of this incompatible couple, who tolerated their collaborations as trifles that helped pay the rent, but hoped and expected to be remembered for more important works (in Gilbert's case, some of his seventy plays; in Sullivan's, his cantatas, songs, and his grand opera *Ivanhoe*).

I am not at all a true Savoyard, in the sense of knowing every song or even every opera. Still, a good production of *Mikado*, *Ruddigore*, *Patience*, or any of a half-dozen others never loses its luster for me. The satire of Gilbert's lyrics is remarkably fresh and pungent today (tell members of the Senate that their seats are henceforth subject to competitive examination, and their reactions would undoubtedly be a fair reenactment of the

Act I finale from *Iolanthe*), while Sullivan's music remains as fresh and warmly appealing as ever it was.

Just as Strauss had his disciples in Vienna, the Gilbert and Sullivan syndrome continued for a while after their partnership had collapsed. Sullivan himself teamed up with Basil Hood in 1899 for something called *The Rose of Persia*, and his protégé, Edward German, also wrote some fine pieces for the Savoy Theatre, including the delightful *Merrie England*.

In the 1920's and 1930's Ivor Novello achieved a pleasing, romantic fusion of operetta and show music, and Noel Coward brought the drawing-room comedy to superb musical life with such bitter-sweet concoctions as *Conversation Piece* and (come to think of it) *Bitter Sweet*. I also am enormously partial to Coward singing Coward, and have been since I stumbled, as a teen-ager, upon his recordings of "Mad Dogs and Englishmen" and the slashingly satiric "Don't Let's Be Beastly to the Germans."

In America the operetta influence came to Broadway for a long run, and later to Hollywood, with the vastly popular shows of Victor Herbert, Rudolf Friml and Sigmund Romberg. All three men were European-born (respectively in Ireland, Czechoslovakia and Hungary), concert-trained (Friml toured America as a classical pianist, while Herbert was the conductor of the Pittsburgh Symphony Orchestra for more than five years), and blessed with a gift for melody which really allowed the lyric theater to live up to its billing.

I came to know their works almost exclusively through the movies. *Naughty Marietta* was my first Jeanette MacDonald-Nelson Eddy film, and perhaps for that reason it remains my favorite Herbert score. From Friml I would choose *Rose Marie*, since I saw it in two different versions. Romberg immediately brings to mind such classics as *The Desert Song*, *The Student Prince*, and *The New Moon*.

I must confess that various stage revivals of these and other American operettas have not tempted me into attendance. I find something terribly dated about the plots, the lines, the whole heart-on-sleeve romantic atmosphere, and I much prefer to hear the lovely scores on disc, unencumbered by all the extramusical trappings. It is either that, or stay up and wait for MacDonald and Eddy to come around on the *Late Show*.

Films

The entire subject of movies is another of those vast categories, which necessarily will have to be short-shrifted here. On the other hand, a significant amount of first-rate light music has been cinematically inspired, and I do want to touch briefly on a little of it.

On October 5, 1927, movies cracked the sound barrier. It was at the old Warner's Theater in New York, and the picture was a creaky bit of soap opera, which cast Al Jolson as *The Jazz Singer*. It started out quietly enough—the first several reels were silent—but then Jolson spoke a soundtrack line heard round the world. "You ain't heard nothin' yet, folks," he roared, launching into "Mammy," one of the songs that heralded the beginning of the end of the silent era. Within months the studios were at work on the first all-talkies, and in 1929 MGM came out with the first "100% All Talking! All Singing! All Dancing!" original film musical. This was *Broadway Melody*, a typical backstage romance, with a score by Nacio Herb Brown and Arthur Freed, and it set a pattern for screen extravaganzas that held for more than a quarter of a century.

The vogue for musicals continued in the 1930's, heightened by the spectacular success of the aforementioned MacDonald-Eddy pictures and the equally famous series with Fred Astaire and Ginger Rogers. The latter films were especially rich in original music, since the roster of composers included such masters of the Broadway musical as Kern, Berlin, and the brothers Gershwin. Richard Rodgers is another stalwart of the Great White Way who has contributed songs to Hollywood films throughout the sound era, from "Lover," "Mimi," and "Isn't It Romantic," which dotted the 1932 hit *Love Me Tonight*, on through the two new ballads he wrote (both words and music) for the Hollywood adaptation of *The Sound of Music*.

By the late 1930's and early 1940's Hollywood was turning out musicals as fast as MGM could feed its lion, but gradually the well then began to run dry. Costs were rising, TV competition became a problem, and talent got scarce. Studios just were not willing to chance an original venture; they preferred to shell out huge sums for what they knew were sure things—the screen rights to such Broadway hits as *My Fair Lady* and *Oklahoma*. Outside of Elvis Presley musicals and similar films, there have not been more than a handful of originals in the past decade or so. *Dr. Dolittle* was the only one of consequence in 1967; then we'd have to go back to *Mary Poppins* in 1964; and I can't think of another really good one before that unless we return to *Gigi* in 1958.

A parallel development in the cinematic world has involved what Aaron Copland once called "a small lamp placed beneath the screen to warm it": the background score. Long before the advent of sound composers wrote incidental music—or at the very least, songs—which were played "live" by the local theater pianists. In more affluent houses, of course, this task might be taken over by a virtuoso at the "mighty Wurlitzer organ," or sometimes even by an orchestra of up to thirty players. When the talkies arrived, background music suffered a temporary setback. For one thing the recording techniques were fairly crude, so a ninety-piece orchestra on the soundtrack might not sound any more imposing than our friend at the Wurlitzer; for another, directors were so engrossed with their new task of putting dialogue on film, they seemed to dump in music as an afterthought, with little consideration for quality, or even awareness of the very real potential of music as an adjunct to the screen drama. Max Steiner was one of the first studio composers to change this concept, with his pioneering scores for *King Kong* and *The Informer* (the latter using *leitmotivs* to help with the flashbacks). Others who joined him in converting film music from a craft to a genuine art form were Alfred Newman, Dimitri Tiomkin, Victor Young, Miklós Rózsa, Erich Korngold, and dozens more as well. Most of them were classically trained musicians, and they brought to the movie score a whole new sense of form and proportion.

More recently a new breed of film composer has taken over; men often associated with the jazz idiom, musicians who can combine the melodic suavity of the old school with the modern sounds and tempos of our atomic age. Alex North, Henry Mancini, Ernest Gold—the list is long, and growing every day. Add to it some of the greatly talented composers of Europe—England's John Barry, France's Maurice Jarre, Italy's Riz Ortolani, etc.—and it becomes clear why movie scores (if not the movies themselves) are better than ever.

I have one final set of recommendations. Our discussion has centered almost entirely about the light music of America and England, with sporadic side trips to France and Austria. Obviously, there is much to explore from other lands as well.

From Spain, listen to some of the zarzuelas. These light-hearted stageworks are the Iberian equivalent of Viennese operetta, and they have much the same blend of frothy tunes and eminently danceable rhythms. Even if you do not like singing, there are plenty of nonvocal samplers about, containing fresh and not frequently encountered overtures, intermezzi, and other instrumental extracts.

Tap the wonderfully wide gamut of popular styles in countries around the world: English music hall ditties, French chansons, Neapolitan ballads, Mexican mariachi bands, the moody fados of Portugal, the pseudoswingy pop tunes of Russia.

Seek out concert music in the lighter vein from faraway places, and delve into some of the fascinating specialty items (several such discs are listed in the discography).

The world of light music, in short, knows no boundaries, and the world of enjoyment it can provide is similarly limited only by your own energy and enthusiasm in seeking it.

10

Jazz

JOHN S. WILSON

I KNOW exactly when I became aware of the joy of jazz. It was the day I stole my first record.

The record was "Wolverine Blues" by the Jelly Roll Morton Trio. I had never heard of Jelly Roll Morton, and I was not aware that what his trio played might be considered jazz. All I knew was what I heard when I cranked up our next-door neighbor's phonograph and lowered the needle on that shiny black shellac disc. A pianist played with a romping, stomping gaiety I found irresistible, followed by a low-register clarinet solo which sang with merriment. The piece was full of little asides and breaks, climaxed by a sudden, brief, high piano note, rapidly repeated, which for some reason sent me into ecstacies (it still does, I am still not sure why, and I have no intention of destroying this cobweb of pleasure by examining it too closely).

No one who lived in our neighbor's house ever played this record—at least, not when I was there. It seemed to me that it would be more convenient for everybody if I took the record home where I could play it at will and the neighbors would not have to listen to it over and over again.

I treasured this record because there was something about it that was different from the other records we had around the house—records that ranged from Wagner and Beethoven through Gilbert and Sullivan and Harry Lauder to "Cohen on the Telephone" and "The Two Black Crows" along with such dance bands as those of Joseph C. Smith, Edwin McEnelly, Joe Raymond, and of course, Paul Whiteman. One Paul Whiteman record stood out from the rest and impressed me almost as much as Jelly Roll Morton's "Wolverine Blues." It was "Mississippi Mud." All through it a trumpet kept appearing, played with a crisp, ringing tone and a punching way of phrasing which had an exciting quality I didn't hear in other dance bands, or for that matter, in Wagner or in Gilbert and Sullivan.

It was not until years later that I learned the trumpeter who had caught my ear was Bix Beiderbecke. By that time I had found out I was a jazz fan, and unwittingly, had been one for some time. On records and radio I had been listening to a wide range of what I thought of simply as "pop" music. But of the "pop" music I encountered in this fashion, the things I responded to most strongly were played by Duke Ellington and McKinney's Cotton Pickers and Red Nichols and Bennie Moten (his "Moten Stomp," played on a portable phonograph through a grating coat of sand on a beach all one summer, was another landmark "new sound" to me, like "Wolverine Blues" and "Mississippi Mud").

Discovering, in retrospect, that these were all jazz bands gave me the first indication that my musical interests were moving in a specific direction. Even the technically nonjazz bands that appealed to me then had some underlying jazz colorations —Coon-Sanders Original Kansas City Nighthawks, Ray Noble's inimitable English recording band (its inimitability proven when Noble came to the United States and recorded with an American band), even Guy Lombardo, whose essentially Dixieland orientation was quite apparent in his early records, are examples.

Because I arrived at jazz in this fashion, totally undirected, responding simply to sounds that provided a kind of stimulation unlike my responses to other music, I tend to look on jazz as an emotional vehicle rather than an intellectual one.

Some Background

In its early days, up until World War II, jazz was functional music, an accompaniment for dancing, and on its own, music that was basically entertaining. When jazz was removed from this functional role after World War II and became concert or listening music, an intellectual view of jazz began to take precedence over the emotional reaction. Along with this came a term that puzzles me, and possibly because it puzzles me, disturbs me.

This term, a descriptive phrase which has turned up frequently in writings about jazz during the past decade, is "the serious jazz listener." I'm not sure what it means. It has such a distant, austere sound I have difficulty relating it to the spontaneous, joyous, thoroughly emotional response I have to a really good jazz performance. And I resent the condescension toward us emotional respondents that the term implies.

I am not suggesting that jazz is not to be taken seriously, that it should be dismissed as something trivial. But I do feel that the best jazz performances are those that stir the blood first, the brain cells later. Lift me out of my seat, out of myself, and if I am so inclined, I will go back afterward and find out how you did it.

In any event, there are usually elements in the best jazz performances that simply cannot be dissected and labeled. The unique texture and intonation produced by Duke Ellington's magnificent growl-trumpet specialist, Cootie Williams, is partially a result of the personal chemistry of this man, Cootie Williams. You can isolate and identify certain aspects of his performance—notes, dynamics, manner of attack—but there is always an unidentifiable, unreproduceable X representing the quality that gives a Cootie Williams performance its individuality.

Jazz is the music of individuals, whether they are playing as improvising soloists or as part of an ensemble. Cootie Williams has his own X quality, and when he is sitting in Duke Ellington's orchestra, he is one of several outstanding and inimitable X's—Johnny Hodges on alto saxophone, Harry Carney on baritone saxophone, Lawrence Brown on trombone, the Duke himself at the piano, each of whom thinks, phrases, and sounds like no other musician. Together they produce an orchestral result that defies analysis or reproduction because there are too many X's involved.

As a result of all these X's the phonograph record has played an important role in the development of jazz—a more essential role, I would judge, than in any other type of music.

It is not possible to convey the vital qualities of a jazz performance in written notes, because the essence of jazz lies both in its improvisational nature and in the individual manner of expression within the improvisation. A jazz performance exists in its finished form only in the moment of its creation, when the musicians play it—and they never play it precisely the same way twice.

If the phonograph record had not come along, jazz would have had no permanence. It originated as a form of urban folk-pop music, played by and for a submerged minority: the Negro. The phonograph record provided both a vehicle for reporting a jazz performance and a means of lifting it beyond its ghetto origins to an audience which otherwise might never have become aware of it.

A Thumbnail History

Until jazz was first recorded in 1917 (by the Original Dixieland Jazz Band, a group of white musicians from New Orleans who were inspired by New Orleans Negro bands), it had apparently gone through relatively little change since it had taken shape as an identifiable musical form about twenty years earlier. But once jazz was recorded, interest in it spread far beyond the Negro neighborhoods of New Orleans, Chicago, New York, St. Louis, Memphis, and Kansas City, where it had its roots.

It reached out to such a distant spot as Ogden, Utah, where young Red Nichols, cornetist son of a traditional bandmaster, tried to emulate Nick LaRocca, the cornetist on the ODJB records. In Davenport, Iowa, Bix Beiderbecke heard the same records and fell under the same influence. And when Beiderbecke, having evolved his own musical personality, began making records, Nichols's playing began to reflect what he heard in Beiderbecke on top of the basic LaRocca inspiration from which both musicians worked.

Through records this chain effect has continued ever since, providing a constant stream of readily available examples for fledgling jazzmen, and whenever a strong and provocative musical personality appears—a Charlie Parker, a Charlie Christian, an Ornette Coleman—the whole body of jazz moves quickly in new directions indicated by these seminal personalities. As a result, the character of jazz has changed quite drastically and frequently since jazz became available on records.

In the twenties, the first recorded decade of jazz, it moved out of the small-group (six to seven pieces) ensemble improvisation which had characterized it until then, splitting in two directions: small groups featuring virtuoso solo improvisation; and orchestrated big-band (thirteen to fourteen pieces) performances, which allowed for short improvised solos. Louis Armstrong was the catalytic figure in the first category, while Fletcher Henderson's orchestra was the groundbreaker in the second.

The thirties were the decade of the big bands, the swing bands, epitomized by Benny Goodman's orchestra. In the forties came the be-bop revolution, led by Charlie Parker and Dizzy Gillespie. New harmonic and rhythmic approaches to jazz were introduced, and small groups returned to a dominant position.

The fifties were characterized by various forms of regression —"cool" jazz, a subdued, withdrawn, return-to-the-womb type of expression, as well as a search for roots. This search led some musicians (Dave Brubeck, John Lewis of the Modern Jazz Quartet) to an exploration of the jazz uses of traditional European musical forms, while others (Horace Silver, Art Blakey, Cannonball Adderley) emphasized the basic blues aspects of jazz, playing what came to be known as "soul jazz."

Freedom has been the focal point of jazz in the sixties—freedom in one degree or another from the traditional disciplines both of jazz and of Western music in general. Ornette

Coleman, John Coltrane, and Cecil Taylor have been in the forefront of these innovations.

Despite these constant changes in the immediate directions of jazz, the music has developed lines of continuity. A musician who reached maturity in one decade usually continued to reflect the jazz mannerisms of that decade for the rest of his career. In the 1960's Louis Armstrong was still a representative of the jazz of the twenties, Benny Goodman continued to play in the style of the thirties, and Dizzy Gillespie reflected the be-bop mannerisms of the forties. In all of these cases, however, as in the cases of most other jazzmen, the passage of time has tempered the playing to some extent. The real thing—Armstrong in the twenties, Goodman in the thirties, Gillespie in the forties—can still be heard on records along with the work of other musicians, who have not survived so long. Records, in fact, carry in their grooves almost the entire history and development of jazz.

Learning to Listen to Jazz

Faced with this opportunity to hear the whole historical panorama of jazz, where should one start? At the beginning— that is, the recorded beginning with the first jazz records by the Original Dixieland Jazz Band?

It might seem logical but I would not recommend it. The contemporary ear must first become adjusted both to the musical style of the Original Dixieland Jazz Band and to the limitations of its acoustical discs.

The best beginning, I think, is the unintentional one—the one in which you hear something that appeals to you, which turns out to be jazz. The next best thing is a reasonable approximation of that situation: Start with whatever jazz you have heard that rouses a responsive interest on your part. This gives you a focal point from which to expand.

Let us say you have heard something by Miles Davis that caught your fancy. You like the pungent tone of his trumpet, and you respond to the attack of his group. This could provide you with an introduction to the avant-garde jazz of the sixties, since Davis's group, as of 1968, was touching the edges of that jazz style. It might lead you to the Third Stream music of the midfifties, through Davis's recordings of big band arrangements by Gil Evans. Or it could take you to the "cool" jazz of the early fifties, which was given identification by an octet Davis led.

If you start here, or anywhere, it is the opening door to adventure. Once you have made some form of personal contact, once you have had a positive reaction of your own, then you are on your way.

You are on your way provided you do not allow yourself to become stuck in the rut of your first discovery. You miss the point completely if you settle for the first jazz sounds you hear, and say, "This is it. I like it. I'm a jazz fan."

You are not a jazz fan yet. There is still a lot more to be discovered. Jazz is a music of constant stimulations. It can provide excitement on a variety of levels, from simple, direct, elementary rhythmic pulsation to highly sophisticated responses.

From whatever your starting point, you can, with the help of recordings, fill in the full panorama. The reason I do not suggest that you start at the recorded beginning, with the Original Dixieland Jazz Band, is the ear adjustments that must be made first. Once you have heard Dixieland recorded by a good band, under more advanced recording circumstances than those primitive beginnings in 1917, you can, quite literally, *hear* much more in the Original Dixieland Jazz Band's 1917 recordings than if you try to listen to them with no preparation.

An ideal introduction is *The Great 16* by Muggsy Spanier and His Ragtime Band (RCA Victor LPM 1295), even though this collection of recordings, made in 1939, was "enhanced" when it was transferred to LP—"enhanced" being an RCA Victor promotional term that means "distorted by the addition of echo." Spanier's band plays many of the very same tunes that were created and recorded by the Original Dixieland Jazz Band, which have become standards of the Dixieland repertory—"At the Jazz Band Ball," "Eccentric," "Bluin' the Blues," and others. In the Spanier versions the basic tune can be heard clearly, and the relationships of the lines of cornet, clarinet, and trombone are quite apparent.

Going from this to the ODJB recordings of the same tunes, you are much more likely to be able to follow what is happening than if you approach the Original Dixieland Jazz Band with nothing to guide you. Superficially, the Original Dixieland Jazz Band recordings might seem to be shrill and repetitious (but undeniably energetic). But if your ear can penetrate beyond the limitations of the recording, if it is aware of the lines the various instruments are taking (all of which is made explicit in the Spanier recordings), then you are much better prepared to absorb early jazz in its original reproductions.

And it is worth doing. The Spanier recordings are good representations of this type of music twenty years after the Original Dixieland Jazz Band made its mark. In fact they have a quality that has been caught by no other group before or since (largely due to Muggsy Spanier's individual X as a jazz musician). Even so, they do not have the same special spark given off by the Original Dixieland Jazz Band. They do not have Larry Shields's singing clarinet (another X quality) or Nick LaRocca's soaring cornet (more X). This differentiation is repeated time and time again in the course of jazz history. The same tunes are played repeatedly by various groups. Entire arrangements may be copied, but the final result is always different. It may be equal. It may even be better. But it is never the same.

Once your ear can supply some of the things that were left out by the acoustical recording system (which prevailed until the late 1920's), you can appreciate the distinctive spirit that enlivened the Original Dixieland Jazz Band. You can sense the drive and depth of King Oliver's Creole Jazz Band, which in recordings made during 1922 and 1923, provided the recorded epitome of the basic New Orleans ensemble jazz style.

Oliver's band, which played and recorded in Chicago, was made up of the cream of New Orleans musicians, including twenty-two-year-old Louis Armstrong on second cornet (Oliver also played cornet). In this context Armstrong can be heard as one of several sparkling elements—as an occasional lead cornetist, in slashing duets with Oliver, and with the additional stimulus of Johnny Dodds's wry and plaintive clarinet.

But the full stature of Armstrong as a creative jazzman was revealed in a series of records by his Hot Five and Hot Seven (recording groups with somewhat varying personnel), made between 1925 and 1929. If you listen to these recordings in chronological sequence—or even just highlights of the series in sequence—you can hear the sound of jazz changing.

The early recordings in this series reflect the traditional ensemble style that had been characteristic of Oliver's band. But as the series moves along, Armstrong's brilliance as a virtuoso soloist steadily takes command. The early ensemble performances change to a series of solos in which Dodds on clarinet, Kid Ory on trombone, and Armstrong, each have equal opportunities. And soon the whole object is to give Armstrong as much of the three-minute time limit of a 78-rpm disc as possible. Thus we hear him in a dazzling display of runs and breaks on "Cornet Chop Suey," his slow, insistent build-up during "Hear Me Talkin' to You," and the incredible excursions he takes on "Potato Head Blues." Tallulah Bankhead is reputed to have survived a long run on Broadway in a revival of *Private Lives* (Miss Bankhead, despite her flamboyant reputation, was not used to long runs), only because she kept Armstrong's record of "Potato Head Blues" spinning on a phonograph in her dressing room.

Armstrong's performances on these records changed the direction of jazz. This music, which had been identified until then with ensemble improvisation, was redirected toward solo improvisation as a result of his virtuosity, a direction that jazz was to follow with increasing concentration for the next forty years.

As a rule the early virtuosos were, like Armstrong, cornetists or trumpeters—Bix Beiderbecke, Red Nichols, and Joe Smith of Fletcher Henderson's band, who was blues singer Bessie Smith's favorite accompanist.

But the only jazz musician whose work in the twenties left as lasting an impression as Armstrong's was Jelly Roll Morton, a pianist, composer, and idea man whose musical conception was so personal, it began and ended with him. Morton's Red Hot Peppers, a group that recorded between 1926 and 1930, paralleled Armstrong's Hot Five and Hot Seven chronologically, and was almost as influential. Morton, a pianist, did not inspire followers, stylistically, as Armstrong did on cornet. Morton's main impact was in bringing an orchestral style to jazz.

His Red Hot Peppers was in the tradition of the small jazz ensemble, seven or eight pieces at most. But instead of turning every man loose on his own, Morton played his musicians as though they were the keyboard of his piano. The Red Hot Peppers were an extension of his own distinctively personal approach to the piano—an orchestration of his use of breaks, fills, runs, and phrasing. He knew precisely what he wanted, and dealing with musicians who were more accustomed to ad libbing than reading, he often had difficulty bending them to his will ("I just want you to play those little black dots," he insisted to a reluctant Sidney Bechet, whose natural inclination was to close his eyes and let his fingers find their own way on his soprano saxophone).

Depending on whom he had at his disposal at his recording sessions, Morton's directions sometimes worked and sometimes did not. When they did, the result was some of the most delightfully inventive jazz recordings ever made by a small group.

By the time Morton made these recordings, he was reaching the peak of a career as a wandering pianist whose mixture of arrogance and talent had lost him at least as many opportunities as it had won. In the Red Hot Peppers recordings he was able to bring together all his capabilities as performer and organizer. At exactly the same time a younger, less experienced pianist, Duke Ellington, was also beginning to create in orchestral terms in much the same way Morton did with his Red Hot Peppers.

Ellington's orchestral approach differed from Morton's in that he worked with larger groups—twelve or thirteen pieces in the early stages and on up to twenty or so in later periods. It also differed from Morton's in that it was less self-centered, and as a result, became threaded with a variety of dazzling colors. Morton's orchestrations were simply an extension of himself. A Morton sideman, given a solo spot, could inject some of his own musical personality into his solo, but he did it within limitations dictated by Morton.

Ellington, on the other hand, built an orchestral style that was based on the distinctive personal sounds of the musicians in his band (the fact that he was able to keep an unusually stable personnel in his band between 1927 and 1942 had a great deal to do with the establishment of an Ellington "sound"). The growl-trumpet style originally brought to the band by Bubber Miley and later carried on by Cootie Williams and Ray Nance; the adaptation of this style to the trombone by Joe Nanton, who was justifiably known as Tricky Sam, since none of his successors in the band since his death in 1944 have had his creative touch with this strange musical tool; the peculiar talent of Johnny Hodges for bending and stretching notes on his alto saxophone; the imaginative use of half-valve positions on cornet by Rex Stewart; the soaring lyricism achieved by Lawrence Brown on trombone; the superb, visceral power in Harry Carney's baritone saxophone; the dark, flowing warmth in Barney Bigard's clarinet—all these and other very individual sounds are the elements out of which Ellington has woven an orchestral style that has taken on an inimitable identity. Ellington is the pianist in the band, and as pianist he contributes his own distinctive sound. But his main instrument, as it was pointed out early in his career, is not the piano—it is his orchestra.

Yet it was not Ellington who made the transition in jazz from the small group to the big band. That was accomplished by Fletcher Henderson's orchestra. Henderson was a pianist with good connections in the New York recording world of the early twenties. He had a band which was primarily a dance band, but because it worked regularly both in dance halls (primarily Roseland Ballroom) and on a variety of recording jobs (his musicians frequently backed Bessie Smith and other blues singers on records), he could get and hold very good musicians. In 1924 Henderson lured Louis Armstrong away from Chicago, where he had been playing with King Oliver.

In the course of a year spent in Henderson's trumpet section, Armstrong helped to transform a dance band into a jazz band. He did it mostly by example and inspiration (Henderson's men were largely Easterners who had not had close contact with the New Orleans-based mainstream of jazz until they met Armstrong) and through the presence of some musicians who were on the verge of blossoming. Coleman Hawkins, for example, can be heard on Henderson's 1923 and 1924 records playing a tenor saxophone that runs a gamut from ordinary to utterly corny, while on the 1926 and 1927 records he has become the first vital and influential tenor saxophonist in jazz.

The enlargement of jazz from its early small-group limitations to big bands involving sections of saxophones and brass was made possible by Henderson's alto saxophonist and arranger, Don Redman, a conservatory-trained musician at a time when this kind of background was rare in jazz. Redman was able to write arrangements that permitted the jazz feeling of a small group to be transformed into a big-band context, though it took a little while for this to become apparent. Henderson's musicians, good as they were, did not begin to translate Redman's arrangements into really viable jazz terms until Armstrong's arrival gave the band a strong jazz voice and an equally strong jazz direction.

The Henderson band, which hit its stride in 1925, set the pattern for big jazz bands, a pattern that dominated jazz in the 1930's and carried on until the end of World War II. Benny Goodman's success in the midthirties—his acclamation as King of Swing and the subsequent arrival of the Swing Era—came very directly from Fletcher Henderson's band because Goodman's initial successes were made with arrangements that had been recorded years earlier by Henderson (this happened because Henderson, in 1935, was a staff arranger for Goodman). You can still rouse some strong arguments about the relative merits of the Henderson and Goodman recordings of such Henderson arrangements as "King Porter Stomp" and "Down South Camp Meeting." Henderson's performances are relatively rough and casual, built on striking solos. Goodman's have occasional solo moments, but their outstanding qualities are polish and smoothness. As a rule the newcomer to jazz prefers the clean impact of the Goodman versions, but as you get deeper into the music, the freewheeling Henderson records may take precedence. And there comes a time, I find, when one can appreciate the special merits of both approaches.

Even though Goodman won public acclaim as the King of Swing, the exemplification of swing in the Swing Era was provided by Count Basie's band, a loose, hungry, and tremendously exciting group when it first came out of Kansas City in 1936.

This was a band that played largely by instinct. There was no money to pay for arrangements, and the band relied on "head" arrangements (extemporized arrangements) based on the blues and built on riffs created on the bandstand. The core of this band was a remarkable rhythm section (Basie, piano; Freddie Green, guitar; Walter Page, bass; Jo Jones, drums), which provided a flowing sense of pulsation as opposed to the heavy, solid, 4/4 beat of other bands of that day.

The Basie rhythm section (and such Basie sidemen as saxophonist Lester Young) formed an important part of the transition from Swing Era jazz to the be-bop style of the 1940's. The easy flow of Basie's rhythm—one step removed from the strict, relatively static beat that preceded it—led in turn to a looser, more varied type of drumming, which came in with be-bop and has continued to be characteristic of jazz ever since.

This change in rhythm, which took place during and just after World War II, is an important dividing line in gauging responses to jazz. The whole aspect of jazz changed at this time. It changed from dance music to listening music. Solo improvisations, which had previously been based on melody, now used chord patterns as a basis. Harmonic structures became more complex. All these aspects of the new jazz of the forties set up barriers for the old jazz listeners—barriers that were intensified by the fact that most of these old listeners were cut off from jazz for three or four years while they served in World War II and came back to civilian life unaware that jazz had changed while they were gone.

At first it seemed to be the lack of traditional "melody" in be-bop that bothered the old listeners (there was melody but it was a new, nervous kind of melody). But the real source of the old listeners' problem with be-bop was, I think, the new approach to rhythm. For the same reason, listeners who have picked up jazz since World War II are apt to find the older jazz, of the Swing Era and before, difficult to appreciate. They are disturbed by rhythm to which they do not respond naturally.

This difference was brought home to me during a series of uninhibited jazz seminars I conducted at the University of Hawaii for several weeks in 1966. The participants—undergraduates and graduate students, some of them in their early thirties—were interested in exploring the various periods of jazz. Their curiosity took them into every decade, but their interest usually flagged when examples from the pre-World War II period were played. Our discussions of why this should be so invariably pointed to the rhythm. To them the rhythm of Benny Goodman's band, which had stirred a generation of youngsters to mad exhilaration, was utterly leaden. They heard it with different ears.

This is one of the challenges that keeps cropping up in jazz. It constantly demands that its listeners have new ears—a willingness to listen to "different" sounds. It is a challenge not all those who have considered themselves jazz fans are willing to meet. The change from ensemble improvisation to an emphasis on soloists, in the twenties, lost some early jazz followers, who would not go along with the new move ("It's not jazz," they said). The appearance of big bands playing jazz disturbed others ("A big band can't play jazz," they said). A really violent upheaval was caused by the arrival of be-bop ("That's got nothing to do with jazz," said the objectors). Every step along the way loses somebody who thought of himself as a jazz fan—the European influences introduced in the 1950's by the Modern Jazz Quartet and Gunther Schuller's Third Stream of music ("That's not jazz"), or the "new thing" of Ornette Coleman in the early sixties ("That's not jazz"), or the free expression, later in the sixties, of Archie Shepp and Albert Ayler ("That's not jazz").

Maybe it is not jazz. Or maybe it is. Or maybe it does not matter, particularly since *jazz*, as a term, has never been pinned down to anyone's satisfaction. (Duke Ellington, for example, does not consider what he plays to be "jazz"—he calls it music.)

But all this is part of the fun of listening to what is, for one reason or another, categorized as jazz. This is a maverick's area. This is the territory for people who don't go by the rules. It was created by musicians who did not know the rules. Even though, down through the years, it has developed traditions of its own, which tend to solidify into rules, the excitement continues to be created by those who are ignoring the rules.

So Charlie Parker and Dizzy Gillespie found their own ways into what became known as be-bop in the forties. To the Jazz

Establishment they were pretty shocking. But they anticipated the musical temper of their times, and the tight, jabbing lines they played are now part of the jazz mainstream. The cycle turned, and in 1960 we find Dizzy Gillespie, the radical of the be-bop era, frowning on the newly arrived, radical Ornette Coleman, who was playing his own set of shocking sounds, and asking, "Is he kidding?" Within five years Ornette Coleman's ideas had joined Gillespie's in the jazz mainstream.

The process of action and reaction goes on constantly in jazz, contributing to its mobility and to its quicksilver elusiveness. Be-bop was a reaction to the apparent (to the be-boppers) dead end at which the swing bands had arrived. The reaction to the nervous agitation of the boppers was "cool" jazz, a dispassionate, vibratoless, withdrawn type of music exemplified by a Miles Davis "Nonet" of 1948 and 1949, which in its style and personnel forecast the influences of jazz in the fifties. The group included Gerry Mulligan, John Lewis (who was to become musical director and pianist of the Modern Jazz Quartet), and Gunther Schuller (the propagator of the idea that there could be a Third Stream of music flowing between European "classical" music and jazz). Gil Evans was the primary arranger for the group. After a lapse of more than six years Evans wrote and conducted some big-band arrangements for Davis (*Miles Ahead*, Columbia CL 1041; CS 8633) which placed the trumpeter in a setting that brought out his lyrical brilliance and helped to establish his present stature in jazz.

During the fifties, jazz—cool, subdued, fumbling back toward its roots—tended to reflect the cautious blandness that affected American life in general in those McCarthy-influenced years. There were a few adventurers—notably Charlie Mingus, the bassist, an individualist who got some attention, and Cecil Taylor, the pianist, a groundbreaker who got none. But it was largely a period of marking time between the explosions of the be-boppers in the forties and the even louder explosions of the free-formites in the sixties.

The major figure who rose in these later years was John Coltrane, a saxophonist who had been around all through the fifties. At first he appeared on the fringes as a capable member of such groups as Johnny Hodges's band, Miles Davis's, and

Thelonious Monk's. Then, starting in 1960, he became the prickly and exploratory leader of his own group, moving rapidly from postbop explorations to an examination of Indian-oriented ideas (played on the soprano saxophone), and just before his death in 1967, moving into the free-form company of Archie Shepp and Pharoah Sanders.

In Coltrane's playing, particularly his last work, I find the feeling of wonder and surprise I first encountered on Jelly Roll Morton's "Wolverine Blues." It is still, to me, the most exciting thing about jazz. When you have listened to jazz over a long period, there are inevitably old, familiar sounds for which you have a very warm feeling. Those sounds are heard now invariably on records, because they are old sounds. Jazz—live jazz—is music of immediacy. You will never hear live jazz today the way it was played yesterday—even by the musicians who played it yesterday. The sense of immediacy will not allow it. When a jazz muscian delves into his past, you will either hear a tired version of something that once had life, or if you and the musician are both lucky, a new, immediate version which offers new wonders and new surprises—something that Duke Ellington, above all others, seems consistently able to do when he reexamines his past successes.

Jazz survives because it continues to be full of these wonders and surprises, whether they are provided by the remarkably varied virtuosity shown by John Coltrane on one of his last LP's, *Kulu Se Mama* (Impulse S 9106), by Erroll Garner remembering tunes he composed twenty years earlier in his 1967 recording, *That's My Kick* (MGM S 4463), or by Wild Bill Davison, showing that the vital juices of a basic but exciting cornet style need never dry up, on *Blowin' Wild* (Jazzology 18).

11

Folk Music

ROBERT SHERMAN

Girls and Folk Music began to interest me at just about the same time, and for some strange reason I have been partial to both ever since. It all began in 1946 or so, when I took my very first full-fledged evening date to my very first hootenanny. I did not know exactly what a hootenanny was then (I'm not sure I do yet), but according to the ad in the paper, it had something to do with singing and it cost only fifty cents. That was an unbeatable combination.

It turned out, musically speaking at least, to be an unbeatable evening too. A number of people I had never heard of got up and sang a number of songs I had never heard, and by the time they sat down again, I was hooked. At intermission I signed up as a member of a new folk-song organization called Peoples Songs, and when the show was over, I spent the wildly extravagant sum of seventy-five cents for a recording by one of the performers who had particularly thrilled me. My poor date had to go without an ice-cream soda that night, but I returned home in an advanced state of euphoria, clutching my membership receipt, my record, and the knowledge that I had stumbled upon a whole new world of music. I still have that 10-inch, 78-rpm disc, by the way. It is a triple header, with Pete Seeger singing "T for Texas," "Keep My Skillet Good and Greasy," and the story-song-with-banjo that was only the most sensational thing I had ever heard in my life, "The Cumberland Mountain Bear Chase."

At this distance in time I cannot say for sure just what excited me so much about folk music. I like to think I was perceptive enough to recognize the more substantial nature of the tunes and the more genuine emotion of the lyrics, as compared with much of the claptrap being spewed out by Tin Pan Alley. I doubt it, though. I suspect it was the vitality of the performers that swept me along. They sang with an infectious sense of joy, a high-spirited exuberance which gave the music a special impact quite apart from its intrinsic merit. There was also something vastly intoxicating about the way in which the audience was part of that music. I was much too shy to sing along myself, but even so, I couldn't help sharing in the electricity flowing so generously back and forth between the folks on stage and those in the hall.

At any rate I started going to hootenannies as often as I could, I became a charter member of the Pete Seeger Fan Club, and I practiced yelling for the "Cumberland Mountain Bear Chase" until I could usually outshout any other encore-seeker in the house.

It was another struggling young balladeer who administered the two-punch to Seeger's one, and completed my wholehearted conversion to folk music—Oscar Brand. One day he came down to my history class at Stuyvesant High School in New York City to sing American folk songs and explain how they had grown out of various episodes in the country's development. It was a great topic (I should know—I used it, in various disguises, for three different term papers in college), and it fired my enthusiasm to new heights. The very idea that something I liked so much could be both Worthwhile and Educational at the same time was folk music to my ears. I do not know about warm puppies, but happiness for me that day was walking my new hero back to the Lexington Avenue Subway, and listening entranced to him talk about his experiences as a minstrel. Needless to say I became a charter member of the Oscar Brand Fan Club forthwith (Pete, forgive me!), and from that date forward, woe betide the villain who came between me and Oscar's regular Sunday night radio show on WNYC.

There was an amusing sidelight to that radio business. Usually Oscar did his show from a small studio, but once a year he would move it to an auditorium and have an audience. Naturally I wrote for tickets, but then, suspecting they would be scarce, I cajoled my mother into sending away for an extra set, just in case. She is a concert pianist, and she used her professional name. Well, I got a form letter back: sorry, no room, try again next year. And Mother? She received a warm, personal note from Oscar, saying how pleased he was that so distinguished a musician appreciated his work, and that of course she could have the tickets and wouldn't she please come backstage afterward and say hello. So, prepared for the worst, Mother reluctantly went with me to a folk concert for the first time in her life. What is more, she enjoyed herself thoroughly (except for complaining that one of the guest singers was off-key), and was able to meet and congratulate Oscar with a clear conscience.

I started drifting away from the hootenannies in the late 1940's, mainly because many of them were becoming political rallies more than songfests, but my interest in folk music continued unabated. I sought out the occasional concerts given in New York by such (then) little-known performers as Josh White, Richard Dyer-Bennet, and Burl Ives, and I bought their recordings on such long-extinct labels as Asch, Charter, and Musicraft. Looking back on it now, I feel we owe a tremendous debt of gratitude to these crusading minstrels who spread the gospel of folk music long before it was either fashionable or profitable to do so. The late Carl Sandburg was another of those valued pioneers; so was John Jacob Niles, who still has a remarkable penchant for writing songs that turn into public-domain folk material almost before the first ASCAP check arrives (he has quietly composed many of our most beautiful "traditional" ballads, including "Black Is the Color," "I Wonder as I Wander," and dozens more). On the distaff side there were Susan Reed, Hally Wood, and Betty Sanders, all of whom have more or less retired now, and Jean Ritchie, who is still a vital personality on the folk scene.

I came to other, more international loves in various ways: Russian music, because our family had a friend in the Don Cossack Choir, and we kept getting free tickets; Welsh music because the New York University Glee Club had a language coach who had been to Wales, and we consequently sang a whole group of Welsh songs; South African music because I developed a violent crush on Miranda and kept going to Marais and Miranda concerts.

I must confess that the music part of folk music always interested me more than the folk. I sat in on one of Henry Cowell's courses on ethnic folk music at the New School, but somehow I could not work up any real enthusiasm for analytical comparisons of different versions of "Barbara Allen." I felt vaguely guilty about not being more fascinated by the field recordings from the Library of Congress and a host of other authentic performances, but unquestionably I preferred the more professional approach. Perhaps because I came to love folk music from the outside, as it were, rather than growing up with it as part of my own background and environment, I wanted a little showmanship with my songs, a certain basic level of refinement.

Now I certainly do not mean to imply that I could not—and do not—appreciate the earthy wit of someone like Woody Guthrie or the gravelly nonvoice of someone like Leadbelly. These men, though, were more than just authentic singers—they were born entertainers! Music was as natural to them as breathing; it reflected their whole life and gave it meaning, and their songs came to an audience imbued with the spark of their very special genius.

Nor do I want to suggest even remotely that ethnic recordings are oddball items, of concern only to the folk scholar. Nothing could be farther from the truth. It is often intriguing to compare an original version of a song with its transfiguration by a professional balladeer, and sometimes you will run across a farmer or a coal miner who sings with more spirit and musicality than half the recitalists at Carnegie Hall. By and large, though, these unpolished, roughhewn, sometimes primitively recorded discs are an acquired taste, and the beginning folk *aficionado* will do better to cast his listening lot with the professionals.

Again, and at the risk of belaboring the point, let me emphasize that there is nothing shameful about being a "professional" folk singer. Purists will argue the issue (and do, incessantly), but a balladeer, as Theodore Bikel once pointed out, is a storyteller, and it is hardly necessary for him to live the story he tells. You do not have to be a cowboy to sing a Western song, or a sailing man to shout a shanty. You do not need to be in love to whisper a love song (although, come to think of it, it might help at that), or be miserable to sing the blues. I grant that the performance of a blues singer with a hefty recording contract in his pocket will be quite different from the mournful wail of a starved-out sharecropper, but that is not to say that it must necessarily be worse.

The medieval troubador—the journeyman minstrel who literally sang for his suppers—was just this kind of storyteller. He did not fight the battles himself, or rescue the damsels or topple the kings, but he made up ballads about those who did, and he sang them just as entertainingly and as beautifully as he could.

So it is, I feel, with the Pete Seegers and the Oscar Brands and the Richard Dyer-Bennets. They are singers of folk songs rather than authentic folksingers, and in this lies their greatest strength. They can sing of many lands, in many styles, even in many languages, and since they are masters of their trade, be convincing in all of them. By combining sincerity and showmanship, they not only capture the essence of the music they sing but convey it glowingly to an audience.

So far as I am concerned, it is to these professionals that we owe the present high level of interest in folk music all over America. By showing that folk songs can be fun, they kindled a new awareness of our treasury of traditional music. By showing that folk songs can be popular, they removed the ballad from its rather suspect position as the darling of small, arty cliques in a few big cities. By showing that folk songs can earn their purveyors a fair number of coins of the realm, they paved the way for the incredible revival that swept the country in the 1950's and 1960's. Thanks largely to their efforts and accomplishments, folk music—which very nearly was a casualty of our ultramodern, ultrasophisticated society—made a dramatic comeback, and now gives every evidence of being here to stay.

The Revival

It is not easy to pinpoint any one person or event as having sparked this great revival, but certainly it would not be far wrong to suggest that the die was cast on the day four modern minstrels decided to form a singing group. They were my old idol Pete Seeger, Ronnie Gilbert, Fred Hellerman, and a rumbling-voiced ex-preacher named Lee Hays, and they called themselves the Weavers. Somehow the Weavers crystallized for me all the things I like best about folk music—the freshness, vitality, humor, depth of feeling and the spontaneous give-and-take among the performers and between performers and audience. I had heard each Weaver sing many times before at various hootenannies, but their work as a team was a revelation.

I remember cheering myself hoarse at their first Town Hall concert. "Wimoweh," a pulsing South African chant, promptly pushed out "The Bear Chase" as my all-time favorite number, and a meltingly beautiful Indonesian lullaby called "Suliram" moved into second place. I liked "Goodnight Irene" so much I even broke down and sang along.

This was in 1949, I believe, and by the following year, something astounding had happened. The Weavers' recordings of "Goodnight Irene" and an Israeli hora called "Tzena Tzena" were back-to-back best sellers, edging out such immortal pop items as "The Thing" and "Music, Music, Music." Folk songs on the Hit Parade! This was an incredible development, quite as inconceivable as jazz at the Philharmonic (this was Before Bernstein, of course), and yet, there it was. From that point the American folk renaissance was on in earnest.

Significantly, if not surprisingly, those early recordings were not really representative of the Weavers' art in actual performance. The big recording companies were scared out of their collective wits by the term *folk music,* and decreed that it must be made as unfolksy as possible in order to get folks to listen to it. The Weavers thus were saddled with flashy arrangements, added choirs, sometimes even jazz-band accompaniments. ("Yours truly has made a lot of records I cannot bear listening to," wrote Pete Seeger a few years ago, "but some of the worst were those which were made under pressure to turn out pop hits.") And yet, despite (or, who knows? because of) those atrocious trimmings, the records sold, and millions of people suddenly were introduced to this strange new music form called folk.

What the Weavers started, other groups and solo singers helped continue. A fellow named Harry Belafonte came along with his sensuous voice and galvanic stage presence, and there were millions of new converts. It was by choice that Belafonte used rich, cleverly sophisticated choral and orchestral backdrops. He never played an instrument because he wanted his hands free to act out his songs and help make his performance a unified theatrical experience. You may like his style or find it oppressively fussy (different Belafonte recordings have led me to each of those conclusions), but there is no denying its impact. Belafonte brought the Calypso craze to America almost singlehandedly, and he went on to place spirituals, blues, even lullabies on the top of the pop charts.

Then, in 1959, the Kingston Trio, a collegiate group that used ballads as a jumping-off point for semipop song stylings, recorded a song called "Tom Dooley," and the simmering folk revival exploded full force. It was just one band out of the dozen on a long-playing disc, but after a few months it caught on, zoomed to overnight popularity, and quickly became a public nuisance. Its syncopated rhythms came blaring out of every jukebox, every record shop, every top-ten radio station. "Tom Dooley Fan Clubs" sprang up in every state (even though the real-life Tom was long since dead and buried) and pilgrimages were undertaken to visit his tomb. The whole affair was the subject of long spreads in the major magazines, and by the end of the year the Kingstons—totally unknown a few months earlier—found themselves the most sought after entertainers in the land.

Far more meaningful than the personal success of the Trio, of course, was the fact that into the spotlight with the group went their folk songs. Dozens of other young performers, smelling gold in them thar ballads, hastened to work the same rich vein. There came the Travelers Three and the Brothers Four, the

Journeymen and the Highwaymen, the Raftsmen and the Shantymen, until the art of folk singing was all but submerged in the swoosh of an arriving fad.

The Nineteen Sixties

To speak of a folk fad is to project a basic contradiction in terms. Traditional music, after all, suggests longevity, while a fad, by definition, is a passing fancy. What happened in the 1960's, though, was far more than the pressing of traditional music into one particular mold; it was its use as a catalyst, a generating force for a long succession of musical vogues. When the craze for folk groups subsided, there was an upsurge of interest in gospel singing. Then came blue-grass music (which Alan Lomax once described as a sort of Southern mountain Dixieland), and the even more jazz-influenced Jug Band music. Joan Baez started what amounted to a cult with her pure soprano, and her stark, intensely concentrated singing. Bob Dylan came along and spawned a budding new crop of protest and topical ballad writers. Lately the pop trends have sped off in still other folk-oriented directions: folk-rock, soul-folk, folk-jazz.

One glorious truth has emerged from all this: Folk music has had, does have, and presumably always will have the resilience to survive both fad and faction. It may be a farfetched analogy, but I cannot help thinking of all the feverish pop-folk activity over the past few years in terms of the fabled Nile River floods. It came on in a rush, with a huge wave that inundated what we might call the heartland of true folk expression. As the swirling currents receded, the trash and trivia washed away with them, but some of the more worthy elements remained, enriching and revitalizing the old traditions. There also was left behind a more fertile soil of receptivity to folk music. People who had been attracted by the surface glitter of the pop trimmings stayed on to enjoy the deeper satisfactions of the folk music at its core. Sure, there were a lot of horrors perpetrated in the name of folk music, but on balance it certainly would seem that the pop interplay has been a good thing. The veteran minstrels have won a host of new admirers, and the crusading newcomers—both singers and songwriters—have given the decade one of the most prolific folksong harvests in history.

The "New" Folk Music

It might not be amiss to dispense a few thoughts on this pesky subject of "new" folk songs. Are we not again dealing in mutually exclusive terms? How can any song bearing a 1967 copyright be called a folk song? That is a good question. In fact, it is a good two questions, and they cannot be answered categorically.

My feeling is that the word "authentic" has many gradations in folk music, and that anonymity and extreme old age are not necessarily attributes of a genuine folk song. If they were, any minstrel who sang "Waterboy" (which is *not* a traditional spiritual, but a composed song by Avery Robinson) would immediately be drummed out of the fraternity. Was it not Mark Twain who said "a folk song is a song nobody ever wrote"? The point of his whimsy is that somebody wrote the song, all right, but nobody can remember who. In the old days that was quite understandable. They did not have publishing societies and publishing offices in the fourteenth century, and ballads served quite a different purpose. They were the newspapers, magazines, and back-fence gossip sessions rolled into one. They told of murders, hangings, wars, political intrigues, and all the other niceties of civilization. They were no more intended for posterity than the news page of today's Late City Edition.

When equivalent songs were penned in the twentieth century, our improved communications systems often meant that they were anonymous no longer, but it did not at all mean that the new songs were inferior to the old. We know that Woody Guthrie wrote "This Land Is Your Land," and John Jacob Niles wrote "Venezuela," and an itinerant entertainer named "Banjo" Patterson wrote "Waltzing Matilda," but the knowledge in no way lessens their status as genuine folk songs. They have entered the oral tradition, and are firmly part of the folk heritage.

What about the protest songs? They too have a parallel in years gone by—the broadside ballads, which not only told a story, but commented on it. They were the editorials, to continue our newspaper analogy, and whether angry, compassionate, or satiric, they bespeak the era that gave them birth. These songs have frequently served as the conscience of a nation and sometimes (as with the union ballads of the 1930's, for instance) they have played a vital role in its history. Old Man Plato knew whereof he spoke when he said (in the *Republic*): "Musical innovation is full of danger to the State, for when modes of music change, the laws of the State always change with them."

The singers of today's topical songs are doing precisely what their counterparts in past centuries have done. They are commenting on their life and times, and more often than not, trying to change them. And so Bob Dylan sings of the generation gap, Tom Paxton of war and peace, Buffy Saint-Marie of the plight of the American Indian. Which of their songs have value primarily as polemics, and which will actually go on to enter the folk mainstream? With a few exceptions (such as Lee Hays and Pete Seeger's "If I Had a Hammer," which has already entered the oral folk tradition in the South as a civil-rights anthem), it is too early to tell. I prefer to think of these contemporary ballads as folk songs in the making—songs, the worth of which will be judged, and the fate of which will be decided, by you and me and people everywhere, through immersion in that mysterious musical melting pot known as the folk process.

12

Music from Latin America

PRU DEVON

People came to the Americas from all over the world, often bringing with them not much but their ambitions, beliefs, and creative abilities. From Mexico and the Caribbean islands down to the Straits of Magellan the dominant influence was Spanish, with the gigantic exception of Portuguese Brazil. Realizing that basic fact, people are inclined to imagine that Latin American music will sound like the fiery flamenco they heard in Spain or the dolorous fado of Portugal. It does not. Rich broth is a blend of good tastes, and Latin American music is like that.

I think one appreciates an unfamiliar art form in direct ratio to one's understanding of it. Rather than a little knowledge being a dangerous thing, I believe it to be the road to deep enjoyment. Thus even a casual grasp of the background of Latin American music increases one's listening pleasure.

Latin America may be the last area, and these might be the last decades in that last area, where genuinely exciting, viable music of the people is a way of life. Up to the present these people have sung their own songs and danced their own dances with a great deal of flair and spontaneity, since relatively few could afford the luxury of commercial entertainment. True, the ubiquitous juke-box made inroads, and movies were available in towns. But these were only drops compared to the avalanche of constantly available sound provided by the inexpensive transistor radio. I brought my transistor with me on my last visit to South America, and I was delighted that most of the radio stations had up to that time escaped serious commercialization and were broadcasting authentic music of the region many hours daily. My dread is that some day the fine sharp differences will become blurred, so that there will be a homogenized genre, a sort of basic Latin American music.

Latin American popular dance rhythms have spread virtually around the globe. (I have a weird little subcollection of tangos from such unexpected countries as Iceland, Australia, Japan, and Saudi Arabia.) Many people get their first taste of Latin American music on the dance floor, finding the tricky rhythm patterns and varied percussion instruments intriguing. Apparently my inner rhythm went counterclockwise and for an ironic reason. When I first heard such innovations as rumba, conga, and son (not a law-firm, the son is a dance), I definitely disliked them! I came from England to the United States in my teens, and I now realize that I was a musical prig. I had had a fine piano and singing teacher who not only got me through the annual Royal Academy exams but also gave me a great enthusiasm for European folk music. I sneered at popular dance music generally, but for some absurd reason I sneered even more haughtily at the vigorous Caribbean dances just coming in at that time.

Later I went to Mexico, where I fell in love with the melodic and richly varied songs. A series of voyages of musical discovery to central South America turned this love affair into an enduring marriage, and I have had the delight and fulfillment of presenting *Nights in Latin America* for more than twenty years.

Folk music traditionally is born "from the soil." I know of no other area in the world so dominated by the dramatic structure of the land as is Latin America. From the Sierra Madres in Mexico, the Central American volcanic chain and the majestic ramparts of the Andes, to enormous, barely passable rain forests and the incredible Amazon, the land itself creates massive barriers. Jungle, pampa, the vast sierras, deep valleys, and canyons all compel much of the population to live in comparative isolation. This is why archaic, curious instruments and strands of melody survive despite the rapid advances of the machine age in and about cities.

The term *folk music* is so elastic, particularly in Latin America, that I prefer to say *regional* unless I am certain there is no known composer or arranger. In South America several composers have specialized in writing in a style that has the qualities of folk music. In other words, they create songs and dances which express the flavor of a specific region in an "enriched" tonality. Two such recordings of unsurpassed beauty listed in my discography are *The South American Suite* based on typical music of Peru, Uruguay, Paraguay, and Argentina, and the magnificent *Misa Criolla* in which the Mass is brilliantly set to authentic Argentine folk forms. On a slighter scale, the opening and closing theme of *Nights in Latin America*, "Los Carnavales," is an example of authentic Indian melody, a Peruvian circle dance known as a Huayño, which was collected by Rosendo Huirse and arranged and orchestrated by his son Jorge.

"Los Carnavales"

The story about "Los Carnavales" that I like best is so fantastic you will find it hard to accept. I swear, however, that every word is true:

Cuzco was the capital city of the Incas (an accepted misnomer, since only the emperor was "the Inca"). The town lies far from Lima, up in the easternmost fold of the Peruvian Andes. Quite far from Cuzco is a village called Pisac, which visitors remember because the men blow conch-shell trumpets there every Sunday. Quite far from Pisac, over a precarious switchback road called *muy sinuouso,* is a tiny hamlet called Paucartambo, which looks as if no white man had ever been there. Its music, played only on pipes and drums, is unadulterated Indian.

The Director of Indian Affairs in Lima had advised me that a unique fiesta took place in July in Paucartambo. So there, after a series of almost-accidents and ludicrous problems, was "your commentator and guide to *Nights in Latin America*," alone and unable to speak the Quechuan Indian tongue of highland Peru. I could write a hundred pages of this enchanted episode, from the moment the burly handsome mayor in pantomime basic Spanish invited me to "sleep with him" (it was a great family dormitory set up for the occasion) to my affectionate leavetaking five days later (at fiesta time jeeps come in one day and out the other because the road is so narrow).

One after another, little groups of costumed Indians arrived, mostly in wonderful, vividly colored costumes, some with huge feathered headdresses, some with weird masks. They came from enormous distances to pay homage to the Virgin of Paucartambo. For three days and the two intervening nights there was rarely a moment of silence, though the people were not vocally noisy at all. It was a trancelike experience, a timeless ballet of oddly simple dances and haunting pentatonic melodies breathed through a variety of flutes and pipes to the occasional thudding of a drum. I was astonished at the acumen of the mayor's tiny grandson, who sat on my lap and identified each dancing group by its special little tune. "Eso es Los Chunchos," he would explain, or "Eso es Los Llameros." After all, he had attended this fiesta each of his six years.

When a small Andean village has a special fiesta it enjoys splurging a bit in the evening and having mestizo entertainment rather than unmixed Indian fare. Lack of electricity rules out loud radios or juke boxes, so the villagers arrange for a truck to come from Cuzco with a generator, a record player, and a selection of locally popular records. The mayor had most graciously invited me to come with him to the opening of the temporary outdoor cantina. We pushed our way through a herd of llamas that had been "parked" while their owners celebrated. And then, just as we entered the enclosure all decorated with paper flowers, fringed tissue paper and rush lanterns, *what* do you suppose came blasting out from the sound truck? With literally hundreds of Huayños to choose from, it was the theme of my program, the Peruvian Huayño "Los Carnavales!" You could say it was sheer coincidence, and I would agree rationally. But I assure you that as the mayor and I solemnly drank each other's health in the fiery chicha, I listened with almost agonized delight to "Los Carnavales" in its native setting, something I will never forget.

Before the white men came, nomadic Indians wandered the land with primitive culture and minimal music. Their instruments were made of cane, earth, bones, and shells. In Mexico and the central Andes, however, there were two advanced and splendid civilizations boasting a highly developed music, which was considered an essential part of a nobleman's life.

The Aztecs and the Incas had the gold that drew the conquistadores and subsequent adventurers and treasure hunters. These men came from Spain without wives or families. They intermarried with the Indian women, thereby starting a new race. African slaves were brought in to cultivate the lucrative tropical crops, and here again new mutations resulted.

To me the rainbow beautifully symbolizes the emotional and musical life of Latin America. While it has pure red, yellow, and blue, the rainbow's loveliness is enhanced by its graduated shadings. Similarly, the blends of the primary Indian, Iberian, and African musical colors rival their basic ingredients in appeal and variety.

Because these three elements and all their prismatic blendings dazzle and at times confuse, for clarity I would like to discuss them separately: Aztec and Inca foundations, Spain the conqueror and catalyst, Africa as a tropical modifier, and Brazil, where Portuguese and African elements combine.

Aztec and Inca

Latin American music owes to the Aztecs and Incas whatever pre-Columbian flavor it has. From the musical point of view it is remarkable how similar these two widely separated civilizations were in their five-toned scale, use of flutes and percussion instruments, and even their attitudes toward singing, dancing, and playing, which they considered virtually inseparable. Neither the Aztecs nor the Incas had any word for *music* as an abstract concept, but both highly valued its performance. The Aztecs, in fact, were known to have put performers to death for a missed dance step, a crude voice, or a false rhythm, because this might well offend the gods!

Both the Aztecs and the Indians used their music ceremonially. It was tied in with their respective sun gods and the pantheon of deities controlled by the powerful priest-aristocracy. It was used for military encouragement and victory celebrations also. For both of these reasons, the pagan music was almost doomed once the Spanish missionaries got to work. What saved it was that many of the priests cleverly adapted the agricultural cycle of festivals to the Catholic cycle of fiestas, exactly as they had superimposed churches on the foundations of temples which they had destroyed. "Operation Superimpose," if I may so call it, affected Mexican music more than Peruvian, Ecuadorian, and Bolivian. I think part of the reason for this is the actual structure of the land.

Mexico, while mostly a high mountainous plateau gouged by occasional canyons, is far more accessible than the Andean altiplano. It was relatively easy for zealous missionaries to infiltrate most of the country and in so doing to affect the music deeply. They did this by introducing guitars and harps to accompany the religious songs and by outlawing instruments directly associated with ritual or the military. They converted the complex dances in elaborate costume, headdress, or mask into something of an Hispanic cast, such as battles between the Moors and the Christians or little Bible stories in pantomime. Thus the dances and costumes fared better than the music. Other elements of pre-Columbian "sound" were quickly absorbed and enriched by the addition of stringed instruments. Today Mexican music is a fusion from which it is impossible to pluck out one melody or one rhythm and say with authority: "This is pure Indian" or "This is pure Spanish."

The Central Andean phases of "Operation Superimpose" developed quite differently from the Mexican. The overpowering ramparts of the Andes tended to discourage missionary work. Exceptions were the great capitals at Cuzco and Quito, where priests flocked to stamp out paganism at its chief centers. As for the highlands generally, they were so vast, and the pastoral valleys where Indians lived were so separated, that relatively few priests penetrated them. Those who did settle in villages had to cover so much territory they simply could not know about the many rituals of sun worship, llama-shearing, plowing, and harvesting. In this manner many of the archaic songs and dances endured.

Even the instruments themselves conspired. The large unique drums, so essential to the Aztecs' complicated dances, were quickly destroyed on the grounds they were flagrantly pagan. The Incas, who stressed melody more strongly than rhythm, used smaller tools: conch shells, flutes of great variety, and above all, superb pipes of pan. These were much easier to conceal, and also much easier to replace if confiscated.

There are recordings that give an idea of how these virtually extinct pre-Columbian instruments sounded, as well as the pan pipes still in use, like those of Carlos Chavez, Ballet Folklorico, GNP, Mexican Fiesta (Monitor), Laura Boulton (Folkways), and Gods and Demons of Bolivia (Vanguard).

A postscript to the Indian chapter of the story: In the mammoth Amazonian jungles and other rain-forest areas there still are nomadic Indians whose lives and music are almost untouched by five centuries of white men's presence. They were untouched also by the high cultural levels of the Aztec and Inca. Theirs is a pragmatic, special-purpose music, used to accompany the grinding of manioc, the roasting of fish, the coming-of-age of children, the propitiation of forest spirits, and the intricate machinations of witchcraft. I know of one tune used exclusively while trimming a chief's headdress with macaw feathers! Another useful and specialized form is animal sounds employed as a hunting lure. This was elegantly utilized by the fabulous but real Yma Sumac, whose superb "Chuncho" jungle song is on the regrettably out-of-print *Voice of the Xtabay* (Capitol W-684). Generally speaking, however, this ethnic music has limited appeal and rarely merges with any other.

European Influence

The second rainbow color or ethnic influence came from the Iberian Peninsula. Spain influenced indigenous music from the moment the first wave of priests followed the conquistadores.

Because the invaders' first step was to obliterate everything associated with the pre-Columbian religions, they destroyed hundreds of instruments and prohibited ritual dancing. Then they contrived to teach the Indians versions of Christianity, which they hoped would appeal to a naïve audience. They used songs and playlets dealing with Bible stories. "Civilized" dancing was introduced, to the accompaniment of the first stringed instruments to be heard in this hemisphere—small portable harps and guitars.

These instruments were a tremendous success almost immediately. Previously, the priests had got nowhere in Paraguay, where the nomadic Guarani tribes slipped through the Chaco like elusive deer. Jesuit missionaries found it was as difficult to pick up quicksilver as to win these people by conversion. But when the priests took to sailing down the rivers on rafts, playing and singing, the lovely sound of their harps completely seduced the Indians, who eagerly crept closer and closer to accept baptism. To this day, the harp is by far the most popular instrument in Paraguay.

By the time colonists were starting to make up a sizable slice of the population, religious music had become well established in Mexico and was making itself heard throughout the conquered areas. The colonists also brought their secular songs and their marvelous, vibrant dances. Spain has always been marked by a dazzling musical diversity, as you will realize if you try to hear in your imagination, say, flamenco seguidillas from Andalucia, a Basque choral group, a fandango from Castile, bagpipes from Galicia, and a vivacious jota from La Mancha. (Incidentally, if you want to make this imagined sampling actual, try to track down a copy of the volume on Spain in Columbia's *World Library of Folk and Primitive Music* [SL 216].)

We skip lightly over several centuries, during which the church gradually relaxed its tight control and various tidal waves of musical impulses swept in from abroad. Soon Viceregal Lima (and to a lesser degree such other emerging cities as Bogota, Caracas, and Santiago) delightedly welcomed various dances that came direct from the courts of Europe. The gavotte, minuet, sarabande, pavana, pasacalle, and chacona, in transmuted form, became the backbone of at least half of southern Latin America's important regional dances. Argentina absorbed these stately forms and sent them radiating from her cities throughout the rural provinces and pampas. Rough gauchos and paysanos, intrigued by these dances' curiously dignified qualities, refurbished them to suit the new environment of pampa or Andean foothill, where they would crash head-on with traditional Inca music.

I have seen gauchos and their Chilean counterparts, called Huasos, dancing the zamba and cueca, gracefully twirling a kerchief overhead, bowing with dignity as their partners curtsy in the correct court manner. Then a few seconds later I have watched them revert to type, and stamp and twirl in their own gusty style more in keeping with their trade. (*Argentine Dances,* Folkways ST 6 7148, and *Gaucho,* Columbia WL 120, give the general flavor.)

The next, much later, important musical impulse was, strangely enough, Italian opera. How often you hear tunes, particularly in Mexico, which are pure Verdi or Rossini. Then there were operetta and musical comedy, known as *Zarzuela,* the latest light music of Spain. On top of these came a deluge of such ballroom dances as the waltz, mazurka, polka, and pasodoble. It was remarkable how distinctively the new musical forms adapted themselves to the new ambience, and how differently they combined with the already intermixed music. A Paraguayan polka, for instance, is not in the least like a Mexican one, which in turn does not sound like one from Bolivia.

Such a Bolivian polka, by the way, might be played on a curious little mandolin made from an armadillo shell, one of the most ingenious instruments produced by Indians anywhere. When I had at last tracked one down in La Paz, its ruddy-cheeked owner did not want to sell it to a gringo. When he relented, he gave me the Cassandra-like warning that my amazingly hairy armadillo was "con pelo buena suerte, pero sin pelo mala suerte" (Should it shed its hair, it would bring me terrible luck). I asked how I could escape such a misfortune, and he explained that to keep the little creature from going bald I should rub it every night with chicha. *Faute de mieux,* I try beer whenever I remember, and so far all is well!

That year the big popular hit in Bolivia was the nicely swinging "O Linda La Paz," extolling the joys of that city two and one quarter miles above the sea. Everybody sang it; it was very catchy. I brought a record home and played it on the program. To my surprise I was swamped with mail and phone calls which made me thoroughly aware of my stupidity in failing to recognize this famous tune, which had apparently encircled the earth. It was known variously as "Sing Everyone Sing" (USA), "O Viene sul Mar" (Italian), "Zwei Augen so Blau" (German), "Zing Faigele Zing" (Yiddish), "Two Lovely Black Eyes" and "My Nellie's Mince Pies" (English), "Poi Lastachka Poi" (Russian), and "Namide No Umibe" (Japanese).

While stringed instruments and religious songs brought new dimensions to pre-Columbian music, perhaps even more important was the Hispanic attitude. This reveling in spirited melodies and this intricate dancing to springy, fiery rhythms formed a new concept. The long story-telling romances—which would translate into corridos in Mexico, decima in Puerto Rico, and estilo in Argentina, songs for children to sing, lullabies, serenades, and all the songs about fishing, plowing, galloping, and even living and dying—were unheard of previously. In the past, one sang and danced because one was told to do so. It was part of one's religious duty. Now one sang and danced because it was a joy!

From the first Catholic fiesta, held at Lake Titicaca, and the moment in 1526 when a companion of Cortéz established a music school in Mexico with professional instructors, the imprint of Spain was stamped on Latin American music in unforgettable fashion.

African Influence

Africans, the third race, the third color in the rainbow, were brought over in a crescendo from the sixteenth to eighteenth centuries. Thanks to the universal popularity of jazz, everybody is thoroughly aware of the superlative rhythmic sophistication of Negro musicians. In the southern new world, the fascinating variety of innumerable percussion instruments fared much better than in the more puritan north. This alone would help to keep the rhythms vital. In addition there was an easier racial assimilation, leading to a stronger musical synthesis.

Once again the structure of the land decided a people's distribution. Slaves were needed in the hot tropical lowlands to produce sugar, coffee, cotton, and fruits. (Africans teemed into the lands bordering on the Caribbean Sea, into coastal Ecuador and Colombia, and overwhelmingly into Brazil, leaving a strong mark on regional music.) On enormous plantations, under varying degrees of tolerance, the slaves managed to keep alive a large proportion of their African heritage of folklore, dance, drumming, and song. Their cults assumed the outer cloak of Catholicism in much the same manner as had the earlier Indian religions. These secret cults (Ñanigo in Cuba, Vodoun in Haiti, and Candomblé in Brazil) preserved, along with their strong African musical elements, intricate drum rhythms, and they affected every dance along the way.

The best-known examples of African-influenced dances are urban, as are the many popular ones that came to us from Cuba and Puerto Rico. They need neither introduction nor champion. They provide a showcase for the strange and ingenious African percussion instruments that form a rhythmic counterpoint to all the many sizes and shapes of drums. There is the slightly macabre-looking quijada, a horse's jawbone complete with rattling teeth, and the marimbola, made from a large wooden box with several metal tongues nailed onto it. Occasionally a large earthenware jug is employed exactly as it was by old-time North American "jug bands." Most widely used and familiar are maracas, which are rattles and claves, two sticks which make a crisp "tic-toc" and are poetically known as "the heart-beat of the Caribbean," and a serrated gourd that is scratched with a fork (guiro).

African-influenced music has a strong dance tradition and is highly syncopated and polyrhythmic. Song is secondary, often a simple chant alternately sung by solo and answering chorus.

Brazil

While there is not space here to discuss the always shifting cultural relationships of each republic individually, it is quite apparent that Brazil must be considered as distinct from the Spanish-speaking lands. Brazil's acculturation story is similar to Spanish America's, but with one striking difference: There were no highly developed pre-Columbian cultures on which to perform "Operation Superimpose." The Indians of that vast land were either Amazon rain-forest tribes or the more advanced Tupi-Burani, who had sweet lyrical songs which occasionally filter into the musical mainstream. (Two of these rarities are on the old Aravel AB 2001, by now a collector's item. They were sung by Los Indios Taba-Jaras.) For practical purposes there are simply two colors of the cultural rainbow in Brazil—Portugal and Africa.

Bandeirantes, bands who pioneered the limitless interior, were followed by agricultural settlers who kept their Portuguese musical traditions alive. Others remained fishermen as they had been at home, with their elegiac songs of lovers parted and husbands drowned at sea. (Dorival Caymmi was to make this genre completely his own in such beautiful recordings as *Cancoes Praieiras*, Odeon LDS 3.004.)

Portuguese aristocrats brought their melancholy fado accompanied by vialao (guitar). These fados, marked by sad yearning, sparked the Brazilian moda, modinha, and toada. This cherished sorrow and homesickness they call *saudades* can be felt in many forms besides fado. There are hundreds of lyrical songs in this mood, nostalgically recalling the immensity of the Amazon, the mysterious beauty of the lush jungle, or the hardships of the sertao. (In listing, note singers Olga Coelho, Clara Petraglia, and Alice Ribeiro.)

Some of the wealthier Portuguese chose to live in towns such as Bahia. Others, if rich enough, became owners of large coastal plantations called *fazendas*, worked by slaves. As early as 1538 the first full shipment of slaves had made the short crossing from the bulge of Africa to the bulge of Brazil. They came from Nigeria, Dahomey, Angola, and Guinea. In the following three centuries over three million slaves were brought to this area. There was an easy-going relationship between owners and field hands. In many cases they were allowed weekends off and could then keep their Candomblé and Macumba rituals intact. There were nonreligious festivities, too, preserving other African musical forms: coco, originally a witchcraft song; batuque, a circle dance accompanied by hand-clapping; and lundu, a rapid song-dance with comic words. All of these were part of the samba family tree. Besides the familiar drums and maracas of Latin dance-bands, Brazil has a whole "bateria" of such curious African instruments as the friction-drum, known as a *cuica* or *pig-squeek,* and chocalho, a very large gourd rattle strung around with conch shells.

Brazil was unique in South America in the 1800's with its transplanted Emperor. (Pedro the First was highly musical, an amateur composer in fact. In 1822 he wrote a hymn of independence and sang it himself in a public performance, accompanied by a chorus!) Cultivated music flourished in this environment. The royal decree abolishing slavery in 1888 immediately impoverished the fazendas but increased the exuberance and musical expression of the masses. The former slaves now migrated in large numbers to towns, where they were introduced to feshta. Like the Spanish fiestas for innumerable saints' days, Portuguese feshta gave many opportunities for musical exchange between the races. Greatest of all feshtas, of course, is carnaval—an unbelievable impetus to the creation of the marchas and sambas that form the backbone of Brazilian popular music.

Brazilian samba and the fragile bossa nova, Argentine tango and an encyclopedia of Caribbean dances, the ubiquitous and romantic bolero and the cheerfully brassy Mexican mariachi band are probably recognized by most aficionados. But there are many stories which must be left untold: how the Mexican Revolution was musically interpreted; how General San Martin (incidentally, an enthusiastic musician and singer) changed the course of Argentina's folk music; the gold rush, which forged an unexpected musical liaison between Chile and Mexico; North American jazz as half-brother to the current bossa nova; a dejected Spanish priest with an Andean llama-bone flute; and even mambo with its peculiar grunts originally attributed to a local piano mover!

There are innumerable other indirect elements that embellish the background, but there is not space here to discuss them. I do want to leave you with an aroused interest in the music of Latin America, and some understanding of how it came to be. Sometimes when you hear it, you might like to try asking yourself such questions as: Which of the three primary racial groups are most represented in this selection? Was there a geographic or historic reason for this? Was it then modified or fertilized by a second or a third ethnic group? How did this come about? Do I enjoy the hybrid more than the components? Why? Indian music can be hauntingly evocative; Spanish, electric and exuberant; African, melodically simple and rhythmically amazing; but it is their myriad combinations that make up the unique, dazzling, and ever-changing spectrum which is Latin American music.

As your interest and perception grow, perhaps you will come to share my hope that electronics will not homogenize this phenomenal variety of songs, dances, chants, and all the diverse sounds of fiesta and carnival. You will, I feel sure, join with me in crying: "Viva las diferencias!"

Discography[*]

OPERA

In every choice of recordings I have made for this list, the performance has been the payoff. I am not concerned here with sophistication of sound, with the subtleties of stereo versus mono. It is the music *per se* that counts.

Bartók, Béla
>*Bluebeard's Castle* (in Hungarian), Christa Ludwig, Walter Berry, London Symphony Orchestra, conducted by Istvan Kertesz   (LONDON OSA 1158)
>> ▶ *Brief, distinguished score, well recorded.*

Beethoven, Ludwig van
>*Fidelio,* Christa Ludwig, Jon Vickers, Walter Berry, Gottlob Frick, Philharmonia Orchestra and Chorus, conducted by Otto Klemperer   (ANGEL S 3625)
>> ▶ *First-rate Beethoven from all concerned, with Ludwig a great Leonore.*

Bellini, Vincenzo
>*Norma,* Gina Cigna, Ebe Stignani, Giovanni Breviario, Tancredi Pasero, Orchestra and Chorus of Torino Radiotelevisione Italiana, conducted by Vittorio Gui   (EVEREST/CETRA S 423/3)
>> ▶ *A rough, rather inelegant prewar performance (reissued in LP), but so very exciting. I find Callas's recorded* NORMA *unpleasant vocally, and Sutherland's not sufficiently dramatic.*
>*Norma,* "Casta Diva" (aria), Rosa Ponselle; "Mira Norma" (duet), Rosa Ponselle and Marion Telva
>>   (RCA VICTOR ALBUM: TEN GREAT SINGERS)
>> ▶ *Classic and distinguished.*

[*] Compiled by the individual contributors to this volume.

I Puritani, Maria Callas, Giuseppe Di Stefano, Orchestra and Chorus of La Scala, conducted by Tullio Serafin   (ANGEL 3502)
▶ *Callas and Di Stefano at their pristine best. An excellent performance.*

La Sonnambula, Joan Sutherland, Nicola Monti, Fernando Corena, Orchestra and Chorus of the Maggio Musicale Fiorentino, conducted by Richard Bonynge   (LONDON OSA 1365)
▶ *Fading score, expertly done.*

Berg, Alban

Wozzeck, Evelyn Lear, Dietrich Fischer-Dieskau, Orchestra of the German Opera, Berlin, conducted by Karl Böhm
(DEUTSCHE GRAMMOPHON GESELLSCHAFT S 138991/2)
▶ *Wonderfully human, accessible performance of a masterpiece.*

Lulu, Evelyn Lear, Patricia Johnson, Dietrich Fischer-Dieskau, Donald Grobe, Orchestra of the German Opera, Berlin, conducted by Karl Böhm
(DEUTSCHE GRAMMOPHON GESELLSCHAFT S 139273/5)
▶ *A problematical opera, gripping yet remote, superbly presented.*

Berlioz, Hector

Béatrice et Bénédict, Josephine Veasey, April Cantelo, John Mitchinson, London Symphony Orchestra and St. Anthony Singers, conducted by Colin Davies   (OISEAU-LYRE S 256/7)
▶ *A charming comedy with sentimental overtones, deftly performed.*

Les Troyens (scenes), Régine Crespin, Guy Chauvet, Paris Opéra Orchestra, conducted by Georges Prêtre   (ANGEL S 3670)
▶ *Badly cut, but gives some idea of the superb score by Berlioz. Crespin is effective as Didon.*

Bizet, Georges

Carmen, Victoria de los Angeles, Janine Micheau, Nicolai Gedda, Ernest Blanc, French National Radio Orchestra, conducted by Sir Thomas Beecham   (ANGEL S 3613)
▶ *If* CARMEN *is your preference, this is the best of its many recordings.*

Boito, Arrigo

Mefistofele. There has been no really adequate recording of this grand old work since the Scala issue of the 1920's with Mafalda Favero, Gianna Arangi-Lombardi, Antonio Melandri, and Nazzareno De Angelis, with Cav. Lorenzo Molajoli conducting (Columbia Operatic Set No. 17, unfortunately not reissued).
▶ *Toscanini directs a splendid performance of the Prologue on RCA Victor LM-1849.*

Borodin, Aleksandr

Prince Igor, Boris Christoff (doubling as Prince Galitsky and Khan Kontchak), Soloists, Chorus, and Orchestra of the National Theatre of Sofia, conducted by Jerzy Semkow

(USSR MELODIYA-ANGEL S 3714)

▸ *A striking performance, with benefit of Western recording techniques.*

Britten, Benjamin

Peter Grimes, Claire Watson, Peter Pears, James Pease, Royal Opera Orchestra, Covent Garden, conducted by Benjamin Britten

(LONDON OSA 1305)

▸ *One could wish for a newer recording, perhaps a different cast, but the current artists are all communicative, and the orchestra under the direction of the composer is first-rate.*

Charpentier, Gustave

Louise, Berthe Monmart, Solange Michel, André Laroze, Louis Musy, Orchestra and Chorus of the Paris Opéra-Comique, conducted by Jean Fournet

(EPIC SC 6018)

▸ *Singers excellent, but the heart of the performance is Jean Fournet's superb conducting.*

Cherubini, Luigi

Medea, Maria Callas, Orchestra and Chorus of La Scala, conducted by Tullio Serafin

(MERCURY SR 3-9000)

▸ *The Callas sound is here acceptable, the interpretation overwhelming.*

Debussy, Claude

Pelléas et Mélisande, Janine Micheau, Rita Gorr, Camille Maurane, Michel Roux, Xavier Depraz, Orchestre des Concerts Lamoureux, conducted by Jean Fournet

(EPIC SC 6003)

▸ *Fournet and the singers score again. Surpasses every other recorded* PELLÉAS.

Donizetti, Gaetano

Don Pasquale, Graziella Sciutti, Juan Oncina, Tom Krause, Fernando Corena, Vienna Opera Orchestra and Chorus, conducted by Istvan Kertesz

(LONDON OSA 1260)

▸ *This recording has its ups and downs, but unfortunately, there is no better available.*

L'elisir d'amore, Mirella Freni, Nicolai Gedda, Mario Sereni, Rome Opera Orchestra and Chorus, conducted by Francesco Molinari-Pradelli

(ANGEL S 3701)

▸ *Sheer joy, as music and performance, from beginning to end.*

Lucia di Lammermoor, Joan Sutherland, Renato Cioni, Robert Merrill, Cesare Siepi, Orchestra and Chorus of L'Accademia di Santa Cecilia, conducted by John Pritchard

(LONDON OSA 1327)

▸ *The definitive modern performance of* LUCIA.

Lucrezia Borgia, Montserrat Caballé, Shirley Verrett, Alfredo Kraus, Ezio Flagello, RCA Italiana Opera Orchestra and Chorus, conducted by Jonel Perlea (RCA LSC-6176)
▶ *Caballé in one of her more congenial assignments.*

Dvořák, Anton
Rusalka, Soloists, Chorus, and Orchestra of the National Theater, Prague, conducted by Zdeněk Chalabala (ARTIA S 89D)
▶ *The last act compensates for all longueurs in the earlier scenes. It is wonderful music, strongly performed.*

Giordano, Umberto
Andrea Chénier, Renata Tebaldi, Mario Del Monaco, Ettore Bastianini, Orchestra and Chorus of L'Accademia di Santa Cecilia, Rome, conducted by Gianandrea Gavazzeni
(LONDON OSA 1303)
▶ *Powerful score in a reputable recording.*
Fedora, Maria Caniglia, Giacinto Prandelli, Orchestra and Chorus of Radiotelevisione Italiana, conducted by Mario Rossi
(CETRA 1222)
▶ *Both opera and performance slightly moldy, but eloquent.*

Gluck, Christoph Willibald
Orfeo ed Euridice, Maureen Forrester, Teresa Stich-Randall, Hanny Steffek, Akademie Choir and Vienna State Opera Orchestra, conducted by Charles Mackerras
(THE BACH GUILD BGS 70686/7)
▶ *Dignified reading, expressively sung.*

Gounod, Charles
Faust, Victoria de los Angeles, Nicolai Gedda, Michel Dens, Boris Christoff, Orchestra and Chorus of the Paris Opéra, conducted by André Cluytens (ANGEL S 3622)
▶ *If it is FAUST you want, this is the best, even with Christoff's heavily accented Méphistophélès.*
Roméo et Juliette (scenes), Rosanna Carteri, Nicolai Gedda, Paris Opéra Orchestra, conducted by Alain Lombard
(ANGEL S 36287)
▶ *Carteri sounds a bit mature as Juliette, with Gedda the perfect Roméo.*

Handel, George Frederick
Alcina, Joan Sutherland, Teresa Berganza, Monica Sinclair, Graziella Sciutti, Mirella Freni, Ezio Flagello, London Symphony Orchestra and Chorus, conducted by Richard Bonynge
(LONDON S 1361)
▶ *A feast of virtuoso singing. Baroque style and ornamentation are imaginatively recreated.*

Hindemith, Paul
Mathis der Maler (scenes), Pilar Lorengar, Dietrich Fischer-

Dieskau, Berlin Radio Orchestra, conducted by Leopold Ludwig   (DEUTSCHE GRAMMOPHON GESELLSCHAFT S 138769)
▶ *This noble work sounds better in excerpts than as an inte-
grated whole, for many of the parts are greater than the sum.*

Janáček, Leoš

Jenufa, Soloists, Chorus, and Orchestra of the National Theater,
Prague, conducted by Jaroslav Vogel   (ARTIA ALPO 80 C/L)
▶ *A strong, but currently overrated opera, adequately per-
formed.*

The Sly Little Vixen, Soloists, Chorus, and Orchestra of the Na-
tional Theater, Prague, conducted by Václav Neumann
(ARTIA ALPO 88 B/L)
▶ *What an affecting mixture of wisdom, satire, and pathos!
So human, and well played.*

Leoncavallo, Ruggiero

Pagliacci, Lucine Amara, Franco Corelli, Tito Gobbi, Mario
Zanasi, Orchestra and Chorus of La Scala, conducted by
Lovro von Matacic   (ANGEL S 3618 B/L)
▶ *Brilliant, consuming performance.*

Mascagni, Pietro

L'Amico Fritz, Ferruccio Tagliavini and Pia Tassinari, Orchestra
and Chorus of Torino Radiotelevisione Italiana, conducted by
Pietro Mascagni   (EVEREST/CETRA S 429/2)
▶ *A charming miniature, well sung. This recording (a reissue)
has the additional interest of the composer on the podium.*

Cavalleria Rusticana, Giulietta Simionato, Mario Del Monaco,
Cornell MacNeil, Orchestra and Chorus of L'Accademia di
Santa Cecilia, Rome, conducted by Tullio Serafin
(LONDON S 1213)
▶ *Good, routine performance, but without much of the ferocity
implicit in the score.*

Massenet, Jules

Hérodiade (scenes), Régine Crespin, Rita Gorr, Albert Lance,
Michel Dens, Orchestra of the Paris Opéra, conducted by
Georges Prêtre   (ANGEL S 36145)
▶ *The best pages of a debatable opera, well performed.*

Manon, Victoria de los Angeles, Henri Legay, Michel Dens, Jean
Borthayre, Orchestra and Chorus of the Paris Opéra-Comique,
conducted by Pierre Monteux   (CAPITOL GDR-7171)
▶ *The standard* MANON *on discs. First-rate.*

Thaïs (scenes), Jacqueline Brumaire, Christiane Gayraud, Michel
Dens, Orchestra of the Paris Opéra, conducted by Pierre
Dervaux   (ANGEL S 36286)
▶ *The opera's important moments, surprisingly well done by a
modest cast.*

Werther, Ninon Vallin, Germaine Feraldy, Georges Thill, Marcel Roque, Orchestra of the Paris Opéra-Comique, conducted by Elie Cohen (PATHÉ FHX 5009/5011)

▶ *The poetry of this prewar recording of* WERTHER *(in an LP reissue) has not yet been surpassed.*

Meyerbeer, Giacomo

Les Huguenots. Marcel's aria "Piff, paff, pouff" from *Les Huguenots* is performed by Nicolai Ghiaurov on his album of French and Russian arias, with the London Symphony Orchestra, conducted by Edward Downes (LONDON OS 25911)

▶ *Bravo!*

Les Huguenots. The Queen's aria "O beau pays de Touraine" is sung by Joan Sutherland on her album *Art of Prima Donna,* with the Orchestra of the Royal Opera House, Covent Garden, conducted by Francesco Molinari-Pradelli (LONDON OS 1214)

▶ *And brava!*

Montemezzi, Italo

L'Amore dei Tre Re, Clara Petrella, Amedeo Berdini, Renato Capecchi, Sesto Bruscantini, Orchestra and Chorus of Radio-televisione Italiana, conducted by Arturo Basile (CETRA 1212)

▶ *The score, though eclectic, is still worth hearing. A good recording.*

Monteverdi, Claudio

L'Incoronazione de Poppea (selections), edited by Raymond Leppard; Magda Laszlo, Frances Bible, Oralia Dominguez, Richard Lewis, Carlo Cava, Glyndebourne Festival Chorus and Royal Philharmonic Orchestra, conducted by John Pritchard (ANGEL SBL 3644)

▶ *Sensitively, magnificently recorded. The closing duet is one of the landmarks in opera.*

Mozart, Wolfgang Amadeus

Così fan tutte, Elisabeth Schwarzkopf, Christa Ludwig, Hanny Steffek, Alfredo Kraus, Giuseppe Taddei, Walter Berry, Philharmonia Orchestra and Chorus, conducted by Karl Böhm (ANGEL S 3631 D/L)

▶ *Polished, persuasive Mozart in today's best performing tradition.*

Don Giovanni, Joan Sutherland, Elisabeth Schwarzkopf, Graziella Sciutti, Eberhard Wächter, Luigi Alva, Giuseppe Taddei, Philharmonia Orchestra and Chorus, conducted by Carlo Maria Giulini (ANGEL S 3605 D/L)

▶ *Same critical comment as on* COSÌ FAN TUTTE.

Idomeneo, Sena Jurinac, Lucille Udovick, Richard Lewis, Leopold Simoneau, Glyndebourne Festival Orchestra and Chorus, conducted by John Pritchard (ANGEL 3574 C/L)

▶ *A dedicated performance of an opera that deserves to be better known.*

The Magic Flute, Tiana Lemnitz, Erna Berger, Helge Roswänge, Gerhard Hüsch, Wilhelm Strienz, Berlin Philharmonic Chorus and Orchestra, conducted by Sir Thomas Beecham
(TURNABOUT [MOZART SOCIETY EDITION] 4111/3)
▶ *A reissue (in LP) of the famous prewar Beecham recording. Still the best* FLUTE *on discs.*

The Marriage of Figaro, Anna Moffo, Elisabeth Schwarzkopf, Fiorenza Cossotto, Eberhard Wächter, Giuseppe Taddei, Philharmonia Orchestra and Chorus, conducted by Carlo Maria Giulini (ANGEL S 3608)
▶ *Same critical comment as on* COSÌ FAN TUTTE.

Musorgski, Modest
Boris Godunov (Rimski-Korsakov version), George London, Irina Arkhipova, Vladimir Ivanovsky, Orchestra and Chorus of the Bolshoi Theater, Moscow, conducted by Alexander Melik-Pashaev (COLUMBIA M4S 696)
▶ *Great performance, sumptuous sound.*

Offenbach, Jacques
The Tales of Hoffmann, Gianna D'Angelo, Elisabeth Schwarzkopf, Victoria de los Angeles, Nicolai Gedda, George London, Ernest Blanc, Jean-Christophe Benoit, Orchestre de la Société des Concerts du Conservatoire, conducted by André Cluytens
(ANGEL SCLX 3667)
▶ *Adequate but frequently uneven recording of a fascinating work. Gedda consistently stylish.*

Ponchielli, Amilcare
La Gioconda, Renata Tebaldi, Marilyn Horne, Carlo Bergonzi, Robert Merrill, Orchestra and Chorus of L'Accademia di Santa Cecilia, Rome, conducted by Lambert Gardelli
(LONDON OSA 1388)
▶ *Vigorous, red-blooded, extrovert performance.*

Poulenc, Francis
Les Dialogues des Carmélites, Denise Duval, Régine Crespin, Rita Gorr, Xavier Depraz, Paul Finel, Orchestra of the Paris Opéra, conducted by Pierre Dervaux (ANGEL 3585)
▶ *Sumptuous recording of an outstanding modern score.*

Prokofiev, Sergei
The Flaming Angel, Jane Rhodes, Irma Kolassi, Xavier Depraz, Orchestra of the Paris Opéra and Chorus of Radiodiffusion-Télévision Française, conducted by Charles Bruck
(WESTMINSTER 1304)
▶ *The Gothic mood is expertly sustained; and the opera itself comes off as one of the major works of our time.*

Puccini, Giacomo

La Bohème, Mirella Freni, Mariella Adani, Nicolai Gedda, Mario Sereni, Rome Opera Orchestra and Chorus, conducted by Thomas Schippers (ANGEL S 3643)
▶ *Tastefully and often movingly sung. Good conducting.*

Gianni Schicchi, Fernando Corena, Renata Tebaldi, Agostino Lazzari, Orchestra of the Maggio Musicale Fiorentino, conducted by Lamberto Gardelli (LONDON OSA 1153)
▶ *Singing only fair, orchestra very good.*

Girl of the Golden West, Birgit Nilsson, Joaõ Gibin, Andrea Mongelli, Orchestra and Chorus of La Scala, conducted by Lovro von Matacic (ANGEL S 3593 C/L)
▶ *Puccini's most important score, with von Matacic firmly in command.*

Madama Butterfly, Renata Tebaldi, Nell Rankin, Giuseppe Campora, Giovanni Inghilleri, Orchestra and Chorus of L'Accademia di Santa Cecilia, Rome, conducted by Alberto Erede (RICHMOND 63001)
▶ *A reissue of Tebaldi's first recorded* BUTTERFLY. *It was this album, with its bloom of vocal youth, that originally, and justifiably, helped build her reputation.*

Manon Lescaut, Licia Albanese, Jussi Bjoerling, Robert Merrill, Orchestra and Chorus of Rome Opera, conducted by Jonel Perlea (RCA LM-6116)
▶ *Puccini* COME SI DEVE. *An impassioned performance.*

La Rondine, Anna Moffo, Graziella Sciutti, Daniele Barioni, Piero Di Palma, RCA Italiana Opera Orchestra and Chorus, conducted by Francesco Molinari-Pradelli (RCA LSC-7048)
▶ *A fragile and frequently appealing little opera, generally well performed.*

Suor Angelica, Victoria de los Angeles, Fedora Barbieri, Rome Opera Chorus and Orchestra, conducted by Tullio Serafin (ANGEL 35748)
▶ *Sensitive projection of a work alternately inert and moving.*

Il Tabarro, Clara Petrella, Antenore Reali, Glauco Scarlino, Orchestra Lirica di Torino della Radiotelevisione Italiana, conducted by Giuseppe Barone (CETRA LPC 50029)
▶ *The oldest, and finest,* TABARRO *on records. No other Giorgietta comes within miles of Clara Petrella for dramatic and vocal penetration. The entire cast and conductor are excellent.*

Tosca, Maria Callas, Giuseppe Di Stefano, Tito Gobbi, Orchestra and Chorus of La Scala, conducted by Vittorio De Sabata (ANGEL 3508)
▶ *Not to be confused with a later stereo release (also by Angel)*

featuring Callas and Gobbi. Here, every one of the artists is at his and her respective best. De Sabata magnificent. Easily the finest recording of TOSCA.

Turandot, Birgit Nilsson, Renata Scotto, Franco Corelli, Rome Opera Orchestra and Chorus, conducted by Francesco Molinari-Pradelli   (ANGEL S 3671)
▶ *Nilsson's big voice meets Puccini's big opera in a perfect union. Stunning performance of an extroverted score.*

Rameau, Jean Philippe
Hippolyte et Aricie, Janet Baker, John Shirley-Quirk, English Chamber Orchestra and St. Anthony Singers, conducted by Anthony Lewis   (OISEAU-LYRE S 286/8)
▶ *Much of the opera is dull, yet some of its scenes have great lyrical beauty.*

Ravel, Maurice
L'Enfant et les Sortilèges, Françoise Ogéas, Michel Sénéchal, Sylvaine Gelma, French National Radio Orchestra, conducted by Lorin Maazel
(DEUTSCHE GRAMMOPHON GESELLSCHAFT S 138675)
▶ *Brilliant, glittering, virtuosic performance.*

L'Heure Espagnole, Jeanne Berbié, Michel Sénéchal, Gabriel Bacquier, French National Radio Orchestra, conducted by Lorin Maazel (DEUTSCHE GRAMMOPHON GESELLSCHAFT S 138970)
▶ *Brilliant, glittering, virtuosic performance.*

Rimski-Korsakov, Nikolai
The Golden Cockerel (*Le Coq d'Or*), Soloists, Moscow Radio Chorus and Radio-Symphony Orchestra, conducted by Alexei Kovalyov   (ULTRAPHONE ULP 108/110)
▶ *Engagingly performed, poorly recorded.*

Sadko, Soloists, Chorus, and Orchestra of the Bolshoi Theater, conducted by Nicolai Golovanov   (ULTRAPHONE ULP 127/130)
▶ *Same critical comment as on* THE GOLDEN COCKEREL.

Rossini, Gioacchino
The Barber of Seville, Victoria de los Angeles, Sesto Bruscantini, Luigi Alva, Carlo Cava, Glyndebourne Festival Orchestra and Chorus, conducted by Vittorio Gui   (ANGEL S 3638)
▶ *This performance is so aristocratic in design as to erase for us every miserable travesty of* THE BARBER *in the past.*

La Cenerentola, Giulietta Simionato, Ugo Benelli, Sesto Bruscantini, Orchestra and Chorus of the Maggio Musicale Fiorentino, conducted by Oliviero de Febritiis   (LONDON OSA 1376)
▶ *Able and sparkling Rossini.*

Le Comte Ory, Jeanette Sinclair, Cora Canne-Meijer, Juan Oncina, Michel Roux, Glyndebourne Festival Orchestra and Chorus, conducted by Vittorio Gui   (ANGEL 3565 B/L)

▶ *A scintillating, jewel-like score. The performance is adequate.*

L'Italiana in Algeri, Teresa Berganza, Luigi Alva, Fernando Corena, Orchestra of the Maggio Musicale Fiorentino, conducted by Silvio Varviso   (LONDON OAS 1376)
▶ *Same critical comment as on* CENERENTOLA.

Semiramide, Joan Sutherland, Marilyn Horne, Joseph Rouleau, London Symphony Orchestra and Ambrosian Opera Chorus, conducted by Richard Bonynge   (LONDON OAS 1383)
▶ *The apex of modern* BEL CANTO *singing is reached by Sutherland and Horne in their great duet.*

Saint-Saëns, Camille

Samson et Dalila, Rita Gorr, Jon Vickers, Ernest Blanc, Paris Opéra Orchestra and Choeur René Duclos, conducted by Georges Prêtre   (ANGEL S 3639)
▶ *Hardly a voluptuous performance, but a good one.*

Shostakovich, Dimitri

Katerina Ismailova, Artists, Chorus, and Orchestra of the Stanislavsky/Nemirov-Danchenko Musical Drama Theatre of Moscow, conducted by Gennay Provatorov
(USSR MELODIYA-ANGEL S 4100)
▶ *A striking performance, with benefit of Western recording techniques.*

Smetana, Bedřich

The Bartered Bride, Soloists, Chorus, and Orchestra of the National Theater, Prague, conducted by Zdeněk Chalabala
(ARTIA S 82 C/L)
▶ *Said by ethnic specialists to be an authentic performance.*

Strauss, Richard

Arabella, Lisa Della Casa, Hilde Gueden, George London, Vienna Philharmonic Orchestra, conducted by Georg Solti
(LONDON OSA 1404)
▶ *Spirited reading of a charming minor work.*

Ariadne auf Naxos, Elisabeth Schwarzkopf, Irmgard Seefried, Rita Streich, Rudolf Schock, Vienna Philharmonic Orchestra, conducted by Herbert von Karajan   (ANGEL 3532)
▶ *Seefried and Streich excel. The orchestral performance is sterling, the over-all mood poetically conveyed.*

Capriccio, Elisabeth Schwarzkopf, Christa Ludwig, Nicolai Gedda, Dietrich Fischer-Dieskau, Hans Hotter, Philharmonia Orchestra, conducted by Wolfgang Sawallisch   (ANGEL 3580)
▶ *An all-star cast lives up to expectations. Brilliantly performed in every way. The opera itself is a tough nut to crack (for the listener) and takes many hearings.*

Elektra, Birgit Nilsson, Marie Collier, Regina Resnik, Tom Krause, Gerhard Stolze, Vienna Philharmonic Orchestra, conducted by Georg Solti (LONDON OSA 1269)
▶ *Much impressive singing, manipulated orchestral sound.*

Die Frau ohne Schatten, Inge Borkh, Ingrid Bjoner, Marta Mödl, Jess Thomas, Dietrich Fischer-Dieskau, Bavarian State Opera Orchestra, conducted by Joseph Keilberth
(DEUTSCHE GRAMMOPHON GESELLSCHAFT S 138911/4)
▶ *A performance recorded "live" at the National Theater, Munich. Much of it is good. Better, as a memento of DIE FRAU in microcosm, is the recording of the duet for the Dyer and his wife (Act III, Scene 1), beautifully sung by Christa Ludwig and Walter Berry, with the orchestra of the German Opera, Berlin, conducted by Heinrich Hollreiser (RCA VICS-1269).*

Der Rosenkavalier (scenes), Lotte Lehmann, Maria Olszewska, Elisabeth Schumann, Richard Mayr, Vienna Philharmonic Orchestra, conducted by Robert Heger (ANGEL GRB-4001)
▶ *The classic prewar performance (reissued in LP), with memorable artists, bearing a mark of authenticity and enchantment not approached by any other recording of ROSENKAVALIER. An added attraction: all the duller scenes in the opera are eliminated, and only its shining pages retained.*

Salome (final scene), Ljuba Welitsch and Metropolitan Opera Orchestra, conducted by Fritz Reiner (ODYSSEY 32160077)
▶ *The model performance in every way (reissued). The complete recording by London (OSA 1218), starring Birgit Nilsson, is for my taste overengineered.*

Tchaikovsky, Pëtr Ilich

Eugene Onegin (scenes), Galina Vishnevskaya and artists of the Bolshoi Theater, conducted by Boris Khaikin (MONITOR S 2072)
▶ *Said by ethnic specialists to be an authentic performance.*

Pique Dame, Soloists, Chorus, and Orchestra of Bolshoi Theater, conducted by Alexander Melik-Pashaev (BRUNO 32004/6L)
▶ *Engagingly performed, poorly recorded.*

Thomas, Ambroise

Mignon (scenes), Jeanne Berbié, Mady Mesplé, Gérard Dunan, Xavier Depraz, Orchestra Lamoureux and Choeur St. Paul, conducted by Jean Fournet
(DEUTSCHE GRAMMOPHON GESELLSCHAFT S 136279)
▶ *So excellently performed is this series of excerpts that one could have wished for the opera complete.*

Verdi, Giuseppe

Aida, Leontyne Price, Rita Gorr, Jon Vickers, Robert Merrill, Giorgio Tozzi, Rome Opera Orchestra and Chorus, conducted by Georg Solti (RCA LSC-6158)
▶ *Conventional, satisfying performance.*

Un Ballo in Maschera, Birgit Nilsson, Giulietta Simionato, Sylvia Stahlman, Carlo Bergonzi, Cornell MacNeil, Orchestra and Chorus of L'Accademia di Santa Cecilia, Rome, conducted by Georg Solti (LONDON OSA 1328)
▶ *Strongly sung and effectively played.*

Don Carlos, Renata Tebaldi, Grace Bumbry, Carlo Bergonzi, Dietrich Fischer-Dieskau, Nicolai Ghiaurov, Royal Opera Orchestra, Covent Garden, conducted by Georg Solti
(LONDON OSA 1432)
▶ *Distinguished cast, well fused.*

Falstaff, Ilva Ligabue, Mirella Freni, Giulietta Simionato, Rosalind Elias, Alfredo Kraus, Geraint Evans, Robert Merrill, RCA Italiana Orchestra, conducted by Georg Solti (RCA LSC-6163)
▶ *Vocally the best* FALSTAFF *on records. In the orchestra, I prefer Leonard Bernstein's reading (Columbia M3S-750) to Solti's.*

La Forza del Destino, Renata Tebaldi, Giulietta Simionato, Mario Del Monaco, Ettore Bastianini, Cesare Siepi, Orchestra and Chorus of L'Accademia di Santa Cecilia, Rome, conducted by Francesco Molinari-Pradelli (LONDON OSA 1405)
▶ *Same critical comment as on* UN BALLO IN MASCHERA.

Luisa Miller, Anna Moffo, Shirley Verrett, Carlo Bergonzi, Cornell MacNeil, Giorgio Tozzi, Ezio Flagello, RCA Italiana Opera Orchestra and Chorus, conducted by Fausto Cleva
(RCA LSC-6168)
▶ *All-around good performance, with Bergonzi excelling as Rodolfo. The final act, musically, is top-rank Verdi.*

Macbeth, Birgit Nilsson, Giuseppe Taddei, Bruno Prevedi, Orchestra and Chorus of L'Accademia di Santa Cecilia, Rome, conducted by Thomas Schippers (LONDON OSA 1380)
▶ *Nilsson's Lady Macbeth is controversial in regard to Italian vocal style, but as characterization, I like its steely quality.*

Nabucco, Elena Suliotis, Tito Gobbi, Bruno Prevedi, Carlo Cava, Vienna State Opera Orchestra and Chorus, conducted by Lamberto Gardelli (LONDON OSA 1382)
▶ *Rough vocalism, but dramatically convincing.*

Otello, Leonie Rysanek, Jon Vickers, Tito Gobbi, Rome Opera Orchestra and Chorus, conducted by Tullio Serafin
(RCA LDS-6155)
▶ *Impressively sung and conducted.*

Rigoletto, Anna Moffo, Rosalind Elias, Alfredo Kraus, Robert Merrill, Ezio Flagello, RCA Italiana Opera Orchestra and Chorus, conducted by Georg Solti (RCA LSC-7027)
▶ *Solid, meat-and-potatoes performance.*

Simon Boccanegra, Tito Gobbi, Boris Christoff, Victoria de los Angeles, Giuseppe Campora, Rome Opera Orchestra and Chorus, conducted by Gabriele Santini (ANGEL 3617)
▶ *A towering opera, for the most part well recorded.*

La Traviata, Anna Moffo, Richard Tucker, Robert Merrill, Rome Opera Orchestra and Chorus, conducted by Fernando Previtali (RCA LSC-6154)
▶ *Same critical comment as on* RIGOLETTO.

Il Trovatore, Antonietta Stella, Fiorenza Cossotto, Carlo Bergonzi, Ettore Bastianini, Orchestra and Chorus of La Scala, conducted by Tullio Serafin
(DEUTSCHE GRAMMOPHON GESELLSCHAFT 138835/7)
▶ *Fluctuating job, but at best quite acceptable.*

Wagner, Richard

Der Fliegende Holländer, Leonie Rysanek, George London, Giorgio Tozzi, Royal Opera Orchestra, Covent Garden, conducted by Antal Dorati (RCA LSC-6156)
▶ *Good, durable, and often eloquent Wagner.*

Lohengrin, Elisabeth Grümmer, Christa Ludwig, Jess Thomas, Dietrich Fischer-Dieskau, Gottlob Frick, Vienna Philharmonic and State Opera Chorus, conducted by Rudolf Kempe
(ANGEL S 3641)
▶ *A poetic, sensitive performance.*

Die Meistersinger, Elisabeth Grümmer, Rudolf Schock, Ferdinand Frantz, Berlin Philharmonic Orchestra, conducted by Rudolf Kempe (ANGEL 3572)
▶ *I cannot recommend unreservedly any complete* MEISTER-SINGER *on records, although the Frantz-Kempe performance will do in a pinch. Better, for savoring the essence of this work, is the reissue of scenes (Angel COLH-137) featuring that incomparable Hans Sachs, Friedrich Schorr.*

Parsifal, Irene Dalis, Jess Thomas, George London, Hans Hotter, Bayreuth Festival Orchestra and Chorus, conducted by Hans Knappertsbusch (PHILLIPS PHS 5-950)
▶ *Wonderfully conducted and played, a good deal of uneven singing. I recommend, as an example of how this music* HAS *been sung, the reissue (Angel COLH-132) of Frida Leider in Kundry's monologue, "Ich sah das Kind."*

Der Ring des Nibelungen
Das Rheingold, Kirsten Flagstad, George London, Gustav Neidlinger, Set Svanholm, Vienna Philharmonic, conducted by Georg Solti (LONDON OSA 1309)

Die Walküre, Birgit Nilsson, Régine Crespin, Christa Ludwig, James King, Hans Hotter, Gottlob Frick, Vienna Philharmonic, conducted by Georg Solti (LONDON OSA 1509)

Siegfried, Birgit Nilsson, Marga Höffgen, Joan Sutherland (Forest Bird), Wolfgang Windgassen, Gerhard Stolze, Hans Hotter, Vienna Philharmonic, conducted by Georg Solti (LONDON OSA 1508)

Götterdämmerung, Birgit Nilsson, Claire Watson, Christa Ludwig, Wolfgang Windgassen, Dietrich Fischer-Dieskau, Gottlob Frick, Vienna Philharmonic, conducted by Georg Solti (LONDON OSA 1604)

▶ *The London* RING *is a monumental project, unmatched on records, with a high standard of performance, but I find much of the sound (via engineering) intrusive and pretentious.*

Tristan und Isolde, Birgit Nilsson, Christa Ludwig, Wolfgang Windgassen, Eberhard Wächter, Marti Talvela, Bayreuth Festival Orchestra, conducted by Karl Böhm (DEUTSCHE GRAMMOPHON GESELLSCHAFT S 139221/5)

▶ *For my taste, the finest orchestral performance on records of* ANY *opera. The singers are good.*

Weber, Karl Maria von

Der Freischütz, Irmgard Seefried, Rita Streich, Richard Holm, Kurt Böhme, Eberhard Wächter, Bavarian Broadcasting Orchestra and Chorus, conducted by Eugen Jochum (DEUTSCHE GRAMMOPHON GESELLSCHAFT S 138639/40)

▶ *Kurt Böhme especially fine as the diabolical Kaspar. Rita Streich an adorable Aennchen.*

ORCHESTRAL MUSIC

Bach, Johann Sebastian

Violin Concerto No. 1 in A minor, Szeryng, Winterthur Collegium Musicum (MERCURY 90466, 50466)

Violin Concerto No. 2 in E, Menuhin, with Masters Chamber Orchestra (CAPITOL SG 7210, G 7210)

Clavier Concerto No. 1 in D minor, Ashkenazy, London Symphony Orchestra, Zinman (LONDON CS 6440, CM 9440)

Six Brandenburg Concertos, Lucerne Festival Strings, Baumgartner (ARCHIVE 73156/7, 3156/7)

Suites for Orchestra, Bath Festival Chamber Orchestra, Menuhin (CAPITOL SGBR 7252, GBR 7252)

Bartók, Béla
  Concerto for Orchestra, New York Philharmonic, Bernstein
                                      (COLUMBIA MS 6140, ML 5471)
  Piano Concerto No. 3, Peter Serkin, Chicago Symphony Orchestra, Ozawa   (RCA LSC/LM 2929)
  Violin Concerto No. 2, Stern, New York Philharmonic, Bernstein
                                        (COLUMBIA MS 6002, ML 5283)
  Music for Strings, Percussion and Celesta, Chicago Symphony Orchestra, Reiner   (RCA LSC/LM 2374)
Beethoven, Ludwig van
  Incidental Music for Egmont, Philharmonia Orchestra, Klemperer   (ANGEL S 3577, 3577)
  The Five Piano Concertos, Fleisher, Cleveland Orchestra, Szell
                                    (EPIC BSC 151, SC 6051)
  Piano Concerto No. 1, Richter, Boston Symphony Orchestra, Munch   (RCA LSC/LM 2544)
  Piano Concerto No. 3, Rubinstein, Boston Symphony Orchestra, Leinsdorf   (RCA LSC/LM 2947)
  Piano Concerto No. 5, Serkin, New York Philharmonic, Bernstein   (COLUMBIA MS 6366, ML 5766)
  Violin Concerto, Francescatti, Columbia Symphony Orchestra, Walter   (COLUMBIA MS 6263, ML 5663)
  Fidelio and *Leonore Overtures,* Cleveland Orchestra, Szell
                        (COLUMBIA MS 7068) stereo only
  Symphony No. 1, Cleveland Orchestra, Szell
                              (EPIC BC 1292, LC 3892)
  Symphony No. 2, Royal Philharmonic Orchestra, Beecham,
                              (ANGEL S 35509, 35509)
  Symphony No. 3, Philharmonia Orchestra, Klemperer
                              (ANGEL 35328) mono only
  ▸ *This earlier performance is far preferable to Klemperer's later rerecording with the same orchestra (Angel S 35853, 35853). If this earlier Klemperer recording is unobtainable, I would recommend the Barbirolli performance (Angel S 36461, stereo only).*
  Symphony No. 4, Columbia Symphony Orchestra, Walter
                              (COLUMBIA MS 6055, ML 5365)
  Symphony No. 5, Amsterdam Concertgebouw Orchestra, Kleiber
                          (RICHMOND 19105) mono only
  ▸ *The best performance of Beethoven's Fifth ever committed to the permanency of recording!*
  Symphony No. 6, Columbia Symphony Orchestra, Walter
                              (COLUMBIA MS 6012, ML 5284)
  Symphony No. 7, Columbia Symphony Orchestra, Walter
                              (COLUMBIA MS 6082, ML 5404)

Symphony No. 8, Marlboro Festival Orchestra, Casals
(COLUMBIA MS 6931, ML 6331)

Symphony No. 9, Vienna Philharmonic Orchestra, Schmidt-
Isserstedt   (LONDON CS 1159, CM 4159)

Berlioz, Hector

Harold in Italy, Primrose, Boston Symphony Orchestra, Munch
(RCA LSC/LM 2228)

Symphonie Fantastique, Boston Symphony Orchestra, Munch
(RCA LSC/LM 2608); or London Symphony Orchestra, Davis
(PHILIPS SR 900101, MG 500101)

Brahms, Johannes

Academic Festival Overture and *Tragic Overture*, Cleveland Orchestra, Szell   (COLUMBIA MS 6965, ML 6365)

Double Concerto for Violin and Cello, Francescatti and Fournier,
Columbia Symphony Orchestra, Walter
(COLUMBIA MS 6158, ML 5493)

Piano Concerto No. 1, Curzon, London Symphony Orchestra,
Szell   (LONDON CS 6329, CM 9329)

Piano Concerto No. 2, Serkin, Cleveland Orchestra, Szell
(COLUMBIA MS 6967, ML 6367)

Violin Concerto, Oistrakh, French National Orchestra, Klemperer   (ANGEL S 35836, 35836)

Serenade No. 1, London Symphony Orchestra, Kertesz
(LONDON CS 6567) stereo only

Serenade No. 2, New York Philharmonic, Bernstein
(COLUMBIA MS 7132) stereo only

Symphony No. 1, Cleveland Orchestra, Szell
(COLUMBIA D3S 758, D3L 358)

▶ *A three-disc set that has all four Brahms Symphonies in
Szell, Cleveland performances.*

Symphony No. 2, Vienna Philharmonic Orchestra, Monteux
(RCA VICS/VIC 1055)

Symphony No. 3, Cleveland Orchestra, Szell, (COLUMBIA MS
6685, ML 6085); or included in (COLUMBIA D3S 758, D3L 358)

Symphony No. 4, Cleveland Orchestra, Szell
(COLUMBIA D3S 758, D3L 358)

Variations on the St. Anthony Chorale, Cleveland Orchestra,
Szell   (COLUMBIA MS 6965, ML 6365)

Britten, Benjamin

Sinfonia da Requiem, New Philharmonia Orchestra, Britten
(LONDON OS 25937, CM 5937)

Young Person's Guide to the Orchestra, London Symphony Orchestra, Britten   (LONDON CS 6398, CM 9398)

Variations on a Theme by Frank Bridge, Bath Festival Chamber
Orchestra, Menuhin   (ANGEL S 36303, 36303)

Bruch, Max
Violin Concerto No. 1, Heifetz, New Symphony Orchestra, Sargent (RCA LSC/LM 2652)

Bruckner, Anton
Symphony No. 4, Columbia Symphony Orchestra, Walter, included in (COLUMBIA M2S 622, M2L 273)
Symphony No. 7, Philharmonia Orchestra, Klemperer
(ANGEL S 3626, 3626)
Symphony No. 8, Berlin Philharmonic Orchestra, Jochum
(DEUTSCHE GRAMMOPHON GESELLSCHAFT 138918/9, 18918/9)
Symphony No. 9, Vienna Philharmonic Orchestra, Mehta
(LONDON CS 6462, CM 9462)

Chopin, Frederic
Piano Concerto No. 1, Rubinstein, New Symphony Orchestra, Skrowaczewski (RCA LSC/LM 2575)
Piano Concerto No. 2, Ashkenazy, London Symphony Orchestra, Zinman (LONDON CS 6440, CM 9440)

Copland, Aaron
Appalachian Spring, New York Philharmonic, Bernstein
(COLUMBIA MS 6355, ML 5755)
Billy the Kid and *Rodeo*, New York Philharmonic, Bernstein
(COLUMBIA MS 6175, ML 5575)
Music for the Theater, New York Philharmonic, Bernstein
(COLUMBIA MS 6698, ML 6098)

Debussy, Claude
Iberia, NBC Symphony Orchestra, Toscanini
(RCA VIC 1246), mono only
La Mer, NBC Symphony Orchestra, Toscanini
(RCA VIC 1246), mono only
Nocturnes, Boston Symphony Orchestra, Monteux
(RCA VICS/VIC 1027)

Dvořák, Anton
Cello Concerto, Casals, Czech Philharmonic Orchestra, Szell
(ANGEL COLH 30), mono only
▶ *One of the truly Great Recordings of the Century.*
Overture Trilogy, Vienna State Opera Orchestra, Somogyi
(WESTMINSTER WST 17072, XWN 19072)
Serenade No. 1, Israel Philharmonic, Kubelik
(LONDON STS 15037) stereo only
Serenade No. 2, Musica Aeterna Chamber Orchestra, Waldman
(DECCA 710137, 10137)
Symphony No. 3, London Symphony Orchestra, Kertesz
(LONDON CS 6525, CM 9525)
Symphony No. 4, London Symphony Orchestra, Kertesz
(LONDON CS 6526, CM 9526)

Symphony No. 6, London Symphony Orchestra, Kertesz
(LONDON CS 6495, CM 9495)
Symphony No. 7, London Symphony Orchestra, Monteux
(RCA VICS/VIC 1310)
Symphony No. 8, Hallé Orchestra, Barbirolli
(VANGUARD 133SD, 133)
Symphony No. 9, NBC Symphony Orchestra, Toscanini
(RCA VIC 1249), mono only
▶ *One of the best of all the Toscanini recordings.*

Dukas, Paul
The Sorcerer's Apprentice, Boston Symphony Orchestra, Munch
(RCA VICS/VIC 1060)

Enesco, Georges
Roumanian Rhapsodies Nos. 1 and 2, Philadelphia Orchestra,
Ormandy   (COLUMBIA MS 6018, ML 5299)

Falla, Manuel de
Nights in the Gardens of Spain, Soriano, Paris Conservatory Orchestra, Burgos   (ANGEL S 36131, 36131)
The Three-Cornered Hat, De los Angeles, Philharmonia Orchestra, Burgos   (ANGEL S 36235, 36235)

Franck, César
Symphonic Variations, Casadesus, Philadelphia Orchestra, Or-
mandy   (COLUMBIA MS 6070, ML 5388)
Symphony in D minor, Chicago Symphony Orchestra, Monteux
(RCA LSC/LM 2514)

Gabrieli, Giovanni
Sonata pian' e forte, London Gabrieli Brass Ensemble
(NONESUCH 71118, 1118)

Gershwin, George
An American in Paris, New York Philharmonic, Bernstein
(COLUMBIA MS 6091, ML 5413)
Piano Concerto, Wild, Boston Pops Orchestra, Fiedler
(RCA LSC/LM 2586)
Rhapsody in Blue, Bernstein, Columbia Symphony Orchestra,
Bernstein   (COLUMBIA MS 6091, ML 5413)

Grieg, Edvard
Piano Concerto, Rubinstein with Orchestra, Wallenstein
(RCA LSC/LM 2566)
Peer Gynt Suite No. 1, Cleveland Orchestra, Szell
(COLUMBIA MS 6877, ML 6277)

Handel, George Frederick
Concerti Grossi, Opus 6, Bath Festival Orchestra, Menuhin
(ANGEL S 3647, 3647)
Royal Fireworks Music, Chamber Orchestra, Mackerras
(VANGUARD BACH GUILD 5046, 630)

Water Music, Bath Festival Orchestra, Menuhin
(ANGEL S 36173, 36173)

Haydn, Franz Josef
Trumpet Concerto, Wobitsch, Zagreb Soloists, Janigro
(VANGUARD BACH GUILD 5053, 641)
Cello Concerto in C, Rostropovitch, English Chamber Orchestra, Britten
(LONDON CS 6419, CM 9419)
Cello Concerto in D, Starker, Philharmonia Orchestra, Giulini
(ANGEL S 35725, 35725)
Symphonies Nos. 6, 7, and 8, Saar Chamber Orchestra, Risten-part
(NONESUCH 71015, 1015)
Symphony No. 13, London Little Orchestra, Jones
(NONESUCH 71121, 1121)
Symphony No. 22, Suisse Romande Orchestra, Ansermet
(LONDON CS 6481, CM 9481)
Symphony No. 39, Esterhazy Orchestra, Blum
(VANGUARD 71123, 1123)
Symphony No. 44, Zagreb Symphony, Janigro
(VANGUARD 2145, 1106)
Symphony No. 49, Zagreb Symphony, Janigro
(VANGUARD 2147, 1108)
Symphony No. 80, London Little Orchestra, Jones
(NONESUCH 71131, 1131)
Symphony No. 86, Cincinnati Symphony Orchestra, Rudolf
(DECCA 710107, 10107)
Last six *London Symphonies Nos. 99 to 104,* Royal Philharmonic Orchestra, Beecham
(ANGEL S 36254/6, 36254/6)

Hindemith, Paul
Mathis der Maler, Philadelphia Orchestra, Ormandy
(COLUMBIA MS 6562, ML 5962)
Symphonic Metamorphosis on Themes of Weber, Philadelphia Orchestra, Ormandy
(COLUMBIA MS 6562, ML 5962)

Ives, Charles
Symphony No. 2, New York Philharmonic, Bernstein
(COLUMBIA MS 6889, ML 6289)
Symphony No. 4, American Symphony Orchestra, Stokowski
(COLUMBIA MS 6775, ML 6175)

Khatchaturian, Aram
Piano Concerto, Hollander, Royal Philharmonic Orchestra, Previn
(RCA LSC/LM 2801)
Violin Concerto, Kogan, Boston Symphony Orchestra, Monteux
(RCA VICS/VIC 1153)
Gayne Ballet, London Symphony Orchestra, Fistoulari
(EVEREST 3052, 6052)

Masquerade Suite, RCA Victor Orchestra, Kondrashin
(RCA LSC/LM 2398)

Liszt, Franz
Piano Concerto No. 1, Richter, London Symphony Orchestra,
Kondrashin (PHILIPS 900000, 500000)
Piano Concerto No. 2, Richter, London Symphony Orchestra,
Kondrashin (PHILIPS 900000, 500000)
Faust Symphony, New York Philharmonic, Bernstein
(COLUMBIA M2S 699, M2L 299)
Hungarian Fantasy, Cherkassky, Berlin Philharmonic Orchestra,
Karajan
(DEUTSCHE GRAMMOPHON GESELLSCHAFT 138692, 18692)
Mazeppa, Boston Pops Orchestra, Fiedler (RCA LSC/LM 2442)
Les Préludes, London Symphony Orchestra, Dorati
(MERCURY SR 90214, MG 50214)

Lully, Jean Baptiste
Le Bourgeois Gentilhomme, Mainz Chamber Orchestra, Kehr
(VOX 501070, 1070)

Mahler, Gustav
Das Lied von der Erde, Vienna Philharmonic Orchestra, Bern-
stein (LONDON OS 26005, CM 36005)
Symphony No. 1, London Symphony Orchestra, Solti
(LONDON CS 6401, CM 9401)
Symphony No. 2, London Symphony Orchestra, Solti
(LONDON CSA 2217, CMA 7217)
Symphony No. 4, New York Philharmonic, Bernstein, (COLUMBIA
MS 6152, ML 5485); or Cleveland Orchestra, Szell
(COLUMBIA MS 6833, ML 6233)
Symphony No. 5, New York Philharmonic, Bernstein
(COLUMBIA M2S 698, M2L 298)
Symphony No. 8, London Symphony Orchestra, Bernstein
(COLUMBIA M2S 751, M2L 351)
Symphony No. 9, Vienna Symphony Orchestra, Horenstein (VOX
VBX 116), mono only, a 3-disc set also containing Horenstein-
conducted performances of *Symphony No. 1* and *Kindertoten-
lieder.*
▶ *An album absolutely indispensable to any Mahler addict,
especially since Horenstein is revealed as one of the great-
est of all Mahler interpreters ever to record any of the
master's music.*

Martinu, Bohuslav
Piano Concerto No. 3, Palenicek, Czech Philharmonic Orchestra,
Ancerl (ARTIA 7205, 205)
Piano Concerto No. 4, Palenicek, Brno State Philharmonic, Pinkas
(ARTIA S 712, 712)

Violin Concerto, Belcik, Prague Symphony Orchestra, Neumann
(ARTIA 7205, 205)
Symphony No. 4, Czech Philharmonic Orchestra, Turnovsky
(PARLIAMENT S 621, 621)

Mendelssohn, Felix
A Midsummer Night's Dream, London Symphony Orchestra, Chorus and Soloists, Maag (LONDON CS 6001, CM 9201)
▶ *Of the several recordings of a Suite from the complete score, my first recommendation would be Cleveland Orchestra, Szell, (Columbia MS 7002, ML 6402).*
Piano Concerto No. 1, Serkin, Philadelphia Orchestra, Ormandy
(COLUMBIA MS 6128, ML 5456)
Violin Concerto in E minor, Szeryng, London Symphony Orchestra, Dorati (MERCURY SR 90406, MG 50406)
Symphony No. 3, London Symphony Orchestra, Maag
(LONDON CS 6191, CM 9252)
Symphony No. 4, Marlboro Festival Orchestra, Casals
(COLUMBIA MS 6931, ML 6331)

Mozart, Wolfgang A.
Piano Concerto No. 9, Ashkenazy, London Symphony Orchestra, Kertesz (LONDON CS 6501, CM 9501)
Piano Concerto No. 15, Bernstein, Vienna Philharmonic Orchestra, Bernstein (LONDON CS 6499, CM 9499)
Piano Concerto No. 19, Serkin, Columbia Symphony Orchestra, Szell (COLUMBIA MS 6534, ML 5934)
Piano Concerto No. 20
▶ *Unfortunately, Bernie Siff has never recorded the score. My second choice, therefore, is Rubinstein with Orchestra, Wallenstein, (RCA LSC/LM 2635).*
Piano Concerto No. 21, Rubinstein with Orchestra, Wallenstein
(RCA LSC/LM 2634)
Piano Concerto No. 23, Casadesus, Columbia Symphony, Szell
(COLUMBIA MS 6194, ML 5594)
Piano Concerto No. 24, Haskil, Lamoureux Orchestra, Markevitch (EPIC BC 1143, LC 3798)
Piano Concerto No. 27, Casadesus, Columbia Symphony Orchestra, Szell (COLUMBIA MS 6403, ML 5803)
Violin Concerto No. 3, Francescatti, Columbia Symphony Orchestra, Walter (COLUMBIA MS 6063, ML 5381)
Violin Concerto No. 4, Heifetz, New Symphony Orchestra, Sargent (RCA LSC/LM 2652)
Violin Concerto No. 5, Stern, Columbia Symphony Orchestra, Szell (COLUMBIA MS 6557, ML 5957)
Divertimento, K 131, Cleveland Orchestra, Szell
(COLUMBIA MS 6968, ML 6368)

Divertimento, K 136, Bath Festival Orchestra, Menuhin
(ANGEL S 36429, 36429)

Divertimento, K 251, English Chamber Orchestra, Davis
(OISEAU LYRE 60029, 50198)

Divertimento, K 287, Vienna Octet   (LONDON CS 6352, CM 9352)

Divertimento, K 334, Berlin Philharmonic Orchestra, Karajan
(DEUTSCHE GRAMMOPHON GESELLSCHAFT 139008, 39008)

Eine kleine Nachtmusik, Columbia Symphony Orchestra, Walter
(COLUMBIA MS 6356, ML 5756)

Serenade, K 239, Lucerne Festival Strings, Baumgartner
(DEUTSCHE GRAMMOPHON GESELLSCHAFT 136480) stereo only

Serenade, K 361, London Wind Soloists
(LONDON CS 6346, CM 9346)

Symphony No. 20, Mainz Chamber Orchestra, Kehr
(TURNABOUT 34002, 4002)

Symphony No. 25, London Symphony Orchestra, Davis
(PHILIPS 900133, 500133)

Symphony No. 28, Cleveland Orchestra, Szell
(COLUMBIA MS 6858, ML 6258)

Symphony No. 29, New Philharmonia Orchestra, Klemperer
(ANGEL S 36329, 36329)

Symphony No. 35, Columbia Symphony Orchestra, Walter
(COLUMBIA MS 6255, ML 5655)

Symphony No. 36, Vienna Philharmonic Orchestra, Bernstein
(LONDON CS 6499, CM 9499)

Symphony No. 38, London Symphony Orchestra, Maag
(LONDON CS 6107), stereo only

Symphony No. 39, Cleveland Orchestra, Szell
(EPIC BC 1106, LC 3740)

Symphony No. 40, Philharmonia Orchestra, Klemperer, (ANGEL
S 36183, 36183); or Columbia Symphony Orchestra, Walter
(COLUMBIA MS 6494, ML 5894)

Symphony No. 41, Columbia Symphony Orchestra, Walter, (CO-
LUMBIA MS 6255, ML 5655); or NBC Symphony Orchestra,
Toscanini   (RCA LM 1030), mono only

Sinfonia Concertante, K 364, Druian and Skernick, Cleveland Orchestra, Szell   (COLUMBIA MS 6625, ML 6025)

Musorgski, Modest

Pictures at an Exhibition (orchestrated by Ravel), Suisse Romande Orchestra, Ansermet   (LONDON CS 6177, CM 9246)

Nielsen, Carl

Symphony No. 3, Royal Danish Orchestra, Bernstein
(COLUMBIA MS 6769, ML 6169)

Symphony No. 5, New York Philharmonic, Bernstein
(COLUMBIA MS 6414, ML 5814)

Offenbach, Jacques
Gaîté Parisienne, Ballet score arranged by Rosenthal, New Philharmonia Orchestra, Munch (LONDON 21011, 55009)
Paganini, Nicolo
Violin Concerto No. 1, Friedman, Chicago Symphony Orchestra, Hendl (RCA LSC/LM 2610)
Prokofiev, Serge
Piano Concerto No. 3, Graffman, Cleveland Orchestra, Szell (COLUMBIA MS 6925, ML 6325)
Violin Concerto No. 1, Stern, Philadelphia Orchestra, Ormandy (COLUMBIA MS 6635, ML 6035)
Violin Concerto No. 2, Perlman, Boston Symphony Orchestra, Leinsdorf (RCA LSC/LM 2962)
Lieutenant Kije Suite, Philadelphia Orchestra, Ormandy (COLUMBIA MS 6545, ML 5945)
Peter and the Wolf, Flanders, Philharmonia Orchestra, Kurtz (CAPITOL SG/G 7211)
Romeo and Juliet (Suites), Minneapolis Symphony Orchestra, Skrowaczewski (MERCURY SR 90315, MG 50315)
Scythian Suite, Boston Symphony Orchestra, Leinsdorf (RCA LSC/LM 2934)
Symphony No. 1, Classical, Philadelphia Orchestra, Ormandy (COLUMBIA MS 6545, ML 5945)
Symphony No. 5, New York Philharmonic, Bernstein (COLUMBIA MS 7005, ML 6405)
Symphony No. 6, Philadelphia Orchestra, Ormandy (COLUMBIA MS 6489, ML 5889)

Rachmaninoff, Sergei
Piano Concerto No. 2, Ashkenazy, Moscow Philharmonic Orchestra, Kondrashin (LONDON CS 6390, CM 9390)
Piano Concerto No. 3, Cliburn, Symphony of the Air, Kondrashin (RCA LSC/LM 2355)
Rhapsody on a Theme by Paganini, Graffman, New York Philharmonic, Bernstein (COLUMBIA MS 6634, ML 6034)
Ravel, Maurice
Bolero, New York Philharmonic, Bernstein (COLUMBIA MS 6011, ML 5293)
Piano Concerto, Katchen, London Symphony Orchestra, Kertesz (LONDON CS 6487, CM 9487)
Daphnis et Chloé, Boston Symphony Orchestra, Munch (RCA LSC/LM 2568)
Rapsodie Espagnole, London Symphony Orchestra, Monteux (LONDON CS 6248, CM 9317)
La Valse, New York Philharmonic, Bernstein (COLUMBIA MS 6011, ML 5293)

Respighi, Ottorino
　Fountains of Rome and *Pines of Rome*, NBC Symphony Orchestra, Toscanini (RCA VIC 1244, mono only); New Philharmonia Orchestra, Munch   (LONDON 21024) stereo only
Rimski-Korsakov, Nikolai
　Capriccio Espagnole, London Symphony Orchestra, Argenta
　　　　　　　　　　　　　　　　　　(LONDON CS 6006, CM 9192)
　Scheherazade, Royal Philharmonic Orchestra, Beecham
　　　　　　　　　　　　　　　　　　(ANGEL S 35505, 35505)
Rossini, Gioacchino
　La Boutique Fantasque, Ballet score arranged by Respighi, Israel Philharmonic Orchestra, Solti   (LONDON CSTS 15005)
Saint-Saëns, Camille
　Cello Concerto No. 1, Fournier, Lamoureux Orchestra, Martinon
　　　　　　　(DEUTSCHE GRAMMOPHON GESELLSCHAFT 138669, 18669)
　Piano Concerto No. 2, Entremont, Philadelphia Orchestra, Ormandy   (COLUMBIA MS 6778, ML 6178)
　Piano Concerto No. 4, Casadesus, New York Philharmonic, Bernstein   (COLUMBIA MS 6377, ML 5777)
　Symphony No. 3, Boston Symphony Orchestra, Munch
　　　　　　　　　　　　　　　　　　(RCA LSC/LM 2341)
Schönberg, Arnold
　Transfigured Night, Southwest German Radio Symphony Orchestra, Horenstein   (VOX 510460, 10460)
Schubert, Franz
　Rosamunde, Incidental Music, Cleveland Orchestra, Szell
　　　　　　　　　　　　　　　　　　(COLUMBIA MS 7002, ML 6402)
　Symphony No. 5, Royal Philharmonic Orchestra, Beecham
　　　　　　　　　　　　　　　　　　(CAPITOL SG/G 7212)
　Symphony No. 8, Columbia Symphony Orchestra, Walter
　　　　　　　　　　　　　　　　　　(COLUMBIA MS 6218, ML 5618)
　Symphony No. 9, London Symphony Orchestra, Krips
　　　　　　　　　　　　　　　　　　(LONDON CS 6061, CM 9007)
Schumann, Robert
　Piano Concerto, Serkin, Philadelphia Orchestra, Ormandy
　　　　　　　　　　　　　　　　　　(COLUMBIA MS 6688, ML 6088)
　Cello Concerto, Rostropovitch, Leningrad Philharmonic Orchestra, Rozhdestvensky
　　　　　　　(DEUTSCHE GRAMMOPHON GESELLSCHAFT 138674, 18674)
　Symphony No. 1, Berlin Philharmonic Orchestra, Kubelik
　　　　　　　(DEUTSCHE GRAMMOPHON GESELLSCHAFT 138860, 18860)
　Symphony No. 4, New York Philharmonic, Bernstein
　　　　　　　　　　　　　　　　　　(COLUMBIA MS 6256, ML 5656)
Shostakovitch, Dmitri
　Piano Concerto No. 1, Previn, New York Philharmonic, Bernstein
　　　　　　　　　　　　　　　　　　(COLUMBIA MS 6392, ML 5792)

Symphony No. 1, Symphony of the Air, Stokowski
(UNITED ARTISTS 8004, 7004)

Symphony No. 5, New York Philharmonic, Bernstein
(COLUMBIA MS 6115, ML 5445)

Symphony No. 10, USSR Symphony Orchestra, Svetlanov
(ANGEL/MELODIYA S 40025, 40025)

Sibelius, Jean
Finlandia and *Swan of Tuonela*, Symphony Orchestra, Stokowski
(CAPITOL SP/P 8399)

Violin Concerto, Heifetz, Chicago Symphony Orchestra, Hendl
(RCA LSC/LM 2435)

Symphony No. 1, Vienna Philharmonic Orchestra, Maazel
(LONDON CS 6375, CM 9375)

Symphony No. 2, Amsterdam Concertgebouw Orchestra, Szell
(PHILIPS PHS 900092, PHM 500092)

Symphony No. 5, New York Philharmonic, Bernstein
(COLUMBIA MS 6749, ML 6149)

Symphony No. 7, Vienna Philharmonic Orchestra, Maazel
(LONDON CS 6488, CM 9488)

Smetana, Bedřich
The Moldau, Symphony Orchestra, Stokowski   (RCA LSC/LM 2471)

Strauss, Richard
Death and Transfiguration, Philharmonia Orchestra, Klemperer
(ANGEL S 35976, 35976)

Don Juan, Stadium Concerts Orchestra, Stokowski
(EVEREST SDBR 3023, LPBR 6023)

Ein Heldenleben, Royal Philharmonic Orchestra, Beecham
(SERAPHIM S 60041, 60041)

Till Eulenspiegel's Merry Pranks, Cleveland Orchestra, Szell
(EPIC BC 1011, LC 3439)

Stravinsky, Igor
The Firebird Suite, Symphony Orchestra, Stravinsky
(COLUMBIA MS 7011, ML 6411)

Petrouchka, Suisse Romande Orchestra, Ansermet, (LONDON CS
6009, CM 9229); or Boston Symphony Orchestra, Monteux
(RCA LSC/LM 2376)

The Rite of Spring, New York Philharmonic, Bernstein
(COLUMBIA MS 6319, ML 5719)

Symphony of Psalms, CBC Symphony, Stravinsky
(COLUMBIA MS 6548, ML 5948)

Symphony in Three Movements, Columbia Symphony Orchestra,
Stravinsky   (COLUMBIA MS 6331, ML 5731)

Tchaikovsky, Pëtr Ilich
Piano Concerto No. 1, Cliburn, Symphony Orchestra, Kondrashin
(RCA LSC/LM 2252)

Violin Concerto, Heifetz, Chicago Symphony Orchestra, Reiner
(RCA LSC/LM 2129)

Capriccio Italien, Symphony Orchestra, Kondrashin
(RCA LSC/LM 2323)

Francesca da Rimini, New York Philharmonic, Bernstein
(COLUMBIA MS 6258), stereo only

Nutcracker Suite, New York Philharmonic, Bernstein
(COLUMBIA MS 6193, ML 5593)

Romeo and Juliet, Boston Symphony Orchestra, Munch
(RCA LSC/LM 2565)

Serenade for Strings, London Symphony Orchestra, Barbirolli
(ANGEL S 36269, 36269)

Sleeping Beauty Suite, New Philharmonia Orchestra, Stokowski
(LONDON 21008, 55006)

Swan Lake Suite, New Philharmonia Orchestra, Stokowski
(LONDON 21008, 55006)

Symphony No. 4, Vienna Philharmonic Orchestra, Maazel
(LONDON CS 6429, CM 9429)

Symphony No. 5, Boston Symphony Orchestra, Koussevitzky,
(RCA LM 2901), mono only; or Philadelphia Orchestra, Ormandy, Columbia   (MS 6109, ML 5435)

Symphony No. 6, Philharmonia Orchestra, Giulini
(SERAPHIM S 60031, 60031)

Variations on a Rococo Theme, Starker, London Symphony Orchestra, Dorati   (MERCURY SR 90409, MG 50409)

Vaughan Williams, Ralph

Fantasia on a Theme by Thomas Tallis, London Sinfonia, Barbirolli   (ANGEL S 36101, 36101)

Symphony No. 2, London, Hallé Orchestra, Barbirolli
(VANGUARD S 134, 134)

Vivaldi, Antonio

Concerti for Diverse Instruments, New York Philharmonic, Bernstein   (COLUMBIA MS 6131, ML 5459)

The Four Seasons, New York Sinfonietta, Goberman
(ODYSSEY 32160132, 32160131)

Wagner, Richard

Miscellaneous Orchestral Works, NBC Symphony Orchestra,
Toscanini   (RCA VIC 1247), mono only

Miscellaneous Orchestral Works, London Symphony Orchestra,
Stokowski   (LONDON 21016), stereo only

MUSIC OF THE BAROQUE

This list of recordings has been chosen with two points in mind: providing a representative sample of Baroque composers, styles, and forms; and including primarily those recordings whose style of performance matches most closely the spirit of the Baroque era.

As we have learned more about the age itself, so have we discovered that the musicians of the seventeenth and eighteenth centuries did not interpret in the style we inherited from our nineteenth-century ancestors. The most obvious differences have to do with ornamentation, phrasing, articulation, dynamics, tempo, instrumental forces, and embellishment. There are quite a few performers today, as distinct from only a few years ago, who have applied themselves to learning about the performance practices of the Baroque age, who understand the necessity for tightening the dotted rhythms of a French Overture, for playing correct ornaments, for phrasing in considerable detail, and for providing embellishments for repeats of a movement. These are the recordings I enjoy the most and which I prefer to recommend.

Albinoni, Tomaso
Concerto a Cinque, Opus 5, No. 5; also includes Handel, *Concerto Grosso, Opus 6, No. 1;* Avison, *Concerto, Opus 9, No. 11;* Manfredini, *Concerto, Opus 3, No. 10;* Telemann, *Concerto in F, (Tafelmusik II)*, Marriner, St. Martin-in-the-Fields Academy   (L'OISEAU-LYRE S 264)
  ▶ *Marriner and his splendid British ensemble bring enormous* ESPRIT *and sensitivity to all their discs.*

Bach, C. P. E.
Concerto in E flat for Harpsichord, Fortepiano, and Orchestra; also includes Fasch, *Sonata for Flute, 2 Recorders, and Continuo;* Quantz, *Trio Sonata in C,* Stadelman, Neumeyer, Wenzinger, Schola Cantorum Basiliensis
                (DEUTSCHE GRAMMOPHON GESELLSCHAFT ARC-73173)
  ▶ *Interesting blend of old and new instruments, illustrating the* GALANT *perfectly.*

Bach, J. S.

Six Brandenburg Concerti, Dart, London Philomusica (2-OISEAU-LYRE S 60005/6); mono version includes *Double Violin Concerto* and *Suites Nos. 3 and 4* (3-OISEAU-LYRE 50167, 50160, 50159); or Harnoncourt, Vienna Concentus Musicus (original instruments) (2-TELEFUNKEN S 9459/60)
▶ *Both stylish, with Harnoncourt using original instruments.*

Cantatas Nos. 4, Christ lag in Todesbanden, and 111, Was mein Got will, Giebel, Höffgen, Rotzsch, Adam, Thomas, Leipzig Gewandhaus Orchestra and Thomanerchor (TURNABOUT 3 4048)

Cantatas Nos. 57, Selig ist der Mann, and 140, Wachet auf! Buckel, Stämpfli, Ristenpart, Saar Choir and Orchestra
(NONESUCH 7 1029)

Cantatas Nos. 159, Sehet, wir geh'n hinauf, and 170, Vergnügte Ruh', beliebte Seelenlust, Baker, Tear, Shirley-Quick, Marriner, St. Martin-in-the-Fields Academy (L'OISEAU-LYRE S 295)

Harpsichord Concerti Nos. 1 in D minor and 2 in E Major, Malcolm, Münchinger, Stuttgart Chamber Orchestra
(LONDON 9392/6392)

Concerto in D minor for Two Violins; Violin Concerti Nos. 1 in A minor and 2 in E Major, Menuhin, Ferras, Masters Chamber Orchestra (CAPITOL S G-7210)

Six French Suites, Dart on clavichord
(L'OISEAU-LYRE 50208/60039)

Goldberg Variations, Kirkpatrick on harpsichord (DEUTSCHE GRAMMOPHON GESELLSCHAFT ARC 7 3138); or Landowska on harpsichord (RCA VICTOR LM-1080)
▶ *Equally valid, with Landowska the more flamboyant but older recording.*

Italian Concerto; also includes *English Suite No. 2, Twelve Little Preludes, Fantasia in A minor, Adagio in G, Prelude and Fughetta in C*, Kipnis on harpsichord (It. Conc. & Suite) and clavichord (remainder) (EPIC LC 3932/BC 1332)
▶ *Good contrast between harpsichord and clavichord, with one brief Prelude played on each instrument.*

Lute Music, Gerwig (NONESUCH 7 1137)

Magnificat; also includes *Cantata No. 78*, Stader, Töpper, Haefliger, Fischer-Dieskau, Richter, Munich Bach Chorus and Orchestra (DEUTSCHE GRAMMOPHON GESELLSCHAFT ARC-73197)

Mass in B minor, Stader, Töpper, Haefliger, Engen, Fischer-Dieskau, Richter, Munich Bach Chorus and Orchestra
(3-DEUTSCHE GRAMMOPHON GESELLSCHAFT ARC-73177/9)

Motets Nos. 2, 3, and 5, Wolters, N. German Singkreis
(NONESUCH 7 1060)

Musical Offering, Menuhin, Bath Festival Orchestra
(ANGEL S 35731)

Organ Music, including *Toccata in D minor, Passacaglia, Preludes and Fugues, Chorales,* etc., Walcha
   (5-DEUTSCHE GRAMMOPHON GESELLSCHAFT ARC S KL 1 306/10)
   ▶ *Excellent selection, played by one of the most distinguished organists of our time.*
Orgelbüchlein (with settings of original chorales), Rilling, Gedaechtniskirche Chorus   (4-NONESUCH 73015)
Partita in B minor; also includes *Concerto after Vivaldi No. 15, Fantasia in C minor, Toccata in F sharp minor,* Puyana on harpsichord   (MERCURY 50369/90369)
St. John Passion, Equiluz, Van t'Hoff, Van Egmond, Villisech, Schneeweis, Gillesberger, Vienna Concentus Musicus (original instruments) (3-TELEFUNKEN S KH-19); or Harwood, Pears, Watts, Willcocks, London Philomusica (in English)
   (3-LONDON 4348/1320)
   ▶ *German versus English performance—former particularly interesting attempt at authenticity.*
Eight Sonatas for Flute, Harpsichord, Larrieu, Puyana (2-MERCURY SR 2 9125); or Shaffer, Malcolm (seven sonatas)
   (2-ANGEL S 36337, 36350)
Six Sonatas for Violin and Harpsichord, Menuhin, Malcolm, Gauntlett   (2-ANGEL S 3629)
Four Suites for Orchestra, Harnoncourt, Vienna Concentus Musicus (original instruments)   (2-TELEFUNKEN S 9509/10)
   ▶ *Like the Concentus Musicus* BRANDENBURGS, *very stylish and controversial, with original instruments in greatly reduced forces.*
The Well-Tempered Clavier, Books I and II, Landowska on harpsichord   (6-RCA VICTOR LM 6801)
   ▶ *A landmark in the extensive Landowska discography.*

Biber, Heinrich Johann
Battalia, Sonata No. 8, Pavern Kirchfahrt, etc.; also includes Muffat, *Concerto Grosso, Suite No. 8,* Harnoncourt, Vienna Concentus Musicus
   (DEUTSCHE GRAMMOPHON GESELLSCHAFT ARC-73262)
Mystery Sonatas for Violin and Continuo, Monosoff, Smith, Scholz, Miller   (3-CAMBRIDGE 1 811)
Böhm, Georg
Organ Music; also includes Buxtehude and Walther Organ Music, Gilbert   (PIROUETTE S 19034)

Boismortier, Joseph Bodin de
Concerto à 5 in E minor, Opus 37; included in *French 18th-Century Concert of Chamber Music,* Paris Baroque Ensemble
   (MUSIC GUILD S 111)
Daphnis et Chloë ballet suite; also includes La Barre, *Flute*

Suite; Leclair, *Violin Sonata (Tombeau);* Mouton, *Lute Suite,*
Seiler, Chamber Orchestra   (HELIODOR S 25018)
▶ *The* DAPHNIS ET CHLOË *suite is an unparalleled charmer.*

Boyce, William
Eight Symphonies, Janigro, Solisti di Zagreb   (BACH GUILD 70 668)
▶ *Brief, delightful, in Handelian style.*

Buxtehude, Dietrich
Five Cantatas, Krebs, Fischer-Dieskau, Gorvin, Bach Orchestra,
Berlin   (DEUTSCHE GRAMMOPHON GESELLSCHAFT ARC-3096)

Carissimi, Giacomo
Jepthe, Judicium Salomonis, Rilling, Spandauer Kantorei
(TURNABOUT 3 4089)

Charpentier, Marc-Antoine
Magnificat, Te Deum, Martinia, Paillard Orchestra, Chorus
(BACH GUILD 70 663)

Corelli, Arcangelo
Twelve Concerti Grossi, Opus 6, Goberman, Vienna Sinfonietta
(3-ODYSSEY 32360001/32360002)

Corrette, Michel
Concertos comique Nos. 3, 4, and 6, Opus 8, for flutes, Rampal,
Baron, Bennett, Schaeffer, Robison, Veyron-Lacroix, Soyer;
also includes Boismortier, *Concertos for Flutes*
(CONNOISSEUR SOCIETY S 362)

Couperin, Louis
Works of, Blanchard Chorus, Chapuis on organ, Mueller on harp-
sichord, Wind ensemble
(DEUTSCHE GRAMMOPHON GESELLSCHAFT ARC-73261)

Daquin, Louis-Claude
Noëls for Organ, Biggs   (COLUMBIA ML 5567, MS 6167)

Frescobaldi, Girolamo
Toccate canzoni, Arie Musicali; also includes Monteverdi,
Madrigals, Curtis, Berkeley Collegium Musicum
(CAMBRIDGE 1 708)

Froberger, Johann
Le Tombeau de M. Blancrocher, Suites, Dart on clavichord
(L'OISEAU-LYRE 50207/60038)
▶ *The sensitivity of the clavichord is wonderfully revealed.*

Fux, Johann
Ouverture, Sonata; also includes instrumental works by Biber,
Legrenzi, and Schmelzer, Harnoncourt, Vienna Concentus
Musicus   (BACH GUILD 70 690)

Gabrieli, Giovanni
Canzonas and other instrumental works; also includes works by
Gabrieli contemporaries, Wenzinger, Schola Cantorum Basil-
iensis (original instruments)
(DEUTSCHE GRAMMOPHON GESELLSCHAFT ARC-73154)

Motets, Negri, Biggs, Smith Singers, Texas Boys Choir
(COLUMBIA MS 7071)
Motets and Canzonas by Giovanni and Andrea Gabrieli, Stevens,
Ambrosian Singers   (ANGEL S 36443)
▶ *Relatively little duplication in these well-recorded collections.*
Geminiani, Francesco
Concerto Grosso, Opus 3, No. 3; also includes Bellini, *Oboe Concerto;* Corelli, *Concerto Grosso, Opus 6, No. 1;* Vivaldi,
Cello Concerto in C minor, Marriner, St. Martin-in-the-Fields
Academy   (L'OISEAU-LYRE S 277)
Handel, George Frederick
Arias, Oberlin, Dunn, Baroque Orchestra   (DECCA 7 9407)
Berenice Overture, "Arrival of the Queen of Sheba" from *Solomon, Oboe Concertos,* Marriner, St. Martin-in-the-Fields Academy   (LONDON ARGO 5 442)
Six Concerti Grossi, Opus 3, Marriner, St. Martin-in-the-Fields
Academy   (LONDON ARGO 5 400)
▶ *One of the most outstanding Baroque discs.*
Twelve Concerti Grossi, Opus 6, Wenzinger, Schola Cantorum
Basiliensis (original instruments) (3-DEUTSCHE GRAMMOPHON
GESELLSCHAFT ARC-73246/8); or Menuhin, Bath Festival Orchestra   (4-ANGEL S 3647)
▶ *Each version commendable; Wenzinger's attempts to be
particularly authentic. A new version by Marriner and the
Academy of St. Martin-in-the-Fields, unissued as of this
writing, promises to be the preferred interpretation.*
*Concerto in C, Alexanderfest; Concerto for Harp, Opus 4, No. 5;
Concerto for Harp and Lute, Opus 4, No. 6,* Jones, London
Philomusica   (L'OISEAU-LYRE 50181/60013)
Dixit Dominus, Willcocks, King's College, Cambridge
(ANGEL S 36331)
Julius Caesar (excerpts), Sutherland, Elkins, Sinclair, Horne,
Conrad, Bonynge, New Symphony
(LONDON 5876/25876)
Messiah, Harper, Watts, Wakefield, Shirley-Quirk, David, London Symphony Orchestra and Chorus, (3-PHILIPS PHM 3 592/
PHS 3 992); or Harwood, Baker, Esswood, Tear, Herincx,
Mackerras, English Chamber Orchestra, Ambrosian Singers
(3-ANGEL S 3705)
▶ *Each is stripped of Victorian overtones; Mackerras more
daring and imaginative in embellishments.*
*Royal Fireworks Music, Concerto for Two Wind Choirs and
Strings,* Mackerras, Wind Band, Pro Arte Orchestra
(BACH GUILD 630/5046)
*Sonatas for Recorder and Continuo, Opus 1, Nos. 1, 2, 4, 7, and
11,* Brüggen, Leonhardt   (TELEFUNKEN S 9421)

Suite in B flat for Harpsichord (Book II); included in collection
of English Harpsichord Music, Kipnis   (EPIC LC 3898/BC 1298)
Water Music (complete), Dart, London Philomusica (L'OISEAU-
LYRE 50178/60010); or Menuhin, Bath Festival Orchestra
(ANGEL S 36173)
▶ *Dart has perhaps the best flavor and lightness.*

Keiser, Reinhard

Croesus (excerpts); also includes operatic excerpts from Handel,
Almira; Mattheson, *Boris Gudenov;* Telemann, *Pimpinone,*
Prey, Otto, Brückner-Rüggeberg, Berlin Philharmonic
(ANGEL S 36273)
▶ *Unusual collection of early 18th-century Hamburg operatic*
excerpts.

Lalande, Michel-Richard de

Symphonies pour les soupers du roi, No. 1; also includes Mouret,
Suites de Simphonies, Scherbaum, Kuentz Chamber Orchestra
(DEUTSCHE GRAMMOPHON GESELLSCHAFT ARC-73233)

Leclair, Jean Marie

Concerto in C, Opus 7, No. 4; also includes *Flute Concerti* by
Grétry, Jacques Loeillet, and Quantz; C. Monteux, Marriner,
St. Martin-in-the-Fields Academy   (L'OISEAU-LYRE S 279)

Locatelli, Pietro

L'Arte del Violino, Opus 3, Concerti Nos. 1 to 4, Lautenbacher,
Kehr, Mainz Chamber Orchestra   (2-VOX 500 500)
Concerto Grosso, Opus 1, No. 9; also includes Corelli, *Concerto*
Grosso, Opus 6, No. 7; Torelli, *Concerto, Opus 6, No. 10;*
Albicastro, *Concerto No. 6 in B flat;* Handel, *Concerto Grosso,*
Opus 6, No. 6, Marriner, St. Martin-in-the-Fields Academy
(L'OISEAU-LYRE 50214/60045)

Louis XIII

Ballet de Merlaison; also includes Charpentier, *Messe pour*
Plusieurs Instruments, Chailley, Instrumental and Vocal Ensemble   (NONESUCH 7 1130)
▶ *Even kings could be composers, though not so distinguished*
as the professionals.

Lully, Jean Baptiste

Le Temple de la paix (ballet); also includes Fischer, *Journal de*
printemps, Opus 1 (Suites); Muffat, *Nobles Jeunesse Suite,* Fro-
ment, L'Oiseau-Lyre Ensemble   (L'OISEAU-LYRE 50136)
▶ *There is relatively little well-performed Lully on discs. This*
is one of the better ones.

Marcello, Alessandro

Oboe Concerto; Concerti Nos. 2, 3, 4, and 6, La Cetra, Cantore
(oboe), I Musici   (PHILIPS WS 9085)
▶ *Competently played, but not the last word in stylistic*
acumen.

Monteverdi, Claudio
Combattimento di Tancredi e Clorinda, Ballo delle Ingrate,
Stevens, Accademia Monteverdiana (EXPÉRIENCES ANONYMES 72)
Lamento d'Arianna and other madrigals; also includes madrigals
by Marenzio, Gesualdo, etc., Deller Consort
(BACH GUILD 70 671)
Madrigals, Deller Consort, Baroque Ensemble, (BACH GUILD
579/5007); or Jürgens, Hamburg Monteverdi Chorus
(TELEFUNKEN S 9438)
Madrigals; also includes Banchieri, *La Pazzia senile,* Sestetto
Italiano Luca Marenzio   (HELIODOR S 25060)
 ▸ *Relatively little duplication in these madrigal collections;
   the Sestetto Luca Marenzio has unusual charm.*
Magnificat for Six Voices, Mass for Four Voices, Malcolm,
Carmelite Priory (London) Chorus   (L'OISEAU-LYRE S 263)
 ▸ *Particular emphasis on emotional impact.*
Orfeo, Krebs, Guilleaume, Wenzinger
(DEUTSCHE GRAMMOPHON GESELLSCHAFT ARC-3035/6)
 ▸ *An old though serviceable recording; at least two new re-
   cordings are in preparation.*
Vespro della Beata Vergine (1610), Hansmann, Jacobeit, Rogers,
Van t'Hoff, Van Egmond, Villisech, Harnoncourt, Jürgens,
Concentus Musicus, Vienna Boys Choir, Hamburg Monteverdi
Chorus, (Original instruments)   (2-TELEFUNKEN S 9501/2)

Pergolesi, Giovanni Battista
Six Concertinos (attrib.), *Two Flute Concerti* (attrib.), Rampal,
Münchinger, Stuttgart Chamber Orchestra
(LONDON 9393 & 9395/6393 & 6395)

Praetorius, Michael
Terpsichore (Dances); also includes Schein, *Banchetto musicale
Suites;* Widmann, *Dances,* Terpsichore Collegium
(DEUTSCHE GRAMMOPHON GESELLSCHAFT ARC-73153)
 ▸ *Beautifully performed collection of early Baroque German
   dances.*

Purcell, Henry
Come Ye Sons of Art; also includes *Anthems,* Deller, Oriana
Chorus and Orchestra   (BACH GUILD 635/5047)
 ▸ *The piece with spectacular duet for countertenors is* SOUND
   THE TRUMPET.
Dido and Aeneas, Baker, Clark, Sinclair, Herincx, Lewis, Cham-
ber Orchestra, St. Anthony Singers (L'OISEAU-LYRE 50216/
60047); or Troyanos, McDaniel, Esswood, Mackerras, NW
German Radio Chamber Orchestra, Monteverdi Chorus
(DEUTSCHE GRAMMOPHON GESELLSCHAFT ARC-198424)
 ▸ *Distinguished performances of Purcell's short but great
   opera.*

Fantasias and Sonatas (selection), Menuhin, Bath Festival Ensemble　(ANGEL S 36270)

Suites from The Gordian Knot Untied and *The Virtuous Wife, Trumpet Sonata, Keyboard pieces,* Kehr, Cologne Rhenish Orchestra, Gerlin (harpsichord)　(NONESUCH 7 1027)

▶ *The orchestral work is quite stylish but heavy-handed keyboard work disappoints.*

Indian Queen, Cantelo, Tear, Brown Patridge, Keyte, Mackerras, English Chamber Orchestra, St. Anthony Singers　(L'OISEAU-LYRE S 294)

▶ *Purcell at both his most humorous and affecting.*

Dioclesian: Incidental Music, Deller, Vienna Concentus Musicus　(BACH GUILD 70 682)

Songs, Oberlin (countertenor) (COUNTERPOINT/ESOTERIC 5 535); *Songs* (also includes instrumental music), Deller, Cantelo, Bevan　(2-BACH GUILD 70 570/1)

Rameau, Jean Philippe

Hippolyte et Aricie, Lewis, English Chamber Orchestra, St. Anthony Singers　(3-L'OISEAU-LYRE S 286/8)

Suite in E minor for Harpsichord; also includes F. Couperin and L. Couperin, *Harpsichord Pieces;* Boismortier, *Suite No. 3 in E,* Kipnis (harpsichord)　(EPIC LC 3889/BC 1289)

Gavotte varié; also includes harpsichord works of C.P.E. Bach, Scarlatti, Fischer, F. and L. Couperin, Chambonnières, Dieupart, and Telemann, Puyana (harpsichord)

(MERCURY 50411/90411)

▶ *The last two discs provide a partial anthology of French Baroque harpsichord music.*

Pygmalion (ballet), Couraud, Lamoureux Chamber Orchestra　(DEUTSCHE GRAMMOPHON GESELLSCHAFT ARC-73202)

Le Temple de la Gloire, Suite; also includes Grétry, *Suite,* Leppard, English Chamber Orchestra　(L'OISEAU-LYRE S 297)

Scarlatti, Alessandro

Concertato in D; also includes concertos by Albinoni, Pergolesi, Tartini, and Vivaldi. Haas, London Baroque Ensemble　(VANGUARD EVERYMAN S 192)

▶ *Excellent Italian repertoire, played fairly well, but also with great conviction.*

Cantata, Su le Sponde del Tebro; also includes Mozart, *Exsultate Jubilate,* etc., Stader, Richter, Munich Bach Orchestra　(DEUTSCHE GRAMMOPHON GESELLSCHAFT 19291/136291)

Toccata No. 7 in D minor for Harpsichord; also includes harpsichord works by Pasquini, Cimarosa, Frescobaldi, Rossi, and Galuppi, Kipnis　(EPIC LC 3911/BC 1311)

Scarlatti, Domenico
  Sonatas for Harpsichord, Kirkpatrick *(60 Sonatas)* (4-ODYSSEY
    32260007, 32260012); or Landowska *(40 Sonatas)*
                                            (2-ANGEL COLH 73/304)
  ▶ *The Landowska 1930's recordings have great atmosphere.*
    Kirkpatrick is the renowned Scarlatti authority.
Schein, Johann Hermann
  Banchetto musicale, Suites Nos. 1 and 2; also includes Prae-
    torius, *Dances,* Conrad Ensemble   (NONESUCH 7 1128)
Schütz, Heinrich
  The Christmas Story, Ehmann, Westphalian Kantorei
                                            (VANGUARD EVERYMAN S 232)
  ▶ *The most accessible Schütz I know.*
  Klein Geistliche Konzerte, Book I, Ehmann, Westphalian Kan-
    torei   (2-NONESUCH 7 3012)
  Cantiones Sacrae, Eighteen Motets, Träder, Hannover Nieder-
    sächsischer Singkreis   (NONESUCH 1062/71062)
Soler, Padre Antonio
  Fandango, Two Sonatas; also includes sonatas by Scarlatti and
    Blasco de Nebra; Kipnis on harpsichord   (EPIC BC 1374)
Stölzel, Gottfried Heinrich
  *Concerto Grosso in D for Six Trumpets, Timpani, Double String
    Orchestra, and Continuo;* also includes Graupner, *Concerto for
    Two Flutes;* Pisendel, *Violin Concerto No. 1,* Redel, Chamber
    Orchestra   (DEUTSCHE GRAMMOPHON GESELLSCHAFT ARC-73266)
  ▶ *The late-Baroque Stölzel has enormous brilliance; the rest
    is somewhat dull.*
Tartini, Giuseppe
  Violin Concertos in D and G; also includes Nardini, *Violin Con-
    certo in E flat,* Melkus, Wenzinger, Vienna Capella Academy
                (DEUTSCHE GRAMMOPHON GESELLSCHAFT ARC-73270)
  Symphony in A; also includes orchestral works of Albinoni,
    Geminiani, and Locatelli; De Stoutz, Zurich Chamber Orchestra
                                            (VANGUARD EVERYMAN S 212)
Telemann, Georg Philipp
  Concerto in D for Horn and Orchestra; also includes Albinoni,
    Oboe Concerto, Opus 9, No. 4; Fasch, *Concerto in D for
    Trumpet;* K. Stamitz, *Clarinet Concerto;* Vivaldi, *Flute Con-
    certo (P. 77),* Penzel, Winschermann, Deutsche Bachsolisten
                                            (NONESUCH 7 1148)
  ▶ *Performance of* HORN CONCERTO *particularly virtuosic.*
  Concerto in C for Recorder, Strings, and Continuo; also includes
    Recorder Concerti by Handel and Vivaldi, Krainis, Marriner,
    London Strings   (MERCURY 50443/90443)
  Concerto in E minor for Recorder, Flute, and Strings; also in-

cludes *Concerto for Four Violins, Concerto for Flute and Oboe d'Amore, Concerto for Three Oboes and Three Violins,* Sparr, Schaeffer, Meyer

(DEUTSCHE GRAMMOPHON GESELLSCHAFT ARC-3109)

▶ *Telemann both old-fashioned and* AVANT-GARDE.

Don Quichotte Suite; also includes Purcell: Suite from *The Fairy Queen;* Haydn: *Echo Divertimento,* Böttcher, Vienna Solisten

(BACH GUILD 70 662)

Musique de Table (Tafelmusik) (Productions 1-3), Brüggen, Concerto Amsterdam (6-TELEFUNKEN S TDL-1 S 9449/54)

▶ *Mostly first-rate Telemann, brilliantly and stylishly recorded.*

Paris Quartets Nos. 1, 4, and 6, Quadro Amsterdam

(TELEFUNKEN S 9448)

Overture No. 1 in G minor for Harpsichord; also includes Pachelbel, *Chorale Partita;* Buxtehude, *Variations;* Kuhnau, *Biblical Sonata No. 1, David and Goliath;* Works by J. S. and C. P. E. Bach, and Kirmaier, Kipnis (harpsichord and clavichord) (EPIC LC 3963/BC 1363)

Suite in A minor for Recorder and Strings; also includes *Concerto for Flute and Recorder in E minor, Overture in G (Nations: Ancient and Modern),* Brüggen, Tilegant, Southwest German Chamber Orchestra (TELEFUNKEN S 9413)

Water Music; also includes *Concerto in A for Flute, Harpsichord, and Continuo; Suite No. 6 for Oboe, Violin, and Continuo; Trio Sonata in E flat for Oboe, Harpsichord, and Continuo;* Wenzinger, Schola Cantorum Basiliensis

(DEUTSCHE GRAMMOPHON GESELLSCHAFT ARC-73198)

Torelli, Giuseppe

Trumpet Concerto in D; also includes trumpet pieces by Alberti, Biber, Manfredini, Haydn, and L. Mozart; Wobisch, Janigro, Solisti di Zagreb (BACH GUILD 641/5053)

Vivaldi, Antonio

Concerto in C for Ottavino (P. 79); also includes *Cello Concerto (P. 434), Concerto for Guitar and Viola d'Amore (P. 266),* and *Concerto for Two Violins (P. 222),* Linde (sopranino recorder), Hofmann, Seiler Chamber Orchestra (DEUTSCHE GRAMMOPHON GESELLSCHAFT ARC-73218); or Brüggen (soprano recorder), Rieu, Amsterdam Chamber Orchestra, which also includes *Concerto alla Rustica (P. 143), Concerti Grossi in A (P. 235), C minor (P. 427),* and *D minor, Opus 3, No. 11*

(TELEFUNKEN S 9426)

▶ *Either version of P. 79 is worth obtaining. The concerto is usually played on piccolo, which was unknown to Vivaldi.*

The Four Seasons, Opus 8, Nos. 1 to 4, Bronne, Monosoff, Kwalwasser, Koutzen, Goberman, New York Sinfonietta, (ODYSSEY

32160131/32160132); or Tomasow, Janigro, I Solisti di Zagreb, (BACH 564/5001); or Corigliano, Bernstein, New York Philharmonic, (COLUMBIA ML 6144/MS 6744); or Buechner, Redel, Munich Pro Arte Chamber Orchestra

(MUSICAL HERITAGE SOCIETY MHS S 579)

▶ *There is as yet no stylistically satisfactory* FOUR SEASONS, *though Redel, in mediocre-sounding monophonic recording, adds more embellishments than most. The rest may be well played but are conservative.*

Concerto in C for Two Trumpets (P. 75); Flute Concertos in G minor, Opus 10, No. 2, La Notte, and *D, Opus 10, No. 3, Il Gardellino; Concerto in B minor for Four Violins, Opus 3, No. 10; Violin Concerto in E minor, Opus 4, No. 2,* Redel, Munich Pro Arte Chamber Orchestra

(MUSICAL HERITAGE SOCIETY MHS S 593)

Concerto in B minor for Four Violins, Opus 3, No. 10; also includes Handel, *Concerto Grosso, Opus 6, No. 4;* Gabrieli, *Canzona noni toni;* Telemann, *Viola Concerto in G,* Marriner, St. Martin-in-the-Fields Academy   (L'OISEAU-LYRE S 276)

▶ *One of great Vivaldi performances for sheer* ESPRIT.

Gloria in D; also includes Pergolesi, *Magnificat,* Baker, Vaughan, Willcocks, King's College Choir   (LONDON ARGO Z 505)

SONATAS AND CHAMBER MUSIC

Bach, Johann Sebastian
Sonatas and Partitas for Unaccompanied Violin, Szigeti
(VANGUARD BACH GUILD 926/9), MONO ONLY
Sonatas for Violin and Harpsichord, Grumiaux and Sartori
(PHILIPS PHS 2-997, PHM 2-597)
Suites for Unaccompanied Cello, Starker
(MERCURY SR 3-9016, OL 3-116)

Bartók, Béla
Six String Quartets, Juilliard Quartet
(COLUMBIA D3S 717, D3L 317)
Sonata for Two Pianos and Percussion, Votapek, Vosgerchian, etc.   (CAMBRIDGE 1803, 803)

Beethoven, Ludwig van
Great Fugue, Fine Arts Quartet   (CONCERT DISC 249, 1249)
String Quartets, Opus 18, Amadeus Quartet
(DEUTSCHE GRAMMOPHON GESELLSCHAFT 138531/3, 18531/3)

String Quartets, Opera 59, 74, 95, Budapest String Quartet
(COLUMBIA M4S 616, M4L 254)
String Quartets, Opera 127, 130/1/2/5, Budapest String Quartet
(COLUMBIA M5S 677, M5L 277)
Septet, Vienna Octet Members (LONDON CS 6132, CM 9129)
Sonatas for Cello and Piano, Fournier and Kempff
(DEUTSCHE GRAMMOPHON GESELLSCHAFT 138993/5), STEREO ONLY
Sonatas for Violin and Piano, Szigeti and Arrau (VANGUARD
1109/12, MONO ONLY); *Kreutzer,* Szeryng and Rubinstein
(RCA LSC/LM 2377)
Trios for Piano and Strings: Kakadu, Senofsky, Trepel, Graffman
(RCA LSC/LM 2715); *Opus 70, Nos. 1 and 2,* Alma Trio
(DECCA 710064, 10064); *Archduke,* Stern, Rose, Istomin
(COLUMBIA MS 6819, ML 6219)

Bloch, Ernest
Piano Quintet, Glazer with Fine Arts Quartet
(CONCERT DISC 252, 1252)
String Quartet No. 3, Edinburgh String Quartet
(MONITOR S 2123, 2123)
String Quartet No. 5, Fine Arts Quartet (CONCERT DISC 225, 1225)
Sonata for Violin and Piano No. 1, Stern and Zakin
(COLUMBIA MS 6717, ML 6117)

Boccherini, Luigi
Quintet in C for Guitar and Strings, Diaz, Schneider, etc.
(VANGUARD 71147, 1147)
Quintet in E for Strings, Schneider, Galimir, etc.
(VANGUARD 71147, 1147)

Borodin, Alexander
Quartet No. 2 in D, Hollywood String Quartet
(CAPITOL P 8187), MONO ONLY

Brahms, Johannes
Three String Quartets, Budapest String Quartet
(COLUMBIA M2S 734, M2L 334)
Piano Quartet No. 1, Quartetto di Roma
(DEUTSCHE GRAMMOPHON GESELLSCHAFT 138104), STEREO ONLY
Clarinet Quintet, Boskovsky and Vienna Octet Members
(LONDON CS 6234, CM 9301)
Piano Quintet, Rubinstein and Guarneri String Quartet
(RCA LSC/LM 2971)
Sextet No. 1 for Strings, Opus 18, Menuhin, Masters, etc.
(ANGEL S 36234, 36234)
Sextet No. 2 for Strings, Opus 36, Heifetz, Baker, etc.
(RCA LSC/LM 2739)
Violin and Piano Sonatas Nos. 1 and 3, Stern and Zakin
(COLUMBIA MS 6522, ML 5922)

Trios for Piano and Strings, Stern, Rose, Istomin
(COLUMBIA M2S 760, M2L 360)
Trio for Horn, Piano, and Violin, Bloom, Serkin and Tree
(COLUMBIA MS 6243, ML 5643)

Chopin, Frederic
Piano Sonatas Nos. 2 and 3, Rubinstein   (RCA LSC/LM 2554)

Corelli, Arcangelo
La Follia, Bress   (FOLKWAYS 3351), MONO ONLY

Debussy, Claude
String Quartet, Juilliard String Quartet   (RCA LSC/LM 2413)
Sonata No. 1 for Cello and Piano, Starker and Sebok
(MERCURY SR 90405, MG 50405)
Sonata No. 2 for Flute, Viola, and Harp, Melos Ensemble Members   (OISEAU LYRE 60048, 50217)
Sonata No. 3 for Violin and Piano, Stern and Zakin
(COLUMBIA MS 6139, ML 5470)

Dvořák, Anton
String Quartet No. 3, Vlach Quartet   (ARTIA S 706, 706)
String Quartet No. 6, Janacek Quartet (LONDON CS 6394, CM 9394)
String Quartet No. 7, Guarneri Quartet   (RCA LSC/LM 2887)
Piano Quintet, Peter Serkin, Schneider, etc.
(VANGUARD 71148, 1148)
Dumka Trio, Dumka Trio   (TURNABOUT 34075, 4075)

Fauré, Gabriel
Piano Quartet No. 1, Pennario, Shapiro, etc. (CAPITOL SP/P 8558)
Piano Quartet No. 2, Babin, Goldberg, etc.   (RCA LSC/LM 2735)
String Quartet, Loewenguth Quartet   (TURNABOUT 34014, 4014)

Franck, César
Piano Quintet, Curzon with Vienna Philharmonic Quartet
(LONDON CS 6226, CM 9294)
Violin and Piano Sonata, Morini and Firkusny
(DECCA 710038, 10038)

Geminiani, Francesco
Sonata for Solo Violin, Staryk   (BAROQUE 2851, 1851)

Handel, George Frederick
Sonatas for Violin and Harpsichord, Opus 1, Olevsky and Valenti   (WESTMINSTER 9064/6), MONO ONLY

Haydn, Franz Josef
String Quartets: Opus 3, No. 5, Janacek String Quartet (LONDON CS 6385, CM 9385); *Opus 33, No. 2, Joke,* Janacek Quartet (LONDON CS 6385, CM 9385); *Opus 33, No. 3, Bird,* Hungarian Quartet (TURNABOUT 34062, 4062); *Opus 64, No. 5, Lark,* Hungarian Quartet (TURNABOUT 34062, 4062); *Opus 76, No. 3, Emperor,* Amadeus Quartet
(DEUTSCHE GRAMMOPHON GESELLSCHAFT 138886, 18886)

Piano Trio No. 1, Cortot, Thibaud, Casals
(ANGEL COLH 12), MONO ONLY

Mendelssohn, Felix
String Quartets Nos. 2 and 3, Juilliard String Quartet
(EPIC BC 1287, LC 3887)
Piano Trio No. 1, Stern, Rose, Istomin
(COLUMBIA MS 7083), STEREO ONLY
Octet, Laredo, Schneider, etc.   (COLUMBIA MS 6848, ML 6248)

Mozart, Wolfgang A.
Quartets Nos. 14-19, "Haydn" Quartets, Juilliard String Quartet
(EPIC BSC 143, SC 6043)
Quartets Nos. 20-23, Budapest String Quartet
(COLUMBIA ML 5007/8), MONO ONLY
Quartets Nos. 22 and 23, Guarneri String Quartet
(RCA LSC/LM 2888)
Piano Quartets No. 1 and 2, Peter Serkin, Schneider, etc.
(VANGUARD 71140, 1140)
Clarinet Quintet, Boskovsky and Vienna Octet Members
(LONDON CS 6379, CM 9379)
String Quintets Nos. 3-6, Griller Quartet and Primrose
(VANGUARD S 158, 194; 158, 194)
String Divertimento, K 563, Italian String Trio
(DEUTSCHE GRAMMOPHON GESELLSCHAFT 139150, 39150)
Quintet for Piano and Winds, Ashkenazy and London Wind
Soloists   (LONDON CS 6494, CM 9494)
Violin and Piano Sonatas, (6 of them), Kroll and Balsam
(OISEAU LYRE 60043/4, 50212/3)
Violin and Piano Sonatas, K 378 and 454, Heifetz and Smith
(RCA LM 1958)

Ravel, Maurice
Introduction and Allegro, Challan, etc.   (ANGEL S 36290, 36290)
String Quartet, Quartetto Italiano   (PHILIPS 900154) STEREO ONLY
Violin Sonata, Oistrakh, Bauer   (PHILIPS 900112, 500112)

Schönberg, Arnold
Four String Quartets, Juilliard String Quartet
(COLUMBIA ML 4735/7), MONO ONLY

Schubert, Franz
Octet, Vienna Octet   (LONDON CS 6051, CM 9110)
String Quartet No. 13, Juilliard String Quartet
(EPIC BC 1313, LC 3913)
String Quartet No. 14, Death and the Maiden, Vienna Philhar-
monic Quartet   (LONDON CS 6384, CM 9384)
String Quartet No. 15, Juilliard String Quartet
(EPIC BC 12360, LC 3860)

Piano Quintet in A, Trout, Peter Serkin, Schneider, etc.
(VANGUARD 71145, 1145)
String Quintet in C, Vienna Philharmonic Members
(LONDON CS 6441, CM 9441)
Sonatinas for Violin and Piano, Schneider and Peter Serkin
(VANGUARD 71128, 1128)
Trio No. 1, Stern, Rose, Istomin   (COLUMBIA MS 6716, ML 6116)
Schumann, Robert
Piano Quartet, Pennario, Shapiro, etc.   (CAPITOL SP/P 8558)
Piano Quintet, Bernstein, Juilliard String Quartet
(COLUMBIA MS 6929, ML 6329)
Smetana, Bedřich
String Quartet No. 1, Guarneri String Quartet (RCA LSC/LM 2887)
String Quartet No. 2, Smetana Quartet
(CROSSROADS 22160112, 22160111)
Tartini, Giuseppe
Violin Sonata No. 10, Didone Abbandonnata, Morini and Pom-
mers   (DECCA 710014, 10014)
Violin Sonata in G Minor, Devil's Trill, Szeryng
(RCA VICS/VIC 1037)
Tchaikovsky, Pëtr Ilich
String Quartet No. 1, Hollywood String Quartet
(CAPITOL P 8187), MONO ONLY

PIANO MUSIC

Albeniz, Isaac
Iberia, (Complete), Alicia de Larrocha   (EPIC SC 6058/BSC 158)
Alkan, Charles-Henri
Symphony for Piano, Raymond Lewenthal   (RCA LM/LSC 2815)
Bach, Johann Sebastian
Chromatic Fantasy and Fugue in D minor, Rudolf Serkin
(COLUMBIA ML 4350)
French Suite No. 5 in G, Emil Gilels   (RCA LM/LSC 2868)
Goldberg Variations, Glenn Gould   (COLUMBIA ML 5060)
Italian Concerto in F, Glenn Gould
(COLUMBIA ML 5472/MS 6141)
Partitas, (Complete), Glenn Gould
(COLUMBIA M2L 293/M2S 693)
Toccata, Adagio and Fugue in C (arranged by Busoni), Vladi-
mir Horowitz   (COLUMBIA M2L 382/M2S 728)
Well-Tempered Clavier, (Complete), Rosalyn Tureck
(DECCA DX 127/8)

Balakirev, Mili
Islamey, Julius Katchen   (LONDON CS 6064)

Barber, Samuel
Piano Sonata, Vladimir Horowitz   (RCA LD 7021)

Bartók, Béla
Out of Doors, Suite, Leonid Hambro   (BARTOK 902)
Sonata for Two Pianos and Percussion, Gyorgy Sandor and Rolf
     Reinhardt, pianists; Otto Schad and Richard Sohm, percussion-
     ists   (TURNABOUT 4036/34036)
Suite for Piano, Opus 14, Béla Bartók   (BARTOK 903)

Beethoven, Ludwig van
Bagatelles, (Complete), Alfred Brendel   (TURNABOUT 4077/34077)
Piano Sonata No. 3 in C, Opus 2, No. 3, *Piano Sonata No. 14
     in C sharp minor,* Opus 27, No. 2 *(Moonlight),* Josef Hofmann
         (ARCHIVE OF PIANO MUSIC X 903)
Piano Sonata No. 8 in C minor, Opus 13, *(Pathétique),* Arthur
     Rubinstein   (RCA LM/LSC 2654)
Piano Sonata No. 21 in C, Opus 53, *(Waldstein),* Vladimir Horo-
     witz   (RCA LM 2009)
Piano Sonata No. 23 in F minor, Opus 57, *(Appassionata),*
     Vladimir Horowitz   (RCA LM/LSC 2366)
Piano Sonata No. 26 in E flat, Opus 81, *(Les Adieux),* Van
     Cliburn   (RCA LM/LSC 2931)
Piano Sonata No. 29 in B flat, Opus 106, *(Hammerklavier),*
     Daniel Barenboim   (COMMAND 11026)
Piano Sonata No. 31 in A flat, Opus 110, *Piano Sonata No. 32
     in C,* Opus 111, Hans Richter-Haaser   (ANGEL S 35749)
Variations in C minor, Alfred Brendel   (VOX SVBX 5416)
Variations on a Theme by Diabelli, Rudolf Serkin
         (COLUMBIA ML 5246)

Brahms, Johannes
Piano Sonatas Nos. 1 and 2, Julius Katchen
         (LONDON CM 9410/CS 6410)
Piano Sonata No. 3 in F minor, Julius Katchen
         (LONDON CM 9482/CS 6482)
*Variations on a Theme by Handel, Variations on a Theme by
     Paganini,* Julius Katchen   (LONDON CM 9474/CS 6474)
Six Intermezzi, Three Rhapsodies, One Capriccio, Artur Rubin-
     stein   (RCA LM 1787)

Chabrier, Emmanuel
Complete Piano Works, Rena Kyrakou   (VOX SVBX 5400)

Chopin, Frederic
Andante Spianato and Grande Polonaise, Vladimir Horowitz
         (RCA LD 7021)
The Four Ballades, Artur Rubinstein   (RCA LM/LSC 2370)

The Etudes, (Complete) Vladimir Ashkenazy (ARTIA MK 203)
Fantaisie in F minor, Van Cliburn (RCA LM/LSC 2576)
The Four Impromptus, Artur Rubinstein (RCA LM/LSC 7037)
The Mazurkas, (Complete), Artur Rubinstein (RCA LM/LSC 6177)
Nocturnes, Moura Lympany (ANGEL S 3602)
Polonaises, Artur Rubinstein (RCA LM/LSC 7037)
Scherzos Nos. 1, 2 and 3, Josef Hofmann
(ARCHIVE OF PIANO MUSIC X 904)
Scherzo No. 4, Vladimir Horowitz (ANGEL COLH 300)
Piano Sonata No. 2 in B flat minor, Vladimir Horowitz
(COLUMBIA KL 5771/KS 6371)
Piano Sonata No. 3 in B minor, Dinu Lipatti (COLUMBIA ML 4721)
Waltzes, Artur Rubinstein (RCA LM/LSC 2726)
Clementi, Muzio
Sonatas, Vladimir Horowitz (RCA LM 1902)
Debussy, Claude
Two Arabesques, Leonard Pennario (CAPITOL S P 8648)
Children's Corner Suite, Walter Gieseking (ANGEL 35067)
En Blanc et Noir, Leonid Hambro and Jascha Zayde
(COMMAND 11013)
Estampes, Walter Gieseking (ANGEL 35065)
Preludes, (Complete), Robert Casadesus
(COLUMBIA ML 4977/78)
Dello Joio, Norman
Piano Sonata No. 3, Frank Glazer (CONCERT-DISC 1217, 217)
Dvořák, Anton
The Slavonic Dances, (Complete), Alfred Brendel and Walter
Klien (TURNABOUT 4064, 34064)
Fauré, Gabriel
Piano Music, (Complete), Grant Johannessen
(GOLDEN CREST 4030, 4046, 4048)
Ginastera, Alberto
Piano Sonata, Hilde Somer (DESTO 6402)
Gottschalk, Louis Moreau
Piano Music, Eugene List (VANGUARD 485)
Granados, Enrique
Spanish Dances, Alicia de Larrocha (EPIC LC 3943/BC 1343)
Grieg, Edvard
Lyric Pieces, Walter Gieseking (ANGEL 35450/1)
Griffes, Charles Tomlinson
Roman Sketches, Leonid Hambro (LYRICHORD 105)
Haydn, Franz Josef
Piano Sonatas, (Nos. 6, 18, 20, 23, 28, 30, 31, 38, 40, 46, and
48), Artur Balsam (L'OISEAU-LYRE S 273/5)
Piano Sonatas Nos. 50 and 52, Nadia Reisenberg
(MONITOR S 2097)

Hindemith, Paul
Piano Sonata No. 3, Paul Badura-Skoda   (WESTMINSTER 9309)
Ives, Charles
Piano Sonata No. 1, William Masselos   (RCA LM/LSC 2941)
Kodály, Zoltán
Dances of Marosszek, Andor Foldes   (DECCA 9913)
Liszt, Franz
Dante Sonata, David Bar-Illan   (RCA LM/LSC 2943)
Hungarian Rhapsodies Nos. 2 and 6, Vladimir Horowitz
(RCA LM 2584)
Hungarian Rhapsody No. 11, William Kapell   (RCA LM 2585)
Hungarian Rhapsody No. 12, Ruth Slenczynska   (DECCA 79991)
Mephisto Waltz, William Kapell   (RCA LM 2588)
Mazeppa, Erwin Nyireghazy   (ARGO DA 43)
Piano Sonata in B minor, Emil Gilels   (RCA LM/LSC 2811)
Transcendental Etudes, Gyorgy Cziffra   (ANGEL 3591)
Mendelssohn, Felix
Allegro Brillant, Leonid Hambro and Jascha Zayde
(COMMAND 11010)
Songs Without Words, Guiomar Novaes   (VOX 12000/512000)
Variations sérieuses, Vladimir Horowitz   (RCA LVT 1043)
Mozart, Wolfgang Amadeus
Fantasia in C minor, (K 396), Lili Kraus   (HAYDN SOCIETY 9044)
Fantasia in D minor, (K 397), Wilhelm Kempff
(DEUTSCHE GRAMMOPHON GESELLSCHAFT 18707/138707)
Fantasia in C minor, (K 475), Daniel Barenboim
(WESTMINSTER 19120/17120)
Piano Sonata No. 8 in A minor, (K 310), Dinu Lipatti
(COLUMBIA ML 4633)
Piano Sonata No. 11 in A (K 331), Guiomar Novaes   (VOX 9080)
Piano Sonata in D for Two Pianos, (K 448), Josef and Rosina
Lhevinne   (RCA LM 2824)
Variations on "Ah, Vous Dirai-Je, Maman," (K 265), Andre
Previn   (COLUMBIA ML 5986/MS 6586)
Musorgski, Modest
Pictures at an Exhibition, Vladimir Horowitz   (RCA LM 2357)
Prokofiev, Sergei
Piano Sonata No. 2 in D minor, Emil Gilels   (ARTIA 163)
Piano Sonata No. 7, Vladimir Horowitz   (RCA LD 7021)
Piano Sonata No. 9 in C, Sviatoslav Richter   (MONITOR 2034)
Rachmaninoff, Sergei
Humoresque, Barcarolle, Polichinelle, Etude Tableau, Opus 39,
No. 6, Sergei Rachmaninoff   (ARGO DA 42)
Prelude in C sharp minor, Prelude in F minor, Etude in E flat,

Opus 33, No. 7, and *Polka de W.R.*, Sergei Rachmaninoff
(RCA LM 2587)
Preludes, Constance Keene   (PHILIPS WS 2 006)
Ravel, Maurice
Gaspard de la Nuit, Vladimir Ashkenazy
(LONDON CM 9472, CS 6472)
Complete Piano Music, Robert Casadesus   (ODYSSEY 323 60003)
Roussel, Albert
Suite pour Piano, Francoise Petit   (L'OISEAU-LYRE 50221/60052)
Scarlatti, Domenico
Sonatas, Vladimir Horowitz   (COLUMBIA ML 6058/MS 6658)
Schubert, Franz
German Dances, Walter Hautzig   (TURNABOUT 4006/34006)
Impromptus, Sviatoslav Richter   (MONITOR 2027)
Piano Sonata in A, Opus 120, Sviatoslav Richter   (ANGEL S 36150)
Piano Sonata in A, Opus Posthumous, Rudolf Serkin
(COLUMBIA ML 6249/MS 6849)
Piano Sonata in A minor, Opus 42, Wilhelm Kempff
(DEUTSCHE GRAMMOPHON GESELLSCHAFT 39104/139104)
Piano Sonata in C minor, Opus Posthumous, Alfred Brendel
(VANGUARD 7 1157)
Wanderer Fantasy, Artur Rubinstein   (RCA LM/LSC 2871)
Schumann, Robert
Andante and Variations in B flat, Vladimir Ashkenazy and Mal-
colm Frager   (LONDON CM 9411/CS 6411)
Carnaval, Artur Rubinstein   (RCA LM/LSC 2669)
Kinderscenen, Benno Moiseiwitsch   (DECCA 10048/710048)
Papillons, Sviatoslav Richter   (ANGEL S 36104)
Symphonic Etudes, Vladimir Ashkenazy
(LONDON CM 9471/CS 6471)
Toccata, Vladimir Horowitz   (ANGEL COLH 72)
Scriabin, Alexander
Piano Sonata No. 9, Vladimir Horowitz
(COLUMBIA M2L 328/M2S 728)
Piano Sonata No. 10, Vladimir Horowitz
(COLUMBIA M2L 357/M2S 757)
Shostakovich, Dimitri
Preludes and Fugues, Dimitri Shostakovich   (SERAPHIM 60024)
Stravinsky, Igor
Concerto for Two Solo Pianos, Arthur Gold and Robert Fizdale
(COLUMBIA ML 5733/MS 6333)
Tchaikovsky, Pëtr Ilich
Piano Music, Philippe Entremont   (COLUMBIA ML 5846/MS 6446)
Wagner, Richard
Piano Music, (Complete), Martin Galling   (VOX SVUX 52022)

CHORAL MUSIC

Bach, Carl Philipp Emanuel
  Magnificat, Prohaska, Vienna State Opera Orchestra
                                                        (BACH GUILD 552)

Bach, Johann Sebastian
  Cantata No. 4, Christ lag in Todesbanden, Wagner, Wagner
    Chorale, Concert Arts Orchestra   (ANGEL S 36014)
  Cantata No. 12, Weinen, Klagen, Sorgen, Zagen, Wöldike,
    Vienna State Opera Orchestra   (BACH GUILD 610, 5036)
  Cantata No. 21, Ich hatte viel Bekümmernis, Lehmann, Berlin
    Motet Choir and Philharmonic
           (DEUTSCHE GRAMMOPHON GESELLSCHAFT ARC-3064)
  Cantata No. 76, Die Himmel erzählen die Ehre Gottes, Scherchen
                        (3-WESTMINSTER S 1019)
  Cantata No. 78, Jesu, der du meine Seele, Prohaska, Bach Guild
    Chorus   (BACH GUILD 537)
  Cantata No. 80, Ein feste Burg ist unser Gott, Prohaska, Aka-
    demiechor   (BACH GUILD 508)
  Cantata No. 104, Du Hirte Israël, höre, Vandernoot, Amsterdam
    Philharmonic Society Orchestra, Bach Chorus
                             (VANGUARD S 219)
  Cantata No. 106, Gottes Zeit ist die allerbeste Zeit, Scherchen,
    Vienna Akademie Kammerchor   (WESTMINSTER 18394)
  Cantata No. 140, Wachet auf!, Prohaska, Vienna Chamber
    Chorus and State Opera Orchestra   (BACH GUILD 598, 5026)
  Cantata No. 198, Trauer-Ode, Scherchen
                        (3-WESTMINSTER S 1019)
  Christmas Oratorio, S.248, Thomas, Detmold Orchestra and
    Chorus   (3-OISEAU-LYRE 50001/3)
  Mass in b minor, S.232, Richter, Munich Bach Orchestra and
    Chorus   (DEUTSCHE GRAMMOPHON GESELLSCHAFT ARC-73177/9)
  St. John Passion, S.245, Richter, Munich Bach Orchestra and
    Chorus
        (3-DEUTSCHE GRAMMOPHON GESELLSCHAFT ARC-73228/30)
  St. Matthew Passion, S.244, Scherchen   (4-WESTMINSTER 4402)

Barber, Samuel
  Stopwatch & Ordnance Map, Opus 15, Golschmann, De Cormier
    Chorus, Symphony of the Air   (VANGUARD 1065)

Bartók, Béla
  Cantata Profana, Süsskind, New Symphony   (BARTOK 312)

Beethoven, Ludwig van

Christus am Oelberg, Opus 85, Scherchen, Vienna State Opera Orchestra and Academy Chorus   (WESTMINSTER 19033, 17033)

Fantasia in C minor for Piano, Chorus, Orch., Op. 80, Somogyi, Vienna State Opera Orchestra and Chorus
(WESTMINSTER 19078, 17078)

Mass in C, Opus 86, Beecham Chorus, Royal Philharmonic
(CAPITOL S G 7168)

Missa Solemnis in D, Opus 123, Bernstein, NY Philharmonic
(2-COLUMBIA M2L 270, M2S 619)

Symphony No. 9 in D minor, Opus 125, Monteux, London Symphony and Chorus (with rehearsal) (2-WESTMINSTER 2234, 234)

Berlioz, Hector

L'Enfance du Christ, Davis, Goldsbrough Orchestra, St. Anthony Singers   (2-OISEAU-LYRE 50201/2, 60032/3)

Requiem, Opus 5 (Grande Messe des Morts), Scherchen, Orchestre Théâtre National Opéra   (2-WESTMINSTER 2227, 201)

Roméo et Juliette, Opus 17, Monteux, Boston Symphony, NE Conservatory Chorus   (2-RCA LD/LDS 6098)

Bernstein, Leonard

Chichester Psalms, for Chorus and Orchestra, Bernstein, NY Philharmonic, Camerata Singers   (COLUMBIA ML 6192, MS 6792)

Bloch, Ernest

Sacred Service, Avodath Hakodesh, Bernstein, NY Philharmonic
(COLUMBIA ML 5621, MS 6221)

Brahms, Johannes

German Requiem, Opus 45, Bamburger, Hamburg No. German Radio Symphony and Chorus   (2-NONESUCH 7 3003)

Liebeslieder Waltzes, Opera 52, 65, Shaw Chorale
(RCA LM/LSC 2864)

Song of Destiny, Opus 54, Beecham, Beecham Choral Society, Royal Philharmonic   (ANGEL S 35400)

Britten, Benjamin

Spring Symphony, Britten, Royal Opera House Orchestra and Chorus   (LONDON 5612, 25242)

War Requiem, Britten, London Symphony and Chorus
(2-LONDON 4225, 1255)

Bruckner, Anton

Mass No. 3 in F minor, Great, Forster, Berlin Symphony
(ANGEL S 35982)

Te Deum, Walter, Westminster Choir, NY Philharmonic
(COLUMBIA ML 4980)

Buxtehude, Dietrich

Missa Brevis, Magnificat in D, Cantata Singers
(URANIA 8018, 58018)

Byrd, William
Ave Verum Corpus, Magnificat, Nunc Dimittis, Willcocks, King's
College Chorus (LONDON ARGO 5 226; LONDON 5725, 25725)
Mass in Three Parts; Mass in Four Parts; Mass in Five Parts,
Little, Montreal Bach Choir (VOX 500 880)

Campra, André
Requiem (Messe des Morts), Frémaux, Paillard Orchestra, Cail-
lard and Caillat Chorales (WESTMINSTER 19007, 17007)

Carissimi, Giacomo
Jepthe, Rilling, Spandauer Kantorei (TURNABOUT 3 4089)

Charpentier, Marc-Antoine
Magnificat, Te Deum, Martini, Paillard Orchestra, Chorus
(BACH GUILD 70 663)

Cherubini, Luigi
Mass in C, Portsmouth Philharmonic (LYRICHORD 28)

Copland, Aaron
In the Beginning, Copland, N.E. Conservatory Chorus
(CBS 32110017, 32110018)

Debussy, Claude
Le Martyre de St. Sébastien, Ormandy, Philadelphia Orchestra
(2-COLUMBIA M2L 353, M2S 753)
Nocturnes (Nuages, Fêtes, Sirènes), Ormandy, Philadelphia Or-
chestra, Temple University Women's Chorus
(COLUMBIA ML 6097, MS 6697)
Trois Chansons de Charles d'Orléans, Concordia Chorus
(CONCORDIA 8, S-2)

Des Prez, Josquin
Mass: L'homme Armé, Venhoda, Prague Madrigal Singers
(CROSSROADS 22160093, 22160094)

Duruflé, Maurice
Requiem, Opus 9, Duruflé, Orchestre Concerts Lamoureux
(EPIC LC 3856, BC 1256)

Dvořák, Anton
Requiem, Opus 89, Ancerl, Czech Philharmonic
(2-DEUTSCHE GRAMMOPHON GESELLSCHAFT 18547/8, 138026/7)
Stabat Mater, Opus 58, Reichert, Recklinghausen Chorus, Westphalian Symphony (2-VOX S VUX 5 2026)

Elgar, Edward
Dream of Gerontius, Barbirolli, Hallé Orchestra and Chorus,
Sheffield Philharmonic Chorus, Ambrosian Singers
(2-ANGEL S 3660)

Falla, Manuel de
Five Songs (and other Spanish music), Luis Morondo, Agrupación
Coral de Pamplona de España (COLUMBIA ML 5278)

Fauré, Gabriel
  Requiem, Opus 48, Frémaux, Monte Carlo Opera National Or-
    chestra, Caillard Chorus   (EPIC LC 3885, BC 1285)
Foss, Lukas
  Psalms; Behold! I Build an House, Wagner Chorale
                    (COMPOSERS RECORDINGS, INC. S 123)
Gabrieli, Giovanni
  Processional and Ceremonial Music, Appia, Gabrieli Fest.
                                  (BACH GUILD 581, 5004)
Gounod, Charles
  Messe Solennelle (St. Cecilia), Markevitch, Czech Philharmonic
    Orchestra and Chorus
          (DEUTSCHE GRAMMOPHON GESELLSCHAFT 39111, 139111)
Handel, George Frederick
  Acis and Galatea, Boult   (2-OISEAU-LYRE 50179/80, 60011/2)
  Chandos Anthems, Mann, Rutgers University Collegium Musicum
                                  (3-VANGUARD S 227/9)
  Israel in Egypt, Waldman, Musica Aeterna   (2-DECCA DX S 7 178)
  Judas Maccabaeus, Abravanel, Utah Symphony
                                  (3-WESTMINSTER 3310/301)
  Messiah, Davis, London Symphony Orchestra and Chorus, (3-
    PHILIPS PHM 3 592, PHS 3 992); or Mackerras, English Cham-
    ber Orchestra, Ambrosian Singers, (3-ANGEL S 3705); or Shaw
    Orchestra and Chorus, (3-RCA VICTOR LM/LSC 6175); or
    Scherchen, London Symphony and Philharmonic Chorus
                                  (3-BACH GUILD 631/3)
  Saul, Wöldike, Copenhagen Boys Choir, Vienna Symphony Or-
    chestra   (VANGUARD 3-BGS 5054/6)
Hanson, Howard
  Lament for Beowulf, Opus 25, Hanson, Eastman-Rochester Or-
    chestra   (MERCURY 50192, 90192)
Harris, Roy
  Symphony No. 4, Folksong, Golschmann   (VANGUARD 1064, 2082)
Haydn, Franz Joseph
  Creation, Waldman, Musica Aeterna   (2-DECCA DX S 7 191)
  Mass No. 3 in C, Missa Sanctae Caeciliae, Jochum
          (2-DEUTSCHE GRAMMOPHON GESELLSCHAFT 138028/9)
  Mass No. 7, Missa in Tempore Belli (Paukenmesse), Wöldike,
    Vienna State Opera Orchestra   (VANGUARD S 153)
  Mass No. 9 in D minor, Missa Solemnis (Nelson Mass), Rossi,
    Vienna State Opera Orchestra   (VANGUARD 470)
  Seasons, Goehr, North German Radio Symphony Chorus
                                  (3-NONESUCH 7 3009)
  Seven Last Words of Christ, Scherchen, Vienna State Opera Or-
    chestra and Academy Chorus   (WESTMINSTER 19006, 17006)

Hindemith, Paul
Requiem "For Those We Love," Hindemith, NY Philharmonic,
Schola Cantorum   (COLUMBIA ML 5973, MS 6573)

Holst, Gustav
Choral Hymns from the Rig-Veda, Opus 26, Holst, English Chamber Orchestra, Purcell Singers   (LONDON ARGO Z NF 6)

Honegger, Arthur
Christmas Cantata, Ansermet, L'Orchestre de la Suisse Romande,
Choruses   (LONDON 5686, 25320)
Judith, Abravanel, Utah Symphony, Chorus   (VANGUARD 7 1139)
Roi David, Abravanel, Utah Symphony
(2-VANGUARD 1090/1, 2117/8)

Janáček, Leoš
Slavonic Mass (M'ša Glagolskaja), Bernstein, NY Philharmonic,
Westminster Chorus   (COLUMBIA ML 6137, MS 6737)

Kodály, Zoltán
Missa Brevis, Hokans, Peloquin Chorale
(GREGORIAN INSTITUTE S 205)
Te Deum, Swoboda, Vienna Chorus and Symphony
(WESTMINSTER 18455)

Lalande, Michel-Richard de
De Profundis, Couraud, Stuttgart Pro Musica and Chorus
(VOX 9040)
Te Deum; Confitemini, Boyd Neel Orchestra, St. Anthony Chorus
(OISEAU-LYRE 50153)

Liszt, Franz
Missa Choralis in A minor, Gillesberger, Vienna Chamber Choir
(VOX 50 1040)

Mahler, Gustav
Symphony No. 2 in C minor (Resurrection), Bernstein, NY Philharmonic, Collegiate Chorale   (2-COLUMBIA M2L 295, M2S 695)
Symphony No. 8 in E flat (Symphony of a Thousand), Bernstein,
London Symphony   (2-COLUMBIA M2L 351, M2S 751)

Mendelssohn, Felix
Elijah, Opus 70, Krips, London Philharmonic, Choir
(3-LONDON 4315)
Midsummer Night's Dream, Incidental Music, Opera 21 and 61,
Maag, London Symphony, Royal Opera House Female Chorus
(LONDON 9201, 6001)

Milhaud, Darius
Choëphores, Bernstein, NY Philharmonic, NY Schola Cantorum
(COLUMBIA ML 5796, MS 6396)
Sabbath Morning Service, Milhaud, Orchestre du Théâtre National de L'Opéra, Choeurs de la Radiodiffusion-Télévision Française   (WESTMINSTER 19052, 17052)

Symphony No. 3, Hymnus Ambrosianus, Milhaud, Conservatory Society Orchestra, Brasseur Chorus
(WESTMINSTER 19101, 17101)

Monteverdi, Claudio
Lagrime d'Amante (from Madrigals, Book VI), Randolph, Masterwork Chorus (WESTMINSTER 9622)
Magnificat a 6 Voci, Wallenstein, Los Angeles Philharmonic, Wagner Chorale (CAPITOL S P 8572)
Vespro della Beata Vergine, Craft, Columbia Baroque Ensemble, Smith Singers, Ft. Worth Tex. Boys Chorus
(2-COLUMBIA M2L 363, M2S 763)

Mozart, Wolfgang Amadeus
Cantata: Eine kleine Freimaurer, K.623, Meyer, Vienna Pro Musica Orchestra, Mulhouse Oratorio Chorus
(3-TURNABOUT 4111/3)
Mass in C, K.317, *(Coronation),* Moralt, Vienna Symphony and Choir Boys (EPIC LC 3415)
Mass in C minor, K.427, *(The Great),* Fricsay, Berlin Radio Symphony
(DEUTSCHE GRAMMOPHON GESELLSCHAFT 18624, 138124)
Requiem, K.626, Walter, NY Philharmonic, Westminster Choir
(COLUMBIA ML 5012)
Sacred Music, Leibowitz, Vienna Academy Chorus and State Opera Orchestra (2-WESTMINSTER 2230, 205)
Vesperae Solennes de Confessore in C, K.339, Ristenpart
(NONESUCH 7 1041)

Orff, Carl
Carmina Burana, Frühbeck de Burgos, New Philharmonic
(ANGEL S 36333)
Catulli Carmina, Smetáček, Prague Symphony, Czech Philharmonic Chorus (CROSSROADS 22160003, 22160004)

Palestrina, Giovanni
Choral Works, De Nobel, Netherlands Chamber Choir
(ANGEL 35667)
Missa Papae Marcelli, Schrems, Regensburg Cathedral Chorus
(DEUTSCHE GRAMMOPHON GESELLSCHAFT ARC-73182)

Pergolesi, Giovanni Battista
Stabat Mater, Rossi (VANGUARD S 195)

Poland
Folk Songs of, Mazowsze Choral Ensemble and Orchestra, Tadeusz Sygietynski (VANGUARD VRS 9061)

Poulenc, Francis
Gloria in G, Prêtre, French National Radio-Television Orchestra and Chorus (ANGEL S 35953)
Mass in G, Whikehart Chorus (LYRICHORD 7 127)
Stabat Mater, Frémaux, Colonne Orchestra (WESTMINSTER 9618)

Prokofiev, Serge
 Alexander Nevsky, Opus 78, Schippers, NY Philharmonic, Westminster Chorus   (COLUMBIA ML 5706, MS 6306)

Purcell, Henry
 Hail! Bright Cecilia (Ode for St. Cecilia), Tippett, Ambrosian Singers   (BACH GUILD 559)
 Music for the Funeral of Queen Mary, Somary, Amor Artis Chorus   (DECCA 7 10114)

Rachmaninoff, Sergei
 The Bells, Opus 35, Ormandy, Temple University Choir, Philadelphia Orchestra   (COLUMBIA ML 5043)

Ravel, Maurice
 Daphnis et Chloé: Suite No. 2, Bernstein, NY Philharmonic, Schola Cantorum   (COLUMBIA ML 6154, MS 6754)
 Trois Chansons, Shaw Chorale   (RCA LM/LSC 2676)

Respighi, Ottorino
 Laud to the Nativity, Wallenstein, Los Angeles Philharmonic
   (CAPITOL S P 8572)

Rossini, Gioacchino
 Messe Solennelle, Vitalini, Societa del Quartetto Orchestra and Chorus   (PERIOD 588)
 Stabat Mater, Schippers, NY Philharmonic, Camerata
   (COLUMBIA ML 6142, MS 6742)

Russia
 National Chorus of Russian Song, A. V. Sveshnikov
   (DECCA DL 9985)

Satie, Erik
 Mass for the Poor, Randolph, Chorus   (COUNTERPOINT 90435)

Scarlatti, Alessandro
 St. John Passion, Boatwright, Yale Orchestra   (OVERTONE 1)

Schönberg, Arnold
 Friede auf Erden, Opus 13, Berlin Radio Chorus (MONITOR 2047)
 Gurre-Lieder, Kubelik, Bavarian Radio Orchestra and Chorus
   (2-DEUTSCHE GRAMMOPHON GESELLSCHAFT 18984/5, 138984/5)

Schubert, Franz
 Mass No. 2 in G, D.167, Froitzheim, Freiburg Orchestra and Chorus   (DECCA 7 10091)
 Mass No. 6 in E flat, D.950, Waldman, Musica Aeterna
   (DECCA 7 9422)
 Rosamunde: Incidental music, Opus 26, Abravanel, Utah Symphony and University Chorus   (VANGUARD 1087, 2114)

Schuman, William
 Carols of Death, Smith Singers   (EVEREST 6129, 3129)

Schütz, Heinrich
 Musicalische Exequien, Gillesberger, Vienna Chamber Chorus
   (VOX ST DL 50 1160)

Stravinsky, Igor
Mass, Davis, English Chamber Orchestra, St. Anthony Singers
(OISEAU-LYRE S 265)
Les Noces, Stravinsky (COLUMBIA ML 5772, MS 6372)
Oedipus Rex, Stravinsky, Washington Opera Society
(COLUMBIA ML 5872, MS 6646)
Symphony of Psalms, Stravinsky, CBS Symphony, Toronto Festival Chorus (COLUMBIA ML 5948, MS 6548)
Telemann, Georg Philipp
St. Matthew Passion, Redel, Swiss Festival Orchestra, Lucerne Festival Chorus (2-PHILIPS PHM 2 594, PHS 2 994)
Thompson, Randall
Peaceable Kingdom, San José Chorus (MUSIC LIBRARY 7065)
Vaughan Williams, Ralph
Flos Campi (Suite for Viola, Small Orchestra and Chorus), Abravanel, Utah Symphony and University Chamber Chorus
(VANGUARD 7 1159)
Mass in G minor, Wagner Chorale (CAPITOL S 8535)
Verdi, Giuseppe
Pezzi Sacri, Giulini, Philharmonic Orchestra and Chorus
(ANGEL S 36125)
Requiem Mass, in memory of Manzoni, Reiner, Vienna Philharmonic (2-RCA LD/LDS 6091)
Vivaldi, Antonio
Gloria in D, Scherchen, Vienna State Opera Orchestra
(WESTMINSTER 18958, 14139)
Juditha Triumphans, Ephrikian, Scuola Veneziana
(3-PERIOD 1043)
Wagner, Richard
Choruses, Pitz, Bayreuth Festival
(DEUTSCHE GRAMMOPHON GESELLSCHAFT 136006)
Walton, William
Belshazzar's Feast, Walton, Philharmonia Orchestra and Chorus
(ANGEL S 35681)

THE ART SONG

Arne, Thomas
Songs to Shakespeare's Plays, Forrester, Young, Priestman, Vienna Radio Orchestra and Chorus
(WESTMINSTER 19075, 17075)
Bach, Johann Sebastian
Songs, Cuénod (CAMBRIDGE 1 702)

Barber, Samuel
Hermit Songs, Leontyne Price, Barber　　(COLUMBIA ML 4988)
Knoxville: Summer of 1915, Steber, Strickland, Dumbarton Oaks
　Chamber Orchestra　　(COLUMBIA ML 5843)
Bartók, Béla
Songs, Opus 15, Laszlo, Hambro　　(BARTOK 927)
Beethoven, Ludwig van
An die ferne Geliebte, Opus 98, Haefliger　　(HELIODOR S 25048)
Songs, (fifteen), Fischer-Dieskau
　　(DEUTSCHE GRAMMOPHON GESELLSCHAFT 139197)
Berg, Alban
Songs (Seven Early Songs), Beardslee
　　(2-COLUMBIA M2L 271, M2S 620)
Brahms, Johannes
Songs, Fischer-Dieskau (Opus 32, Nos. 1 through 6, and 9)
　　(ANGEL 35522)
Songs for Alto, Viola, Piano, Opus 91, and Opus 47, No. 1;
　Opus 94, No. 4; Ferrier　　(LONDON 5098)
Britten, Benjamin
Les Illuminations for Solo Voice and Orchestra, Opus 18, J.
　Harsanyi, N. Harsanyi, Princeton Chamber Orchestra
　　(DECCA 7 10138)
*Seven Sonnets of Michelangelo, The Holy Sonnets of John
　Donne*, Alexander Young, Watson, Westminster　(ARGO RG 25)
Serenade for Tenor, Horn, Strings, Opus 31, Pears, Tuckwell,
　Britten, London Symphony　　(LONDON 9398, 6398)
Songs (Six) from the Chinese, Opus 58, Pears　(RCA LM/LSC 2718)
Canteloube, Joseph
Songs of the Auvergne, Grey, Cohen, Orchestra　(ANGEL COLC 152)
Chanler, Theodore
Epitaphs, (nine), Curtin　　(COLUMBIA ML 5598, MS 6198)
Chausson, Ernest
Poème de l'Amour et de la Mer, Opus 19, Verna
　　(MUSIC LIBRARY 7009)
Copland, Aaron
Twelve Poems of Emily Dickinson, Addison
　　(CBS 32110017, 32110018)
Couperin, Francois
Leçons de Ténèbres (Lamentations of Jeremiah), Cuénod, Sinim-
　berghi, Holetschek, Harand　　(WESTMINSTER 9601)
Cowell, Henry
Toccanta for Soprano, Flute, Cello, and Piano, Boatwright,
　Ensemble　　(COLUMBIA ML 4986)
Hymn and Fuguing Tune No. 5, Randolph Singers (included in
　English Madrigals and American Part Songs)
　　(CONCERT HALL SOCIETY CHC-52)

Debussy, Claude
Songs, Fischer-Dieskau
(DEUTSCHE GRAMMOPHON GESELLSCHAFT 18615, 138115)
Songs, Teyte   (ANGEL COLH 134)
Dowland, John
Lute Songs, Oberlin, Iadone   (EXPÉRIENCES ANONYMES 34)
Duke, John
Songs, (four), Tassie   (MUSIC LIBRARY 7117)
Duparc, Henri
Songs, (twelve), Souzay   (PHILIPS 500027, 900027)
Falla, Manuel de
Seven Popular Spanish Songs, De Los Angeles   (ANGEL S 35775)
Fauré, Gabriel
Songs, (six), Curtin   (CAMBRIDGE 1 706)
Flagello, Nicholas
Songs, (three), Reardon   (SERENUS 1019, 12019)
Grieg, Edvard
Songs, Nilsson, Bokstedt, Vienna Opera Orchestra
(LONDON 5942, 25942)
Hindemith, Paul
Marienleben (Song Cycle), Opus 27, Lammers
(2-NONESUCH 7 3007)
Italian and Spanish Songs of the 16th and 17th Centuries, Cuénod,
Leeb   (WESTMINSTER WL 5059/9611)
Janáček, Leoš
Diary of One Who Vanished, Haefliger, Griffel, Women's Chorus,
Kubelik (DEUTSCHE GRAMMOPHON GESELLSCHAFT 18904, 138904)
Loewe, Karl
Ballades, Prey   (VOX 5 510)
Mahler, Gustav
Kindertotenlieder, Fischer-Dieskau
(DEUTSCHE GRAMMOPHON GESELLSCHAFT 18879, 138879)
Das Lied von der Erde, Lewis, Forrester, Reiner, Chicago Sym-
phony   (2-RCA LM/LSC 6087)
Songs of a Wayfarer, Fischer-Dieskau, Furtwängler, Philhar-
monia Orchestra   (ANGEL 35522)
Monteverdi, Claudio
Songs (Duets), Schwarzkopf, Seefried   (ANGEL 35290)
Musorgski, Modest
Nursery (song cycle), Dorlyak   (MONITOR 2020)
Songs and Dances of Death, Davrath   (VANGUARD 1068)
Songs and Dances of Death, London
(COLUMBIA ML 6134, MS 6734)
Poulenc, Francis
Songs; also includes Chabrier, Debussy, and Satie, Bernac,
Poulenc   (COLUMBIA ML 4484)

Ravel, Maurice
Chansons Madécasses, Fischer-Dieskau
(DEUTSCHE GRAMMOPHON GESELLSCHAFT 18615, 138115)
Shéhérazade, Tourel, Bernstein, NY Philharmonic
(COLUMBIA ML 5838, MS 6438)
Schubert, Franz
Die Schöne Müllerin, Opus 25, D.795, Fischer-Dieskau
(2-ANGEL S 36283S)
Schwanengesang, D.957, Fischer-Dieskau   (ANGEL S 36127)
Winterreise, Opus 89, D.911, Fischer-Dieskau
(2-DEUTSCHE GRAMMOPHON GESELLSCHAFT 139201/2)
Schumann, Robert
Dichterliebe, Opus 48, Fischer-Dieskau
(DEUTSCHE GRAMMOPHON GESELLSCHAFT 139109)
Frauenliebe und Leben, Opus 42, Stader
(WESTMINSTER 19029, 17029)
Shostakovich, Dmitri
From Jewish Folk Poetry, Dolukhanova, Dorlyak, Maslenikov
(MONITOR 2020)
Spain
Five Centuries of Spanish Song, Victoria de Los Angeles
(RCA LM 2144)
Strauss, Richard
Songs, (seventeen), Souzay   (PHILIPS 500060, 900060)
Wagner, Richard
Wesendonck Songs, Farrell, Bernstein, NY Philharmonic
(COLUMBIA MS 6353)
Warlock, Peter
Curlew (song cycle), Young, Solomon, Graeme, Sebastian
(LONDON ARGO 26)
Wolf, Hugo
Italienisches Liederbuch, Berger, Prey   (2-VOX 5 532)
Songs, (seventeen, miscellaneous), Lear
(DEUTSCHE GRAMMOPHON GESELLSCHAFT 18979, 138979)

MUSICAL THEATER

Annie Get Your Gun (Irving Berlin), Ethel Merman, Bruce Yar-
nell   (RCA LOC/LSO 1124)
Babes in Arms (Richard Rodgers, Lorenz Hart), Mary Martin, Jack
Cassidy, Mardi Bayne   (COLUMBIA OL 7070/OS 2570)

Bells Are Ringing (Jule Styne, Betty Comden, Adolph Green), Judy Holliday, Sydney Chaplin   (COLUMBIA OL 5170/OS 2006)

The Boy Friend (Sandy Wilson), Julie Andrews in her Broadway debut   (RCA LOC 1018)

The Boys from Syracuse (Richard Rodgers, Lorenz Hart), Portia Nelson, Jack Cassidy   (COLUMBIA OL 7080/OS 2580)
  ▶ *My preference is for the 1963 Off-Broadway cast recording on Capitol, but this has been discontinued.*

Brigadoon (Frederick Loewe, Alan Jay Lerner), Shirley Jones, Jack Cassidy, Frank Poretta, Susan Johnson
   (COLUMBIA OL 7040/OS 2580)

Bye Bye Birdie (Charles Strouse, Lee Adams), Chita Rivera, Dick Van Dyke, Paul Lynde, Dick Gautier
   (COLUMBIA OL 5510/OS 2025)

Cabaret (John Kander, Fred Ebb), Joel Grey, Lotte Lenya, Jack Gilford, Jill Haworth   (COLUMBIA KOL 6640/KOS 3040)

Camelot (Frederick Loewe, Alan Jay Lerner), Julie Andrews, Richard Burton, Robert Goulet
   (COLUMBIA KOL 5620/KOS 2031)

Candide (Leonard Bernstein, Richard Wilbur, John Latouche), Barbara Cook, Robert Rounseville, Irra Pettina, Max Adrian
   (COLUMBIA OS 5180/OS 2350)

Carousel (Richard Rodgers, Oscar Hammerstein II), John Raitt, Eileen Christy, Reid Shelton, Susan Watson
   (RCA LOC/LSO 1114)

Cinderella (Richard Rodgers, Oscar Hammerstein II), Julie Andrews, Jon Cypher, Edie Adams   (COLUMBIA OL 5190/OS 2005)
  ▶ *While not written as a stage musical, this rates inclusion because its songs are in the best theater tradition.*

The Desert Song (Sigmund Romberg, Otto Harbach, Oscar Hammerstein II), Edmund Hockridge, June Bronhill
   (ANGEL 35905) (M&S)

Do I Hear a Waltz? (Richard Rodgers, Stephen Sondheim), Sergio Franchi, Elizabeth Allen, Carol Bruce
   (COLUMBIA KOL 6370/KOS 2770)

Fanny (Harold Rome), Ezio Pinza, Walter Slezak, William Tabbert, Florence Henderson   (RCA LOC/LSO 1015)

The Fantasticks (Harvey Schmidt, Tom Jones), Jerry Orbach, Rita Gardner, Kenneth Nelson   (MGM 3872) (M&S)

Fiddler on the Roof (Jerry Bock, Sheldon Harnick), Zero Mostel, Maria Karnilova, Julia Migenes, Bert Convy
   (RCA LOC/LSO 1093)

Finian's Rainbow (Burton Lane, E. Y. Harburg), Ella Logan, Donald Richards, David Wayne   (COLUMBIA OL 4062/OS 2080)

Gigi (Frederick Loewe, Alan Jay Lerner), Maurice Chevalier, Leslie Caron, Louis Jourdan, Hermione Gingold   (MGM 3641) (M&S)

Girl Crazy (George Gershwin, Ira Gershwin), Mary Martin, Louise
    Carlyle, Eddie Chappell   (COLUMBIA OL 7060/OS 2560)
Guys and Dolls (Frank Loesser), Robert Alda, Isabel Bigley,
    Vivian Blaine, Sam Levene   (DECCA 9023) (M&S)
Gypsy (Jule Styne, Stephen Sondheim), Ethel Merman, Jack Klug-
    man, Sandra Church, Paul Wallace

(COLUMBIA OL 5420/OS 2017)
Hello, Dolly! (Jerry Herman), Carol Channing, David Burns,
    Charles Nelson Reilly, Eileen Brennan   (RCA LOCD/LSOD 1087)
High Society (Cole Porter), Bing Crosby, Frank Sinatra, Grace
    Kelly, Louis Armstrong, Celeste Holm   (CAPITOL W 750) (M&S)
Hit the Deck (Vincent Youmans, Clifford Grey, Leo Robin), Tony
    Martin, Jane Powell, Debbie Reynolds, Vic Damone (MGM 3163)
House of Flowers (Harold Arlen, Truman Capote), Diahann Car-
    roll, Pearl Bailey, Rawn Spearman, Juanita Hall

(COLUMBIA OL 4969/OS 2320)
The King and I (Richard Rodgers, Oscar Hammerstein II), Ger-
    trude Lawrence, Yul Brynner, Dorothy Sarnoff, Larry Doug-
    las, Doretta Morrow   (DECCA 9008) (M&S)
Kismet (Robert Wright, George Forrest—based on Borodin), Al-
    fred Drake, Lee Venora, Richard Banke   (RCA LOC/LSO 1112)
Kiss Me, Kate (Cole Porter), Alfred Drake, Patricia Morison,
    Harold Lang, Lisa Kirk
        (COLUMBIA OL 4140/OS 2300, or CAPITOL TAO 1267) (M&S)
    ▶ *Same principals in both versions.*
Lady in the Dark (Kurt Weill, Ira Gershwin), Gertrude Lawrence
    in very condensed version   (RCA LPV 503)
Little Mary Sunshine (Rick Besoyan), Eileen Brennan, William
    Graham, John McMartin   (CAPITOL WAO 1240) (M&S)
Lost in the Stars (Kurt Weill, Maxwell Anderson), Todd Duncan,
    Inez Matthews, Frank Roane   (DECCA 9120) (M&S)
Mame (Jerry Herman), Angela Lansbury, Beatrice Arthur, Jerry
    Lanning, Frankie Michaels,   (COLUMBIA KOL 6600/OS 3000)
Man of La Mancha (Mitch Leigh, Joe Darion), Richard Kiley,
    Joan Diener, Robert Rounseville, Irving Jacobson

(KAPP 4505) (M&S)
The Merry Widow (Franz Lehar), Lisa Della Casa, John Reardon,
    Laurel Hurley, Charles K. L. Davis

(COLUMBIA OL 5880/OS 2280)
The Most Happy Fella (Frank Loesser), Robert Weede, Jo Sul-
    livan, Art Lund, Susan Johnson
    (COLUMBIA OL 5118/OS 2330, or O3L-240 COMPLETE VERSION)
The Music Man (Meredith Willson), Robert Preston, Barbara
    Cook   (CAPITOL W 990) (M&S)
My Fair Lady (Frederick Loewe, Alan Jay Lerner), Rex Harrison,
    Julie Andrews, Stanley Holloway (COLUMBIA OL 5090/OS 2015)

The New Moon (Sigmund Romberg, Oscar Hammerstein II), Dorothy Kirsten, Gordon MacRae   (CAPITOL W 1966) (M&S)

No Strings (Richard Rodgers), Richard Kiley, Diahann Carroll   (CAPITOL O 1695) (M&S)

Oh, Kay! (George Gershwin, Ira Gershwin), Barbara Ruick, Jack Cassidy, Allen Case   (COLUMBIA OL 7050/OS 2550)

Oklahoma! (Richard Rodgers, Oscar Hammerstein II), Alfred Drake, Joan Roberts, Celeste Holm   (DECCA 9017) (M&S)

On a Clear Day You Can See Forever (Burton Lane, Alan Jay Lerner), Barbara Harris, John Cullum, Clifford David   (RCA LOCD/LSOD 2006)

On the Town (Leonard Bernstein, Betty Comden, Adolph Green), Nancy Walker, Betty Comden, Adolph Green, Cris Alexander, John Reardon   (COLUMBIA OL 5540/OS 2828)

On Your Toes (Richard Rodgers, Lorenz Hart), Jack Cassidy, Portia Nelson   (COLUMBIA OL 7090/OS 2590)

110 in the Shade (Harvey Schmidt, Tom Jones), Inga Swenson, Robert Horton, Stephen Douglass   (RCA LOC/LSO 1085)

One Touch of Venus (Kurt Weill, Ogden Nash), Mary Martin, Kenny Baker   (DECCA 9122) (M&S)

Paint Your Wagon (Frederick Loewe, Alan Jay Lerner), James Barton, Olga San Juan, Tony Bavaar   (RCA LOC/LSO 1006)

The Pajama Game (Richard Adler, Jerry Ross), John Raitt, Janis Paige, Eddie Foy, Jr., Carol Haney   (COLUMBIA OL 4840)

Pal Joey (Richard Rodgers, Lorenz Hart), Vivienne Segal, Harold Lang   (COLUMBIA OL 4364)

Peter Pan (Mark Charlap, Jule Styne, Carolyn Leigh, Betty Comden, Adolph Green), Mary Martin, Cyril Ritchard   (RCA LOC/LSO 1019)

Porgy and Bess (George Gershwin, Ira Gershwin, DuBose Heyward), Lawrence Winters, Camilla Williams, Avon Long (complete version)   (COLUMBIA OSL 162)

The Red Mill (Victor Herbert, Henry Blossom), Eileen Farrell, Felix Knight   (DECCA 8016)

Roberta (Jerome Kern, Otto Harbach, Dorothy Fields, Jimmy McHugh), Joan Roberts, Jack Cassidy, Stephen Douglass, Kaye Ballard   (COLUMBIA OL 7030/OS 2530)

She Loves Me (Jerry Bock, Sheldon Harnick), Barbara Cook, Daniel Massey, Barbara Baxley, Ludwig Donath   (MGM 4118) (M&S)

Show Boat (Jerome Kern, Oscar Hammerstein II), Barbara Cook, John Raitt, Anita Darian   (COLUMBIA OL 5820/OS 2220)

The Sound of Music (Richard Rodgers, Oscar Hammerstein II), Film version, starring Julie Andrews   (RCA LOC/LSO 1032)

South Pacific (Richard Rodgers, Oscar Hammerstein II), Mary Martin, Ezio Pinza, Juanita Hall, William Tabbert
(COLUMBIA OL 4180/OS 2040)

Street Scene (Kurt Weill, Langston Hughes), Anne Jeffreys, Brian Sullivan, Polyna Stoska
(COLUMBIA OL 4139)

The Student Prince (Sigmund Romberg, Dorothy Donnelly), Jan Peerce, Roberta Peters, Giorgio Tozzi
(COLUMBIA OL 5980/OS 2380)

Sweet Charity (Cy Coleman, Dorothy Fields), Gwen Verdon, John McMartin, Helen Gallagher, Thelma Oliver
(COLUMBIA KOL 6500/KOS 2900)

A Tree Grows in Brooklyn (Arthur Schwartz, Dorothy Fields), Shirley Booth, Johnny Johnston, Marcia Van Dyke
(COLUMBIA OL 4405)

Up in Central Park (Sigmund Romberg, Dorothy Fields), Eileen Farrell, Wilbur Evans
(DECCA 8016)

West Side Story (Leonard Bernstein, Stephen Sondheim), Carol Lawrence, Larry Kert, Chita Rivera
(COLUMBIA OL 5230/OS 2001)

Wish You Were Here (Harold Rome), Jack Cassidy, Patricia Marand, Sheila Bond
(RCA LOC/LSO 1108)

Wonderful Town (Leonard Bernstein, Betty Comden, Adolph Green), Rosalind Russell, Edie Adams, George Gaynes
(DECCA 9010) (M&S)

Miscellaneous Songs by One Composer

Noel Coward, Joan Sutherland, Noel Coward, John Wakefield
(LONDON 5992/25992)

Rudolf Friml, featuring composer as pianist and conductor
(WESTMINSTER 6069/15008)

George Gershwin, Barbara Cook, Bobby Short, Elaine Stritch, Anthony Perkins
(MGM 4375) (M&S)

Victor Herbert, Robert Shaw Chorale and Orchestra
(RCA LM/LSC 2515)

Jerome Kern, Barbara Cook, Bobby Short, Harold Lang, Nancy Andrews
(COLUMBIA OL 6440/OS 2840)

Jerome Kern, Reid Shelton, Susan Watson, Danny Carroll
(MONMOUTH-EVERGREEN MES 6808)

Cole Porter, Mabel Mercer
(ATLANTIC 1213)

Cole Porter, Cesare Siepi
(LONDON 5705/25705)

Arthur Schwartz, Nancy Dussault, Karen Morrow, Clifford David, Neal Kenyon
(MONMOUTH-EVERGREEN 6604/5) (M&S)

Kurt Weill (American shows), Lotte Lenya
(COLUMBIA KL 5229)

Vincent Youmans, Nolan Van Way, Ellie Quint, Bob Quint
(MONMOUTH-EVERGREEN 6401/2) (M&S)

In addition to the Victor Herbert album listed above, the Robert Shaw Chorale and Orchestra have recorded two miscellaneous collections of operetta and musical comedy songs, beautifully performed in fine arrangements by Robert Russell Bennett. Several of the songs are not available in any other version. There are on Victor LM/LSC 2231, and Victor VCM/VCS 7023. Also recommended is a *Treasury of Great Operettas*, a set containing condensed versions of eighteen operettas, performed by Anna Moffo, William Lewis, Jeannette Scovotti, Rosalind Elias, Stanley Grover, etc., with musical direction by Lehman Engel. Available only directly from *The Reader's Digest* in Album # RD 40.

LIGHT MUSIC

This list of recommended recordings will follow the general outlines already established in Chapter 9: Part I will consider some of the important arranger-conductors, Part II is a composer's corner, Part III deals with music from the movies, and Part IV is a rapid roundup of light music on the international scene.

Naturally there will be some duplication of artists (Arthur Fiedler, for instance, shows up in Parts I, II, and III), but otherwise I have limited the selections to one, or occasionally two discs per man. This will, I hope, emphasize what must already be clear: The list is only a suggested sampling intended as a guide and not an index. If you like one recording by somebody, the chances are excellent that you will enjoy others, and you are hereby urged to take a Schwann-dive into the many more currently available.

Part I: The Conductors

Black, Stanley
  Music of France   (LONDON 44090) STEREO ONLY
Chacksfield, Frank
  New Limelight   (LONDON 3421, STEREO 44066)
Dragon, Carmen
  Fiesta!   (CAPITOL 8335) MONO AND STEREO

Farnon, Robert
  Music from the Emerald Isle (LONDON 3050) MONO ONLY
Fennell, Frederick
  Popovers (MERCURY 50222, STEREO 90222)
Fiedler, Arthur
  Evening at the Pops (RCA 2827) MONO AND STEREO
Goldman, Richard Franko
  Greatest Band in the Land (CAPITOL 8631) MONO AND STEREO
   ▶ *A fascinating assortment of original and rarely heard music for band, including a march by Stephen Foster and a nonmarch—"The Presidential Polonaise"—by John Philip Sousa.*
Gould, Morton
  Beyond the Blue Horizon (RCA 2552) MONO AND STEREO
Kostelanetz, Andre
  Promenade Favorites (COLUMBIA ML 6206, STEREO MS 6806)
Lane, Louis
  Pop Concert, U.S.A. (EPIC 3539, STEREO 1013)
Mitchell, Howard
  Music to Have Fun By (RCA 2813) MONO AND STEREO
Mantovani
  Folk Songs Around the World (LONDON 3360, STEREO 360)

Part II: The Composers

Anderson, Leroy
  Anderson Conducts Anderson (DECCA 8865, STEREO 78865)
  Anderson Conducts His Music (DECCA 8954, STEREO 78954)
   ▶ *Between them, these two albums contain the most popular Anderson miniatures, some two dozen in all.*
Coates, Eric
  London and *London Again Suites*, Eric Johnson, conductor
         (WESTMINSTER 18951, STEREO 14132)
  3 Elizabeths and *4 Centuries Suites*, Eric Coates, conductor
         (LONDON 9065) MONO ONLY
Coward, Noel
  Noel and Gertie, with Gertrude Lawrence
         (ODEON 1050) MONO ONLY
  Joan Sutherland Sings Noel Coward
         (LONDON 5992, STEREO 25992)
   ▶ *The Odeon disc is vintage Coward, recorded in 1936, with songs and dialogue from* PRIVATE LIVES, RED PEPPERS *and other shows. Also included are two of his great specialty numbers: "Mrs. Worthington" and "Mad Dogs and Englishmen." The London album is, of course, something of an anachronism, but it is lots of fun anyway.*

Friml, Rudolf
Indian Love Call   (WESTMINSTER 6069, STEREO 15008)
> ▶ *A bouquet of memorable tunes, with composer Friml doubling as pianist and conductor.*

German, Edward
Merrie England (excerpts), *Dances from Henry VIII,* and *Nell Gwynn,* Victor Olof, conductor   (LONDON 772) MONO ONLY
> ▶ *This disc was discontinued a few years ago, but it is a fine one, and worth a hunt. The complete* MERRIE ENGLAND *was recorded in England, and with a little bit of luck, can be located in import specialty shops; its label is Odeon, 1311/2.*

Gershwin, George
An American in Paris and *Rhapsody in Blue,* Leonard Bernstein, pianist and conductor   (COLUMBIA 5413, STEREO 6091)
Variations on "I Got Rhythm," Cuban Overture, and *Second Rhapsody,* Leonard Pennario, pianist; Alfred Newman, conductor   (CAPITOL 8581) MONO AND STEREO
> ▶ *Also see under Morton Gould, below.*

Gilbert and Sullivan
Overtures, Sir Malcolm Sargent, conductor
      (ANGEL 35929) MONO AND STEREO
Pineapple Poll, Charles Mackerras, conductor
      (CAPITOL 8663) MONO AND STEREO
> ▶ *Sullivan's music is gloriously served in both albums, the second being a ballet derived by Mackerras from sundry themes in the operas. The full operas are, of course, heartily recommended, and only space limitations preclude their listing here. If stylistic perfection is what you want, go with the d'Oyly Carte productions on the London label; if vocal beauty is of greater concern, the Angel series with soloists and chorus of the Glyndebourne Festival is preferable.*

Goldman, Edwin Franko
March Time, Frederick Fennell, conductor
      (MERCURY 50170, STEREO 90170)

Gould, Morton
Interplay and *Fall River Legend,* Morton Gould, conductor
      (RCA 2532) MONO AND STEREO
Latin American Symphonette, and *Porgy and Bess Suite* by Gershwin, Howard Hanson, conductor
      (MERCURY 50394, STEREO 90394)

Grofé, Ferde
Grand Canyon Suite, Eugene Ormandy, conductor
      (COLUMBIA 5286, STEREO 6003)

Herbert, Victor
The Immortal Victor Herbert, Robert Shaw Chorale
      (RCA 2515) MONO AND STEREO

Kálmán, Emmerich
Countess Maritza and *Czardas Princess* (Excerpts), Soloists, Vienna Symphony Chorus and Orchestra
(WESTMINSTER 18966, STEREO 14147)

Lehár, Franz
The Merry Widow (complete), Schwarzkopf, Gedda, *et al.*
(ANGEL 3630) MONO AND STEREO
Waltzes, Robert Sharples, conductor
(RCA 1106) MONO AND STEREO

Lumbye, Hans Christian
Copenhagen Pops, Lavard Friisholm, conductor
(CAPITOL 7253) MONO AND STEREO

Novello, Ivor
Ivor Novello's Music Hall, Eric Johnson, conductor
(WESTMINSTER 18953, STEREO 14134)

Offenbach, Jacques
Operetta Overtures, Hermann Scherchen, conductor
(WESTMINSTER 19035, STEREO 17035)
Gaîté Parisienne, Charles Munch, conductor
(LONDON 55009, STEREO 21011)

Romberg, Sigmund
A Night with Romberg, Lois Hunt and Earl Wrightson
(COLUMBIA 1302, STEREO 8102)

Sousa, John Philip
Sousa Forever, Morton Gould, conductor
(RCA 2569) MONO AND STEREO
Sound Off, Frederic Fennell, conductor
(MERCURY 50264, STEREO 90264)

Stolz, Robert
The Vienna of Robert Stolz, Robert Stolz, conductor
(EPIC LN 3374) MONO ONLY

Strauss, Johann, Jr.
Gypsy Baron and *Die Fledermaus Suites*, Arthur Fiedler, conductor
(RCA 2130) MONO AND STEREO
Die Fledermaus (complete), Gueden, Resnik, *et al.*
(LONDON 4249, STEREO 1249)
Tales of Old Vienna, Willi Boskovsky, conductor
(LONDON 9340, STEREO 6340)
▶ *This sparkling set also contains music by Papa Strauss, and Johann Jr.'s two younger brothers, Josef and Eduard.*
The Blue Danube, Josef Krips, conductor
(LONDON 9232, STEREO 6007)

Suppé, Franz von
Overtures, Henry Krips, conductor
(ANGEL 35427) MONO AND STEREO

Waldteufel, Emil
Waldteufel Waltzes, Henry Krips, conductor
(ANGEL 53426) MONO AND STEREO

Part III: Music from the Movies

FEATURE PRESENTATIONS
(original soundtrack scores)

The Alamo, Dimitri Tiomkin   (COLUMBIA 1558, STEREO 8358)
Cleopatra, Alex North
(20TH CENTURY FOX 5008) MONO AND STEREO
Gigi, Lerner and Loewe   (MGM 3641) MONO AND STEREO
Gone with the Wind, Max Steiner   (MGM 1E10) MONO AND STEREO
Hans Christian Andersen, Frank Loesser
(DECCA 8479, STEREO 78479)
How the West Was Won, Alfred Newman
(MGM 1E5) MONO AND STEREO
Lawrence of Arabia, Maurice Jarre
(COLGEMS 5004) MONO AND STEREO
Mary Poppins, Sherman and Sherman
(BUENA VISTA 4026) MONO AND STEREO
Those Magnificent Men in Their Flying Machines, Ron Goodwin
(20TH CENTURY FOX 3174, STEREO 4174)
Windjammer, Morton Gould   (COLUMBIA 1158, STEREO 8651)
Wizard of Oz, Arlen and Harburg   (MGM 3996) MONO ONLY
Zorba the Greek, Mikis Theodorakis
(20TH CENTURY FOX 3167, STEREO 4167)

STAR ATTRACTIONS
(Nostalgia, Incorporated)

Astaire, Fred
Nothing Thrilled Us Half as Much   (EPIC 13103, STEREO 15103)
Cantor, Eddie
Cantor Sings   (CAMDEN 870) MONO AND STEREO
Chevalier, Maurice
The Best of Chevalier   (MGM 4205) MONO AND STEREO
Garland, Judy
Hollywood Years   (MGM 4005) MONO ONLY
Jolson, Al
Rock-a-bye Your Baby   (DECCA 9035, STEREO 79035)
Kaye, Danny
The Best of Kaye   (DECCA 175, STEREO 7175)
MacDonald, Jeanette, and Nelson Eddy
Original Recordings   (RCA 526) MONO ONLY

Temple, Shirley
Animal Crackers in My Soup
(20TH CENTURY FOX 3006) MONO ONLY

Tucker, Sophie, Gloria Swanson, Fanny Brice, Dennis King, et al.
Stars of the Silver Screen, 1929-1930   (RCA 538) MONO ONLY

SELECTED SHORT SUBJECTS
(miscellaneous collections)

Black, Stanley
Film Spectacular   (LONDON 3313, STEREO 44025)

Farnon, Robert
Great Movie Themes   (PHILIPS 200,098, STEREO 600,098)

Fiedler, Arthur
Music from Million Dollar Movies   (RCA 2380) MONO AND STEREO

Gold, Ernest
Film Themes   (LONDON 3320, STEREO 320)

Kleiner, Arthur
Musical Moods from the Silent Films
(GOLDEN CREST 4019) MONO ONLY
▶ *Until his recent retirement, Kleiner presided at the piano for all the silent film showings at the Museum of Modern Art, in New York. This intriguing collection includes music from* THE KID, BIRTH OF A NATION, COVERED WAGON, *etc.*

Korngold, Erich
Film Themes   (WARNER BROS. 1438) MONO AND STEREO

Mancini, Henry
The Academy Award Songs, 1934-1964
(RCA 6013) MONO AND STEREO

Muller, Werner
International Film Festival
(WARNER BROS. 1548) MONO AND STEREO

Ortolani, Riz
Made in Rome   (UNITED ARTISTS 3360, STEREO 6360)

Rozsa, Miklos
Great Movie Themes   (MGM 4112) MONO AND STEREO

Shaindlin, Jack
Fifty Years of Movie Music   (DECCA 9079, STEREO 79079)
▶ *A most intriguing excursion, including Chase and Newsreel Music, "Charmaine" on the Mighty Wurlitzer, and the Max Steiner scores for* KING KONG *and* THE INFORMER.

Young, Victor
Love Themes from Hollywood   (DECCA 8364) MONO ONLY

Part IV: International and Specialty Items

Africa
Drum Fever, Saka Acquaye ensemble
(CRESTVIEW 805, STEREO 7805)

England
Cheers, Tessie O'Shea   (COMMAND 872) MONO AND STEREO
Trooping the Colour, Band of the Grenadier Guards
(LONDON SP 44044) STEREO ONLY

France
The Best of Edith Piaf   (CAPITOL 2616) MONO ONLY
Sixty French Girls Sing Encore, Les Djinns Singers
(ABC PARAMOUNT 368) MONO AND STEREO

Indonesia
Bali Island and *Ceylon Island Suites,* composed by Saburo Iida
(LONDON 91379, STEREO 99379)

Italy
San Remo's Greatest Hits   (EPIC 18047, STEREO 19047)
Songs of Venice, I Gondolieri Chorus
(LONDON 91391, STEREO 99391)

Lebanon
Evening in Beirut   (CAPITOL 10189) MONO ONLY

Malaya
Popular Music of the Far East   (CAPITOL 10256) MONO ONLY

Mexico
Hottest Mariachi in Mexico   (REQUEST 8041) MONO AND STEREO

Portugal
Lisbon by Night   (MONITOR 393) MONO AND STEREO

Russia
Pops à la Russe   (MONITOR 591) MONO ONLY

South America
South American Suite, composed and conducted by Waldo de los
Rios   (COLUMBIA 5162, STEREO 1862)
▶ *One of the most inventive scores of its type, and a work
that has proved to be a great favorite with WQXR audiences.
The recording was out-of-print for several years, and I sus-
pect that it was the clamor by disappointed listeners that
prompted Columbia to reissue the Suite.*

Spain
Zarzuela Arias, Montserrat Caballé (RCA 2894) MONO AND STEREO
Zarzuela Preludes and Intermezzi, conducted by Rafael Frühbeck
de Burgos   (LONDON 9424, STEREO 6424)
Bullfight! sounds and music   (LONDON 44082) STEREO ONLY

Tahiti
Dream Island   (CAPITOL 10281) MONO ONLY

Sweden
  Swinging Swedish Schottisches and Waltzes
                              (CAPITOL 10172) MONO ONLY
Yugoslavia
  Hit Parade   (MONITOR 601) MONO ONLY

JAZZ

The 1920's

Armstrong, Louis
  The Louis Armstrong Story   (4-COLUMBIA CL 851/4)
  ▸ *Classic small group jazz played by Armstrong's Hot Five and Hot Seven between 1925 and 1929, showing emergence of Armstrong as a virtuoso soloist.*
  In the '30's and '40's   (RCA LPM/LSP 2971)
  ▸ *Mostly with big bands.*
Beiderbecke, Bix
  The Bix Beiderbecke Story   (3-COLUMBIA CL 844/6)
  ▸ *A style-setting trumpeter shining through groups that are less interesting than he is.*
Henderson, Fletcher
  A Study in Frustration   (4-COLUMBIA C4L 19)
  ▸ *A ten-year survey of the first of the big jazz bands, a star-studded group, tracing the development of the jazz potential of a large ensemble.*
Jazz, Vols. 1-11   (FOLKWAYS 2801/11)
  ▸ *A unique series of discs presenting aspects of jazz from African origins to World War II.*
Johnson, James P.
  Father of the Stride Piano   (COLUMBIA CL 1780)
  ▸ *A magnificent "stride" pianist, teacher of Fats Waller, in solo and small-group performances.*
Jugs, Washboards and Kazoos   (RCA LPV 540)
  ▸ *Groups using simple or homemade instruments that reflect the early jazz era before recordings.*
Morton, Jelly Roll
  King of New Orleans Jazz   (RCA LPM 1649)
  Stomps & Joys   (RCA LPV 508)
  Hot Jazz, Pop Jazz, Hokum and Hilarity   (RCA LPV 524)
  Mr. Jelly Lord   (RCA LPV 546)

Jelly Roll Morton   (MAINSTREAM 56020, 6020)
> ▶ *The RCA's contain almost all the work of Morton's Red Hot Peppers (1926-1930), fascinating expressions of his pioneering orchestral style, plus solos, trios, and oddities of "hokum." The Mainstream disc is a definitive collection of Morton as piano soloist, composer, and singer.*

Moten, Bennie
Count Basie in Kansas City   (RCA LPV 514)
> ▶ *Greatest of the Midwestern bands at its peak with young Count Basie at the piano.*

Nichols, Red
The Red Nichols Story   (BRUNSWICK 54047)
> ▶ *Small groups loaded with stars on the rise (Teagarden, Goodman, Krupa, Jimmy Dorsey) playing a crisp, bright extension of Dixieland.*

Oliver, King   (EPIC 16003)
> ▶ *Acoustical recordings, made in 1923, of a superb band playing New Orleans ensemble style with Louis Armstrong on second cornet.*

Original Dixieland Jazz Band   (RCA LPV 547)
> ▶ *A landmark—first jazz records ever made (1917), played by a group that established a style and repertory which is still being heard half a century later.*

The 1930's

Basie, Count
The Best of Count Basie   (2-DECCA DX S 7 170)
Basie   (ROULETTE S 52003)
> ▶ *The loose, swinging excitement of the original Basie band of the thirties is on the Decca discs; the Roulette is a peak effort of a second, more polished, but less provocative, Basie band of the fifties and sixties.*

Berigan, Bunny
Great Dance Bands of the '30's   (RCA LPM 2078)
> ▶ *Berigan's classic recording of I CAN'T GET STARTED and other examples of his lusty trumpet-playing with his big band.*

Crosby, Bob
Greatest Hits   (DECCA 7 4856)
> ▶ *Big band Dixieland crossed with swing.*

Ellington, Duke
The Beginning (1926-28), Vol. 1   (DECCA 7 9224)
The Ellington Era, Vol. 1   (3-COLUMBIA C3L 27)
The Ellington Era, Vol. 2   (3-COLUMBIA C3L 39)

Music of Ellington   (COLUMBIA CL 558)
▶ *The two* ELLINGTON ERA *albums trace the development of
Ellington's band and his work as a composer from 1926 to
1939. Columbia CL 558 collects high spots of the same
period.*

Goodman, Benny
  King of Swing   (2-COLUMBIA OSL 180)
  Carnegie Hall Jazz Concert   (2-COLUMBIA OSL 160)
  Small Groups   (RCA LPV 521)
  ▶ *The Swing Era is recaptured at its height and with audi-
  ence excitement in the 1937-1938 radio broadcasts on* KING
  OF SWING. *The Concert, first of its kind in Carnegie Hall,
  was a significant musical event of the thirties. The small
  groups are the original Goodman trio and quartet (Teddy
  Wilson, Gene Krupa, Lionel Hampton).*

Hampton, Lionel
  Swing Classics   (RCA LPM 3318)
  ▶ *All-star recording groups in superb jam sessions.*

Hawkins, Coleman
  Body and Soul   (RCA LPV 501)
  ▶ *Highlights covering thirty-six years in the career of the first
  major jazz saxophonist.*

Holiday, Billie
  Golden Years   (3-COLUMBIA C3L 21)
  Golden Years, Vol. 2   (3-COLUMBIA C3L 40)
  Billie Holiday   (MAINSTREAM 56000, 6000)
  ▶ *One of the greatest jazz vocalists (the first who was not
  basically a blues singer) in the performances that established
  her. On the* GOLDEN YEARS *sets, she is accompanied by many
  of the major jazzmen of the thirties; the Mainstream includes
  her famous* STRANGE FRUIT.

Lunceford, Jimmie
  Lunceford Special   (COLUMBIA CL 2715, CS 9515)
  ▶ *A big band with a distinctive style that joined subtlety and
  wit to a strongly rhythmic attack.*

Reinhardt, Django
  Best of Django Reinhardt   (2-CAPITOL T 10457/8)
  ▶ *A gypsy guitarist, the first European to win international
  recognition in jazz, playing with the Quintet of the Hot
  Club of France as well as some visiting Americans.*

Russell, Pee Wee
  A Legend   (MAINSTREAM 56026, 6026)
  ▶ *A highly individualistic clarinetist in definitive perform-
  ances in a Dixieland-swing style.*

Spanier, Muggsy
   The Great 16   (RCA LPM 1295)
     ▸ *A magnificent set of small group recordings that epitomize the latter-day Dixieland style.*

Teagarden, Jack
   King of the Blues Trombone   (3-EPIC SN 6044)
   Jack Teagarden   (RCA LPV 528)
     ▸ *Surveys of the work of a masterful trombonist and singer from the late twenties through the thirties (Epic) and into the forties and fifties (Victor).*

Waller, Fats
   '34/'35   (RCA LPV 516)
   Valentine Stomp   (RCA LPV 525)
   Fractious Fingering   (RCA LPV 537)
   Smashing Thirds   (RCA LPV 550)
     ▸ *Fun, swing, and a jazz piano style that has had an effect on almost every jazz pianist since the midtwenties.*

Webb, Chick
   Vol. 1, Legend (1929-36)   (DECCA 7 9222)
   Vol. 2 (1937-39)   (DECCA 7 9223)

The 1940's

Bechet, Sidney
   Jazz Classics   (BLUE NOTE 1201)
   Blue Bechet   (RCA LPV 535)
     ▸ *One of the great jazz originals, a clarinetist and soprano saxophonist who played with a fierce overpowering lyricism, in the performance that established him (SUMMERTIME on Blue Note 1201) and with various small groups.*

Christian, Charlie
   With the Benny Goodman Sextet   (COLUMBIA CL 652)
     ▸ *Performances that established the electric guitar in jazz and set a guitar style that dominated jazz for twenty years.*

Ellington, Duke
   At His Very Best   (RCA LPM 1715)
   The Indispensable Duke Ellington   (2-RCA LPM 6009)
     ▸ *The Ellington band at one of its highest points (possibly the highest) coincides with an unusually fertile period for the Duke as a composer.*

Gillespie, Dizzy
   Groovin' High   (SAVOY 12020)
   Jazz at Massey Hall   (FANTASY 8 6003)
     ▸ *These two and the Parker recording, listed later in this sec-*

tion, are three definitive be-bop recordings by its two most vital proponents. The Savoy discs, made in the midforties, are the basic be-bop statements. The Fantasy reports a concert in 1953 at which Gillespie, Parker, Bud Powell, Max Roach, and Charlie Mingus play the best recorded versions of their be-bop successes of the forties.

Herman, Woody
The Thundering Herds   (3-COLUMBIA C3L 25)
Hines, Earl
Grand Terrace Band   (RCA LPV 512)
Kenton, Stan
Artistry in Rhythm   (CAPITOL T-167)
Milestones   (CAPITOL T-190) OUT OF PRINT
Krupa, Gene
Drummin' Man   (2-COLUMBIA C2L-29)
  ▸ *Big bands that carried the Swing Era into the forties. Hines' band, 1940-1941, is a crisply swinging group, just on the verge of taking on some early signs of be-bop. Krupa's and Herman's midforties bands show the vitality of the new blood then entering jazz, while Kenton was exploring distinctive sounds—rich sonorities and blazing walls of brass.*

Parker, Charlie
The Genius of Charlie Parker   (SAVOY 12009, 12014)
Powell, Bud
The Amazing Bud Powell, Vol. 1, Vol. 2   (BLUE NOTE 1503, 1504)
  ▸ THE *pianist of the be-bop movement in the performances that gave him his stature.*

Watters, Lu
San Francisco Style   (3-GOOD TIME JAZZ 12001/3)
  ▸ *The primary source of the traditional jazz revival of the late forties and the prototype of almost all revivalist bands since then.*

Young, Lester
Memorial Album   (2-EPIC SN 6031)
  ▸ *Recordings by the original Count Basie band featuring Young's tenor saxophone playing, which formed a bridge between the swing period and the post-bop cool jazz era of the fifties.*

The 1950's

Brown, Clifford
The Immortal Clifford Brown   (LIMELIGHT 28201, 28601)
  ▸ *A varied collection by a trumpeter who influenced trumpeters of the fifties and sixties as Armstrong and Beider-*

becke influenced those of the twenties and thirties and as Gillespie influenced those of the forties.

Brubeck, Dave

Jazz Goes to College   (COLUMBIA CL 566)

▶ *The most consistently successful jazz group of the fifties and sixties in live performances which project the group's relationship and response to its audience.*

Davis, Miles

Birth of the Cool   (CAPITOL TT 1974)
Miles Ahead   (COLUMBIA CL 1041, CS 9633)
Kind of Blue   (COLUMBIA CS 1355, CS 8763)

▶ *Three aspects of one of the dominant trumpeters of post-World War II jazz: leading a nonet (BIRTH OF THE COOL), which established the "cool" jazz idiom of the early fifties; in big band settings by Gil Evans which brought out Davis' lyrical resources; leading a hard-driving small group which has been his usual vehicle since the late fifties.*

Garner, Erroll

Concert by the Sea   (COLUMBIA CL 883)

▶ *The first disc to capture the full flavor of Garner's highly personal piano style. Along with THAT'S MY KICK, (MGM S 4463), recorded a decade later (1966), the definitive Garner.*

Lewis, George

Concert!   (BLUE NOTE 1208)

▶ *A group of veteran New Orleans musicians, the sturdiest remnants of the traditional jazz revival of the forties. They had a widespread influence on European jazz musicians and were the prime source of the "trad" bands that were THE popular fare in England until the Beatles came along.*

Modern Jazz Quartet

European Concert   (2-ATLANTIC S 1385/6)

▶ *High points in the repertory of a group that often draws on European forms (particularly the fugue) as much as it does on jazz but manages to give its precise, subtle performances a compellingly swinging character.*

Mulligan, Gerry

The Genius of Gerry Mulligan   (PACIFIC JAZZ 8)

▶ *The original records by Mulligan's pianoless quartet in 1952 and examples of subsequent Mulligan groups through 1957.*

Outstanding Jazz Compositions of the 20th Century
                                          (2-COLUMBIA C2L 31, C2S 831)

▶ *Never mind the title. The set is largely devoted to efforts at Third Stream music (drawing on both jazz and European music) by Gunther Schuller, the chief proponent of Third Stream music, Jimmy Giuffre, Milton Babbitt, George Rus-*

sell and others. As a bonus there's a long, thoroughly mainstream work by Duke Ellington, IDIOM '59.

Silver, Horace
Blowin' the Blues Away   (BLUE NOTE 8 4017)
▶ The driving, blues-rooted "hard bop" that came as a reaction
to the withdrawn qualities of "cool" jazz in the midfifties.

Tatum, Art
This Is Art Tatum   (2-20TH CENTURY FOX 3162/3)
▶ A pianist with extraordinary facility and a fertile imagination
in informal performances which show him at his best.

The 1960's

Allen, Red
Feelin' Good   (COLUMBIA CL 2447, CS 9247)
Davison, Wild Bill
Blowin' Wild   (JAZZOLOGY 18)
▶ A trumpeter (Allen) and a cornetist (Davison) whose basic
styles were formed in the twenties, playing with tremendous
vitality, freshness and enthusiasm in the sixties. Excellent
examples of the long-lasting potential of what might have
become dated playing.

Coleman, Ornette
At the Golden Circle   (2-BLUE NOTE 8 4224/5)
▶ The pioneer of the modern jazz idiom of the sixties in the
performances that lifted him from the status of a curiosity
to the ranks of the unquestioned jazz greats.

Coltrane, John
My Favorite Things   (ATLANTIC S 1361)
Kulu Se Mama   (IMPULSE S 9106)
▶ The final, climactic phases of Coltrane's consistent develop-
ment during his thirty-year career: his amalgamation of
Indian influences and jazz in his use of the soprano saxo-
phone (MY FAVORITE THINGS) and his polar position in the
AVANT-GARDE of the sixties (KULU).

Dolphy, Eric
Last Date   (LIMELIGHT 82013, 86013)
▶ A summation of an exceptionally versatile and exploratory
saxophonist, flutist, and clarinetist who had had a strong influence on the direction of the jazz in the sixties when he
died in 1964 at the age of thirty-six.

Ellis, Don
Electric Bath   (COLUMBIA CL 2785, CS 9585)
▶ A big band that colors a strong, basic, swinging attack with
odd time signatures, electronic devices, and unusual instrumentation.

Evans, Bill, and Hall, Jim
  Undercurrent   (UNITED ARTISTS 14003, 15003)
   ▶ *Piano and guitar duets by a pair of unusually well-grounded, subtle, and technically adroit jazzmen.*

Fitzgerald, Ella
  At Juan Les Pins   (VERVE 6 4065)
   ▶ *The jazz-derived phrasing that colors Miss Fitzgerald's ballad-singing and the warm lyricism in her rhythm numbers are caught at their best in this relaxed, "in-person" recording.*

Getz, Stan
  Jazz Samba   (VERVE 6 8432)
   ▶ *This disc was a major factor in popularizing* BOSSA NOVA *and in turning Getz toward a more deeply lyrical use of his saxophone. Good on both counts and for a third—the presence of Charlie Byrd, playing guitar in the classical, finger-plucking manner.*

Hines, Earl
  The Real Earl Hines   (FOCUS S 335)
   ▶ *Recording of a concert in 1964, the first Hines had ever given, which showcased his talents so brilliantly that it brought him back into the jazz limelight after a decade of obscurity.*

Lloyd, Charles
  At Monterey   (ATLANTIC S 1473)
   ▶ *A tenor saxophonist who is one of the more readily communicative members of the* AVANT-GARDE *of the sixties with a quartet that features an extremely provocative pianist, Keith Jarrett.*

Mingus, Charles
  The Black Saint and the Sinner Lady   (IMPULSE S 1385/6)
   ▶ *A fascinating jazz iconoclast who has built a highly personal form of ensemble expression on a foundation of church music, the blues, and Duke Ellington. The Ellington influence is particularly strong in this well-developed set.*

Monk, Thelonious
  Two Hours with Thelonious   (2-RIVERSIDE 9 460/1)
   ▶ *A collection of solo and quartet performances by a pianist and composer who has a wry and individualistic approach.*

Shepp, Archie
  Mama Too Tight   (IMPULSE S 9134)

Taylor, Cecil
  Unit Structures   (BLUE NOTE 8 4237)
   ▶ *Two of the foremost jazzmen in the* AVANT-GARDE *of the sixties in sets that exemplify their work.*

Blues Singers

Charles, Ray
  Live Concert   (ABC S 500)
  ▶ *This and the King recording, listed later in this section, are*
    representative of the Blues.
Johnson, Robert
  Delta Blues   (COLUMBIA CL 1654)
  ▶ *The country Blues of the thirties.*
King, B. B.
  Blues Is King   ·   (BLUESWAY S 6001)
Rushing, Jimmy
  Listen to the Blues   (VANGUARD 3007, 73007)
  ▶ *This and the Turner recording, listed later in this section,*
    are representative of the Urban Blues of the thirties and
    forties.
Smith, Bessie
  The Bessie Smith Story   (4-COLUMBIA CL 855/8)
  ▶ *The Classic Blues of the twenties.*
Turner, Joe
  Boss of the Blues   (ATLANTIC S 1234)
Vinson, Eddie "Cleanhead"
  Cherry Red   (BLUESWAY S 6007)

FOLK

As we get down to the specific business of suggesting the
wherewithal of a basic folk library, things start getting complicated. There are, literally, thousands of albums to choose
from, in an endless variety of styles, categories, languages, and
repertoires. What I plan to do, then, is simply set down an
assortment of recordings that have been a source of pleasure to
me over the years. Most of them, incidentally, seem to have
struck a similarly responsive chord in the hearts of listeners to
WQXR's *Folk Music of the World* program. We have an all-
request show once a month and we keep pretty good tabs on
the songs and singers our audience likes best.

Enjoyment, or if you will, listenability is the keynote. I have
specifically refrained from listing albums merely because they

are historically important or educationally valid or anything except sources of highly agreeable music. Admittedly, it is a highly subjective list, too. You won't find Bob Dylan on it, for instance, even though he has exerted a vast influence on the younger generation of ballad composers. This is because, as much as I admire many of Dylan's songs, I personally find his singing whiny, mumbly, and bleaty, and would much rather recommend other performances of his music.

I have tried to choose albums that will be fun for the casual folknik as well as the connoisseur. For this reason, and others already mentioned, I have generally steered away from ethnic field recordings and other esoteric material (*i.e.*, Indian ragas) likely to appeal to specialized tastes. I have also eliminated the host of albums by such singers as Trini Lopez and such groups as The Byrds, since they are really geared more to the pop trade than to the folk.

Essentially, this leaves us with the traditional-style performances of professional folk singers (whether individually, in small groups, or as a chorus), and the rather more sophisticated concert interpretations of trained musicians. I do not really want to get into a discussion of the relative merits of the two, *per se*, except to suggest that both have their place. I feel the test of a valid performance is the degree to which it succeeds in conveying the basic emotional content of a given song. This is true whether the singer happens to be a farmer in Kentucky or a star of the Metropolitan Opera, and this is why you will find on the list both a Kentucky farmer and a contralto who sang at the Met.

For reasons of clarity, convenience and—considering the huge discography at hand—self-preservation, I have divided my recommendations into four major compartments.

Part I lists ten of my very favorite albums—recordings I have found particularly meaningful and appealing, and the ones to which I seem to keep returning time and again. There is no attempt at a preferential order within this category.

Part II contains fifty American soloists and groups (a few are Canadian), representing among them virtually every shade of musical opinion in the folk field. The solo singers are listed first in alphabetical order, then the groups and choirs.

Part III maintains the setup of Part II, except that it taps the
wonderfully rich heritage of Great Britain and Ireland.

Part IV is at once the most extensive and restricted compila-
tion of all; extensive because it ranges over music from a couple
of dozen countries, restricted because no list of fifty albums can
even begin to suggest the full international array currently available for the record-buyer here in the U.S.A.

I think I need hardly stress again that these are personal
choices, which I feel will provide the nucleus of a well-rounded
and (most importantly) an easily expandable library of folk
recordings. There are many deserving artists and recordings
which, for reasons of space or (I apologize in advance) over-
sight, have not been included. Please do not look on this selection as definitive or all-inclusive. Use it, rather, as a tentative
guide. If it helps you to a wider appreciation of folk music in
even one of its myriad guises, it will have served its purpose well.

Part I: Favorites

Belafonte, Harry
Love Is a Gentle Thing   (RCA 1927) MONO AND STEREO
▸ *Belafonte's soothing, meltingly tender songside manner
works wonders with eleven wistful tunes of love lost and
found.*

Bibb, Leon
Cherries and Plums   (LIBERTY 3358, STEREO 7358)
▸ *More love songs, including an exquisite modern romance
called "The Honey Wind." Bibb's singing is gentle, his
musicianship impeccable.*

Bikel, Theodore
Jewish Folk Songs   (ELEKTRA 141, STEREO 7141)
▸ *These are the songs his mother taught him, and Bikel re-
calls them with affection and uncommon warmth.*

Damari, Shoshana
Shoshana!   (VANGUARD 9126, STEREO 2144)
▸ *The vibrant Israeli* CHANTEUSE *has long been an incompar-
able interpreter of Jewish and Israeli music. Here she
widens her tonal horizons to include songs from Turkey,
Romania, and South America as well.*

Gibson, Bob
There's a Meeting Here Tonight   (RIVERSIDE 830) MONO ONLY

▶ *A light, fluid voice, boundless energy, and a knack for pick-*
ing good songs are among Gibson's attributes. Add a gener-
ous supply of personal charm, and you have the story of this
buoyant album. It may be hard to find, incidentally, but it
IS *still listed in the Schwann Catalogue, and it is worth the*
hunt.

Hinton, Sam
Whoever Shall Have Some Good Peanuts
(FOLKWAYS FC 7530) MONO ONLY

▶ *One of those children's albums guaranteed to captivate us*
erstwhile kiddies too. Hinton is among the most underrated
balladeers in America today, and his witty assemblage of
songs, stories, and sundry musical oddments is sheer delight.

Kennedy, Calum
Islands of Scotland
(LONDON 91322) MONO ONLY

▶ *I think this must be my favorite of all favorite albums—a*
totally enchanting garland of songs from the Hebrides. The
arrangements are tasteful, the performances by Kennedy
(himself a native of the Isle of Lewis) serene, sensitive, and
radiant.

The Soviet Army Chorus and Band
(ANGEL 35411) MONO AND STEREO

▶ *Rip-roaring songs à la Russe by the best chorus in the world,*
along with two delicious extras: "O No John" and "It's a
Long Long Way to Tipperary," both sung in English (of
sorts).

Tracey, Andrew, et al.
Wait a Minim!
(LONDON 58002, STEREO 88002)

▶ *What is a nice show album doing in a folk discography like*
this? Simple. The original cast recording of the South African
revue is made up entirely of international ballads. The ar-
rangements by Andrew Tracey are fresh and inventive; the
performances have enormous flair.

The Weavers
At Home
(VANGUARD 9024, STEREO 2030)

▶ *My favorite among the many fine Weavers albums, this one*
also boasts first-rate solo turns by Pete Seeger ("Empty
Pockets Blues") and Ronnie Gilbert ("Every Night").

Part II: America

Anderson, Marian
He's Got the Whole World in His Hands
(RCA 2592) MONO AND STEREO

Baez, Joan (VANGUARD 9078, STEREO 2077)
> ▸ *Baez's solo album debut contains all traditional songs, and is still a winner. For a more representative sampling of her later style, with its switch in emphasis to newly composed material, try* FAREWELL ANGELINA *(Vanguard 9200, stereo 79200). Included are four Bob Dylan ballads, and one each by Pete Seeger, Lee Hays, and Woody Guthrie.*

Belafonte, Harry
Swing Dat Hammer (RCA 2194) MONO AND STEREO

Bikel, Theodore
From Bondage to Freedom (ELEKTRA 200, STEREO 7200)

Bok, Gordon
Johnny Todd and Other Songs
(VERVE-FOLKWAYS 3016) MONO AND STEREO
> ▸ *A new talent, and a fine one.*

Brand, Oscar
Laughing America (TRADITION 1014) MONO ONLY
> ▸ *Oscar's predilection for making history come alive is also revealed in the equally entertaining* ELECTION SONGS OF THE U.S.A., *(Folkways 5280), mono only.*

Collins, Judy
The Fifth Album (ELEKTRA 300, STEREO 7300)
> ▸ *A top-notch collection of contemporary ballads, beautifully sung.*

Dobson, Bonnie
For the Love of Him (MERCURY 20987, STEREO 60987)

Dyer-Bennet, Richard
Of Ships and Seafaring Men
(DYER-BENNET RECORDS #12) MONO ONLY

Felix, Julie
Debut Album (LONDON 3395, STEREO 395)

Guthrie, Woody
Dust Bowl Ballads (FOLKWAYS 5212) MONO ONLY
> ▸ *A classic recording by America's greatest ballad composer.*

Hinton, Sam
Songs for Men (FOLKWAYS 2400) MONO ONLY

Houston, Cisco
I Ain't Got No Home (VANGUARD 3006, STEREO 73006)
> ▸ *The last testament of a superb balladeer, recorded less than two months before he died of cancer, at the age of forty-two. Another fine Houston album is* WOODY GUTHRIE SONGS *(Vanguard 9089, stereo 2131).*

Ives, Burl
The Wayfaring Stranger (COLUMBIA 628, STEREO 9041)
> ▸ *The old master, in the halcyon days before he turned pop singer.*

Jackson, Mahalia
The World's Greatest Gospel Singer
(COLUMBIA 644, STEREO 8759)
▶ *The title says it.*

Langstaff, John
Songs for Singing Children   (HMV 1604) MONO ONLY
▶ *An imported disc, probably available only at specialty shops, this rollicking songfest stands among the best children's recordings ever made.*

Leadbelly
Take This Hammer   (VERVE-FOLKWAYS 9001) MONO AND STEREO

McCurdy, Ed
Treasure Chest of American Song   (ELEKTRA 205) MONO ONLY

Mitchell, Howie
Folk Songs   (FOLK-LEGACY 2) MONO ONLY
▶ *Pleasing, unaffected singing in traditional style. Mitchell can also be heard, with seven friends, in a refreshingly spontaneous round of group music-making, called "Golden Ring" (Folk-Legacy 16, mono only).*

Niles, John Jacob
I Wonder as I Wander   (TRADITION 1023) MONO ONLY
▶ *Niles, with his eccentric manner and eerily high-pitched voice, is the very model of an unauthentic folksinger, but his compelling personality holds your attention unflaggingly. The album is named for one of the many famous tunes Niles has "collected" from his own fertile imagination; others here include "Black Is the Color," "Go Way from My Window," and "Venezuela."*

Odetta
At Carnegie Hall   (VANGUARD 3003, STEREO 73003)

Paxton, Tom
Ain't That News!   (ELEKTRA 298, STEREO 7298)
▶ *Our most talented young folk composer, Paxton has a gift both for incisive lyrics and affecting melodies.*

Reed, Susan
Folk Songs   (ELEKTRA 116) MONO ONLY

Ritchie, Jean
A Time for Singing   (WARNER BROS. 1592) MONO AND STEREO

Robeson, Paul
Favorite Songs   (MONITOR 580) MONO ONLY
▶ *The resonant Robeson voice imparts a rare grandeur to these spirituals and other folk songs.*

Sainte-Marie, Buffy
Little Wheel Spin and Spin   (VANGUARD 9211, STEREO 79211)
▶ *Another gifted young singer-composer.*

Sandburg, Carl
    Folk Songs   (LYRICHORD 66) MONO ONLY
    ▶ *Rumbling, rambling versions of seventeen ballads, love songs, and what Sandburg called "darn fool ditties."*

Seeger, Pete
    Birds, Beasts, Bugs and Bigger Fishes
                     (FOLKWAYS 711) MONO ONLY
    ▶ *Choosing one "best" Pete Seeger record is akin to selecting one best book to be marooned with on a desert island—it just cannot be done. This disc has the ineffable advantage of containing "The Cumberland Mountain Bear Chase," but I will not be at all insulted if you prefer Pete's later and more socially significant collections. Especially recommended among these are* STRANGERS AND COUSINS *(Columbia 2334, stereo 9134),* DANGEROUS SONGS!? *(Columbia 2503, stereo 9303), and* GOD BLESS THE GRASS *(Columbia 2432, stereo 9232).*

Terri, Salli
    I Know My Love   (CAPITOL 8556) MONO AND STEREO

Washington, Jackie
    Folk Songs   (VANGUARD 9110) MONO ONLY

Watson, Doc
    Southbound   (VANGUARD 9170, STEREO 79170)

Wheeler, Billy Edd
    Billy Edd, U.S.A.   (MONITOR 354) MONO ONLY
    ▶ *A protégé of John Jacob Niles, Wheeler writes lovely songs, and sings them most effectively. He shares billing here with sultry-voiced Joan Sommer (who subsequently changed her style to pop-blues and her name to Joan Tolliver).*

White, Josh
    Spirituals and Blues   (ELEKTRA 193, STEREO 7193)

Addiss, Steve, and Crofut, Bill
    Folk Songs   (COLUMBIA 2611, STEREO 9411)
    ▶ *Ballads from many lands by two personable young singers who have been touring the world on State Department-sponsored trips for a good many years now.*

The Baby Sitters
    Folk Songs for Babies, Small Children and Parents
               (VANGUARD 3002, STEREO 73002)
    ▶ *Charming songs for the younger set.*

The Beers Family
    An American Folk Tradition   (COLUMBIA 6105, STEREO 6705)

DeCormier Singers
Folk Album (COMMAND 897) MONO AND STEREO
▶ *A little overblown, but exciting performances nonetheless.*
Gene and Francesca
Love and War Between the Sexes (ELEKTRA 164) MONO ONLY
Ian and Sylvia
Northern Journey (VANGUARD 9154, STEREO 79154)
▶ *One of the best albums by the duo before their recent (and lamented) conversion to pop, country-and-western, and folk-rock stylings.*
Kathy and Carol
Folk Songs (ELEKTRA 289, STEREO 7289)
Kingston Trio
Folk Era (CAPITOL 2180) MONO AND STEREO
▶ *A three-disc set chronicling the work of this popular group, from "Tom Dooley" on down. If that's too big a dose, one of the Trio's best single albums is their early in-concert performance* FROM THE HUNGRY I *(Capitol 1107), mono only.*
The Limeliters
14 Karat Folk Songs (RCA 2671) MONO AND STEREO
Luboff Choir, Norman
Songs of the World (COLUMBIA C2L-13) MONO ONLY
▶ *Lush, but lovely choral settings of folk favorites from twenty-four countries.*
Marais, Josef, and Miranda
In Person (DECCA 9026) MONO ONLY
▶ *Songs of the South African veld, and many other lands too. A companion album, also recorded in actual performance, is also excellent (Decca 9027, mono only).*
Mitchell Trio
Slightly Irreverent (MERCURY 20944) STEREO 60944
▶ *I liked the Trio much better when it was named for (and led by) Chad Mitchell, so my choice is the group's last album before Chad left it, in 1965.*
Paton, Sandy and Caroline
Folk Songs (FOLK-LEGACY 30) MONO ONLY
▶ *Charming duets, family style.*
Peter, Paul and Mary
See What Tomorrow Brings
(WARNER BROS. 1615) MONO AND STEREO
de Paur Chorus
Dansé Calinda! (MERCURY 50418, STEREO 90418)
▶ *Exciting choral versions of Creole songs and Negro Spirituals.*

The Weavers
Reunion at Carnegie Hall (VANGUARD 2150, STEREO 9130)
▶ *I just could not let the list go without a final wave to The Weavers. This marvelous set contains "Wimoweh," "Guantanamera," "Goodnight Irene," and "If I Had a Hammer."*
The Womenfolk
Never Underestimate the Power (RCA 2919) MONO AND STEREO

Part III: Britain and Ireland

Clancy, Liam
Folk Songs (VANGUARD 9169, STEREO 79169)
▶ *One of the Clancy boys (see below) takes off on his own with a beguiling bouquet of Irish song.*
Deller, Alfred
Wraggle Taggle Gipsies (VANGUARD 1001) MONO ONLY
▶ *The strangely pure, semifalsetto timbre of a counter-tenor's voice is not to everyone's taste, but Deller's performances are impeccable.*
Ferrier, Kathleen
English Folk Songs (LONDON 5411) MONO ONLY
▶ *Glowing concert performances by the beloved contralto.*
MacColl, Ewan
Songs of Robert Burns (FOLKWAYS 8758) MONO ONLY
McCormack, John
Irish Songs and Ballads (ANGEL 124) MONO ONLY
▶ *The greatest Irish tenor of them all.*
McKellar, Kenneth
Songs from Scotland (LONDON 91331, STEREO 99331)
O'Dowda, Brendan
Immortal Irish Ballads (CAPITOL 10213) MONO AND STEREO
O'Duffy, Michael
Songs of Ireland (AVOCA 122) MONO AND STEREO
O'Hara, Mary
Songs of Ireland (TRADITION 1024) MONO ONLY
▶ *Winsome and winning.*
O'Shea, Tessie
Cheers (COMMAND 872) MONO AND STEREO
▶ *Bright, brassy memories of the British music hall.*
Redpath, Jean
Laddie Lie Near Me (ELEKTRA 274, STEREO 7274)
Stewart, Andy
A Scottish Soldier (EPIC 18027, STEREO 19027)
▶ *Highland songs with a swagger, by modern Scotland's answer to Sir Harry Lauder.*

Thomas, Thomas L.
Welsh Traditional Songs (LONDON 5172) MONO ONLY

Cameron, Isla, and Britton, Tony
Songs of Love, Lust and Loose Living (LONDON 5808) MONO ONLY
▶ *Not for the kiddies.*

Ian Campbell Folk Group
The Rights of Man (ELEKTRA 309, STEREO 7309)

Clancy Brothers and Tommy Makem
The First Hurrah (COLUMBIA 2165, STEREO 8965)
▶ *One of many first-rate albums by these four exuberant, exultant, irrepressible sons of the auld sod.*

Corrie Folk Trio and Paddie Bell
The Promise of the Day (ELEKTRA 304, STEREO 7304)

Galliards
England's Great Folk Group (MONITOR 407) MONO AND STEREO

Hall, Robin, and MacGregor, Jimmie
Two Heads Are Better Than One (MONITOR 365) MONO ONLY
▶ *Fine songs and singing by the talented pair who later founded the Galliards.*

Morriston Orpheus Choir
The Glory of Wales (EPIC 18039, STEREO 19039)
▶ *One of the most marvelous male choirs in a land of marvelous male choirs, the Morriston Orpheus offers thrilling versions of such favorites as "Ar Hyd Y Nos" and "Rhyfelgyrch Gwyr Harlech" (or, if you insist, "All Through the Night" and "Men of Harlech").*

Part IV: Other Lands

AFRICA
(see also Marais and Miranda, Part II)

Fodeba, Keita, et al.
Voices and Drums of Africa (MONITOR 373) MONO ONLY

Makeba, Miriam
Folk Songs (RCA 2267) MONO AND STEREO
▶ *This delectable album, which also contains international as well as South African songs, just missed my list of top-ten favorites in Part I by the proverbial whisker. Makeba's "Suliram" is not to be missed.*

de Paur Chorus
Songs of New Nations (MERCURY 50382, STEREO 90382)

Troubadors of King Baudouin
Misa Luba and *Native Songs of the Congo*
(PHILIPS 206, STEREO 606)
▶ *The* MISA LUBA *is absolutely fascinating. The form and Latin words of the traditional Catholic Mass are fused with the pulsing drums, intricate cross-rhythms, and improvised themes of tribal Africa.*

ARMENIA

Various Soloists
Armenian Folk Songs   (MONITOR 303) MONO ONLY

AUSTRALIA

Clauson, William
Songs of Australia   (MONITOR 424) MONO ONLY
Harris, Rolf
The Court of King Caractacus   (EPIC 24110, STEREO 26110)

AUSTRIA

The Engel Children (Die Engelkinder)
Music from the Tyrol   (VOX 15050, STEREO 515050)
Tauber, Richard
21 Favorite Volkslieder   (CAPITOL 10369) MONO ONLY
▶ *German and Austrian songs by the pride of old Vienna.*

CANADA

Les Feux Follets
Canadian Mosaic   (RCA 1088) MONO AND STEREO
▶ *It will probably take some hunting in imported record shops to locate a copy of this release, but it contains an entertaining panorama of music from various areas of the country. Les Feux Follets is Canada's national folklore ensemble.*
Mills, Alan
Folk Songs of Newfoundland   (FOLKWAYS 8771) MONO ONLY

CHINA

Chang, Grace
Nightingale of the Orient   (CAPITOL 10272) MONO ONLY

CZECHOSLOVAKIA

Melnik Folk Ensemble
Czechoslovakia in Song and Dance   (MONITOR 329) MONO ONLY

FRANCE

Davrath, Netania
Songs of the Auvergne (VANGUARD 9085, STEREO 2090)
▶ *The wonderful settings by Joseph Canteloube and Davrath's luxurious singing make this set, and its companion Volume II (Vanguard 9120, stereo 2132), a treat from beginning to end.*
Malkine, Sonia
French Songs from the Provinces (FOLKWAYS 8743) MONO ONLY

GERMANY

Kunz, Erich
German University Songs, Vol. II (VANGUARD 1010, STEREO 2009)
▶ *There are five volumes of these robust songs of wine and women, all of them delightful.*
Prey, Hermann
Famous German Folk Songs (ANGEL 36414) MONO AND STEREO

GREECE

Fleury
Isles of Greece (VANGUARD 9168, STEREO 79168)
Yapapa, Stella
Love Ballads and Folk Songs of Greece
(MONITOR 369) MONO ONLY

HUNGARY

Horvath, Toki
King of the Gypsies (ANGEL 65040) MONO ONLY
▶ *Fabulous fiddling, and some good songs by Mihaly Szekely.*
Sandor Lakatos Ensemble
The Gypsies Are Singing (WESTMINSTER 19022, STEREO 17022)

ISRAEL

Ahroni, Hanna
Songs of Israel (DECCA 8937, STEREO 78937)
Schlamme, Martha
Israeli Folk Songs (VANGUARD 9072, STEREO 2070)

ITALY

Bastianini, Ettore
Songs of Italy (LONDON 91412, STEREO 99412)
Corelli, Franco
Memories of Naples (ANGEL 36126) MONO AND STEREO

JEWISH-YIDDISH

Bernardi, Herschel
Chocolate Covered Matzohs   (VANGUARD 9074) MONO ONLY
▸ *Songs and hilarious comedy routines by the noted actor whose most recent Broadway triumph was in the role of Tevye, in* FIDDLER ON THE ROOF.

Davrath, Netania
Yiddish Folk Songs   (VANGUARD 9117, STEREO 2127)

LATIN AMERICA
(with apologies to Pru Devon)

Buchino, Maria Luisa
Music of Chile   (MONITOR 342) MONO AND STEREO

Curtin, Phyllis
Cantigas y Canciones   (VANGUARD 1125, STEREO 71125)
▸ *Concert arrangements and composed songs in folk style by Villa Lobos, Ginastera, and other Latin American masters. Beautiful performances.*

Jimenez, Alfonso Cruz
Folk Songs of Mexico   (FOLKWAYS 8727) MONO ONLY
▸ *Gentle, almost intimate singing by a blind street minstrel from the state of Oaxaca.*

Petraglia, Clara
Songs from Brazil   (WESTMINSTER 9807) MONO ONLY

Various Artists
Latin American Festival   (MONITOR 390) MONO ONLY

PHILIPPINE ISLANDS

Bayanihan Ensemble
Songs and Dances from the Philippines
        (MONITOR 322) MONO AND STEREO

POLAND

Slask Ensemble
Songs and Dances of Poland   (MONITOR 325) MONO ONLY

PORTUGAL

Marques, Maria, and Fernandes, Manuel
Fados and Folk Songs   (MONITOR 340) MONO AND STEREO

Rodrigues, Amalia
World's Greatest Fado Singer   (KAPP 1310, STEREO 3310)

ROMANIA

Ciocarlia Ensemble
Rumanian Folk Songs and Dances   (MONITOR 304) MONO ONLY

▶ *Enesco's "Rumanian Rhapsody"* AU NATUREL, *and other musical enticements.*

RUSSIA

Piatnitsky Chorus
Ballads and Balalaikas   (ARTIA 192) MONO AND STEREO
Various Artists
Moscow Nights   (MONITOR 590) MONO ONLY
▶ *The pop scene, Russian style.*

SCANDINAVIA

Clauson, William
Swedish Songs   (MGM 4198) MONO AND STEREO
Saga Sjöberg and Arne Dørumsgaard
Scandinavian Folk Songs   (MONITOR 333) MONO ONLY
▶ *Gracious settings (by Dørumsgaard) and warmly appealing singing, too.*

SPAIN

Berganza, Teresa
Airs of Aragon and the Basque Country
                                (LONDON 5543, STEREO 25116)
Herrero, Miguel
Creaciones   (MONTILLA 104) MONO ONLY
Montero, Germaine
Canciones de Espana   (VANGUARD 9050) MONO ONLY
Plata, Manitas de
Flamenco Guitar   (CONNOISSEUR SOCIETY 263) MONO AND STEREO

SWITZERLAND

Various Artists
Alpine Festival   (COLUMBIA 159) MONO ONLY
Various Artists
Swiss Mountain Music   (CAPITOL 10161) MONO ONLY
Various Artists
A Visit to Switzerland   (CAPITOL 10264) MONO AND STEREO

YUGOSLAVIA

Radio Zagreb Children's Choir
Yugoslav Melodies and Folk Songs
                                (VANGUARD 9138, STEREO 79138)
Various Artists
Folk Songs and Dances of Yugoslavia   (MONITOR 312) MONO ONLY

MUSIC FROM LATIN AMERICA

Twenty years ago you could buy very little authentic Latin American music in the United States. Now, however, there is an incredible number of popular dance and sentimental songs very readily available. Because such popularity flickers, and supply and demand has its own mysterious dynamics, I have left this classification virtually untouched. Similarly, the various popular solo or trio performers, whose output is prodigious and somewhat standardized, have been given short shrift just because their discs are so numerous. (Note that the words "and others," appearing in parentheses, signify that the artist or artists have many similar releases.) With these things in mind, and twenty years of answering listener's inquiries, I have listed material that is characteristic and generally less commercially exploited.

Some of these will be currently stocked by the large record shops, and they will order the others for you. Two labels that may be unfamiliar to you are SMC, Spanish Music Center, 319 West 48th Street, New York, New York, 10036, and Folkways, 701 Seventh Avenue, New York, New York 10036. The latter company has a listing of some sixty-five albums from the entire inclusive area of Latin America, in many cases not represented at all elsewhere. They generally include excellent pamphlets of explanation. However, their musical appeal varies; often they are of more value to the ethnomusician than to the typical WQXR listener. If concerned, I suggest you obtain their catalogue.

I confess to a certain inconsistency in my alphabetizing. This is due not to indifference to order, but the knotty problem concerning which word should be the key to the reader, *i.e.*, "Guitar" under G, or the name of the record, its composer, or its performer, all frequently unknown here.

This list as an introductory guideline should add to your appreciation and enjoyment of a music of tremendous vitality, excitement, and variety.

Assorted Countries

Alma del Bandoneon (el)   (SMC 1104)
▶ *Instrumental featuring distinctively Argentine type of accordion.*
Boleros y Folklore (and others), Los Hermanos Silva
(RCA MKL 1203)
Bravo Hi-Fi, Morton Gould, George Gershwin, Robert McBride
(MERCURY MG 50166)
▶ *Striking non-Latin Latin Americana.*
Cantigas y Canciones, Phyllis Curtin
(VANGUARD VRS 1125, STEREO VSD 71125)
▶ *Beautifully sung Villa-Lobos, Barrios, etc.*
Caramba (and others), Los Machucambos   (LONDON INT, SP 44084)
Exitos de Sudamerica   (DECCA DL 4722)
▶ *There are several Paraguayan groups who present recordings of great variety. This is one of the best.*
Greatest Hits (and others), Los Paraguayos
(PHILIPS PHM 200-235, STEREO PHM 200-235)
Guitar Classics, Elias Marreiro   (SMC 1111, 1112, 1113)
▶ *Classic composers of Europe, Spain, Latin America.*
Guitar Moods, Jorge Morel   (SMC 1110)
Himnos Nacionales   (MONTILLA FM 95)
▶ *All of the National Anthems.*
Latin American Best Sellers (and others), Trio Los Panchos
(COLUMBIA EX 5183, STEREO ES 1883)
Latin American Festival   (MONITOR MF 390)
▶ *Wide, characteristic sampler.*
Latin American Fiesta, Villa-Lobos, Guernieri
(COLUMBIA ML 5914, STEREO MS 6514)
▶ *Fernandez, Chavez, Revueltas.*
Maravilloso, Los Indios   (EPIC LN 3530)
Pan American Folk Dances   (SMC 1030)
▶ *Includes songs, words, and dance instructions.*
Panorama Folklorico, Los de Ramón   (RCA MKL 6001)
▶ *Astonishingly varied assemblage from everywhere.*
Xango, Olga Coelho   (DECCA DL 10018)
▶ *Predominantly from the renowned singer's Brazil repertoire.*

Andean Republics (Ecuador, Peru, Bolivia)

Cancionero Incaico, Vols. 1 and 2   (SMC 518, 557)
Canciones Peruanas   (SMC 1105)
Ecos de los Andes   (SMC 1043)

Gods and Demons of Bolivia   (VANGUARD VRS 9054)
  ▶ *Extremely interesting and well documented.*
Incaica, Vols. 1 and 2   (SMC 1089, 1090)
Musique Indienne des Andes   (BAM LD 349-M)
Realm of the Incas, Elisabeth Waldo (GNP 603) MONO AND STEREO
  ▶ *Good "re-creation" using authentic themes and instruments.*
Songs and Dances of Bolivia   (FOLKWAYS FW 6871)
Traditional Music of Peru   (FOLKWAYS FE 4456)

Argentina

Argentina, Maria Luisa Buchino   (MONITOR MF 343)
Argentine Folkdances   (FOLKWAYS FW 8841)
Aromas de Pampa   (SMC 1103)
  ▶ *Instrumental, featuring harp.*
Cantata para America Magica, Alberto Ginastera
                          (COLUMBIA MS 6447, STEREO ML 5847)
  ▶ *Striking. Contemporary yet pre-Columbian in concept. So-
    prano and wild instruments.* (TOCCATA FOR PERCUSSION, *by
    Carlos Chavez, on reverse.*)
Color en Folklore, Los Fronterizos
                   (PHILIPS PHS 600-246, STEREO PHM 200-246)
Danzas Folkloricas Argentina
                   (RCA INTERNATIONAL FPM 165, STEREO FSP 165)
  ▶ *Superb instrumental.*
Folklore Argentino, Maria Luisa Buchino   (SMC 1096)
Folklore Argentino (el)   (SMC 558)
Guitarra (una), Eduardo Falú
                   (PHILIPS PHM 200-244, STEREO PHS 600-244)
Misa Criolla, Ariel Ramírez   (PHILIPS PCC 219)
  ▶ *Magnificent creation, the traditional Mass magically set in
    folklore lyrics and rhythms.*
Nuestro Folklore en Hollywood, Los Chalchaleros   (RCA AVL 3554)
  ▶ *Do not be put off by the title. This is entirely authentic.*
South American Suite, Waldo de los Rios
                       (COLUMBIA EX 5162, STEREO ES 1862)
  ▶ *A symphonic tone-poem, with some folk-themes used. Para-
    guay, Uraguay, and Peru are included.*
Trovadores (los)   (COLUMBIA EX 5169)
  ▶ *Irresistible quintet. South American prizewinners.*
Tangos, Lo Mejor de Carlos Gardel   (RCA MKLA 34)
Tangos (and others), Amor en la Sombra, Libertad Lamarque
                                                 (RCA MKL 1245)
Tangos (and others), Sarita Montiel   (COLUMBIA EX 5071)
Tangos, Julio Sosa   (COLUMBIA EX 5164)
Tangos, Instrumental   (MONTILLA FMS 2100)

Tangos, Besos Brujos, Blanca Mooney   (COLUMBIA EX 5041)
Tangos, (more Argentine), Instrumental   (CAPITOL T 10303)
Tangos (and others), Los Cinco Latinos   (COLUMBIA EX 5086)
▶ *Young, nontraditional, swingers.*

Brazil

Bonfá, Luiz, Guitar   (EPIC LN 24124)
Bonfá, O Vialaõ de   (COOK 1134)
Bossa Nova, Miltinho   (AUDIO FIDELITY AFLP 1984)
Brasil e Samba, Instrumental   (RCA BBL 1173)
Debut, "Poly," Guitar and Winds   (EPIC LN 24193)
Esto es Carnaval   (COLUMBIA EX 5083)
Jequibau   (EPIC LN 24192)
▶ *Instrumental in current off-beat 5/8 and other odd time.*
Songs of Brasil, Clara Petraglia   (WESTMINSTER 9807)
▶ *Delicate songs, guitar accompaniment.*
Tren do Caipira (el), Villa-Lobos
     (EVEREST LPBR 6041, STEREO SDBR 3041)
▶ *Beguiling descriptive nostalgia from Bachianas Brasileiras. Argentine Ginastera on reverse with two Ballets.*
Uirapuru, Villa-Lobos   (EVEREST LPBR 6016)
▶ *Symphonic synthesis for ballet drawn from strange Brazilian folk legend.*
Xango and Eight Brasilian Folk Songs   (WESTMINSTER 9807)
▶ *Jose Siqueira's richly textured contemporary Negro cantata. On reverse, soprano Alice Ribeira sings.*

Caribbean

Bomba   (MONITOR MF 355)
▶ *Mostly interesting Puerto Rican and Haitian.*
Caribbean Calypsos   (CAPITOL T-10071)
Caribbean Folkmusic   (FOLKWAYS FE 4533)
▶ *Two-disc broad sampling of rustic material.*
Cuba, Rapsodia de, Esther Borja   (MONTILLA LD 21)
Cuban Ballet, Tambó   (MONTILLA FM 92)
Cuban Nights, Miguelito Valdes   (DECCA DL 8716)
▶ *This and MACHITO Y SUS AFRO-CUBANS, listed below, include old-style Afro-Cuban dance hits of the past.*
Haiti (Fiesta en), Jean León Destiné   (ELEKTRA EKL 130)
Haitian Folksongs, Lolita Cuevas   (FOLKWAYS FP 811)
Homenaje a Los Santos   (SEECO SCLP 4269)
▶ *This, and NAÑIGO and ORIZA, listed below, are reasonably authentic Afro-Cuban examples. They are semiritual and semisocial.*

Jamaican Children's Songs (FOLKWAYS FC 7250)
Jamaican Folk Songs, Louise Bennett (FOLKWAYS FP 6846)
Machito y sus Afro-Cubans (DECCA DL 4505)
Nañigo, Ruth Fernandez (MONTILLA FM 54)
  ▸ *Famous ultra contralto of Cecilia Valdez.*
Oriza (SEECO CELP 4260)
Panama (Sylvia de Grasse en) (MONTILLA FM 161)
Petite Musicale (la), Olive Walkes (RCA LPS 3001)
  ▸ *Trinidad and Tobago in well-modulated chorus.*
Puerto Rico (Sons and Dances of) (FOLKWAYS FP 80-2)
Steel Band (the Original Trinidad) (ELEKTRA 139)
Trinidad (Limbo from)

(RCA LPB 3013, STEREO LPS 3013)
Trio Vegabajeño (RCA LPR 1009)
  ▸ *So very typical of Puerto Rican Bolero.*

Chile

Chile, Maria Luisa Buchino and group (MONITOR MF 342)
  ▸ *Sterling, vital, and regional.*
Folklore Chileno (el), Los Quincheros (SMC 562)
Folk Songs of Chile (FOLKWAYS FW 8817)
Peña de los Parra (MUSIC HALL 12 586)
Traditional Songs of Chile (FOLKWAYS FW 8748)

Colombia

Canta un Tiple, Pacho Benavides (MONTILLA FM 89)
  ▸ *Instrument resembling guitar but with twelve strings, divided in groups of four.*
Cumbia (a bailar la) (COLUMBIA EX 5136)
Cumbia (Señorita) (COLUMBIA EX 5148)
Flores Negras, Carolos Ramirez sings (SMC 541)
Pajaros (los) (PHILIPS PHM 200-240, STEREO PHS 600-240)

Mexico

Bailes Regionales, Instrumental (RCA MKL 1448)
Ballet Folklorico de Mexico (RCA MKL 1530, STEREO MKS 1530)
Cancionero Mexicana, Vols. 1 and 2, includes words

(SMC 559, 560)
Cantos de las Posadas, includes words (FOLKWAYS FC 7745)
Corridos de la Revolución (RCA MKL 1309)
Fantasia Mexicana, Mariachi (MONTILLA DM 1115)
Fiesta Mexicana, Mariachi (MONITOR MF 472, STEREO MFS 472)

Folklore de Mexico (lo Mejor del)   (RCA MKLA 46)
▶ *Three-disc cross-section of all regions.*
Lourdes, Maria de Mariachi   (COLUMBIA EX 5067)
Mejia, Miguel Aceves   (RCA MKL 1140)
Mexican Folk Songs, Trio, words included   (SMC 1059)
Mexican Panorama   (VANGUARD VRS 9014)
Mexican Rancheras, Dora Maria   (CAPITOL T-10102)
Mexico, Carlos Chavez   (COLUMBIA LL 1015)
▶ *Famed concert of 1940 in superbly illustrated book. Includes re-created Aztec music and Paloma Azul.*
Mexico, Alta Fidelidad   (VANGUARD VRS 9009)
▶ *Like* MEXICAN PANORAMA, *listed above, an authentic group of songs.*
Mexico, Music of   (DECCA DL 9527)
▶ *Sinfonia India, El Sol, Oberatura Republicana, Carlos Chavez, Huapango, José Pablo Moncayo.*
Misa en Mexico (la)   (COLUMBIA EX 5155)
▶ *Exciting rendition of traditional Mass set in folklore forms.*
Negrete, Jorge (and others)   (RCA MKL 1157)
▶ *Marvelously vigorous and typical singer.*
Salon Mexico, Aaron Copland   (RCA LM 1928)
Sones de Mexico   (FOLKWAYS FP 15)
Viva Mexico   (CAPITOL T-10083)
▶ *Four fine contemporary composers: Galindo, Moncayo, Revueltas, Ayala.*

Paraguay

Azucena con los Comuneros del Paraguay   (DECCA DL 4722)
Chiriguanos (los)   (ELEKTRA EKL 202)
Guantanamera, Los Tres Paraguayos   (MONITOR MFS 490)
Guaranies (los)   (VENEVOX BL 411)
Maravilloso, Los Indios   (EPIC LN 3530)
Trio del Paraguay with Digno Garcia (and others)
        (MONTILLA FM 131)

Venezuela

Dances of Venezuela   (FOLKWAYS FW 8844)
▶ *One of my favorites in the Folkways Catalogue.*
Por los Caminos de Venezuela, Adilia Castillo
        (COLUMBIA EX 5063)
Venezuela, Vols. 1 and 2   (SMC 1044, 1045)
▶ *Very typical orshera and male singer.*
Venezuelan Fiesta, Salon Orchestra   (RCA LPM 1203)

Index

Adams, Lee, 168
Adderly, Cannonball, 188
Albanese, Licia, 12
Albéniz, Isaac, 64, 116
Albert, Eugene d', 103
Albinoni, Tomaso, 80, 82
Alexander, Cris, 165
Anderson, Leroy, 174
Apollinaire, Guillaume, 140
Arlen, Harold, 162–163
Armstrong, Louis, 188–189, 191–192, 194–195
Ashkenazy, Vladimir, 111, 115
Astaire, Adele, 160
Astaire, Fred, 149, 160, 181
Auber, Daniel-François, 29–30
Ayler, Albert, 197

Babbitt, Milton, 116
Bach, Carl Philipp Emanuel, 44
Bach, Johann Christian, 44
Bach, Johann Christoph, 103
Bach, Johann Sebastian, xxii, 40–44, 56, 69, 71–80, 82, 86, 95, 102–105, 107, 113, 115, 117–119, 121–123, 129, 143, 170
Baez, Joan, 207
Balakirev, Mily, 63
Balfe, Michael, 26
Ballet Folklorico, 216
Balsam, Artur, 107
Balzac, Honoré de, 29
Bankhead, Tallulah, 192
Barber, Samuel, 116, 144
Barbieri, Fedora, 12
Barenboim, Daniel, 106, 108

Barnum, P. T., 14
Barry, John, 183
Bartók, Béla, 65, 97, 99–100, 112, 115–117
Basie, Count, 195–196
Battistini, Mattia, 17
Beatles, The, 173
Bechet, Sidney, 193
Beecham, Sir Thomas, 18, 120, 121
Beethoven, Ludwig van, xvi–xviii, xxii–xxiii, 26–28, 49–54, 57–58, 61, 69, 75–76, 85, 89–95, 98, 100, 107–109, 112–113, 117, 119–120, 124–127, 136, 170, 172, 179, 184
Beiderbecke, Bix, 185, 187–188, 191–193
Belafonte, Harry, 206
Bellini, Vincenzo, xxiii, 3, 18, 28–29
Berg, Alban, 3, 38, 98, 101, 115
Bergonzi, Carlo, 10
Berlin, Irving, 151–152, 159, 167, 181
Berlioz, Hector, 23, 29, 31, 54–57, 127, 138–139
Bernac, Pierre, 145
Bernstein, Leonard, 56, 68, 91, 116, 133, 165, 205
Biber, Heinrich von, 76, 86
Bigard, Barney, 194
Bikel, Theodore, 203
Bing, Rudolf, 12
Bizet, Georges, xvii, 64
Bjoerling, Jussi, 11
Black, Stanley, 173
Blakey, Art, 188

Bloch, Ernest, 97, 99–100, 131
Boccherini, Luigi, 86–87, 93
Bock, Jerry, 168
Bodanzky, Artur, 6–7, 26, 128–129
Bogan, Robert, 7
Bogatyryev, Semyon, 61
Bohnen, Michael, 27
Boismortier, Joseph Bodin de, 72, 83
Boito, Arrigo, 25, 37
Bolton, Guy, 150
Bonelli, Richard, 10
Bookspan, Martin, xxiii, 39–68, 84–101
Bori, Lucrezia, xvii, 9
Borodin, Aleksandr, 36, 63, 97, 113, 149
Boulez, Pierre, 116
Boult, Adrian, 120
Boulton, Laura, 216
Boyce, William, 44, 170
Brahms, Johannes, 57–59, 75, 85, 95–96, 109, 111, 113–114, 117–118, 128, 134, 136–138, 144
Brand, Oscar, 201–202, 204
Branzell, Karin, 6
Britten, Benjamin, 38, 65, 68, 116, 142–143
Brothers Four, 206
Brown, Lawrence, 187, 194
Brown, Lew, 159–160, 167
Brown, Nacio Herb, 181
Brubeck, Dave, 188
Bruckner, Anton, 4, 57, 59–60
Busch, Fritz, 18, 25
Busoni, Ferruccio, 78, 103
Byrd, William, 39
Byron, George Gordon, 56

Caballé, Montserrat, 29
Cage, John, 65–66
Callas, Maria, 12–13, 26, 29
Caniglia, Maria, 12
Cannabich, Christian, 44
Carissimi, Giacomo, 76
Carney, Harry, 186–187, 194
Carter, Elliott, xxiii, 116
Caruso, Enrico, xv–xvi, 10, 23
Casadesus, Robert, 114
Casals, Pablo, xiv
Caymmi, Dorival, 221
Chabrier, Emanuel, 140
Chacksfield, Frank, 173
Chaliapin, Feodor, 19
Charpentier, Gustave, 124
Charpentier, Marc-Antoine, 82–83, 124
Chausson, Ernest, 64

Chavez, Carlos, 216
Cherubini, Luigi, 25–26
Chopin, Frederic, xvi, xviii–xix, xxiii, 29, 109–112
Christian, Charlie, 188
Christofori, Bartolomeo, 102
Cleopatra, 170
Cliburn, Van, 111
Coates, Eric, 170–171, 174
Coelho, Olga, 221
Cohan, George M., 149
Coleman, Ornette, 188–189, 197–198
Collin, Heinrich Josef von, 53
Coltrane, John, 189, 198–199
Comden, Betty, 165
Cooke, Deryck, 63
Coolidge, Elizabeth Sprague, xxiii
Coon-Sanders Original Kansas City Nighthawks, 185
Cooper, Lillian Kemble, 158
Copland, Aaron, 58–59, 65–68, 116, 170, 173, 182
Corelli, Arcangelo, xxii, 41, 73, 77, 81–82, 86
Corelli, Franco, 11
Cortéz, Hernando, 219
Couperin, François, 73, 77, 80–82
Coward, Noel, 148, 159, 180
Cowell, Henry, 143–144, 203
Crespin, Régine, 11, 35, 145
Cui, Cesar, 63

Dale, Alan, 149–150
Dallapiccola, Luigi, 38
Davis, Miles, 189–190, 198
Davison, Wild Bill, 199
Debussy, Claude, 18, 31, 65, 98–99, 113–115, 133, 139
Delacroix, Ferdinand, 29
Delibes, Léo, 31
Del Monaco, Mario, 12
De Luca, Giuseppe, 10
De Sica, Vittorio, 37
De Sylva, Buddy, 159–160, 167
Devon, Pru, 210–223
Dietz, Howard, 160–161
Di Stefano, Giuseppe, 12
Distler, Hugo, 133
Dittersdorf, Carl Ditters von, 44
Dodds, Johnny, 191–192
Don Cossack Choir, 202
Donizetti, Gaetano, xix, 3, 18, 28–29
Dowland, John, 117
Downes, Olin, 9
Dragon, Carmen, 173
Dreyfus, Max, 149
D'Urfey, Thomas, 142

Dvořák, Anton, 37, 57, 60–61, 95–97, 113, 133
Dyer-Bennet, Richard, 202, 204
Dylan, Bob, 207, 209

Ebb, Fred, 168
Eddy, Nelson, 180–181
Einstein. Alfred, 47
Elizabeth I, Queen, 170
Ellington, Duke, 185–187, 193–194, 197, 199
Elmo, Cloe, 12
Evans, Gil, 190, 198
Eysler, Edmund, 178

Falla, Manuel de, 116, 132
Farnon, Robert, 173
Farrar, Geraldine, 19
Farrell, Charles, 167
Faulkner, T. A., 177
Fauré, Gabriel, 64, 98, 116, 128, 139
Favero, Mafalda, 12
Felsenstein, Walter, 20
Fennell, Frederick, 173
Ferber, Edna, 150
Ferrier, Kathleen, 23
Fiedler, Arthur, 171–173
Fields, Dorothy, 161, 167
Filtz, Anton, 44
Firkusny, Rudolf, 61
Fischer-Dieskau, Dietrich, 145
Fizdale, Arthur, 116
Flagstad, Kirsten, xvii, 7, 10–11, 27
Flaubert, Gustave, 29
Foss, Lukas, 133
Francis, Arthur, 155
Franck, César, 64, 98
Freed, Arthur, 181
Fremstad, Olive, 23
Frescobaldi, Girolamo, 81
Friedberg, Carl, 113
Friml, Rudolf, xix, 147–148, 180
Froberger, Johann Jakob, 71, 73

Gabrieli, Andrea, 39–40
Gabrieli, Giovanni, 39, 69, 71–72, 81
Gabrilowitsch, Ossip, 106
Gama, Vasco da, 30
Garden, Mary, 19
Garner, Erroll, 199
Gatti-Casazza, Giulio, 9, 12
Gaultier, Denis, 81
Gautier, Théophile, 29, 139
Gaynor, Janet, 167
Gedda, Nicolai, 11
Geminiani, Francesco, 80–82, 86
Gençer, Leyla, 29

George I, King, 43
German, Edward, 180
Gershwin, George, 152–155, 160, 162, 165, 167, 174–175, 181
Gershwin, Ira, 154–155, 163, 167, 181
Ghiaurov, Nicolai, 13
Gibbons, Orlando, 39
Gieseking, Walter, 114
Gigli, Beniamino, 10
Gilbert, Ronnie, 205–206
Gilbert, William Schwenk, xix, 148, 170–171, 179–180, 184–185
Gilels, Emil, 112
Gillespie, Dizzy, 188–189, 197–198
Gilman, Lawrence, 9
Ginastera, Alberto, 30
Giordano, Umberto, 37
Giulini, Carlo Maria, 25
Glinka, Mikhail, 63
Gluck, Christoph Willibald, 3, 23–24, 29
Goethe, Johann Wolfgang von, 53, 56
Gold, Ernest, 182
Gold, Robert, 116
Goldberg, Isaac, 153
Goldman, Edwin Franko, 176
Goodman, Benny, 188–189, 195, 197
Gorin, Igor, 141
Gossec, François Joseph, 23
Gould, Glenn, 104–105, 115
Gould, Morton, 116, 174–175
Gounod, Charles, 31
Granados, Enrique, 64, 116
Green, Adolph, 165
Green, Freddie, 196
Greuze, Jean Baptiste, 2
Grieg, Edvard, 64, 98, 113, 148–149, 171–172
Grisi, Giuditta, 29
Grofé Ferde, 174–176
Gruen, John, 144
Guthrie, Tyrone, 19
Guthrie, Woody, 203, 208

Haefliger, Ernst, 145
Halévy, Jacques, 31
Hambro, Leonid, 116
Hammerstein, Oscar, II, 149–151, 157–158, 167
Handel, George Frederick, ix, xxi, xxiii, 3, 22, 40–44, 73, 75–77, 79–82, 86, 105, 113, 117, 119–121, 124, 170
Hanson, Howard, 117, 119
Harburg, E. Y., 166–167

Harding, Warren G., 4
Harms, T. B., 149
Harnick, Sheldon, 168
Haroun al Raschid, 9
Hart, Lorenz, 156–157, 160, 167
Hart, Moss, 163
Hawkins, Coleman, 194–195
Haydn, Franz Josef, 41, 44–45, 50–
    51, 59, 82, 84, 86–88, 105–108,
    124–125
Hays, Lee, 205–206, 209
Heifetz, Jascha, xiv, 85
Heine, Heinrich, 29, 135
Hellerman, Fred, 205–206
Henderson, Fletcher, 188, 192, 194–
    195
Henderson, Ray, 159–160, 167
Herbert, Victor, 60, 147–148, 180
Herman, Jerry, 168
Highwaymen, 207
Hindemith, Paul, 138
Hitler, Adolf, xvii
Hodges, Johnny, 186, 194, 198
Hoffman, E. T. A., 5
Hofmann, Josef, 108, 110, 112
Hofmannsthal, Hugo von, 25, 36
Hogan, John V. L., ix–x
Holman, Libby, 160
Holzbauer, Ignaz, 44
Hood, Basil, 180
Horowitz, Vladimir, xiv, xviii–xix,
    xxiii, 105, 107–108, 110, 115–
    116
Huirse, Jorge, 212
Huirse, Rosendo, 212

Ibsen, Henrik, 64
Indio Taba-Jaras, Los, 221
Indy, Vincent d', 64
Istomin, Eugene, 85, 94
Ives, Burl, 202
Ives, Charles, 65

Janáček, Leoš, 37, 128–129, 140–
    141
Jannings, Emil, 4
Jarre, Maurice, 183
Jeritza, Maria, 5
Johnson, Edward, 12
Jolson, Al, 181
Jones, Jo, 196
Jones, Tom, 168
Journeymen, 207
Joyce, James, 144
Jullien, Louis Antoine, 171–172

Kabalevsky, Dmitri, 116, 141
Kálmán, Emmerich, 147, 178
Kander, John, 168
Kapell, William, 112
Kappel, Gertrude, xvii, 6–9, 11, 35
Karajan, Herbert von, 19–20
Katchen, Jules, 114
Kaufman, George S., 153
Kern, Jerome, 146, 149–151, 153,
    156, 158, 162, 167, 181
Kingston Trio, 206
Kipnis, Alexander, 27, 34
Kipnis, Igor, xxiii, 40, 69–83, 105
Kirkpatrick, Ralph, xxiii, 105
Kleiber, Erich, 18
Klemperer, Otto, 18
Köchel, Ludwig, 48
Kodály, Zoltán, 133
Korngold, Erich, 182
Kostelanetz, André, 173
Koussevitzky, Serge, 51–52, 66–67
Kreisler, Fritz, 85, 98
Kreutzer, Rudolphe, 92

Lachmann, Franz, 26
Lalande, Michel-Richard de, 124
Lalo, Édouard, 64
Lamartine, Alphonse, 57
Landowska, Wanda, xxiii, 105
Lane, Burton, 166–167
Lane, Louis, 173
Lang, Paul Henry, 50
LaRocca, Nick, 187–188, 191
Laubenthal, Rudolf, 6
Lauder, Harry, 184
Lauri-Volpi, Giacomo, 10–11
Lawrence, Gertrude, 154
Lawrence, Robert, xvi–xvii, 1–38
Leadbelly, 203
Lear, Evelyn, 13, 145
Lehár, Franz, 147, 178–179
Lehmann, Lotte, xv, xvii, 10–11,
    27
Leider, Frida, 7, 10–11, 35
Leinsdorf, Erich, 6–7
Leinsdorf, Mrs. Erich, 6–7
Leoncavallo, Ruggiero, 37
Leopold, Prince, 42
Lerner, Alan Jay, 166–167
Lewis, John, 188, 198
Lind, Jenny, 14
Lipatti, Dinu, 11
Liszt, Franz, 29, 57, 103, 109, 112–
    113
Locatelli, Pietro, 73, 80, 82, 86
Loesser, Frank, 163–165

Loewe, Frederick, 166–167
Lomax, Alan, 207
Lombardo, Guy, 185
Louis XIV, King, 40
Lubin, Germaine, 7, 19
Ludwig, Christa, 11, 27, 35
Ludwig, Christian, 42
Lully, Jean-Baptiste, 29, 42, 73, 81, 124, 170
Lumbye, Hans Christian, 178
Lympany, Moura, 111–112

MacDonald, Jeanette, 180–181
McEnelly, Edwin, 185
McKinney's Cotton Pickers, 185
Mahler, Gustav, 26, 57, 62–63, 137–138
Maison, René, xvii
Mancini, Henry, 182
Manfredini, Francesco, 82
Mantovani, Annunzio Paulo, 173–174
Marais & Miranda, 203
Marcello, Alessandro, 80
Marcello, Benedetto, 80
Marek, George, 7
Marie Antoinette, Queen, 29
Marsh, Lucy Isabelle, 146
Martinelli, Caterina, 124
Martinelli, Giovanni, 10
Martinu, Bohuslav, 68
Mascagni, Pietro, 37
Mason, Edith, 10
Massenet, Jules, 2, 31
Matzenauer, Margaret, 23
Melchior, Lauritz, 34
Mendelssohn, Felix, xxii, 56–57, 84, 93–94, 109–110, 170
Merman, Ethel, 164
Meyer, Kerstin, 23
Meyerbeer, Giacomo, 3, 24, 30–31
Milan, Luis, 138
Milanov, Zinka, 12
Miley, Bubber, 194
Milstein, Nathan, xv
Mingus, Charlie, 198
Mitchell, Howard, 173
Mitropoulos, Dimitri, 91
Modern Jazz Quartet, 188, 197–198
Molière, 40
Monk, Thelonious, 199
Monteverdi, Claudio, xxii, 22, 24, 32, 69, 71, 75, 81–82, 124
Morley, Thomas, 117
Morondo, Luis, 132

Morton, Jelly Roll, 184–185, 192–193, 199
Moten, Bennie, 185
Mozart, Leopold, 45–46
Mozart, Marianne, 45
Mozart, Wolfgang Amadeus, xiii, xxi–xxii, 3, 5, 22–25, 28, 32, 41, 45–51, 69, 82, 84, 86–89, 93, 105–106, 108, 113, 117–118, 124–125, 129, 136, 169–170
Mudarra, Alonzo de, 138
Müller, Wenzel, 92
Mulligan, Gerry, 198
Munch, Charles, 54–55, 58–59
Murphy, George, 153
Murphy, Lambert, 146
Musorgski, Modest, 2–3, 36, 63, 90, 140–141
Musset, Alfred de, 29
Muzio, Claudia, 10

Nance, Ray, 194
Nanton, Joe, 194
Napoleon I, 29
Nero, Emperor, 170
Newman, Alfred, 182
Nichols, Red, 185, 187–188, 192
Nielsen, Carl, 65–66
Niles, John Jacob, 202, 208
Nilsson, Birgit, xvii, 11, 27
Noble, Ray, 185
North, Alex, 182
Novello, Ivor, 180

Offenbach, Jacques, 5, 170–171, 179
Oliver, King, 191–192, 194
Olszewska, Maria, 10
Original Dixieland Jazz Band, 187, 189–191
Ormandy, Eugene, 4, 126, 147
Ortolani, Riz, 183
Ory, Kid, 192

Paderewski, Ignace, 171
Paganini, Nicolò, 73
Page, Walter, 196
Pagnol, Marcel, 162
Palestrina, Giovanni Pierluigi da, 129
Parker, Charlie, 188, 197–198
Patterson, "Banjo," 208
Paxton, Tom, 209
Pedro the First, Emperor, 222
Peerce, Jan, 11

Pergolesi, Giovanni Battista, 80
Pertile, Aureliano, 10
Petraglia, Clara, 221
Piatigorsky, Gregor, 85
Pinza, Ezio, 10, 33
Plato, 209
Ponchielli, Almicare, 3, 37
Pons, Lily, xix–xx
Ponselle, Rosa, 9, 28
Ponte, Lorenzo da, 24–25
Porter, Cole, 158–159, 162, 167
Poulenc, Francis, 20, 31, 132, 139–140
Presley, Elvis, 182
Prey, Hermann, 145
Price, Leontyne, 13, 144
Prokofiev, Sergei, xxii–xxiii, 38, 65, 67, 115–116
Puccini, Giacomo, 2–3, 5, 16, 37–38
Purcell, Henry, 81–82, 86, 117, 142, 170
Puyana, Rafael, 105

Rachmaninoff, Sergei, 85, 98
Raftsmen, 207
Rameau, Jean Philippe, 29, 73, 77, 80–81
Randolph, David, xxiii, 41, 117–145
Raskin, Judith, 145
Rasumovsky, Count Andrei Kyrillo-vitch, 89
Rathaus, Karol, 36
Ravel, Maurice, 65, 99, 113, 115, 133
Raymond, Joe, 185
Redman, Don, 195
Reed, Susan, 202
Reiner, Fritz, 18, 35
Reisenberg, Nadia, 107
Reisman, Leo, 160
Rembrandt, xxii
Rethberg, Elisabeth, 9
Reyer, Louis Étienne, 31
Ribeiro, Alice, 221
Richter, Franz, 44
Richter, Sviatoslav, 61
Richter-Hasser, Hans, 108
Rimbaud, Arthur, 142
Rimski-Korsakov, Nikolai, 36, 63, 65
Ritchie, Jean, 202
Robinson, Avery, 208
Rodgers, Richard, 149, 151, 156–158, 160, 162, 167, 181

Rogers, Ginger, 149, 181
Romberg, Sigmund, xix, 147–148, 180
Rome, Harold, 161–162
Rose, Leonard, 85, 94
Rosenthal, Manuel, 179
Rosenthal, Moriz, 85, 113
Rosetti, Francisco Antonio (F. A. Rössler), 44
Rossini, Gioacchino Antonio, 3, 28–31, 218
Rózsa, Miklós, 182
Rubens, Peter, 2
Rubinstein, Anton, 171
Rubinstein, Artur, xv, xviii, 107–108, 110–112
Rudolf, Archduke, 91, 94
Runyon, Damon, 164
Rysanek, Leonie, 27

Saint-Marie, Buffy, 209
Saint-Saëns, Camille, 31, 64, 116, 170
Salmaggi, Alfredo, 16
Salmaggi, Felix, 16
Salomon, Johann Peter, 45
Sammartini, Giuseppe, 44, 80
Sand, George, 29
Sandburg, Carl, 202
Sanders, Betty, 202
Sanders, Pharoah, 199
Sanger, Elliott M., x–xi
Sargent, Malcolm, 120
Satie, Erik, 133, 140, 170
Sayao, Bidu, 12
Scarlatti, Alessandro, xxiii, 3, 138
Scarlatti, Domenico, 80, 86, 102, 105
Scherchen, Hermann, 122–123
Schickaneder, Emmanuel, 25
Schiller, Friedrich von, 51
Schipa, Tito, 10
Schmidt, Harvey, 168
Schönberg, Arnold, 30, 61, 65, 74–75, 96–97, 100, 115
Schorr, Friedrich, 6
Schubert, Franz, xiii, xv, xxii, 53–54, 84, 93, 109–113, 134–135, 138, 170
Schuller, Gunther, 197–198
Schuman, William, 119
Schumann, Clara, 56, 113, 171
Schumann, Robert, xxii, 52, 56, 84, 93–95, 109, 112–113, 134–135
Schütz, Heinrich, 82
Schwartz, Arthur, 160–161, 167

Schwarzkopf, Elisabeth, 145
Seeger, Pete, 200–201, 204–206, 209
Serkin, Rudolf, xv, 58–59, 108, 110
Shakespeare, William, xxii, 57, 141–142, 170
Shantymen, 207
Shaw, George Bernard, 166
Shepp, Archie, 197, 199
Sherman, Robert, 169–183, 200–209
Shields, Larry, 191
Shostakovich, Dmitri, 36, 65–67, 99, 116, 141, 170
Sibelius, Jean, xxi–xxii, 64, 68, 170
Siff, Bernie, 48
Siloti, Alexander, 103, 113
Silver, Horace, 188
Simionato, Giulietta, 23
Simon, Alfred, xix, 146–169
Skulnik, Menasha, 162
Smetana, Bedřich, 37, 63, 95–96, 149
Smith, Bessie, 192, 194
Smith, Joe, 192
Smith, Joseph C., 185
Sondheim, Stephen, 163–164
Sousa, John Philip, xvi, 176–177
Souzay, Gerard, 145
Spanier, Muggsy, 190–191
Spontini, Gasparo, 3, 29, 31
Stader, Maria, 145
Stamitz, Carl, 44
Stamitz, Johann, 44
Steber, Eleanor, 12
Steiner, Max, 182
Stern, Isaac, 85, 94
Stevens, Risë, 23
Stevens, Wallace, 144
Stewart, Rex, 194
Stockhausen, Karlheinz, 116
Stokowski, Leopold, 78
Stolz, Robert, 178
Straus, Oscar, 147, 178
Strauss, Johann, xvi, xx, 170, 174
Strauss, Johann, Jr., 64, 170, 177–180
Strauss, Richard, 3, 14, 18, 23, 35–36, 64, 116
Stravinsky, Igor, xxii, 38, 65, 112, 115–116, 129, 131–132
Strehler, Giorgio, 20
Strouse, Charles, 168
Styne, Jule, 163–164
Sullivan, Arthur, xix, 148, 170–171, 179–180, 184, 185

Sumac, Yma, 216
Suppé, Franz von, 178
Süssmayer, Felix, 125
Sutherland, Joan, xxiii, 13, 29
Sveshnikov, A. V., 133
Sygietynski, Tadeusz, 133
Szell, George, 96

Taglioni, Filippo, 29
Tallis, Thomas, 130
Tartini, Giuseppe, 73, 80, 86
Taubman, Howard, xiii–xxiii
Taubman, Mrs. Howard, xxi
Taylor, Cecil, 189, 198
Tchaikovsky, Peter Ilich, xix, 36, 57, 61–62, 97, 113–114
Tebaldi, Renata, 7, 12–13
Telemann, Georg Philipp, 69, 73, 77–78, 80, 82, 170
Terry, Sir Richard, 120
Theodor, Karl, 44
Thomas, John Charles, 10
Thompson, Oscar, 9
Thorborg, Kerstin, 23
Tibbett, Lawrence, 9–10, 33
Tiomkin, Dimitri, 182
Torelli, Giuseppe, 41, 82
Toscanini, Arturo, xiv–xv, xvii–xviii, xxi–xxiii, 7, 17–19, 23
Tovey, Sir Donald Francis, 94
Traubel, Helen, 12
Travelers Three, 206
Troyer, Count Ferdinand, 94
Tucker, Richard, 11
Tureck, Rosalyn, 104–105
Turina, Joaquín, 116
Twain, Mark, 179, 208

Varèse, Edgar, 65
Vaughan Williams, Ralph, 68, 130–131
Veit, Ivan, ix–xi
Veracini, Francesco Maria, 86
Verdi, Giuseppe, xvii–xviii, xx, 2–4, 12, 16, 18, 29, 32–34, 37, 120, 127, 218
Viardot-García, Pauline, 23
Vickers, Jon, xvii, 27
Victoria, Queen, 176
Vivaldi, Antonio, 40–41, 45, 69, 72, 75–78, 80–82, 86, 120
Voltaire, 165

Wagner, Richard, xvii, xx, 2, 3, 5–6, 9, 16, 18–19, 23, 26–27, 30, 32, 34–35, 51, 58, 103, 116, 176, 184–185

Wagner, Wieland, 19
Waldstein, Count Ferdinand von, 107
Waldteufel, Emil, 178
Walker, Nancy, 165
Walter, Bruno, xv, xvii–xviii, 18, 25, 28
Walton, William, 129–130, 170
Warren, Leonard, xvii
Webb, Clifton, 160
Weber, Carl Maria von, 27–28, 109–110
Webern, Anton von, xxii, 75, 101, 115
Weill, Kurt, 163–164
Weinberger, Jaromir, 149
White, George, 159

White, Josh, 202
Whiteman, Paul, 185
Wilbye, John, 117
Wilheim, August, 42
Williams, Cootie, 186, 194
Wilson, John S., 184–199
Wodehouse, P. G., 150
Wolf, Hugo, 134, 137
Wood, Grant, 158
Wood, Hally, 202

Youmans, Vincent, 155, 162
Young, Lester, 196
Young, Victor, 182

Zayde, Jascha, xviii, 89, 102–116